# R E A D I N G
# Inca
# H I S T O R Y

Reading Inca History

*24.95*

*Less*  *20%*

*20.00*

Purchased by: _____

# READING Inca HISTORY

## CATHERINE JULIEN

UNIVERSITY OF IOWA PRESS Ψ IOWA CITY

University of Iowa Press,
Iowa City 52242
Copyright © 2000 by the
University of Iowa Press
All rights reserved
Printed in the United States of America
Maps by Pat Conrad
http://www.uiowa.edu/~uipress

The publication of this book was generously
supported by the University of Iowa Foundation.

The Burnham Macmillan Fund of the Department
of History, the Dieter S. Haenicke Center for
International and Area Studies, and the Preparation
and Publication of Papers and Exhibition of
Creative Works Fund, all at Western Michigan
University, have provided publication support for
this book.

Printed on acid-free paper

Library of Congress
Cataloging-in-Publication Data
Julien, Catherine J.
Reading Inca history / by Catherine Julien.
p.    cm.
Includes bibliographical references and index.
ISBN 0-87745-725-5 (cloth), ISBN 0-87745-797-2 (pbk.)
1. Incas—Historiography.    2. Incas—Genealogy.
3. Incas—Kings and rulers.    I. Title.
F3429.J85    2000
985'.019'072—dc21
                                                    00-039246

02   03   04   P   5   4   3   2   1

*A mi hija Clara, y a su Cuzco*

# Contents

# Acknowledgments

This project has been a long time in coming. It began with my first exposure to interpretations of the Inca past. Almost the first thing I read was María Rostworowski's monograph on Pachacuti, and ever since I have been looking for different points of view within the dynastic descent group itself. There never was agreement on "what happened" in the Inca past, not even among the Incas.

At the time, I was studying anthropology with John Howland Rowe, who combines history and archaeology in his own work and who could compare the physical remains of the Inca empire to the representations of it that were collected from Inca sources in Cuzco and find a resonance between them. At the same time, Rowe treated the Spanish narratives as problematic, for, of course, an anthropologist knows that the Spaniards were not in Cuzco doing ethnography, and what they wrote does not reflect more than a superficial knowledge of the rules and practices of the people with whom they lived. Still, the Spanish authors — and the native Andeans who wrote Spanish narratives — captured Inca genres, and these genres reflect the Inca past in some way. Rowe has written mainly about the Incas, not about how we work or about the sources through which we study the Incas, even though he has generated his own source criticism and worked within this personal body of knowledge. Perhaps he made a mistake in not writing more about the Spaniards, just as it may be a mistake to attempt a study like this without more knowledge about how Spanish authors worked. I would argue that the attention paid to Spanish authors has far outweighed what has been given to Inca sources and that these sources are deserving of attention. My greatest intellectual debt in this enterprise is to Rowe, although the scholarly efforts of people like María Rostworowski, Franklin Pease, John Murra, and Tom Zuidema have clearly stimulated the thinking which underlies the present work.

Some of the material in chapters 5 and 6 was published in an essay on the Incas, published as *Die Inka* by C. H. Beck in Munich (1998), and I thank the publishers for permission to publish in English. I also thank the Humboldt Foundation for a research fellowship that allowed me to spend two years at the Seminar für Völkerkunde of the University of Bonn. Near the beginning of my tenure in Bonn (a stay that lengthened to five years), a group of students, including Kristina Angelis, Bärbel Konerman, and Gerlinde Pilgrimm, asked me questions about the social organization of Cuzco and how to read what had been written about it. These interests led to a seminar in which the present work germinated. One of the students, Alexander Voss, was assigned a paper on Inca genealogy. He avidly traced all the contradictions in the various accounts of Inca genealogy, making me aware, as I never had been before, of how controversial a subject dynastic descent actually was. During this time I was the recipient of a voluminous correspondence from John Rowe on a variety of matters related to the present work. I had more contact with him on these matters than I had had on my dissertation, despite being an ocean away. I owe this book to the fertile period I spent in Bonn.

The time I spent abroad was also intellectually stimulating because of the many encounters I had with colleagues. The list would be long were I to mention everyone, but I will mention some, including Ute Baumgart, Michael Tellenbach, Eva König, Antonio Nodal, Wiebke Ahrndt, Martin Volland, Albert Meyers, Heiko Prümers, Roswith Hartmann, Vera Stähle, Christine Scholten, and, particularly, Sabine Dedenbach-Sálazar Sáenz, Hanns Prem, Kristina Angelis, and Kerstin Nowack. Moreover, the Bonn seminar was graced by the presence of Luis Lumbreras and Marcela Rios for an entire year while I was there. Rossana Barragán and David Pereira were there for some of that time. A little-known fact is that I was one of the greatest beneficiaries of these arrangements. I spent time visiting colleagues who influenced or contributed to this work in one way or another. I especially want to recall Fermín del Pino, Juan José Villarías, Frank Meddens, Marius Ziolkowski, and Inge Schjellerup. Spain is a point of reunion for Andeanists who work in archives, and I was fortunate to cross paths with Jorge Flores, Teodoro Hampe, Manuel Burga, Tom Abercrombie, Gary Urton, Frank Salomon, Christine Borchart, David Cook, Susan Ramírez, Chantal Caillavet, and María Susana Cipolletti. I will not soon forget sitting in the Seville streets, drinking coffee with Gary Urton, Frank Salomon, and Tom Abercrombie and wondering at the constellation of circumstances that had connected our lives. I also owe a debt to the Archivo General de Indias in Seville for their gracious reception and meticulous attention to my requests.

While a great deal of the thought that went into the present study was generated on the other side of the Atlantic, the manuscript itself was written while I was a member of the Department of History at Western Michigan University. Conversations with students there provided stimulation, too, and I want to acknowledge Michael Martin for remarking on two particular points in a graduate seminar in which I presented the information on Inca dates. John Monaghan, my Mesoamerican colleague here, also read and commented on the manuscript, helping me formulate points of difference with what has been going on in his field. I am also grateful to my department for granting me time for research and for having so graciously received me into the historians' guild. The view from within is different, and occupying this new place is a stimulating intellectual experience in its own right.

John Rowe read and commented on the present manuscript in nearly final form, offering comments that have helped me in its revision. He has done a great deal of work on the very sources I am using and has been particularly helpful to me in sorting out what sources can be identified in Cobo. I have had the best kind of criticism from him, and my argument that Cobo may have gotten his Inca history from Polo has been strengthened by his arguing against it. The matter is not resolved, nor will it be unless more manuscript sources are found. With regard to manuscript sources, I was able to check certain passages in the Betanzos manuscript, thanks to Roland Hamilton. Finally, I want to thank Susan Niles and Holly Carver. Both have contributed in their own ways to the creation of this book, the former by making numerous comments that were extremely useful in revising the manuscript and the latter by nursing the project and the author through the various stages that have led to this point. There is magic afoot when such forces come together.

Quito

ECUADOR

Tomebamba

Chachapoyas

Cajamarca

Trujillo

PERU

Huánuco Pampa

Pachacamac

Ayacucho

Urubamba R.

CUZCO

Andahuaylas
Urcos

BOLIVIA

N

Hatuncolla
Lake Titicaca

Arequipa
Tiahuanaco

Incallacta

0   100   200   300   400   500
KILOMETERS

CUZCO

# READING

# Inca

# HISTORY

# I Introduction

The nobles tell very great stories about Inca Yupanqui and Topa Inca, his son, and Huayna Capac, his grandson, because these were the rulers who proved themselves to be the most valiant. Those who would read about their deeds should know that I put less in my account than I knew and that I did not add anything, because I do not have any other sources for what I write than what these Indians tell me. And for myself, I believe what they say and more because of the traces and signs left by these kings and because of their great power, which is an indication that what I write is nothing compared to what actually happened, the memory of which will endure for as long as there are native Andean people.

Muy grandes cosas quentan los orejones deste Ynga Yupangue e de Topa Ynga, su hijo, e Guaynacapa, su nieto porque éstos fueron los que se mostraron más valerosos. Los que fueren leyendo sus acaeçimientos crean que yo quito antes de lo que supe que no añadir nada, y que, para afir[marlo por çierto], fuera menester verlo, ques causa que yo no afirme más de que lo escrivo por relación destos yndios; y para mí, creo esto y más por los rastros y señales que dexaron de sus pisadas estos reyes y por el su mucho poder, que da muestra de no ser nada esto que yo escrivo para lo que pasó, la qual memoria durará en el Perú mientras oviere honbres de los naturales. (Cieza de León [1553], chap. 48; 1986 : 140)

Pedro de Cieza de León wrote in the early 1550s and was one of the first Spaniards to write about the Inca past in any detail. He was a soldier, but he took upon himself the task of recording what had gone on before he arrived in Peru. Most of what he wrote was about fighting among Spanish factions, but one part of his much longer work was a narrative of the Inca past, beginning with the origins of a group of siblings from a cave at Pacaritambo and extending to the time of the Spanish arrival in Cuzco, twelve generations later.

The narrative tells the story of the Inca imperial expansion. Structured by the genealogy of the dynastic line, it is peopled by the Inca rulers and their close kin. Cieza says he took all of his material from native sources. Obviously he translated — with the aid of translators — what he was told by particular individuals, since the Incas had no form of writing, and other forms of recording were unintelligible to the Spaniards. Cieza names one Inca informant, Cayo Topa ([1553], chap. 6; 1986:38), and he occasionally indicates divergent stories, so he talked to others while he was in the Andes. They could have been eyewitnesses to some of the events Cieza wrote about, but no one living could have a memory of the period before the last two, or possibly three, generations.

Cieza recovered some kind of material from oral historical genres. Like other Spaniards who wrote narratives structured by the genealogy of the Inca dynastic descent group, he collected this material from Inca sources. Like other Spaniards, he assumed that the material reflected a knowledge of the Inca past. He had firsthand acquaintance with the landscape of the Inca empire and could convince himself of the truth of the story he told. The story Cieza told explained the rise of Inca power — a power which was then still obvious. Like other Spaniards, Cieza did not refer to his sources except in a general way. Because of the filters of language and culture, even if he transcribed what he was told, the content was irrevocably altered. By making the stories he was told intelligible to another audience and by writing them down in a manuscript, both the meanings associated with the original genre or genres and the context of their transmission were lost.

Something may remain, but whether aspects of the underlying original can be recovered depends on how Cieza worked. Did he retell what he was told by informants who were transmitting material from Inca genres, injecting his own comments or interpretations at its margins? Or did he do "history" as we do it, taking material from whatever sources he had, reworking and reconceptualizing it to craft a narrative that fulfilled his own canons of historical writing, including notions of sequence and dynastic succession? To what extent did he bring the Inca past into line with the canons of universal history, a history that began with the book of Genesis? He was the first Spaniard to tread on new literary territory. As far as we know, he was the first to produce what was a new genre: the Spanish historical narrative of the Inca past.

In the years that followed, other Spaniards and two native Andeans were to craft some version of the same project. The Jesuit Bernabé Cobo, who wrote about the Incas in the mid–seventeenth century, said he could still collect the story of the dynastic past from the Incas of Cuzco, though he chose to work with manuscript sources in the creation of his own text ([1653], chap. 2; 1892:119). Although a memory of the Inca past underlay the movement of Topa Amaro in the eighteenth century to restore the Inca empire, the bishop of Cuzco, Manuel Moscoso y Peralta, wrote that local knowledge of the Inca past was taken largely from what Garcilaso de la Vega had written about it (Moscoso in Valcárcel 1983:276–277; Brading 1991:491). The genealogical tradition had survived, but it had survived through both visual representation — a series of portraits of the twelve rulers from Manco Capac to Huascar — and performance — processions of the same sequence of rulers (Pease García Yrigoyen 1992:321; Fane 1996:238–241; Gisbert 1994:149–157). These forms of remembrance were still powerful media for the representation of Andean autonomy and were recognized as such at the time of the Topa Amaro revolt in the 1780s (Rowe 1955:10, 26–27; Brading 1991:491).

Cieza's optimism about the durability of local knowledge of the Inca past — and, specifically, about the story he told of the deeds of the Inca rulers who expanded the authority of Cuzco across a large Andean territory — seems unwarranted in the late twentieth century. If the story he recorded drew from local knowledge in Cuzco, even if translated in word, format, and purpose, that knowledge does not appear to have survived among the descendants of the Incas. The stories that anthropologists have collected in the Cuzco region refer to Inkarrí, a word meaning "Inca rey," but do not reproduce the content of the Spanish historical narratives to any meaningful degree (see essays and transcriptions by Arguedas and Roel Pineda, Núñez del Prado, Valencia Espinoza, Flores Ochoa, and Pease García Yrigoyen in Ossio 1973). At the core of the Spanish historical narratives is a genealogical sequence, beginning with the origins of the dynastic line at the time of Manco Capac and his brothers and sisters — the Ayar siblings — and ending with the death of Huayna Capac, the eleventh ruler in the line of dynastic descent, when a civil war between his sons, Atahuallpa and Huascar, the twelfth Inca, began. The genealogical sequence that structures the Spanish historical narratives is not in evidence in the Inkarrí accounts.

Cieza and the other Spaniards who wrote about the Incas sometimes referred to the stories they were repeating as "fables," even as they narrated events in the lives of persons they took to have been living human beings. They were uncertain about the reliability of their material, and understandably so, since they could not have witnessed or had written testimony of the events they described. When the authors of these accounts referred to the Chanca attack on Cuzco — when the stones themselves turned into warriors — they could understand the battle as a historical event, even if clearly fabulous elements were part of the story. Just so they understood the assistance of St. James or the Virgin in the defeat of Manco Inca in the siege of

Cuzco when these elements were incorporated into the narratives of events that were written after the fact. Where the "fabulous" elements remained fabulous in their narration of stories about the Incas, those that fit within Spanish canons of acceptable explanation could be believed.

Spaniards or Andean authors like Garcilaso Inca de la Vega who were educated had classical texts to provide them with models for the Inca empire. In their minds, the empire, par excellence, was Rome. It was a paradigm by which they could explain the Incas. The comparison between the Incas and Rome was evident in the physical remains of roads, bridges, and canals, but it went further. Inca imperial organization was perceived as "a positive cultural, religious and political force"; it had been a "good thing" (MacCormack 1998:8–10). Moreover, an acquaintance with classical texts gave these authors a touchstone by which they could interpret stories about the Inca past. They could read classical historians who dealt with fabulous origin stories and legends alongside accounts of historical events and, like them, recognize that "the deeds of gods and heroes had been interwoven with those of human beings, with the more reliable history of recent events" (MacCormack 1998:19). The incorporation of fabulous elements was not an obstacle to accepting the historicity of an account of the past.

A lot has changed. Some modern readers greet the fabulous elements and the plausibly historical content alike as myth. The denial of the historical content of works on the Inca past is expressed in two ways. One is the rejection of the descriptive categories used by Spaniards like Cieza in their narratives. When the Spaniards use terms like "king" to describe the Inca ruler or "empire" to describe the Inca project, they are forcing an Andean reality into alien categories (Rostworowski de Diez Canseco 1999:ix–x, 1988:13–14; Pease García Yrigoyen 1995:72–78, 126–127). The second form of denial asserts that Spanish authors misunderstood what they heard: the stories they were told by the Incas of Cuzco had no historical content; rather, they encoded the social organization of Cuzco or reflected other aspects of local knowledge (Zuidema 1964, 1995; Pease García Yrigoyen 1995:71–78; Urton 1990:6).

The first form of denial stems from a doubt about the capacity of Spaniards to interpret a fundamentally foreign world and is exacerbated by the difficulties of translating the meaning of foreign categories into another language. If we had source materials in the Inca language that revealed the nature of what the Spaniards termed "empire," we could partially mitigate this problem because we would gain an approximate understanding from these sources of what it was the Spaniards lacked the words to describe. Even if words get in the way, the Spanish historical narratives offer a perspective on Inca history that must be considered; the existence of an Inca state cannot be denied, and the last several rulers were documented both by the narratives and by witnesses who knew and served them (Rostworowski de Diez Canseco 1999:22–36, 65–91, 178–179).

The second form of denial is a more serious challenge to interpreting the written sources that deal with the Inca past. It denies the existence of an Andean "history." History only arrived in the Andes with the Spaniards. Franklin Pease has used the shallowness of Spanish interest in the Inca past in the first years of their presence in the Andes as the core of his argument that the detailed later accounts of "Inca history" were driven by Spanish historiographical practice, that is, that the Spaniards gave the Incas a past by applying their own canons of universal history to what were essentially Inca myths (1995:72–78). Since the Spaniards were in close contact with the Incas from the beginning, their delay in using Inca sources as the foundation for an account of the Inca past provokes the conclusion that the histories they later wrote were their own invention.

The denial of the historical content of Inca sources was first put forward by Reiner Tom Zuidema in 1964. At that moment, Zuidema was not interested in explaining how the Spaniards reinterpreted what they heard from Inca sources. His denial simply cleared the way for the presentation of an alternative reading of the same texts: Zuidema would read them as myth, and as myth that encoded social organization or local knowledge (Nowack 1998a:133–143; Zuidema 1995, 1964; Urton 1990:6). The logic underlying this argument is that, since social organization is assumed to be immutable or nearly so, a temporal sequence that posits the entire evolution of a social order over only twelve generations must be wrong. If the end product reflects certain durable patterns of thought or explanation, then the end product cannot be something that came into existence through a stepwise evolution over a relatively short span of time. The denial of the historicity of an underlying Inca account is thus closely linked to the needs of the new interpretation: the Inca rulers did not succeed each other in real time but represent segments of the descent group that were always there.

If I may be so bold as to interpret the underlying logic of this argument again: it is based on a literalist reading of the dynastic "history" and does not take into account the possibility that the story was a representation of the past that was created at a specific moment. Even though a mechanism in each generation was the basis for defining *panacas*, or segments of the dynastic descent group, there was no gradual accrual of *panacas*. Rather, a new order was created by reinterpreting past practice according to a new set of rules. Two Spanish authors describe the creation of a historical record during the time of Pachacuti, the ninth Inca (Sarmiento de Gamboa [1572], chap. 9; 1906:3–31; chap. 30; 1906:68; Betanzos [1551–1557], chap. 17; 1987:85–86). An account of the dynastic past crafted then would have explained the particular configuration of Cuzco that that Inca had imposed on the dynastic descent group and the other inhabitants of the Inca city after the Incas had launched an empire.

Rather than a faithful reflection of the past, it was a story which represented a new social order in historical terms. The "history" crafted at this time reflected the interests of a particular group, but it rewrote material that was known or believed about the past in line with new explanations of the rise to power of a segment within the larger group that was identified as Inca. The new history relied on a knowledge of actual dynastic descent and of the events associated with each generation of the dynastic descent group, but it incorporated a perspective that benefited a group that had emerged as uniquely powerful.

That the Incas preserved a knowledge of the line of dynastic descent through a form of genealogy — which is what the Spanish accounts explicitly tell us — cannot be denied so quickly. Clearly, the Spaniards worked from within the framework of their own sociology of knowledge. Just as clearly, whatever form of recorded memory that was found in the Andes answered different needs and purposes and had evolved in a different way from the historical practice of the sixteenth-century Spaniard. Still, there is a growing body of archaeological research, particularly on Inca architecture, that is establishing a concordance between material remains and the list of Inca rulers. The corpus of architecture associated with Pachacuti can now be distinguished on stylistic grounds from what was built during the rule of Huayna Capac, his grandson (Protzen 1993:257–269; Niles 1993:155–163, 1999:262–297). There are also indications that the Inca ceramic style will reflect the succession of Incas associated with the imperial expansion, both in Cuzco and the provinces (Julien 1993:181–199).

The denial of genealogical practice is very specific to the area of Inca studies. Mesoamericanists have not denied the historicity of the recorded memories of their Prehispanic subjects. Some are hard at work studying native lineages and their genealogies. Dates and writing bring the Maya, the Aztecs, and the Mixtecs into our world. Given that their tools resemble ours, it is perhaps easier to accept the historical content of their texts. In the case of the Maya, the written record is associated with monumental sites built long before the arrival of Europeans. "Long count" dates that used a fixed point of reckoning gave the Maya past a chronology that lent itself to conceptualization in much the same way as conventional history (Morley 1983 [first published in 1946]). Scholars extended this conceptual framework by correlating other sequences with the European calendar (Caso 1949). As the twentieth century neared its end, the casting of the Maya past in the same terms as European history was critically reexamined (Boone and Mignolo 1994; Gillespie 1989). However, this reexamination occurred only after advances in the interpretation of Maya writing allowed the texts on stelae — not just the dates — to be read. Stelae associated with sites like Tikal and Copan tell about the lifetimes of particular Maya rulers and their families; the burial sites of particular rulers have been identified (Schele and Miller 1986; Schele and Freidel 1990). That a Maya history developed for its own reasons has not been denied, perhaps because the recording process took place long before the arrival of Europeans and not decades afterward, as in the case of the Spanish historical narratives about the Inca past.

As will be argued in the conclusions, the Spanish historical narratives incorporate sources that reflect an Inca historical consciousness. Whether my argument is accepted or not, there is another matter that underlies the divergent interpretations of the Spanish historical narratives by students of the Incas. They are ultimately a product of different forms of conceptualization, one derived from historiography and the other from a structuralist anthropology. To place the Incas in an anthropological framework, Zuidema had to describe their social organization in much the same terms used by anthropologists when describing small-scale societies elsewhere in the world: the unit of analysis had to be reconceptualized (Nowack 1998a:129–133; Kuper 1988:231). The baggage that came along with this was the notion that such societies were timeless or changed only at the pace of evolution (Thomas 1989:9–17). In part, this reconceptualization of the Incas brought with it a heightened awareness of difference. We, like the Spaniards, had accorded the Incas the same kind of historiographical status as the Romans, that is, as a group distant merely in time but intelligible in terms of cultural behavior. If the Incas were more like the Gê or the Bororo, then we could apply what anthropologists had learned about such societies.

That structuralist anthropology did not incorporate a theory of change or historical process. When a small-scale society becomes an empire, things change. People reinvent themselves, the social order, and the past. To adjust the Incas to an anthropological paradigm that does not take a theory of change into account and that classifies them in the same terms as groups that have survived a long history of colonial domination is to colonize the Prehispanic past. On the other hand, the anthropological knowledge that alerts us to the impossibility of our facile understanding of the Inca and even the Roman past does serve to reorient our search for a meaningful Inca history.

Zuidema's analysis of Inca Cuzco was published in 1964. During the time between the book's first appearance and its republication in Spanish in 1995, he has elaborated aspects of his work and extended the analysis to the Inca calendar and other systematic forms of knowledge. Zuidema constructed a Cuzco that had that same, timeless existence as other communities studied by anthropologists. To this day Zuidema continues to deny the historicity of the dynastic genealogy (1995:35–38). The transformation of Cuzco from a small-scale society to the largest American empire ever created has not been a topic in Zuidema's work.

If the list of Incas does not reflect a temporal sequence, even if structured only by lifetime and not by chronology, what was it that the Spaniards heard that led them to construct a historical sequence? An idea was initially formulated in Zuidema's 1964 work — that the list of eleven or twelve Inca rulers commonly included in the Spanish historical narratives and usually classified into two groups labeled Hanan and Hurin should be read as two parallel dynastic lines — was later developed by Pierre Duviols as an alternative reading of the standard list of Inca rulers. In a sense, this theory reestablished a kind of historical "truth" (Duviols 1979, 1980). The parallel series of rulers were taken to be historical personages who governed the two halves of Cuzco in some sort of sequence. No effort was made to use other aspects of their biographies in rewriting Inca "history," so the new reading of the narratives was limited to denying the truth of the conventional reading. The resulting hypothesis of dual kingship undergirds the interpretation of the Inca past in a number of prominent works (Zuidema 1995:53–58; Pease García Yrigoyen 1992:60–61, 69–70; Rostworowski de Diez Canseco 1999:177–181).

The various forms of denial have attacked a straightforward reading of the Spanish historical narratives. Simple readings of these sources as history are no longer possible. At the same time, those who have attacked how the narratives were read have only offered alternative readings. They have not examined in any more than a cursory way what kind of Inca source material was incorporated in the narratives themselves. The comparison of texts for literary borrowings or dependencies on other texts has been attempted, if only rarely (Wedin 1966: 60–73; Aranibar Zerpa 1963; Rowe 1985b:207–216; Pärssinen 1992:50–70), but no attempt has been made to compare the narratives for the purposes of establishing and identifying underlying Inca source materials. Perhaps such efforts have been inhibited by the idea that a text that has passed through the double filters of language and culture cannot reflect its underlying source.

Before returning to this problem, I want to note one current that has developed from Zuidema's work: an interest in local knowledge. To a degree, this interest has centered on astronomy and mathematics (Urton 1981, 1997), but a related development is ethnographic study of the transmission of memory in the Andes, a field that has blossomed in recent years (Allen 1988; Salomon 1997; Rappoport 1990; Harrison 1989; Abercrombie 1998). A denial of the historicity of the Spanish narratives is not necessarily a denial of Inca historical consciousness, and some of those who pursue the subject from an ethnographic base are deeply interested in how memory was recorded over the *longue durée* (Urton 1998; Salomon 1997).

A great deal of this interest has settled on the *quipo*, a series of knotted cords suspended from a central cord that, through color, technique, or position, can be "read" for the information it contains. So far, only the encoding of numerical information has yielded itself to meaningful interpretation (Ascher and Ascher 1981; Pärssinen 1992:31–50). Recently, the search has turned to the capacity of the *quipo* to encode narrative. Gary Urton has argued that *quipo* construction shows a degree of uniformity that belies the often-stated conclusion that they were mnemonic devices "read" only by the individuals who kept them, that is, that the symbolic system had few generally recognizable features. Rather, Urton notes that the content of *quipos* that were transcribed into Spanish administrative records is evidence that Inca *quipos* could encode subject/object/verb constructions (1998:410–412). Not only were there grammatical constructions that could record what happened, that is, events, *quipos* had the "capacity . . . to denote the temporal relationship between events, which is the basic requirement for establishing a relative chronology" (Urton 1998:426–427).

This line of investigation may yet lead us to revolutionary insight into the Inca past, and we have great hopes for what was recorded on *quipos* (MacCormack 1997:289–290). However, *quipos* were not the only format for recording Inca memory. Both Cieza de León and Pedro Sarmiento de Gamboa describe the composition of Inca narrative, giving a number of specifics about how it was transmitted and in what form. Cieza compared the recitations about Inca rulers to *cantares*, thus equating them to a form of epic poetry that circulated in print and manuscript in the Spain of his day. He also described what was recorded about the Inca rulers as *romances* and *villancicos*, genres "of legendary and historical poetic narration in medieval Castile" (Niles 1999:7–11, 45–51; MacCormack 1997:286–287; Cieza de León [1553], chap. 11; 1986:27). Cieza, at least, is clear about the filters of language and culture through which he understood Inca efforts to preserve a memory of their past. He also refers to the controlled, edited quality of the transmissions and the conscious forgetting of individuals whose deeds did not measure up to some standard (MacCormack 1997:288–289). When Cieza writes about fundamentally foreign historical practice, he distances his own practices from it and develops a sharper image through comparison.

Another medium for recording memory was described by Sarmiento de Gamboa and Cristóbal de Molina. A series of painted wooden tablets that represented the lives of the individuals through whom dynastic descent was traced was kept by the dynasty. Access to it was limited (Sarmiento de Gamboa [1572], chap. 9; 1906:31; Molina [1576]; 1989:49–50). Oral performance, history, and visual art at the same time, this form has been impossible to study or sufficiently value in the absence of any physical record (Julien 1999:62–63, 76–78).

That the Incas recorded and orally transmitted some kind of memory does not seem to be in doubt. What is contested is the content of such records. But how can anything be learned about their content? One point of entry is a textual analysis of the Inca content of the Spanish historical narratives themselves. No one has yet done a textual analysis of these narratives for the purposes of identifying underlying oral sources. Franklin Pease has authored critical editions of sixteenth-century works, including the complete works of Cieza (Cieza de León [1550] 1984, [1553] 1986, 1987, 1994), who gave a standard account of Inca genealogy, and an impressive study of historical writing in the Andes (Pease García Yrigoyen 1995), but neither he nor other authors have dealt with the specific nature of the Inca sources that nourished the Spanish narratives. If there were formally recorded and transmitted memories of the Inca past, then these narratives may have captured, *grosso modo*, their structure and even their content. If the historical narratives written in Spanish draw from a genre or genres of Inca history, we can develop images of them.

Because we are exploring later texts to retrieve earlier sources, the method can best be described as a kind of archaeology of the source materials. How do we excavate a text? One of the methods used to recover the underlying textual sources of manuscripts is through comparison of two manuscripts dependent on the same source. The same method can be used to uncover dependency on an oral genre. The degree of consistency between some of the accounts is an indication that these narratives incorporate Inca genres, perhaps in their entirety. For comparative analysis to be profitable, works whose authors used material from the same Inca genres must be compared. Even given the filters of language and culture through which any Inca genres were put, the format or structure of a genre and, even, a general approximation of its contents may have been detected.

The idea that some Spanish historical narratives will yield Inca genres when subjected to comparative analysis may be difficult to accept. They were written after — often decades after — control of the Inca empire had been successfully usurped by Pizarro and other Spaniards who followed. The Spanish arrival, however, is a false boundary. Inca sovereignty was recognized until 1572. Initially, the genre or genres performed at public events were performed before the Spaniards (False Estete 1924; Cieza de León [1553], chap. 11; 1986:29). Those Inca genres that were recorded in some form were not dependent on performance, however. Even when the performance tradition ended, the record can have remained. For example, some Inca genres were *quipo*-based. A *quipo* recounting the lords and fortresses conquered by Topa Inca, the tenth ruler on the dynastic list, was presented by his descendants in 1569 (Rowe 1985b). A *quipo* that recorded the events of the life of Pachacuti was collected by a Spanish *corregidor* in 1559 (see chapter 4).

The survival of recorded memory and the processes involved in transmitting it from one generation to the next is, of course, an essential precondition to our enterprise. Since we do not know when and under what circumstances the transmission process stopped, our only means of assessing the survival of generic material is in the analysis of the Spanish historical narratives themselves. The proof, as it were, is in the pudding.

What we can learn about Inca genres is dependent on what was incorporated in Spanish texts. If there were various Inca genres with historical content, then authors can have mixed these materials to construct their histories. Today good historical practice requires the evaluation of the quality of source material but little respect for its integrity. We do history much the way we make soup: choosing the best ingredients, chopping them up, and throwing them all together in one pot. How did sixteenth-century authors work? They say very little on that score, so we must try to reconstruct their habits. The authors who wrote about the Incas seldom refer to source material. On occasion, they say they relied on a particular source (Cieza de León [1553], chap. 6; 1986:13; Cobo [1653], bk. 12, chap. 2; 1892:116; Cabello Valboa [1586], pt. 3, chap. 9; 1951:260; Acosta [1590], bk. 6, chap. 1; 1940:281). We have assumed that these authors — in the absence of specific information to the contrary — worked like modern historians. However, even when authors had various texts at their disposal, they often elected one as their primary source. The integrity of the source — its authority — was respected.

For example, Cabello Valboa, who set his Inca history against a backdrop of world history, could have followed modern historical practice, evaluating source materials on the Incas and then crafting a wholly new work from pieces of the sources he privileged, stringing them together and reconciling the differences between them. However, what Cabello appears to have done was to choose reliable sources and then follow them. He had a manuscript by Polo de Ondegardo, whom he credited for his knowledge of native beliefs and ceremonies. He also had a manuscript by Cristóbal de Molina that dealt with the "origins of the Incas" ([1586], pt. 3, chap. 9; 1951 : 258–260). By comparing Cabello's account of the Inca past with that contained in a manuscript by the Mercedarian Martín de Morúa, a sharper image of the Molina account can be obtained. These authors preserved the structure and much of the content of the underlying text. Cabello can have changed the meaning of what Molina wrote in subtle ways, but he transmitted much of what Molina wrote without substantial change.

As we begin the process of identifying Inca genres, then, we also begin to learn something about how particular authors composed their narratives. One author, Sarmiento de Gamboa, created a pasticcio of Inca sources, compiling his text from various Inca genres. Since our argument about Sarmiento is intimately tied to comparison with other texts that drew from Inca sources, the reader is referred to the contents of chapters 3–5 for a full exposition of what his text contains.

Knowing how an author worked or, at least, having a hypothesis about what was incorporated in a particular text is an important precondition for reading that work. The Spanish narratives of the Inca past are complex constructions, and those texts that purport to represent Inca history as related by the Incas especially so. Any kind of recorded memory about the past necessarily encapsulates two time periods: the time of what is remembered, and the time the memory is recorded. A composition process occurs in the latter period. When an Inca genre is incorporated in a Spanish text, a third time period and another composition process are embedded. For each episode of composition we have an author or authors. We have to be aware of the history of composition and the complex authorship of such works. Change can be introduced in the transmission process, but the major events in the history of these texts are the composition episodes.

Writing is purposeful activity. The product is never neutral and may contain a wide variety of messages. Sometimes the messages are explicit arguments, the text serving as a vehicle for advocacy. Other times the messages may simply be tacitly held assumptions or explanations that are noncontroversial to the intended audience but that receive legitimation by the simple acknowledgment that they can be tacitly held. Because the transmission of the text reaches other audiences, these messages acquire another status: they are communications across a cultural divide. What we are dealing with is the transmission of "truths" generated from within a foreign sociology of knowledge that may not have been recognized by the translators. There is, therefore, a lot to be gained from learning how to read these texts. To the degree that the authors who wrote narratives in Spanish respected the integrity of underlying Inca source material, they may have transmitted some of the messages conveyed in these texts as well. When we read their texts, we have to develop an ear for embedded messages.

At issue is how we read the Spanish historical narratives. They have been read for their historical content (Rowe 1946, 1985a, 1985b; Julien 1983, 1985; Rostworowski de Diez Canseco 1953, 1999). They have been appreciated for what they can tell us about Europeans attempting to describe a fundamentally foreign world (Pease García Yrigoyen 1995). They have been read as myth encoding social organization (Zuidema 1964, 1995). What I propose to do here is develop an analysis of the sources that drew from Inca genres, identifying these genres in the process (chapters 3–5), and then read these sources explicitly for the themes and messages they contain (chapters 6–8).

Because the analysis offered here is dependent on what Spanish authors captured in their texts, it is the product of a particular historical moment. Two manuscripts have been published in recent years which greatly extend our ability to identify Inca genres. One is the complete manuscript of the Inca history of Juan de Betanzos ([1551–1557] 1987). Until its publication in 1987, only eighteen chapters of a much longer work were known (1880). Betanzos's manuscript is the key to understanding a life history genre (see chapter 4), as well as other aspects of dynastic practice that are intimately bound up with historical consciousness among the Cuzco Incas. The second source is the reading of a *quipo* of the conquests of Topa Inca, the tenth ruler on the dynastic list, contained in a petition put forward by his descendants in 1569. In this case, we have the direct transcription of a historical record kept by members of the dynastic descent group. That the material from this *quipo* also found its way into the historical narratives of Sarmiento, Cabello Valboa, and Morúa was demonstrated by John Rowe, who found this document and created a concordance between it and these sources (1985b). To be fair to earlier authors, the puzzle that we attempt to unravel here may not have been possible to take apart until 1987. Given the obvious importance of these new sources, we may entertain the hope that our analysis of the reliance of Spanish texts on Inca sources can be extended as more relevant source material is found.

What I am putting on the table is an alternative reading of a selected group of sources. I find that the Incas possessed a historical consciousness of their

own. It revolved around the origins of the dynastic descent group and a recognized genealogy of twelve generations. It involved various oral genres, some
of which were supported by physical records.

Others who work with the Incas will notice that a number of controversial issues are dealt with in rather summary fashion here. One issue is the existence of a god who created not just the Incas but the heavens and the earth
and all its peoples. This issue is discussed summarily in chapter 8. Another issue is the dual kingship hypothesis (Zuidema 1995:53–56, 227–234; Duviols
1979, 1980). My interpretation denies dual kingship. The dual kingship hypothesis was originally based on the argument that Polo de Ondegardo collected an account of dynastic succession that was substantially different from
what other Spaniards got; Polo got it right, while all of the others misunderstood. However, we do not have what Polo himself wrote; he has been interpreted through the use of his work by Joseph de Acosta. Polo testified that the
genealogical account recorded by Sarmiento de Gamboa substantially matched
his own understanding of dynastic succession (Rowe 1993–1994:105; Montesinos [1642]; 1882:246, 252–253), so Acosta appears to have got it wrong.
These matters will be dealt with in chapter 3; they are peripheral to the central
purpose of this work, but those interested will find the bare bones of an argument here and are encouraged to draw their own conclusions.

While debating certain differences of interpretation or use of sources might
be productive, other issues cannot be resolved by arguing the details. The
present work proposes an alternative reading of the Spanish historical narratives. As such, it does not attempt to rebut other approaches. Even when an
underlying understanding of how to read the historical narratives has been
achieved, students of the Incas manage to disagree with each other (Duviols
1997:128–129). It makes little sense to argue the details when differences hinge
on totally different modes of reading.

OUTLINE

I will begin at the end and end at the beginning. Perhaps it is logical to
ask the question of why the Incas were interested in representing their past
only after we have examined those representations. Since what is problematic
is not just how but whether the past was being represented, the order of ques-
tioning is reversed. What Inca purpose was served by creating and transmitting particular versions of the dynastic past? Since the historical narratives are

all grounded in genealogy, we begin by exploring the calculation of a particular status that was transmitted through the dynastic line of descent. Those descended from Manco Capac through the male line were recognized as possessing a degree of *capac* status.

This quality was both connected to and responsible for the success of the dynastic group in extending the authority of the Incas over a large Andean territory. The recognition that the line possessed this status was coincident with Inca success; the assertion of *capac* status, when it came, explained a present state of affairs. Just as this mode of explanation waxed with Inca power, it waned as the dynasty lost control to European invaders. In chapter 2 we will examine dynastic assertions of *capac* status through the period of empire. This period does not end with the miraculous appearance of Pizarro's expedition in the Andes. That the Spaniards tapped into the rationale behind this claim into the decade of the 1570s is probably at least partially a result of their recognition of Inca sovereignty up until that time. Claims to sovereignty were supported by genealogical arguments, hence, dynastic memory of the direct line of descendants from Manco Capac to Huascar was still strong. Calculations of genealogical distance to the dynastic line were a reason to instill a knowledge of the history of descent in every Inca generation even after the argument that the Incas were powerful because they were *capac* no longer made any sense.

Just as *capac* status changed with the trajectory of Inca power, it was interpreted differently by different segments of the dynastic descent group in the same period. Betanzos drew from sources in Capac Ayllo, the descent group of Topa Inca, tenth in the dynastic genealogy, and his account reflects the bias of those with carefully husbanded *capac* status against others who were *capac* on their father's side alone. Because claims to status were contentious and because the dynastic genealogy could be recast to favor particular groups or individuals, there was a very good reason for formalizing an account of dynastic descent. One has to ask, after all, why it was necessary to formalize an account of only twelve generations. The physical remains of the individuals in the direct line of descent were periodically arranged in public space; any resident of Cuzco knew who they were and in what order they had lived. As will be seen over the course of this work, descent was contested ground, and the past could be rewritten to favor alternative explanations. By creating and retelling an official version of the dynastic past and by performing it publicly, other claims could be forestalled. When we examine Spanish historical narratives that drew from Inca sources (as we do in chapters 3–5), we will be plumbing the texts for information about an Inca genre that served as a permanent record of the dynastic descent group, as well as about other Inca genres. A painted history was kept inside a building near Cuzco. This painted history, as long as it remained in place, was a standard of truth. Whose truth? Whoever put it there.

Since we do not have any direct testimony about the content of this painted history, our efforts to gain a knowledge of it are concentrated on texts that reiterate its subject matter: the genealogy of the dynastic descent group. In chapter 3 we begin the excavation of Spanish historical narratives for their underlying Inca sources. The knowledge that the Incas were interested in genealogy is our point of departure, so our first concern is to define an Inca genealogical genre. The results of that effort have been alluded to above: the "text" of this genre was a painted history kept privately by the dynastic descent group. Our method is comparative. First we privilege Spanish historical narratives that drew from Inca sources. Then we compare the genealogical information transmitted in these and other narratives.

Our method is an extractive process. Once the genealogical genre is defined and recognized, it can be extracted from a text so that other kinds of Inca sources begin to come into view. The term "genre" has been used loosely here. For example, the genealogical genre may have been limited to a unique artistic work: a series of painted wooden tablets. Can a single work be called a genre? Here we are using the word to distinguish one kind of Inca source from another, regardless of whether the form was used more than once. If we can identify a genealogical genre *grosso modo*, then we know which Spanish historical narratives drew from it — or a transmission of it — and which did not.

Our course of discovery leads to another Inca genre: the life history (chapter 4). Since we have an idea of what material was transmitted in the genealogical genre, its absence in Betanzos's narrative indicates that he drew from another type of source. His account of the Inca past is dominated by the life of Pachacuti, the ninth ruler of the dynastic list. The structure of the Betanzos narrative closely parallels the structure of the account of Pachacuti in the historical narrative of Sarmiento. What Betanzos relates is material from the life history genre. Sarmiento had the life history of Pachacuti and accommodated it into a larger project that also drew from the genealogical genre. Once we understand that Sarmiento was compiling material and we know the contribution of two Inca genres, we can see the outline of others. The problem of compilation is particularly acute in Sarmiento's account of the life of Topa Inca, the tenth ruler in the descent list. We have used comparison as a means of extracting an image of the life of Topa Inca that might reflect a life history of this Inca, but there are other Inca sources clouding the picture.

Dimly reflected in Sarmiento and in other narratives are other genres: stories that do not appear to be part of the life history or genealogy genres, and information about military campaigns and ordinances that may have been incorporated from *quipo* sources, bringing to four or five the number of genres we can identify. The analysis of the genres besides the life history and the genealogical genre is not attempted, only their identification.

If the compilation of Inca sources obscures the outlines of underlying Inca genres when our lens focuses on Topa Inca, it has a similar effect on the first seven Incas of the dynastic list (chapter 5). At this point we will rely on a theory of composition that was introduced in the text of the Spanish historical narratives. It is that Pachacuti, the ninth Inca, composed the histories of the first seven rulers. The perspective in the Inca accounts of the earlier history of the dynasty is situated in the period of expansion under this theory of composition. We should analyze the material with this theory in mind, if only to find inconsistencies that would disprove it. Our problem is that, following its logic, Pachacuti organized the recording of both the life histories and the painted history. Certainly they were formally separate, but what about content? We can detect compilation in the compositions of the Spanish narratives, but here we cannot easily separate the material from the two Inca genres. Sequencing problems for the period when lifetimes overlapped indicate that both genres were organized around the lifetime of the individuals who were the subject matter. If the composition of material about each ruler occurred after death, then the painted tablets related to the later rulers were also life histories, albeit set in genealogical order. The circumstances of composition of generic material related to the seven earlier Incas were different, and we take them into account when we try to discern what messages the narratives contain.

The method we use for extracting oral genres is comparison, the same method used to compare texts for underlying written sources. In fact, we use it in chapter 5 to compare the narratives of Miguel Cabello Valboa and Martín de Morúa in order to reconstruct an underlying text, the lost historical narrative written by Cristóbal de Molina. What we find are similarities in structure and content. In this case, similarities in wording may also be sought, and a good deal more may be gleaned from these texts about their source than what is attempted here.

Finally, although our purpose is to recover Inca genres, we are also studying the Spanish historical narratives created in Cuzco during the later sixteenth and early seventeenth centuries. Those historical narratives constitute a genre that is not strictly European in either nature or origin. The enterprise of the Spaniards and the two Andean authors who wrote historical narratives is similar to our own: they used Inca sources, recasting them in a form intelligible to Spanish readers and interpreting them according to canons of historical writing. In the sixteenth century, these canons dictated adherence to a universal, biblical history. In one famous case — the manuscript prepared by Sarmiento de Gamboa for the viceroy Francisco de Toledo — an author used Inca sources to justify a view that the Incas were tyrants who had only recently usurped authority over the Andean territory. Another author, Betanzos, may have twisted an Inca account to fit his wife's genealogical claims. In this case, an Inca source appears to have been used to suit an Inca, not a Spanish, purpose. The question of Inca history is more complex than we have heretofore been willing to imagine. We return to the nature of Inca history in the conclusions.

Our purpose in examining the Spanish historical narratives for their underlying Inca sources is so that we can read them. In chapters 6–8 we examine themes and messages in the Spanish historical narratives that drew from Inca sources in an effort to create a feedback relationship between the source analysis and our reading. We have been reading the narratives all along for information about the context of the material that was transmitted. By reading the narratives for messages and themes, we can learn more about the narratives.

The first reading (chapter 6) is to examine what Sarmiento wrote about the emergence of the Incas. According to the theory of composition outlined above, the story of early Cuzco was composed after the Inca expansion had begun. It explained how the Incas of the dynastic descent group had, from the time of origins, manifested their indomitable nature. In the backdrop of this story is another history. The chapter examines how the Inca account masks but does not obliterate a vision of the past in which they were subordinate to other powers. After the Incas are able to dominate their own political neighborhood, the story shifts to the obstacles to their quest for power on a much larger stage. These obstacles were identified by titles that incorporate the word *capac*. Whether or not these other Andean lords constructed *capac* status in the way the Inca dynasty did, the Incas recognized them as claimants to what appears to have been an exclusive status in their eyes. The expansion may simply be an effort to unseat these lords. What Sarmiento understood by the term *capac* does not appear to be what Betanzos understood, so we are applying Betanzos's understanding to Sarmiento's text. The voice that explains the Inca expansion in terms of unseating other lords with claims like the Incas' may not be Sarmiento's.

The next major theme we will explore is the transformation of Cuzco, and that subject is examined in chapter 7. It is embedded in the life history of Pachacuti, told by both Betanzos and Sarmiento. Again, Betanzos provides us with a different reading of the same material and one that goes far beyond what a Spaniard would find to be significant about the Inca project. Betanzos describes what is in effect a consecration of the city and its people. Moreover, the redesign of urban space represents the Inca past. That urban forms were vehicles for representing the past and not just archaeological remnants of earlier periods is something that was fundamentally foreign to Spaniards. The transformation of Cuzco was a complete retelling of the past, and the coincidence of the composition of both the genealogical and the life history accounts of earlier periods with this period of reinvention alerts us to the purpose of the encoded messages we have already read in chapter 6. A new past was created to explain the rise to power of the Incas. That rise, however, was a great deal more than just the conquest of Andean space. The dynastic story explains how a group of siblings, apparently subject to no greater authority, progressively achieved dominion over everything around them, moving from one plane to the next. Some of the story is in Sarmiento, but the story of the revelation of *capac* status cannot be understood without Betanzos's account of the transformation of Cuzco.

To a certain extent chapter 8 is also about what the Incas are not telling about their early history. It deals with the origin myth and with inconsistencies in its telling. These inconsistencies are a window into other versions and other strata of explanation. The Inca accounts of origin are an example of pasticcio: a work or style produced by borrowing fragments or motifs from various sources. Two stories are involved: the emergence of the Ayar siblings at Pacaritambo and the creation of everything by Viracocha at Tiahuanaco. These stories derive from Andean sources, but just as the Pacaritambo story appears to have changed with the transformation of Cuzco, the creation story appears to have been affected by the assault mounted by Christianity on Inca belief. New systems of explanation evolve from the old, so it is still possible to excavate older strata. In addition to the narratives, material from the lists of *huacas* preserved by Cobo and Albornoz and descriptions of dynastic rituals from the account of fables and rites by Molina is used to look for the cast of characters of other stories about origins. What we have done is to apply a theory of change to the diverse sources that refer to the characters described in the stories of Inca origins. As in chapter 2, we have expanded our frame of reference to include the period after the Spanish arrival, since change that occurred after the arrival of Pizarro and his band in Cuzco is critical to our understanding of the sources generated in their wake.

Rather than extracting a model of social organization from these sources or studying a system of thought, we are attempting to recover Inca knowledge about their past. At the end we return to the subject of Inca history. Since what we have learned can help to define it, we make that attempt. Comparison always brings differences into sharp relief, so we cast our definition against a general definition of history as a sixteenth-century Spaniard would have known it. There is change in the way history has been practiced by those who wrote in European languages, and new standards of truth and explanation have developed since the time the historical narratives about the Inca past were composed. It is wise not to forget that standards of truth and explanation are historically contingent.

## A NOTE ON TERMS AND SPELLING

In the text which follows terms like "empire" have been used that convey a meaning specific to English usage and which may not adequately describe the political configuration that existed in the Andes when Pizarro arrived in Cuzco in 1533. The term is used here as an approximation and assumes only that -- as in the case of European empires — a larger territory was governed in some way by a smaller group within it who had extended their authority by force or threat of force. The name given by the Incas to the whole was Tahuantinsuyo, so the unit was locally defined and can be expected to have been conceptualized in a manner specific to particular historical circumstances. Other terms like "king" have been avoided, even though the Incas and other Andean groups appear to have had hereditary rulers that Spaniards readily equated with monarchs. Writing about the Incas in any language other than the Inca language of the sixteenth century will have these same pitfalls, and readers must always remember that the underlying meanings are something that those who work with the Incas are trying to refine and distill from a variety of sources and by a variety of methods. Local ideas about the nature of sovereignty may be among the tacitly held assumptions we can read in the Spanish historical narratives that drew from Inca genres.

Except where noted, all native names have been Hispanicized and spelled in a consistent manner. There may be issues involved in the spelling of these names, but those interested in such issues will need to consult the original texts.

Finally, material inserted in square brackets [], such as dates or other versions of names, is an identification made by the author based on current information or expertise.

# 2 Capac

All versions of the Inca past stress descent through the male line from an apical pair: Manco Capac and a sister-wife. The Spanish historical narratives of the Inca past list approximately twelve generations spanning the time from origins to the Spanish arrival. All the accounts are structured by genealogy, even when an author attempts to correlate the Andean past with calendar years or European history. Genealogy was a structuring principle familiar to Europeans, but was this structure imposed by Spaniards on narrative material that had a very different purpose in its original context, or was the genealogical structure a feature of the underlying Inca source? Clearly, the Spaniards and the native Andeans who wrote narrative accounts of the Inca past had their own purpose in mind when they sat down to write. Just as clearly, these purposes cannot explain Inca practice. If the Incas kept an account of dynastic genealogy, what Inca purpose was served?

In this chapter, I will argue that the Incas kept an account of dynastic descent from Manco Capac because it was used as a reference in calculating *capac* status, a hereditary status that passed through the male line to each new generation of Inca brothers and sisters in the dynastic line. The status can only be imperfectly known, but clearly, both men and women were conduits for it. Because we have access to information that bears on Inca dynastic practice, it may seem that it was reckoned only by the group of people descended from Manco Capac. Certainly, they tried to make exclusive claims to *capac* status within the larger group of people who were Inca. At the same time, other non-Inca groups are identified as *capac* in the Spanish historical narratives. These peoples were rivals of special importance to the Incas and will be discussed in chapter 6.

The reckoning of descent was important in determining who was *capac* and to what degree, and this reckoning was embedded in more general practices related to affiliation. How the Incas determined who was Inca and how a person was classified within the broader group are at issue, but our approach will be to examine *capac* status in light of what we can glean about affiliation from early written texts, paying attention to particular instances where individuals asserted claims based on principles of descent or affiliation. The terms used to classify individuals or members of groups will enter into the analysis, although our use of them is subordinate to other approaches. Since we do not have ethnographic access to sixteenth-century practitioners, our expectation is that we will barely penetrate the conceptual universe in which these individuals operated. However, our interest is not to examine Inca practice in light of general models or even to develop a competing model but to trace the historical trajectory of *capac* status and understand what we can about how it was calculated.[1]

## AFFILIATION

The Incas of Cuzco — both those who were *capac* and those who were not, and including both males and females — were affiliated through the male line. While the dual nature of gender was fully utilized by the Incas in systems of symbolic representation, the descendants of Manco Capac, male and female, still traced their descent through the male line to their forebear and his sister-wife.[2] A woman's sons and daughters are members of their father's descent group. A son is *churi* to his father. A daughter is *huarmi churi* (literally, "a female churi") or *ususi* to her father. In contrast, a woman's children are *huahua*, the generic term for offspring used when referring to animal as well as human offspring (González Holguín [1607]; 1842: fols. 96v–97).

Several terms mark membership in the descent group as well as refer to a class of relatives. One is *huaoque*. While it means a man's brother or cousin, it also means a member of his descent group of the same age or older. The term *pana* was used by a man to refer to his sister, a cousin, or any woman of his patrilineage (González Holguín [1608]; 1952:270). *Churi* is the name used by men to refer to all members of their descent group younger in age than themselves. It is significant that a man called his daughter *huarmi churi*, which we have already noted means "female *churi*" (González Holguín [1608]; 1952:122, 184, 270, 359). She was a member of his descent group.

When the Spaniards arrived in Cuzco, the descent group of Manco Capac was further subdivided into eleven or twelve groups called *panacas*, derived from the word *pana*. Each one traced descent from one of the generations of direct descendants of Manco Capac. In the narrative of Sarmiento, the life history of each ruler is followed by a reference to the name of his *panaca* and to its representatives who lived in Cuzco when Sarmiento wrote. The segmentation process which created the *panacas* is part of the narrative and may be the most important theme of the genealogical genre. A clear pattern of marriage alliance with non-Inca groups is evident until the generation of Pachacuti, the ninth Inca, as will be discussed in chapters 3 and 6. Pachacuti married his son Topa Inca to his full sister Mama Ocllo and allowed the pair to succeed him in his lifetime. From the time of Pachacuti onward, the pair through whom the succession passed was, ideally, to be a full brother and sister, children of the Inca and the Coya. Clearly, the marriage strategies of the dynasty changed at this time, when the dynastic line also took on the project of imperial expansion.

Before the institution of sister-marriage, Inca women were members of the same segment of the dynastic descent group as their brothers, but when they married, a new relationship was created between a woman's descent group and her husband's. The term *caca* or *cacay* was used by the men of her descent group to mark various men who were related to the descent group through marriage. For example, a man called his father-in-law *caca* (Pérez Bocanegra 1631: 611–613; González Holguín [1607]; 1842: fols. 96v, 99). A man and his brothers-in-law called each other *cacay*. The Incas also used the term *caca* to refer to the mother's brother, who, in the same way as the husband of a sister, was not a member of the descent group. For example, the men related to Anahuarqui, the wife of Pachacuti, were called *cacacuzcos* in a colonial lawsuit (see below) (Rostworowski de Diez Canseco 1993: 135). They were related by marriage to the dynastic line. Because Sarmiento tells us something about the origins of each of the women who married the head of the dynastic line in each generation, we can tentatively identify other groups of *cacacuzcos*.

By defining an apical ancestor, a descent group could mark precisely who was a member and who was not. There would be no overlap. Clearly, there were various groups of people who lived in Cuzco who did not trace their descent to Manco Capac, including groups descended from two of his brothers (Sarmiento de Gamboa [1572], chap. 11; 1906: 33–34). While these people were still Inca, and the tie to the dynastic line may have been conceived of as genealogical in some sense, their members were not part of the dynastic descent group.

This interpretation of Inca affiliation practice differs from the view offered by Irene Silverblatt in *Moon, Sun, and Witches* (1987). Silverblatt does not reanalyze Inca affiliation practice but, rather, draws from earlier work by Reiner Tom Zuidema. In a 1967 study, Zuidema analyzed baptismal records from Anta, a town north of Cuzco, and found that men were often given their father's surnames while women received their mother's. The records began in the 1570s, before the 1583 Church Council that decreed this practice as official policy (Lisi

1990:133; Lounsbury 1986: 133–134). Zuidema concluded, therefore, that the practice was autochthonous. Parallel descent is not the only mechanism that would explain a parallel transmission of names, however. If a patrilineal descent group customarily chose women from another local patrilineage, then when a woman chose a surname for baptism it might well reflect her patrilineal affiliation. Zuidema's hypothesis countered earlier assertions that descent among those identified as Inca was patrilineal (see Webster's references to earlier literature, 1977:29, n. 2). It begged for a fuller inquiry into affiliation practice in the decades after Pizarro's arrival in Cuzco, but the matter has not generated related research on sixteenth-century sources.[3]

Rather than construct a general model of affiliation practice in the Andes or even among those identified as Inca, I will limit my inquiry to the transmission of *capac* status through the dynastic line. Inca men and women traced their descent through the male line back to Manco Capac and a sister-wife, the progenitors of the Inca dynasty and the conduit through which *capac* status passed. Where arguments are based on affiliation terms, these should not be viewed as unproblematic. Rather, they should be taken as tentative statements. We cannot get broad ethnographic confirmation, so our test is how well the explanation fits the specific cases we can find. Descent groups, reckoned patrilineally, appear to have characterized the larger population identified as Inca, regardless of any other calculations that may have been made through female lines. In an Inca creation story set at Tiahuanaco, the ancestors of all Andean peoples were sent out to the particular points on the landscape at which they were to emerge (Betanzos [1551–1557], pt. 1, chap. 1; 1987:11–12; Sarmiento de Gamboa [1572], chap. 7; 1906:26–28; chap. 11; 1906:33). For the Incas, at least, the world was peopled by a series of descent groups who traced their ties back to apical ancestors. There were other dynastic lines that the Incas marked with the term *capac* (see chapter 6), a tacit recognition by the Incas that the practice of other Andean groups bore some similarity to their own. How the Incas classified people is one thing, however. How non-Incas actually determined affiliation or the transmission of any special status is another.

The source materials we have focus on the Cuzco Incas, so that is a logical place to begin if we hope to unravel affiliation practice. At issue is how to read the narratives drawn from dynastic sources. Should they be read for what they reveal about social organization, or can they be read for what they purport to tell us about the Prehispanic past? At this moment I am reading them for what they reveal about *capac* status and how it developed over time. After introducing the concept of *capac*, I will explore specific instances of its transmission.

Since both males and females were conduits for *capac* status, as will be seen, the contribution of women is of particular interest and will be considered through several discrete examples. The story does not end with the arrival of the Spaniards, and I will also examine the behavior of individuals in concrete situations in early Spanish Cuzco. Using the explanatory value of an idea as a test of its validity is an anthropological approach. Trying to recast it in the context of the changed circumstances in which the Inca elite found themselves following the Spanish arrival is a historical exercise.

## CAPAC

The term *capac* referred to a class of people and not to a single individual. It was also used as part of a title that denoted a hereditary ruler. In 1572, when Sarmiento de Gamboa used the terms "Chimo Capac" or "Colla Capac," he referred to the hereditary ruler of Chimor or of the Colla, as if he had said the "Capac of Chimor" or the "Capac of the Colla."[4] These terms were supplied to him by well-born Incas who may have simply equated the practices other people used to identify a ruling line with their own, explaining foreign practice through reference to their own. What we can learn, as is most often the case with Cuzco sources, is about the Incas.

What did the term mean when applied to the Incas themselves? The one author who explored the usage of this term in detail was Juan de Betanzos, who devoted a chapter to it in his narrative history ([1551–1557], pt. 1, chap. 27; 1987:131–132). Betanzos, who can be placed in the Andes as early as 1531 (Calancha 1974–1981, vol. 1:240), soon developed competence in the Inca language and served in official capacities as an interpreter (Domínguez Faura 1994; Lohmann Villena 1997:129; Nowack 1998:513). He was married to a woman who claimed to be a member of Capac Ayllo, the descent group of Topa Inca, the tenth Inca. His narrative account of Inca history, completed in 1551, appears to have drawn heavily from a genre of Inca oral tradition, perhaps a life history of the Inca Pachacuti (see chapter 4). His history is not without detectable deformations, which will be noted below when the subject is his wife.

What is important here is that Betanzos interrupts his narrative with a chapter titled "In which is treated how Topa Inca Yupanqui was named Capac, and more particularly, how he was named Capac and what this name Capac means" (Betanzos [1551–1557], pt. 1, chap. 27; 1987:131–132). In it he describes the preparations made for the marriage and coronation of Topa Inca. Betanzos appears to be assimilating the meaning of the term to the Spanish term "king." Later in the same chapter, the subject turns to the child born to Topa Inca Yupanqui and Mama Ocllo, his sister. When the child was about six months old he was given a fringe headdress by his grandfather Pachacuti that signified "king and lord" and was similar to the one Pachacuti wore. The child also received the name Huayna Capac. It is at this point that Betanzos launches his commentary on the term *capac*.

> The term "Inca" properly means king, and this is the name by which all of the lords [*orejones*] of Cuzco are called, and each one of them, and to differentiate the Inca [here: king] or when they speak to him they call him Çapa Inca which means "only king." And when they want to confer a greater status upon him than king they call him *capac*. Everyone guesses at what this term means, but what I understand is that it is an expression that means "very much more than king." Some who do not understand the speech, stopping to consider what Huayna Capac means, to summarize their conclusion [about the use of this term] they say it means "rich young man." They don't understand, because, if it were *capa* without the final *c* they are right because *capa* means rich, [but] *capac* with the *c* is an expression that means very much more than king. And so Yamqui Yupanqui named the child Huayna Capac when he placed the royal fringe on him. And when they want to say emperors or monarchs in our sense of these terms, they say *capacuna*. And this is what *capac* means, according to what I know of the speech.

> Lo que quiere dezir Ynga dice propiamente rrey y ansi llaman a todos los orejones del Cuzco e a cada uno dellos y para diferençiar dellos al Ynga llamanle çapa ynga /fol. 65/ o cuando le quiere hablar que dize solo rrey y cuando le quieren dar mayor ditado que rrey llamanle capac lo que quiere dezir capac presuma cada uno que quiere ser que lo que yo entiendo dello es que quier[e] dezir un ditado mucho mas mayor que rrey y algunos que no entienden el hablar parandose a considerar que quiere decir Guaina Capac en rresolucion de lo que ansi han pensado dizen que dize mançebo rrico y no lo entienden porque si dixera capa sin çe postrera tenían rrazon porque capa dize rrico y capac con ce dize un ditado mucho mas que rrey e ansi le puso Yamque Yupangue quando ansi le fue dada la borla deste niño Guaina Capac y quando ellos quieren dezir como nosotros decimos los emperadores o monarcas dizen ellos capaccuna ansi que esto es lo que

quiere dezir capac segun que yo dello entiendo y de su hablar. (Betanzos n.d. [1551–1557], pt. 1, chap. 27, fols. 64v–65; 1987:132)

Betanzos faced the usual dilemma of those who translate terms loaded with meaning into another language. The word "Inca" could mean ruler, but a whole class of people in Cuzco, here called "orejones," was described by this term. In Spanish, the term "king" referred to a single individual, so Betanzos is clearly extending the meaning of a Spanish word to another context.

He calls the class of people who were Inca "orejones." There are numerous documentary references to *orejones*, Spanish for "big ears," the name given to wearers of golden ear spools. What members of this group had in common was an initiation ceremony during which their ears were prepared to receive ear spools. There were other people who were initiated in the Cuzco region who were Inca in a broader sense and who wore wool or something else, not gold, in their ears (Garcilaso [1609], bk. 1, chap. 23; 1990:40). They were also part of the group broadly defined as Inca but may not all have been recognized by the Spaniards as such and may have been excluded from the designation *orejones*. Betanzos appears to use the term "Inca" in a narrower sense to mean those who wore golden ear spools. He further differentiates among members of this group, defining two terms that marked status within it. One term was *çapa*: Çapa Inca meant "unique Inca" and referred to the person who was ruler. The other term was *capac*. Finding no equivalents in the Spanish lexicon for it, Betanzos twice tried to convey its meaning with the ambiguous statement that it meant "very much more than king" ([1551–1557], pt. 1, chap. 27; 1987:132). Fortunately, Betanzos provides other information about dynastic affiliation practice that can be used to contextualize the term *capac*. It is probably no coincidence that the question arises when he is discussing the infant Huayna Capac. Other authors have explained the meaning of this name as "rich prince." Betanzos debates their usage precisely in this case.

Before considering why this child was *capac*, information about the nature of the dynastic descent group must be taken into account. In the various Spanish narratives that trace a genealogical sequence from Manco Capac to Huascar, two different theories of dynastic practice are presented. One is that each new ruler was the product of a union between a full brother and sister (cf. Morúa [1590] 1946; Guaman Poma [1615] 1987). The other identifies a brother-sister marriage in the generation of Manco Capac, then traces a pattern of marriage to women from other, often non-Inca groups before turning to a pattern of sister-marriage in the generation of Topa Inca, the tenth Inca, and afterward (cf. Sarmiento de Gamboa [1572] 1906; Cabello Valboa [1586]

1951; Murúa [1611–1615] 1987; Pachacuti Yamqui Salcamaygua [early seventeenth century] 1993). Huayna Capac was the first ruler born to the union of a brother and sister from the preceding dynastic generation. If *capac* status was passed down the line of individuals directly descended from Manco Capac, then this child got a rather strong dose of it.

Here our hypothesis is that a concentration of *capac* status resulted from pairing individuals who were closest, in descent terms, to the dynastic line.[5] A full sister fulfilled this requirement better than anyone, but the Inca term *pana* extended to half-sisters and to cousins who traced their descent from Manco Capac, and these women may also have been conduits for *capac* status, especially when they were connected to the dynastic line on both their father's and mother's sides. Because only eleven generations were reckoned to have descended from Manco Capac at the time of Huayna Capac's birth, it was a relatively simple matter to determine the proximity of any individual to the dynastic line. Arguably, many individuals had some degree of *capac* status.

Some individuals were more *capac* than others, however. In Betanzos's narration of the social and physical reengineering of Cuzco that occurred at the time the imperial expansion began, he describes how Pachacuti populated the two precincts of the Inca city, called Hanan and Hurin Cuzco. Pachacuti had faced the Chanca invasion — the event that preceded Pachacuti's usurpation of rule from his father, Viracocha — with three friends, named Apo Mayta, Vica Quirao, and Quilliscachi Urco Huaranga. Later, Pachacuti rebuilt Cuzco and resettled its inhabitants in two districts, called Hanan and Hurin Cuzco. His three friends were resettled in the Hurin Cuzco precinct:

> He ordered the plan of the city and painting that he had had made of clay brought to him; and, having it in front of him, he distributed the already-finished houses and blocks, made as you have heard, to all of the citizens and residents of Cuzco, all of whom were lords, descendants of his lineage and of the other kings who had succeeded before him since the time of Manco Capac, settling them and ordering them to settle in the following manner: the three lords, his friends, were to populate the area from the houses of the Sun downhill toward the confluence of the two rivers — in that residential space fashioned between the two rivers, and from the houses of the Sun downhill — and he ordered that the place be called Hurin Cuzco, which means the lower part of Cuzco; and the very tail end of this neighborhood he ordered be called *pumapchupa*, which means "tail of the puma," in which place these three lords and those of their lineage

were ordered to settle, from whom and from each of whom the three lineages of Hurin Cuzco descended. These lords were named Vica Quirao, Apo Mayta, and Quilliscachi Urco Huaranga. From the houses of the Sun uphill — all the part occupied by the two arroyos up to the hill where the fortress is now — he distributed lands to the lords who were his closest relatives and who were descended directly from his lineage, children of the lords and ladies of his very descent group and lineage, because the three lords who were settled below the houses of the Sun, as you have already heard, were the bastard sons of the lords, although they were members of his lineage, born to women foreign to the Inca nation and of low birth. The Incas called the children so born *guacchaconcha*, which means "relatives of poor people of low status," and such children, although they are children of the Inca himself, are given this name. Neither the male nor the female children are taken for or held by the other lords as anything other than nobles of the common sort.

Mando traer alli la traça de la çiudad e pintura que ansi auia mandado hazer de barro e tiniendo delante de si dio e rrepartio las casas e solares ya edificados y hechos como oydo aueis a los señores del Cuzco y a los demas vezinos e moradores de todos los cuales heran orejones deçindientes de su linaje e de los demas señores que hasta el auian subçedido desde el prinçipio de Mango Capac poblandolos e mandandolos poblar en esta manera que los tres señores sus amigos poblasen desde las casas del sol para abaxo hazia la junta de los dos rrios en aquel espaçio de casas que entre los dos rrios se hizieron y desde las casas del sol para abaxo al cual sitio mando que se llamase Hurin Cuzco que dize lo baxo del Cuzco y el rremate postrero de la punta desto mando que se nombrase pumapchupa que dize cola de leon en el cual sitio poblaron estos tres señores ellos e los de su linaje de los cuales /fol. 36/ y de cada uno por si comenzaron e diçindieron los tres linajes de los de Hurin Cuzco los cuales señores se llamaron Vicaquirao y el otro Apomayta y el otro Quilis Cache Urco Guaranga e de las casas del sol para arriba todo lo que tomauan los dos arroyos hasta el çerro do agora es la fortaleza dio e rrepartio a los señores mas propicos deudos suyos e deçendientes de su linaje por linea rrecta hijos de señores e señoras de su mesmo deudo e linaje porque los tres señores de las casas del sol para abaxo mando poblar segun que ya aueis oido eran hijos bastardos de señores aunque eran de su linaje los cuales auian auido en mujeres estrañas de su naçion e de baxa suerte a los cuales hijos ansi auidos llaman

ellos guacchaconcha que quiere dezir deudos de pobre gente e baxa gene-
raçion y estos tales aunque sean hijos del Ynga son llamados ansi e no son
tenidos ni acatados ninguno destos ansi hombres como mugeres de los
demas señores sino como por vn orejon de los otros comunes. (Betanzos
n.d. [1551–1557], pt. 1, chap. 16, fols. 35v–36; 1987:77–78)

The status distinctions among those who were Inca required a genealogical
calculation. For the descendants of Manco Capac, it was the bloodline of
the mother, not the father, that would determine a greater or lesser degree of
*capac* status.[6] If before the dynastic line had been reproduced through alliance
with non-Inca women, now it would be reproduced by pairing individuals
from the dynastic descent group itself. However, the same father could produce "common" or "bastard" Incas as well as "noble" or "legitimate" ones.

Redefining the marriage rules was a form of social engineering. As time
went on, the composition of the Inca elite began to change. In a series of
ordinances attributed to Pachacuti, Betanzos tells us about how status was
marked to reflect it:

> He ordered and ruled that those of his lineage, his descendants, being
> properly *orejones* on both the father's and mother's side and from the city
> itself (he said this because he had given certain of his daughters to lords
> and many other daughters of the lords of his lineage, marrying the [pro-
> vincial] lords to these daughters to put them in the service and dominion
> of Cuzco, and what he ordered did not apply to these), would wear
> one or two falcon plumes on their heads as a sign so that they would be
> known and held and treated by the people of the land as his descendants,
> and if any other person should put on the feather or sign indicating he
> was from Cuzco, and of the most principal people, he would die for it.

> Hordeno y mando que los de su linaje y deçendientes siendo propiamente
> orejones de padre y madre de dentro de la çiudad del Cuzco dijo aquesto
> porque habia dado ciertas hijas suyas a caçiques señores y otras muchas
> hijas de señores de su linaje y casandolos con ellas por traellos a su serui-
> dumbre y dominio del Cuzco y no se entendia con los hijos destas esto
> que ansi mandaua y hera que truxesen vnas dos plumas de halcon por
> señal en la cabeça para que fuesen conoçidos y tenidos y acatados por
> toda la tierra por sus deçendientes y que si otra cualquier persona se la
> pu[si]ese la tal pluma o señal en que fuese del Cuzco y de los mas princi-

pales muriesse por ello. (Betanzos n.d. [1551–1557], pt. 1, chap. 20, fol. 56; 1987:110)

Betanzos speaks of another status designator: the wearing of two feathers. Since golden ear spools marked those who were *capac*, the two feathers apparently designated those who were residents of Cuzco. Later on (see quote below), he makes it clear that these people were also his descendants through the conduit of his son and daughter, Topa Inca and Mama Ocllo.

Betanzos alludes to marrying Inca daughters to provincial lords as a means of subjecting them to Inca authority. Marriage, as will be discussed again in chapter 7, was an alliance between two social groups, but it was an alliance that was not symmetrical: the woman's group was at least symbolically superior. Betanzos mentions this practice in passing, but there are many references in the Spanish historical narratives to the marriage of Inca daughters to provincial men. Guaman Poma was the product of one such union (1987:819 [833]). The creation of mixed-blood children was the result of a marriage policy that symbolized subordination. There is another side to this program of social engineering, however. If receiving an Inca daughter was a sign of subjection to Inca authority, what of the Inca men who took women, perhaps now only as secondary wives or concubines, who were not Inca? Betanzos brings up the problem of the status of those born to these sorts of mixed unions at the point in his narrative where Topa Inca begins to act on his own after the death of Pachacuti. Betanzos does not leave the topic there but expands on what had changed since then.

> After the death of his father, Topa Inca ordered that none of the descendants of Inca Yupanqui [Pachacuti], his father, should live outside the space between the two arroyos of Cuzco; and the descendants of Inca Yupanqui were called from then on Capac Ayllo Inca Yupanqui Hahuaynin, which means "lineage of kings, descendants, and grandsons of Inca Yupanqui." These [individuals] are more respected and highly held among the people of Cuzco than any other lineage, and these are the people who were ordered to wear two feathers on their heads. As time went on, this generation of *orejones* multiplied and created certain titles and honorifics like *mayorazgos*, and they took diverse family names, marrying themselves to women who were not of their lineage. Seeing this, those of Inca Yupanqui ordered that those who would mix their blood with that of outsiders would call themselves by another family name so

that they [those of Inca Yupanqui] could cleanly call themselves Capac
Ayllo and descendants of Inca Yupanqui. When the Spaniards would
come and ask, "What lineage do you belong to?" the problem grew, and
both the real members and the others gave their lineage in the manner
described above.

Y mando Topa Ynga Yupangue despues de la muerte de su padre que
ninguno de los deçindientes de Ynga Yupangue su padre poblase de la
parte afuera de los dos arroyos del Cuzco y a los deçindientes deste Ynga
Yupangue llamaron desde entonces hasta hoy capac aillo ynga yvpangue
haguaynin que dice de linaje de rreyes deçindientes y nietos de ynga
yupangue y estos son los mas sublimados y tenidos en mas entre los del
Cuzco que de otro linaje ninguno y estos son a quien fue mandado traer
las dos plumas en la cabeza y como andando el tiempo fueron multipli-
cando esta generacion de orejones vuo y ay el dia de hoy muchos que
hicieron cabeças y nombradias como mayorazgos y tomaron apellidos di-
versos casandose con mujeres que no heran de su linaje y viendo esto los
de Ynga Yupangue hordenaron que los que ansi mezclasen sangre ajena
que apellidasen nuevo apellido y sobrenombre para que ellos pudiesen lin-
piamente nombrarse capac caillo y deçindientes de ynga yupangue y como
viniesen los españoles todo esto se acresento [o alardeo] que ansi los vnos
como los otros se nombran de aquel linaje en la manera que ya aueis oydo
esto quando los españoles se lo preguntan de que linaje son. (Betanzos
n.d. [1551–1557], pt. 1, chap. 32, fol. 73v; 1987:150)

Children born to Inca men and non-Inca women were to be distinguished
from those born of unions where both parents were Inca in some sense.[7] Since
descent was reckoned patrilineally, the children of an Inca father were theo-
retically members of his *panaca*. Purity, however, had become important to
"those of Pachacuti," so names were used to distinguish subgroups within
Capac Ayllo. The view put forth in Betanzos is certainly partisan and reveals a
degree of prejudice by those with the right bloodlines toward others in the
dynastic descent group.

Betanzos's story embeds a view of affiliation practice within a historical
framework. If we can accept it, then the emphasis on descent through both
male and female lines developed at the same time Cuzco was transformed into
an imperial capital. The same Inca who is credited with reorganizing the capital was also said to have organized Inca history, formalizing the historical traditions related to his forebears, painting tablets with depictions of both kings

and queens, and organizing initiation rites to mark the special nature of the descendants of Manco Capac (Betanzos [1551–1557], pt. 1, chap. 17; 1987: 85–86; Sarmiento de Gamboa [1572], chaps. 30–31; 1906: 68–69). The historical genre not only recalled past glory, it located members of the Inca descent group with relation to one another and to the other residents of Cuzco, privileging those descended from Manco Capac through both father and mother and defining them as legitimate in comparison with other Incas descended from Manco Capac only through the paternal line. What we can learn about the internal divisions of the larger group called Incas from the incorporation of Inca source materials in Spanish historical narratives is not the topic here; it will be an important topic in chapters 6–8.

At this juncture we must ask, Has Betanzos framed Inca practice within a larger conceptual framework that is not Inca but Spanish? This question is technically unanswerable, but the likelihood is great that he did not. Inca practice after the reorganization of Cuzco privileged marriage between men and women of the descent group of Manco Capac. Though Spaniards determined affiliation bilaterally, rulership was a hereditary status that passed through the male line. The women closely related to the line through which succession passed typically married into other dynastic lines, despite the inbreeding that resulted from exchanges between dynasties in later generations. Inca women made a contribution to each generation of the ruling line. Children born to other women were Inca but of the "common" sort.

## INCA WOMEN

So far I have asserted — without offering much support for the assertion — that women also traced their descent through the dynastic line of Manco Capac. The genealogies of a number of highly born women indicate that such was the case, and several will be examined here. The woman or women whose birth qualified them as a possible spouse for the Inca were *coya*. The term is not parallel to the Spanish "queen," because to become a queen one had first either to inherit rule or to marry a king. Enough examples exist of the use of the term *coya* to refer to women who never married a ruler or ruled in their own right, so that we can conclude that women who were *coya* acquired the status in another way.

Before turning to specific examples of women who were *coya*, let us look at what Betanzos said about the status. Immediately after his description of the settlement of Cuzco in which he describes the settling of people of mixed ancestry in Hurin Cuzco (cited above), he describes the qualities of the person espoused to the Inca:

> The reader should know that the Inca who becomes ruler has a principal wife, and she must be a sister or a first cousin from his parentage or lineage; and they call this woman *piwi huarmi*, and by another name, *maman huarmi*; and the common people call this woman, as befits the principal wife of the king, when they enter to greet her *pacsa indi usus çapai coya huaccha coyac*, "Moon and daughter of the Sun and unique queen, friend of the poor." And this woman had to be directly related to the Inca through both the mother and the father without any spot or trace of *guaccha concha*, which is what you have already heard about; and this woman was received by the Inca as wife the day he received the fringe of state and royal insignia. The children of this woman were called *piwi churi*, which is the same as if we said "legitimate children."

> Abran de saber que el Ynga que ansi es señor tiene una muger principal y esta a de ser de su deudo e linaje hermana suya o prima hermana suya a la cual muger llaman ellos piuiguarmi y por otro nombre mamanguarme y la gente comun como a tal muger prinçipal del señor llaman quando ansi la entran a saludar paxxa yndi usus çapaicoya guacchacoyac luna e hija del sol e sola rreyna amigable a los pobres y esta tal señora *auia de ser de padre e madre derechamente señora e deuda del ynga sin que en ella vuiese rrasa ni punta de guaccha concha que es lo que ya aueis oydo y esta tal señora*[8] rresçibia el Ynga por muger prinçipal suya el dia que tomaua la borla del estado e ynsignia rreal e los hijos que ansi tal señora auia se nombrauan piuichuri que dize como si dixesemos hijos lixitimos. (Betanzos n.d. [1551–1557], pt. 1, chap. 16, fol. 36; 1987:78)

At the end of this passage Betanzos uses "legitimate" in the Spanish sense of being the legitimate issue of a marriage, since other children of the Inca could be legitimate in the Inca sense, that is, they were descended from Manco Capac on both father's and mother's sides.

Among the names used to address this woman is the term *inti usus*, glossed by Betanzos as "daughter of the Sun."[9] Here I must put this usage in the context of Inca affiliation terms. A number of authors refer to the Incas as *intip churi*, often translated as "son of the Sun" (Sarmiento de Gamboa [1572], chap. 29; 1906:66). Given that *churi* could also designate younger members of the same lineage, the term is better glossed as "younger members of the Sun's patrilineage" in the same way *inti usus*, used above by Betanzos, was glossed as "daughter of the Sun." It denotes women who are members of a lineage tied ultimately to a solar supernatural and who trace that relationship through genealogical descent from Manco Capac and his sister. The title incorporating this term reflects both the recognition of Inca affiliation with a solar supernatural and the concern with selecting marriage partners from the dynastic descent group.

Betanzos does not specifically tie this designation to the Inca expansion, but I will argue that *capac* status was something the dynastic descent group could only claim as a result of their success abroad (see chapter 7). Just as the assertion was a reflection of their success, it became difficult to make when their fortunes reversed. The Inca claim to *capac* status has a historical trajectory, and that is what we must try to unravel. To do so, let us look at the genealogies recorded for a number of Inca women. An analysis of how they are constructed and what they represent reveals the role played by women in the determination of status. The cases will be taken in chronological order.

### Anahuarqui

Anahuarqui was from Choco, a village very near Cuzco in the Huancaro valley (Sarmiento de Gamboa [1572], chap. 34; 1906:72). She was not a descendant of Manco Capac, if we correctly interpret a document from the late sixteenth century. Claims to land filed in 1589 asserted that the lands had belonged to Mama Anahuarqui, "*coya* and legitimate wife, according to their law, of Inca Yupanqui [Pachacuti]."[10] The claimants, a group of men, identified themselves as *cacacuzcos*. *Caca* is a term that means mother's brother or a man's brothers-in-law, "his wife's brothers and cousins" (González Holguín [1607]; 1842: fols. 97–98v), that is, the men of her patrilineage. The men who claimed to be "grandsons and descendants" of Anahuarqui were, following a patrilineal theory of descent, not her descendants at all. Under a system of parallel descent, they could not claim to be her descendants either. Given the basic intranslatability between Spanish and Inca practice, the best way to read the claims of the group of men self-identified as "*cacacuzcos*, residents in the parish of San Jerónimo . . . grandsons and descendants of Anahuarqui" would be to understand them to be members of her patrilineage. *Cacacuzcos* were the lineages from whom the principal spouses of the Incas came prior to the change in dynastic practice which prescribed marriage to a principal wife who was descended on both mother's and father's sides from Manco Capac.

Another reason for thinking Anahuarqui was not a member of the dynastic descent group is that she is never mentioned by Betanzos. As noted above, Betanzos represents the point of view of Capac Ayllo, the descent group claimed by his wife, Angelina, and which vaunted its own purity. As will be shown in chapter 5, he drew from a life history of Pachacuti. That he never names the woman who was, like Pachacuti, a progenitor of Capac Ayllo is significant.

The birth of Capac Ayllo was the linchpin in the reform of dynastic practice which accompanied the Inca expansion, the topic of chapter 7. Although we know very little about *panaca* formation before this moment, that is, about the specific parentage of the individuals who were the first generation of a new *panaca*, we know something about the first generation of Capac Ayllo. A petition was presented in 1569 by the "grandsons of Topa Inca Yupanqui." Because of the support given by the *panaca* of Topa Inca to Huascar's cause, Atahuallpa's generals had killed many adult members of the *panaca*. When the Spaniards arrived, the lands belonging to Topa Inca's *panaca* were easier to usurp than other, better-defended *panaca* lands (Rowe 1985b). What is interesting to note about the organization of the *panaca* indicated in the petition is that the descent group was formed not just by the descendants of Topa Inca but by those of his two full brothers as well.[11] It has heretofore been argued that the descendants of a ruler formed his *panaca* (Rowe 1946:202). The inclusion of all three sons of Pachacuti and Anahuarqui in Capac Ayllo is a clue that the generation of children produced by the preceding Inca pair was the basis of a new *panaca*, at least from this time forward. The origin of the *panaca*, like the origins of the dynastic line itself (see chapter 8), was a set of siblings. No mention was made of any sisters, because they were not conduits for *panaca* affiliation, but Mama Ocllo was their full sister.

What should not be forgotten is that these were the children of Anahuarqui, too. Earlier Incas had chosen spouses from other groups in the Cuzco region, as will be discussed below, so choosing a mother who was Inca, even if she were not a descendant of Manco Capac, would at least avoid ties to other groups created by marriage. However, when Pachacuti prescribed marriage with female descendants of Manco Capac, he conferred a lower status on his own *panaca*, when viewed from the perspective of Capac Ayllo. Capac Ayllo was the descent group of Topa Inca, not Pachacuti. The specific *panaca* of Pachacuti was Iñaca Panaca or Hatun Ayllo (Sarmiento de Gamboa [1572], chap. 47; 1906:93; chap. 54; 1906:102). Although Betanzos specifically gives the name as Capac Ayllo Inca Yupanqui Hahuaynin, glossing it as "lineage of kings, descendants, and grandsons of Inca Yupanqui" and clarifying its relationship to Pachacuti, he uses Capac Ayllo as synonymous with "los de Pachacuti" (Betanzos n.d. [1551–1557], pt. 1, chap. 32, fol. 73v; 1987:150, cited above).

In a very real sense, those of Capac Ayllo descended directly from Pachacuti through the conduit of his children, Topa Inca and Mama Ocllo.

### Mama Ocllo

Mama Ocllo was a full sister of the three progenitors of Capac Ayllo. She was perhaps the woman most revered by the Incas. There were shrines in Cuzco that were related to her, a golden image was made of her which had an active life after her death, and there was an elaborate funeral ceremony, or *purucaya*, held in her honor (Rowe 1979:10; Cabello Valboa [1586], pt. 3, chap. 20; 1951:360; pt. 3, chap. 22; 1951:174; Betanzos [1551–1557], pt. 1, chap. 44; 1987:189–190). Her *capac* status was unproblematic.

### Pallacoca and Rahua Ocllo

In the next generation, a problem arose. Because of it, arguments from genealogy were advanced that illustrate the logic of descent reckoning. The son of Topa Inca and Mama Ocllo, named Huayna Capac, had numerous children, but his principal wife bore no sons (Sarmiento de Gamboa [1572], chap. 60; 1906:105–106; Cabello Valboa [1586], pt. 3, chap. 21; 1951:364; pt. 3, chap. 24; 1951:394; Murúa [1611–1615], chap. 31; 1987:111–112). The question then arose, Which of the children of other wives had the best genealogical claims to succeed as Inca? The story is usually told as a political contest between two sons of Huayna Capac named Atahuallpa and Huascar. There is a genealogical angle to the story, however. Atahuallpa, according to Betanzos, was the son of Pallacoca. Her father was Llapcho, a grandson of Pachacuti and a member of Capac Ayllo. Huascar, on the other hand, was the son of Rahua Ocllo. Her specific parentage is not given. She was described as being from Hurin Cuzco and related to many of the lords of that division, although she was "a little bit related" to Pachacuti. Who her father or mother was is not mentioned (Betanzos [1551–1557], pt. 1, chap. 46; 1987:194; pt. 1, chap. 47; 1987:197–198). Following Betanzos, we would conclude that she was descended from one of the *panacas* of Hurin Cuzco, with some tie to the *panaca* of Pachacuti through intermarriage. Very probably there were other women in Cuzco who had a genealogical position equal to or better than Rahua Ocllo's; Pallacoca, for one.

### Angelina Yupanqui

If Betanzos offers insight into the logic of *capac* status, the story he tells about the genealogy of his own wife is problematic. However, even if we regard her genealogy as a falsification, it still reveals something about the logic of descent.

Betanzos was married to Angelina Yupanqui, and his manuscript is, at least in part, a means of asserting his wife's claims to direct descent from the line of Manco Capac. The Betanzos narrative may well have been written as the backdrop for a story about Angelina's descent (Nowack 1998b:514). The story begins with the birth of Angelina's forebear Yamqui Yupanqui, presented in the text as the eldest son of Pachacuti and one of two sons by the wife he took when he received the royal fringe, that is, by his principal wife. The second son was Topa Inca ([1551–1557], pt. 1, chap. 20; 1987:99). This story is contradicted in a document presented in 1569 by the members of Capac Ayllo, documenting the status of the descendants of Capac Ayllo (Rowe 1985b:195–196, 222–223). Yamqui Yupanqui is not one of the three sons mentioned in the petition. The same three sons are specifically mentioned as the product of the union of Pachacuti and Anahuarqui by two authors who drew from Inca sources (Murúa [1611–1615], bk. 1, chap. 21; 1987:80; Sarmiento de Gamboa [1572], chap. 37; 1906:77; chap. 40; 1906:83; chap. 42; 1906:84; chap. 47; 1906:93). In one of these accounts, the three full brothers of Topa Inca are mentioned, immediately followed by a reference to Yamqui Yupanqui (Murúa [1611–1615], bk. 1, chap. 21; 1987:80); if he had been a full brother, he would have been included with the others. Betanzos weaves Yamqui Yupanqui and his descendants seamlessly into his historical narrative, putting him at the very heart of dynastic affairs. For example, the Betanzos story represents Yamqui Yupanqui as Pachacuti's successor, who, recognizing his younger brother's virtues, passes along the royal fringe and the woman elected to be the principal wife, abdicating rule himself.[12]

The casting of Yamqui Yupanqui and his son, also named Yamqui Yupanqui, who was Angelina's father, as major players on the Inca stage is decidedly a deformation of the genealogy-cum-history of the Incas. However, whether the story is an utter fabrication or not, the argument itself is structured in a way that reflects a consciousness of how *capac* status was transmitted. Angelina traced her descent through the male line back to Pachacuti and claimed membership in Capac Ayllo.

### Francisca Ynguill

The case of another Inca woman, Francisca Ynguill, illuminates our understanding both of Inca practice and of the difficulties of the period after the death of Huayna Capac, when a civil war broke out between his sons Atahuallpa and Huascar. In a lawsuit over the claims of Juan Pizarro's descendants in Cuzco, information about the genealogy of Francisca Ynguill, the woman who bore his children, was presented. A series of Spaniards testified, but it was a group of Inca witnesses who supplied information about her genealogy. Some witnesses were better informed than others, but all said she was affiliated with the *panaca* of Inca Roca, the sixth Inca of the dynastic series and the first Inca of Hanan Cuzco.

The first witness was Anton Ruiz Urco Guaranga, an Inca who resided in the parish of San Jerónimo. No *panaca* affiliation was supplied for him. The year was 1572, the year the parish was created. *Panacas* from both Hanan and Hurin Cuzco had been settled there, so even his affiliation at the level of *suyo* cannot be identified (Julien 1998:85–86). He noted that Francisca Ynguill was the daughter of Guamanta Issi Capac, who was himself a "son and grandson" of "Atun Inga Roca Capac" and who had been a "first cousin" of Huayna Capac (Archivo General de Indias, Patronato 90B, no. 1, ramo 55, fol. 109v). He was seconded in his testimony by don Garcia Aparamti, identified as a lord of Hanan Cuzco (Archivo General de Indias, Patronato 90B, no. 1, ramo 55, fols. 110–110v). A later witness, don Francisco Guaman Rimache, an Inca who had been in charge of the people of Larapa, a settlement near San Jerónimo in the Cuzco Valley that had just been moved to San Jerónimo, also named Guamanta Yssi Capac as "son and grandson" of "Ynga Roca Ynga," specifying that the latter had been a "natural lord" of the land (Archivo General de Indias, Patronato 90B, no. 1, ramo 55, fol. 110v). This Ynga Roca Ynga is the Inca Roca who was sixth on the genealogical list that began with Manco Capac. Elsewhere, Guaman Rimache identifies himself as the brother of Ynguill (Guillén Guillén 1994:274).

The Spanish relationship terms make no sense. Someone cannot be both son and grandson of the same person. If the terms are taken as indicative of lineage affiliation, what is being specified at the most general level is that someone is a direct descendant of that person and a member of that *panaca*. Guaman Rimache is telling us that Francisca Ynguill is a direct descendant of Inca Roca, the sixth Inca. If Inca Roca was the great-great-great-grandfather of Huayna Capac, it would be difficult to describe his descendant Guamanta Yssi Capac, the father of Ynguill, as the "first cousin" of Huayna Capac. Again, what is being translated does not fit easily into Spanish. If the Inca term for brother could extend to mean men of a man's patrilineage of his generation or older, then perhaps the Spanish term "primo hermano" was being used to define a person of the same patrilineage who was not, strictly speaking, a first cousin.

Anton Ruiz Urco Guaranga also testified that Francisca Ynguill was "very young" and that she had been kept in seclusion by Manco Inca "because she was of his descent and lineage, to create in her his caste and children" (Archivo

General de Indias, Patronato 90B, no. 1, ramo 55, fol. 109v). Manco Inca became ruler after Pizarro arrived in Cuzco. He was a young man, and since accession and marriage were conflated, he would have soon chosen the person through whom the dynastic succession would pass. Ynguill was too young to be married, so Manco was waiting for her to mature before taking her as principal wife. That apparently never happened. Juan Pizarro took her to wife instead.

The witnesses tell us nothing about who Ynguill's mother was. We have already learned that a calculation of the mother's genealogical nearness to the line through which Inca rule passed was important. There were daughters of Huayna Capac in Cuzco that Manco Inca might have married, although perhaps they, too, were being monopolized by Spaniards. We can also assume that there were direct descendants of Pachacuti and Topa Inca who survived the cataclysmic events of the Inca civil war. However, the choice of a young girl descended on the male side from Inca Roca would suggest that what set her apart from other possible candidates was the affiliation of her mother. Perhaps Manco did not suspect that the Spaniards would attack the dynasty by appropriating the women through whom *capac* status passed,[13] thus making it much more difficult to assert respectable genealogical claims. In the post–Inca civil war, post–Spanish arrival world, where serious losses had already been incurred among the very people who embodied a status that may have been an essential qualification for rulership, finding individuals with these qualities became increasingly difficult.

### NEW RULERS, NEW RULES

Not only did it become difficult to reproduce the dynasty following the old rules, but the Spaniards who arrived in Cuzco came with a new set of rules for determining affiliation and succession. While they recognized that succession to Inca rule was inherited through a dynastic line that was traced back to a particular ancestor, they did not understand or did not honor the contribution of Inca women to the status that was being inherited. If a man was a direct descendant of the last Inca ruler, then in Spanish eyes he had a legitimate claim to govern. Marriage to a sister was unthinkable, and marriage to a first cousin was not permitted without special dispensation. Both the interference of Pizarro in electing a new Inca and the dilution of *capac* status would have caused problems for the dynasty. A large number of people would also have had a modicum of *capac* status, but perhaps no one had such a clear concentration of it that they would stand out as an obvious candidate for rule on the basis of their genealogy. The problem rapidly worsened, given the competition for power within the dynasty that was unleashed when the Spaniards arrived in Cuzco.

Pizarro met a young son of Huayna Capac named Manco Inca prior to his arrival in Cuzco and decided that he would support Manco's claim to sovereignty. To what extent Pizarro's sponsorship affected Manco's success in asserting his claim is unknown, but, by the criteria we have been exploring, Manco had a less than ideal pedigree. A son of Huayna Capac, he was Hanan Cuzco on his father's side only. His mother was a native of Anta, a place in the valley just north of the city of Cuzco (Betanzos [1551–1557], pt. 2, chap. 28; 1987:289). The people of Anta were Incas (Guaman Poma [1615]; 1987:347), but they may not have been descendants of Manco Capac.[14] Hence, if we judge Manco Inca by the standards of Capac Ayllo, as we understand them from Betanzos, Manco's genealogical claim was even weaker than Huascar's.

In the years that followed Pizarro's recognition of Manco, a competing claim to Inca sovereignty would be asserted by another son of Huayna Capac: Manco's half-brother Paullo. Paullo was the son of Añas Colque, a very well born woman from Huaylas (Betanzos [1551–1557], pt. 2, chap. 19; 1987:260; Varón Gabai 1997:175–177). However well born she might have been in Huaylas, by the standards of Capac Ayllo her son was a "bastard." Here we are using the word "bastard" as the opposite of "legitimate" as this term was used by Betanzos, that is, to refer to people whose fathers descended from Manco Capac but whose mothers were non-Inca. Guaman Poma, who wrote long after Paullo's death, also uses the term "bastard" to describe Paullo, whom he calls "a bastard son of Huayna Capac" ([1615]; 1987:181). Guaman Poma defines *capac apo* as "perfect king" and *auquicona* as "bastards — *auquiconas* — and they were called *mestizo*," referring specifically to Paullo ([1615]; 1987:117–118; cf. Garcilaso de la Vega [1609], bk. 1, chap. 26; 1990:45). At the time Guaman Poma wrote, the term *mestizo* referred to a person of mixed Spanish and Indian blood. Guaman Poma used its meaning in Spanish as a reference to persons of mixed blood to refer to Paullo, but this time the mixture was of Inca and non-Inca lines.

Paullo did not have a claim to rule under Inca rules of succession. He was no threat to Manco Inca. In fact, in the early years of the Spanish occupation of Cuzco, Paullo was the steward of Manco Inca and carried out his brother's wishes, which may even have included committing murder (Betanzos [1551–1557], pt. 2, chap. 28; 1987:290). Manco sent Paullo with Diego de Almagro on an expedition in 1535 which reached Chile. Someone who could not assert a claim to rule would have been a better choice for such an assignment than a person who had the genealogical qualifications to rule and who might use this opportunity to raise a claim that would compete with Manco's.

As we know from history, Manco's choice was not as safe as he thought. When Paullo returned to Cuzco at the time of Manco's revolt, Almagro gave him the *borla* — the fringe that was worn by the Inca ruler (Temple 1937a: 219– 226). What had happened? The most logical explanation of this turn of events is that Paullo had learned that, in Spanish eyes at least, the genealogical contribution of his mother was not a liability. Following the logic of Spanish rules of succession, he was an acceptable alternative to Manco.

In a recent study by Gonzalo Lamana (1997), a strong case is made that Paullo was also acceptable to many non-Incas. While the Inca civil war may have originated at least to some degree in the status differences between Hanan and Hurin Cuzco, the rise of Paullo was a different sort of contest over status. We cannot assume that the distinction the Incas made between those descended from Manco Capac on both sides and those who traced descent through the patrilineage alone meant anything beyond Cuzco. In fact, the very high status of Paullo's mother in Huaylas may have given him a claim to rule that non-Incas could support. His mixed-blood status may have won him acceptance by others of mixed Inca blood, and perhaps even of Hurin Cuzco. Paullo's acceptance, albeit briefly, as Inca and the support he generated among non-Incas indicate fissures in Inca claims to legitimacy that could open and engulf the empire in fratricidal wars.

The contest between Manco and Paullo continued long after their deaths in the 1540s. Manco died in Vilcabamba, leaving three sons who successively became regent or ruler (Guillén Guillén 1976–1977: 49–55). Paullo died in Cuzco after successfully negotiating a relationship with Francisco Pizarro — despite his having been allied with Almagro — after Almagro's death. He died a wealthy man, with a large *encomienda* worth what some of the more principal Spaniards in Cuzco held. His sons by several women were legitimated by royal decree, and he married the mother of his eldest son, Carlos. Carlos was well educated. He spoke and wrote Spanish as well as anyone and had also learned Latin (Temple 1940, 1948b). However, Paullo's claims to rule were not recognized by Pizarro and those who governed Peru after Pizarro. Instead, the Spanish crown recognized the sovereignty of the descendants of Manco. From the time Manco Inca had retired to Vilcabamba, to the overthrow of his third son, the Inca Topa Amaro, the Spanish crown negotiated with the line of Manco, recognizing it to hold a legitimate claim to Inca sovereignty. Spanish recognition of Inca sovereignty only came to an end when Topa

Amaro was captured and executed in 1572, at the time Viceroy Toledo was in Cuzco (Guillén Guillén 1976–1977:49–55).

On the eve of Topa Amaro's capture two incidents occurred which indicate that ideas about *capac* status continued to animate claims to Inca sovereignty up to the bitter end.

### *Toledo's* Paños

One of these incidents occurred in January 1572, when Viceroy Toledo assembled a group of those descended from Manco Capac to validate a history and a genealogy of the Inca dynastic lineage. The history, painted on three large cloths (approximately 3.5 x 3 m square), portrayed the Incas and Coyas from Manco Capac and his sister to Huascar, who Toledo claimed was the last legitimate Inca. The genealogy was painted on a single, long cloth (approximately 5.5 x 1.5 m) and traced the same line from the time of Manco Capac and his sister to what was then the present (Julien 1999; Montesinos [1642]; 1882:244–259; Sánchez Cantón 1956–1959, vol. 2:252).

The point that Huascar was the last legitimate Inca was strongly made to the people there assembled. Toledo appears to have understood that the Incas had their own definition of legitimacy. In a letter that accompanied the *paños*, he noted that he had proved that the line of legitimate rulers "was finished and that no descendants remained except those who were descended transversely or bastards" (Levillier 1924, vol. 4:54–55). Toledo understood that Manco Inca's claim to rule — following an Inca reckoning — was weak. Toledo's argument that Huascar was the last legitimate ruler was echoed in the written historical narrative prepared by Sarmiento de Gamboa under the viceroy's sponsorship and sent as a gift to Philip II at the same time as the *paños* ([1572] 1906). By declaring Huascar to be the last legitimate Inca, Toledo derailed the claims of any other son of Huayna Capac. Not only the sons of Manco and Paullo but the sons of Atahuallpa, who were under the guardianship of the crown at that time, were denied the possibility of asserting claims to sovereignty.

It is doubtful that the Incas agreed with Toledo that, with the death of Huascar, the status that flowed through the line of Manco Capac had been eliminated. What caused a problem at the authentication, however, was the depiction of the descendants of Paullo in a position superior to that of the descendants of Manco Inca. During the act of authentication, María Cusi Huarcay, the full sister and widow of Saire Topa (Villanueva Urteaga 1970), the eldest son of Manco Inca, protested the positioning of a daughter of Paullo, named doña Juana, "above" her own portrait. The *paños* have not survived, so we cannot know how the *paño* depicting Inca genealogy was painted, but clearly the descendants of Manco understood that they had been subordinated to people who were not "legitimate" in Inca terms. During the authentication, María Cusi Huarcay is reported to have said: "And how can it be borne that the father of don Carlos [Paullo] and he are in a more prominent place, and his sister, being bastards, than my father [Manco] and I, being legitimate." Toledo is said to have responded: "Don't you see, doña María, that don Carlos and his father always served the king, and your father and brother have been tyrants and have remained hidden in the mountains" (Archivo General de Indias, Lima 270, fols. 532–533; Urbano 1997:239–241; Temple 1948b:168–171). Toledo had conveniently forgotten that the Spanish crown had recognized the rights of Saire Topa and Cusi Huarcay as Inca sovereigns and had negotiated with Titu Cusi as sovereign as late as 1565 (Guillén Guillén 1976–1977). He was not ignorant of the status differentiation between Manco and Paullo, as indicated by his own statement that only transverse descendants and "bastards" remained. His use of the term "bastards" in the citation above may well refer to a legitimacy determination that followed Inca rules.

### Melchor Carlos Inca

Toledo's knowledge of what *capac* status was is also evident in the case of Melchor Carlos Inca's baptism. Melchor Carlos was the son of Carlos Inca and María de Esquivel, a Spanish woman whom Carlos married following the customary Spanish rules (Temple 1937b:300; 1948a:113–114; 1948b:155–160; 1949–1950a:632–634). According to one source, Toledo was the baptismal godparent (Baltasar de Ocampo in Maúrtua 1906, vol. 7:308–309).

In the months following the baptism, Toledo had Carlos and other Incas arrested and tried for their complicity in the Vilcabamba rebellion (Nowack and Julien 1999). The suit has not survived, but the notary who prepared the documentation later testified that Carlos, his brother Felipe Saire Topa, and others had been charged by Gabriel Loarte, the criminal prosecutor, with acknowledging Melchor Carlos to be *capac*: "and furthermore, the said don Carlos and the said don Felipe and others had sworn a son that had been born to him as *capac*, which means king" [y ansimismo el dicho don Carlos y el dicho don Filipe y otros a vn hijo que le nasçio al dicho don Carlos le avian jurado por capac que quiere dezir rrey] (Archivo General de Indias, Lima 29, no. 6, fols. 70v–71).[15] This situation is nothing short of astonishing. The child, of course, was a *mestizo* in the Spanish sense. He was the son of Carlos Inca and a Spanish woman. Following the criteria of Capac Ayllo, this child could not have been *capac*: he had a non-Inca mother. Carlos could only have called his son *capac* under the logic of a Spanish rule of succession.

The strategies of Paullo and his sons are revealing. For Paullo, the old rules seem to have been a motivating factor in his behavior. Whether or not Paullo was part of an aggrieved class of mixed-blood Incas, his own behavior demonstrates that he tried to reconcentrate *capac* status in his descendants. On his way to Chile with Almagro, Paullo married a woman of excellent Inca pedigree from the Copacabana sanctuary. She may have been descended from Viracocha Inca, the eighth Inca in the line of Manco Capac (Ramos Gavilán [1621], bk. 1, chap. 12; 1988:85; chap. 31; 1988:85). Apparently this woman bore him no children. The woman who bore Carlos and Felipe, two sons who were considered the issue of his principal wife, was Catalina Tocto Ussica, who descended from Inca Roca, the sixth Inca, whose *panaca* was affiliated with Hanan Cuzco (Temple 1948b:135–141; Varón Gabai 1997:175–177; Nowack and Julien 1999). Under the old rules, the children of this marriage would have had a better claim to rule than their father. On the other hand, Carlos's choice of spouse indicates a very different mentality. Carlos had found a place within the *encomendero* society of Spanish Cuzco, of which he was an established member. When he and other Incas recognized his son Melchor Carlos as *capac* at his baptism, they were constructing an argument based on Spanish, not Inca, rules.

It was certainly the wrong moment for any kind of assertion of sovereignty. Toledo was to generate various texts denying sovereignty to the Incas. In the ceremony authenticating the *paños*, he would serve official notice to the dynasty that the last legitimate Inca — Huascar — had died at the hands of Atahuallpa just as the Spaniards had arrived in the Andes (Montesinos [1642] 1882; Julien 1999). The suit against Carlos and other Cuzco Incas was conducted concurrently with the Vilcabamba campaign. At the same time Topa Amaro was captured, Carlos and the others awaited sentencing. It was too late to argue claims to sovereignty — by any rule whatsoever.

## INCA HISTORY

Following the historical trajectory of *capac* status through the period of Toledo's challenge to Inca sovereignty is an essential step in arguing for the existence of Inca history. The need to calculate one's nearness to the dynastic line is a sufficient reason for keeping a record of dynastic descent. What is more, the determination of who was *capac* did not end when Spaniards suddenly appeared in Cuzco. There was good and sufficient reason for the continuation of Inca practice during the time Inca sovereignty was recognized by the Spanish crown.

The devaluation of *capac* status occurred only after Toledo asserted that the Incas were not natural lords. Betanzos wrote well within the period when *capac* status was recognized by the Spanish crown and from the perspective of Capac Ayllo. Pedro Sarmiento de Gamboa wrote at the very end of that period ([1572] 1906). His historical narrative bolstered Viceroy Toledo's argument that the last legitimate Inca was Huascar. It was constructed from Inca sources and authenticated by members of the *panacas*. Rather than an argument about *capac* status, which Sarmiento appears not to have understood, his central argument was that the Incas were tyrants and had annexed the Andean territory only recently, by force. They were not natural lords. It is the account of Betanzos, not Sarmiento, which allows us to penetrate the logic of *capac* status.

Even though Inca sovereignty had been dealt a serious blow, affiliation by *panaca* was recognized and continued long after Toledo (Julien 1998b). New ideas about succession had also been learned, well before Toledo's arrival in the Andes, by those who could not make a claim under the old rules. Since the Spanish rule recognized descent in the male line (but only direct descent from the last recognized ruler and not the accretion of a particular status through inheritance), only those who traced descent to Huayna Capac could put forward claims that stood a chance of being recognized. Under an Inca rule, there may have been descendants of Pachacuti or Topa Inca — and especially Topa Inca or his brothers — who had more *capac* status than Manco Inca. Even at this very early moment, being a son of the former ruler — a Spanish prerequisite for kingship — can have outweighed Inca preferences. Manco Inca was, at least to some degree, chosen by Pizarro.

We now have a historical trajectory for the recognition of *capac* status, even if we do not really have any deep understanding of what it meant to be *capac*. We have also identified reasons for Inca interest in the preservation of a standard genealogy of the generations through which this status passed: genealogical knowledge buttressed claims made by individuals to authority in Cuzco and, while it lasted, over an Andean empire. Genealogy is a form of history. By its nature it incorporates a chronological sequence, whether or not a correlation is made to any kind of time scale. Spaniards like Betanzos, Sarmiento, and others may have captured an Inca genre that recorded a dynastic genealogy.

# 3 Genealogy

Of the written sources that deal in some way with the Inca past, those that seem most like history are the accounts structured around the genealogy of the descent group of Manco Capac and his sister-wife, the apical pair through whom *capac* status passed. Genealogy, by its very nature, incorporates a historical sequence. The Spaniards learned about Manco Capac, the Chancas, the *pururaucas*, and, even, the war between Huascar and Atahuallpa from the Incas of Cuzco. When they wrote a "history" of the Incas that began only twelve generations before, what they wrote was antithetical to a Christian belief that all mankind had its origins in Adam and Eve. There was no European model for what they wrote; rather, some Inca source underlies the genre of historical narrative that developed in Cuzco.

In this and the following two chapters, we will be examining the historical narratives for information about Inca sources. A recent effort was initiated by Gary Urton to try to work on this problem by studying *quipos* (1998). It may be possible to learn the symbolic system encoded in these knotted devices and approach the question of historical knowledge with this tool. However, our inquiry is more broadly focused. For example, a formal account of dynastic genealogy was kept, but it does not appear to have relied to any great degree on *quipo* recording. Songs with historical content may have been transmitted without any kind of recording device. Moreover, our concern is with content, not with the means of transmission. The general premise is that the content of Inca source materials and, perhaps, discrete genres can be distinguished, *grosso modo*, in the texts that drew from them: in the same way that a Cabello Valboa could draw material from a text like Molina, an author could incorporate material from Inca sources into a narrative account of the Inca past.

We have begun this enterprise by launching an argument that dynastic practice relied on a knowledge of genealogy. Genealogy is the structuring device of all the historical narratives written in Spanish. Our initial hypothesis, then, is that the Incas had a formal mechanism for transmitting knowledge of dynastic descent. Groups who trace descent from a particular ancestor — or, in this case, generation — may articulate an ideology of descent. Was the Inca account a straightforward genealogy, or was it more? Did it articulate an ideology of descent? Our approach to these questions is to excavate the Spanish historical narratives for their Inca content. By comparing the narratives themselves, the structure of underlying Inca genres may become visible. We will also read what some Spanish authors said about recording and transmitting material on the Inca past, but what they said will be tested against what we can learn about Inca sources from the narratives.

A fundamental step in this process is the selection of sources; narratives that were explicitly drawn from Inca sources will be preferred. Authors who knew something about Inca genres may have had direct access to bearers of material that had origins in these sources. Authors who knew the Inca language are also important; even when they translate material into Spanish, they have a better grasp of the concepts they are translating. We have already encountered Juan de Betanzos: he will be one of our principal sources for information on Inca genres. When he tried to explain the misunderstandings of other authors, as he did when he explained what *capac* status was, he helped us to resituate our own perspective so that it is closer to the point of view of the Inca sources.

The idea that some source materials are better than others is an old one. Almost everyone who has worked with the historical narratives on the Inca past exhibits a preference for some texts while tacitly or explicitly rejecting others. Some authors have classified sources in such a way as to make their biases explicit. For example, Philip Ainsworth Means (1928) assessed authors on the basis of where their sympathies appeared to lie: authors close to Viceroy Toledo, who was hostile to the Incas, were regarded as less reliable than other authors who extolled the accomplishments of the Incas or were otherwise sympathetic to their descendants. Others who have classified the authors who wrote narratives on the Incas have ordered them chronologically or grouped them by the social role of the principal author (Porras Barrenechea 1986; Pease García Yrigoyen 1995). Such treatments provide a useful historical context for the activities of the Spanish and indigenous authors who wrote about the Inca past.

For our purposes, what makes a source valuable is the degree to which it drew from underlying Inca genres, regardless of the messages the author tried to embed in the text. Since the transmission of Inca genres may have come to an end at a particular time, nearness in time to the transmission of Inca generic material — even if the material had evolved in some way after the Spaniards arrived — is also a factor. Some authors borrowed wholesale from earlier source materials and so may transmit material whose structure and content reflect the underlying Inca genre. These accounts are more valuable for our purposes than early sources that are primarily based on eyewitness material. Such narratives contain valuable material about the past, but they do not tell us much about Inca genres.

We will take at face value the statements of Spanish authors that they drew their material from Inca informants in Cuzco. Their narratives offer us a starting point. Our project is to try to recover Inca genres in whatever form they were used as sources for Spanish historical narratives. After selecting narratives that drew their material from Inca sources, the second fundamental step is to compare them. The order and kind of events chosen for inclusion are what will be compared. Even if an account of the past is reinterpreted through a new cultural filter, we may be able to recover the underlying event structure of an Inca source and detect themes or messages. Although we would like to know about how the material was transmitted or performed, the texts we are analyzing are not good sources of information about those practices. The performance that resulted in the inclusion of Inca source material in a Spanish historical narrative would have occurred in a radically different context from the venues in which the same material was performed for an Inca audience. What we can hope to recover is some information about the content of recorded genres.

Most of the genealogical accounts we will examine were collected between the late 1540s and the 1570s. In all cases, time had passed since the Spanish arrival. The first decades after the Spanish arrival were a time of intense cultural confrontation. Even before Pizarro and his band arrived in Cuzco, the Incas were engaged in a conflict that appears to have affected what members of the dynastic descent group told Spaniards about their past. However, because of the nature of genres (they embed a format or features that limit or define them), they will evolve within these parameters, or they are no longer Inca genres. We have to be aware of several sources of instability: although the processes of transmission established before the Spaniards arrived can have continued, we do not necessarily expect that the Spaniards tapped into these lines of transmission. The Spaniards may have simply written down what particular informants remembered of the genres, particularly after any formal transmission processes came to an end. Authors who had some access to Inca genres, that is, to material that had been organized in a particular format and was transmitted orally, with or without the aid of recording devices, may have introduced their own interpretations or read new values and meanings into an old story but would still preserve the structure of the underlying genre and, possibly, some of its themes and messages. These conjectures serve only as reminders of what processes can have affected the material that was used in the construction of

Spanish narratives. However, the only way to learn about them is through the narratives themselves, so we return to our point of departure.

First we will select the authors who structured their accounts using dynastic genealogy, then we will examine the genealogical information they contain. Many accounts also include information about the Inca *panacas*. We know something about a painted history from descriptions of it and from a series of painted cloths made in emulation of it as an accompaniment to the historical narrative of Pedro Sarmiento de Gamboa. Since the painted history included, at the very least, the Incas and Coyas through whom succession passed, it may be the underlying source of genealogical material for the Spanish historical narratives. Our purpose, then, is to examine what the narratives might have to tell us about this Inca genre.

Two authors specify length of rule in years and try to correlate the rule of each Inca with their own calendar years. Their efforts will be discussed in a section at the end of chapter 5. In most of the accounts, the passage of time is marked by events in the lifetime of a particular ruler. In all cases, dates or allusions to the passage of time measured in years are subordinate to the genealogical sequence. Genealogy, not chronology, is what gives the historical narratives their temporal order.

## SPANISH HISTORICAL NARRATIVES

An interest in using Inca source materials or using them as the backbone of a narrative in Spanish began to develop only after the Spaniards had been in the Andean region for almost two decades. The awareness of a distinct historical tradition dawned slowly, hindered by its very different nature and by the language barrier. Many of the Spaniards who came with Pizarro acquired facility in the Inca language as time went by. Their understanding of the language increased their ability to tap Inca genres that extended backward in time beyond the reach of their own memories or, even, the memories of the eldest Incas then alive. Juan de Betanzos and Cristóbal de Molina, the parish priest who was the chief agent of evangelization of the native inhabitants of Spanish Cuzco from 1556 on, spoke the Inca language as well as understood it (Pease García Yrigoyen 1995 : 27–28, 36; Porras Barrenechea 1986 : 349; Julien 1998b:85). Once Spaniards began to collect information from Inca sources, they developed a new style of historical narrative that was structured by the dynastic account of descent. An Inca genre, extending backward to the time of origins, twelve generations prior to Pizarro's arrival, quickly became the device that provided a structure for historical narratives written in Spanish.

The first historical narrative about the Incas to utilize a genealogical format was authored by Cieza de León. Cieza spent the years from 1541 to 1550 traveling in the Andes. He traveled first in northern South America but clearly spent time in Peru during the time Governor Pedro de La Gasca campaigned against Gonzalo Pizarro and reorganized Spanish administration (1547–1550). The first part of Cieza's *Crónica del Perú*, published in Seville in 1553, was based on his travels. The second part, written before Cieza's death in 1554 but not published until 1873, was a narrative of Inca history. Cieza's project also included a "chronicle" of the wars between Spaniards prior to La Gasca's campaign, later published as parts 3 and 4 of his *Crónica del Perú* (Pease García Yrigoyen 1995:191–226).

What is of interest to us here is Cieza's account of the Inca past ([1553] 1986). He begins with a discussion of the great variety of "fables" the peoples of the Andes tell about their past. He quickly turns to the subject of human origins, telling a story about a Creator deity called Ticci Viracocha. Then he tells the story of Inca origins from a cave at Pacaritambo, near Cuzco. The story of the Incas continues through the line of descent of Manco Capac and ends after the death of the eleventh ruler, Huayna Capac, in the middle of the civil war between Huayna Capac's sons Huascar and Atahuallpa. There are chapters about how the Incas organized their empire that may be descriptive digressions, but the underlying structure of his account is provided by genealogy. The genealogy includes the names of each Inca ruler and his principal spouse, or Coya.

Cieza had traveled widely in the Andes and had questioned people in Cuzco and the provinces about the Incas. However, he specifically notes in his historical narrative that he took his information from "Cayo Topa and other Incas." He described Cayo Topa as "the one living male descendant of Huayna Capac in Cuzco in 1550" (Cieza de León [1553], chap. 6; 1986:13).[1] Cieza's narrative contains more information about Viracocha Inca, the eighth Inca, than other accounts do, so he may have had access to sources with particular information about this Inca.

We have already met Juan de Betanzos in chapter 2. Betanzos came to the Andes before Cieza but wrote during the 1550s. The most complete manuscript of his work on the Incas appears to have been written between 1551 and 1557. In it he does not identify his specific sources. He was married to Cusi Rimay Ocllo, known then as doña Angelina Yupanqui (Pease García Yrigoyen

1995 : 228). She belonged to the *panaca* called Capac Ayllo (see chapter 2). Betanzos's account, then, may well reflect the point of view of a particular group within the larger dynastic descent group. What is interesting is that, although Betanzos mentions the names of the Incas from the time of Manco Inca to the death of Huayna Capac, after the generation of the second Inca (Sinchi Roca) he neglects to mention the name of the woman through whom succession passed and her origins, an essential part of the genealogical format, as will be seen below. Betanzos apparently did not incorporate what we will argue is an Inca genealogical genre in his text. Instead, he used another kind of Inca source, the life history (see chapter 4).

Neither Cieza's nor Betanzos's manuscripts circulated widely, despite awakening interest in the subject of Inca history in the following decades. Cieza's manuscript on Inca history was requisitioned by the Council of the Indies, and he never got it back. It was used extensively in the later historical narrative of Antonio de Herrera y Tordesillas and was consulted by Garcilaso de la Vega in Spain. The only author to cite Betanzos was Gregorio García, who wrote more than half a century afterward (Pease García Yrigoyen 1995 : 314).

Spaniards continued to mine Inca source material in the following decades. One of the most important individuals to write about the Incas was Polo de Ondegardo. He was a royal administrator, or *corregidor*, in Cuzco from 1559 to 1560. In 1559 he was given the task of collecting information about the Incas by the viceroy Marqués de Cañete and the archbishop Jerónimo de Loaysa. Several manuscripts authored by Polo have survived, but none of these is an Inca history. The two most important manuscripts we have are not historical accounts but opinions ( *pareceres*) written as counsel to the viceroys of Peru in two distinct periods. Polo was a jurist. The opinions he authored, though expressed in a Spanish that makes their precise interpretation difficult, open a door into the mind of someone who knew a great deal about the Incas and, especially, about aspects of Inca administration in the provinces (Pease García Yrigoyen 1995 : 34, 40; Porras Barrenechea 1986 : 335–343).

What Polo wrote about the Inca past has survived only through its interpretation by two later authors. One is Joseph de Acosta. Acosta appears to have had several Polo manuscripts, among them a manuscript on marriage and other "rites and ceremonies" that Polo sent to Archbishop Loaysa ([1590], bk. 5, chap. 4; 1940 : 221; bk. 5, chap. 23; 1940 : 256; bk. 6, chap. 18; 1940 : 304), a manuscript Polo wrote on the Bolivian frontier in 1574 at the time of the Chiriguaná war ([1590], bk. 7, chap. 27; 1940 : 372), another that contained material about dynastic descent ([1590], bk. 6, chaps. 19–23; 1940 : 304–311), and, possibly, a report about the removal of the remains of Inca rulers from *panaca* control in Cuzco ([1590], bk. 5, chap. 6; 1940:226–227). What Polo wrote about the Inca past has survived only in Acosta's paraphrasing of Polo in his *Historia natural y moral de las Indias* (1590), in which he specifically states that he follows Polo "in the things of Peru" ([1590], bk. 6, chap. 1; 1940:281), and in the *Confesionario*, a work prepared by Acosta using material from Polo (1585). In both, a list of Inca rulers, sorted by their affiliation with the Hanan/ Hurin Cuzco division, is included (Acosta [1590], bk. 6, chaps. 20–23; 1940: 306–311; Polo de Ondegardo 1585:8).

What Acosta paraphrased in that work has given rise to a new hypothesis about how to read the list of Inca rulers. First, Reiner Tom Zuidema (1964, 1995) made an argument that all of the *panacas* were contemporary, that they were not the product of successive generations, but, rather, Acosta's representation reflected separate dynastic lines in Hanan and Hurin Cuzco. Pierre Duviols (1979) embraced the hypothesis, basing his argument on Acosta's transmission of Polo. Acosta can be read in this manner, but Polo himself, when called upon to authenticate a manuscript that was structured around the genealogy of twelve consecutive Inca rulers, clearly stated that that version accorded with what he knew (Rowe 1993–1994:105; Montesinos [1642]; 1882: 246, 252–253).

There is another writer who had access to a Polo manuscript that may have followed a genealogical format similar to that found in other Spanish historical narratives. Bernabé Cobo, a Jesuit who worked largely from manuscript materials in the seventeenth century, included an Inca history in a much longer work entitled *Historia del nuevo mundo* (1653). Cobo said he had a copy of the manuscript Polo sent to Archbishop Loaysa in 1559. In his eleventh book, in a chapter which immediately precedes his Inca history, Cobo discusses the principal sources for his books 12 to 14, his books on the Incas. Polo is the first manuscript source he mentions, and clearly he privileges Polo above the others. Polo had called an assembly of the oldest individuals he could find, including the most important Incas as well as those versed in Inca religion and *quipocamayos*, the "historians of the Incas." According to Cobo, Polo's witnesses had access to *quipos* and paintings for some of the material they were questioned about ([1653], bk. 12, chap. 2; 1892:116–117). Cobo structures his account with the same genealogical format used by other authors; the story begins with Inca origins and covers the period spanned by the lifetimes of Manco Capac to Huayna Capac, the "last Inca king" ([1653], bk. 12, chaps. 3–17; 1892:121–191). If Cobo drew his Inca history from Polo, and there is a fair chance that he did, it had the same genealogical format common to other Spanish accounts.[2]

A decade after Polo collected his information on the Incas, Viceroy Francisco de Toledo organized another collecting effort. Toledo himself conducted a series of interviews during the initial stages of an administrative survey, or *visita*. Toledo left Lima in 1571 for Cuzco. On the way, in various places on the road to Cuzco, he assembled groups of individuals and asked them specific questions about the Incas. Then, in Cuzco and Yucay, between March and September of the same year, he assembled additional groups and asked similar questions as well as new ones about burial practices and sacred objects (*huacas*) and other customs. Later, in January and February 1572, he developed a special questionnaire to be administered to groups of non-Incas about who had resided in the Valley of Cuzco and who had been there when, according to Inca accounts of their past, the Incas had first arrived in the valley (Levillier 1940, vol. 2 : 15–193).

At the same time, Pedro Sarmiento de Gamboa, a cosmographer who had been commissioned to write a geographical description of the Andean region ([1572]; 1906 : xxxiii, 9–10), collected information from Inca sources to be used in a historical narrative that was titled part 2 of a *Historica indica* (1572).[3] Sarmiento spoke — with the aid of translators — to representatives from different Cuzco groups, presumably the *panacas*, and wrote a series of *memoriales* that served as the basis for his manuscript ([1572], chap. 9; 1906 : 31–32). Part of this project involved painting a narrative of the dynastic past to the time of Huascar, composed of words and pictures, and painted on three cloths called *paños*. A fourth cloth depicted the genealogy of the Inca line to the present, that is, to 1572, and included women as well as men (Julien 1999 : 62–63, 76–78).

Toledo's interviews were forwarded to the Council of the Indies. Sarmiento's manuscript, bound in green leather and lined with red silk, was hand-carried back to Spain from Cuzco soon after its composition in 1572 and delivered to the king by a personal envoy of the viceroy (Montesinos [1642]; 1882 : 257–259; Sarmiento de Gamboa [1572]; 1906 : xxxix; Levillier 1924, vol. 4 : 54–55). The four *paños* were delivered with it. The book and the painted cloths were a gift from Toledo to Philip II of Spain.

Although both were a gift to the king, they were also part of a means of authenticating a version of the Inca past told by the Incas themselves. To authenticate the *paños*, Toledo assembled a group of people descended from each of the *panacas* on 14 January 1572. What was depicted on them was specifically described as having been "written and painted on these four cloths, made to be sent to the king, of the descent and origin of the Incas and how they tyrannically subjected all of the natives of these kingdoms" (Montesinos [1642]; 1882:246). The cloths were painted by Indian painters.[4] Before an assembly in which all of the *panacas* were represented, all of what was written and painted on these cloths was read and described, "both the busts [*bultos*, alternatively, full-length figures] of the Incas and the medallions of their wives and descent groups [*ayllos*]" and, in the borders, that which had happened in the time of each one. On the first cloth was the myth of Inca emergence from Tambotoco and stories about the creations of Viracocha, the supernatural Creator. What was written bore the rubric of Alvaro Ruíz de Navamuel, principal notary of the Toledo government, "except that which is declared or explained about the history and the wind roses to indicate the sites of the towns," which were the work of Pedro Sarmiento de Gamboa, who did not read or explain them, since "the Indians do not understand it." The entire graphic display was "read" to those assembled in their language, and the group confirmed what was painted in every detail (Montesinos [1642]; 1882:249–251; Sarmiento de Gamboa [1572]; 1906:xxxviii–xl, 130–134; Iwasaki Cauti 1986:72–73). A month later, on 19 February 1572, a similar procedure was carried out with a different assemblage of *panaca* members, this time asked to authenticate Sarmiento's book ([1572]; 1906:131–132). The purpose of this elaborate performance was to secure Inca authentication of a text. Much had been written about the Inca past, but Toledo was the first to attempt to get members of the dynastic descent group, en masse, to approve what was written (Julien 1999:85).

The relationship between Sarmiento's book and the *paños* has not been sufficiently appreciated by modern scholars. Toledo obtained *panaca* approval of Sarmiento's narrative by presenting it first in a format that had been in use during the lifetimes of those called upon to authenticate it: an Inca painted genre. Cristóbal de Molina described it:

> They [the Incas] kept in a house of the Sun called Poquen Cancha, which is near Cuzco, the life of each one of the Incas and the lands he conquered, painted in their figures on some tablets and [also] what their origins were. And among these paintings was a painting of the following fable.

> Y tenían en una casa de el Sol llamada Poquen Cancha, que es junto al Cuzco, la vida de cada uno de los yngas y de las tierras que conquistó, pintado por sus figuras en unas tablas y qué origen tuvieron y entre las dichas pintures tenían asimismo pintada la fábula siguiente. ([1576]; 1989:49–50)

Molina then relates an Inca creation myth. Regardless of the style of representation used, Toledo adapted a format familiar to the Incas. The *paños* reproduced the subject matter of the tablets: the lives of the Incas, their conquests, and the Inca origin myth.

Not surprisingly, Sarmiento also describes a pictorial version of Inca history painted on wooden tablets. At the very beginning of his narrative of Inca history, he states that Pachacuti, the ninth ruler, gathered people who were knowledgeable about it and had what was most noteworthy painted on a series of large wooden tablets. These tablets were kept in a room of one of the houses of the Sun, perhaps the same Poquen Cancha named by Molina. Particular individuals were charged with preserving a knowledge of what was represented on them and declaring it when permission was granted by the Inca ruler (Sarmiento [1572], chap. 9; 1906:31). The panels served as an official dynastic account of their past, and that may be why Toledo chose to emulate them.

Sarmiento does not say he saw these tablets. Neither does Polo de Ondegardo, who was present when the *paños* were authenticated and who may have actually seen the wooden tablets in Cuzco in the late 1540s. However, even the memory of wooden tablets that depicted Inca history would have been sufficient as inspiration for a later series. Because of this effort to create an Inca version of their own past (and one that was in some way equivalent to a painted historical genre), Sarmiento's narrative may be a source of information about it.

Following closely on Toledo's effort, the bishop of Cuzco, Sebastián de Lartaún, requisitioned a narrative on the Inca past from Cristóbal de Molina, priest of the hospital parish (Nuestra Señora de los Remedios) in the city of Cuzco. According to Cobo, Molina also assembled informants who had been alive during the rule of Huayna Capac. The result, again according to Cobo, was substantially the same as Polo's and Sarmiento's accounts. Cobo notes that Molina also included a lengthy description of the "rites and fables of the gentile period" ([1653], bk. 12, chap. 2; 1892:118–119). Molina's historical narrative has not been located, but an account of the "rites and fables" of the Incas is known, probably excerpted from the longer account described by Cobo ([1576] 1989).[5]

Long ago Francisco de Loayza noted that the account of Cabello Valboa was based on a lost historical narrative authored by Molina (1943:xv). Cabello stated that he followed Molina ([1586], pt. 3, chap. 9; 1951:259–260). John Rowe has also noted correspondences between Cabello Valboa and one of the Morúa manuscripts ([1611–1616], bk. 1; 1987) and suggested that the similarities are due to borrowing from the lost historical narrative of Molina (1985b:194, 200–201).

There may be yet another missing manuscript that drew on Cuzco sources in the same period. In a letter to the king dated 14 March 1575, the provincial of the Mercedarian order wrote that a friar of his order had written on the origins of the Incas (Morúa [1605]; 1946:34, n.). That friar may or may not have been Martín de Morúa. Very little is known about the whereabouts of Morúa at any given moment, but he served as parish priest in several parishes in Cuzco and may have held the post of *arcediano* in the cathedral chapter. He devotes an entire chapter to Cuzco, recording all of the prelates who had served as bishop, and another to the history of the Mercedarian order in the viceroyalty of Peru, without making a single personal reference. He may have been in Cuzco in the 1570s: when he tells about the arrival of Topa Amaro to Cuzco in 1572, he describes Toledo watching the procession from the window of Diego de Silva's house as if he, Morúa, had been there. He wrote at least two different manuscripts; both incorporate materials from other texts.[6] Because of structural resemblances to the account of Cabello Valboa (see table 4.3 and chapter 5) as well as closely similar wordings, one of Morúa's manuscripts appears to have drawn its Inca history from the lost account of Cristóbal de Molina (see Murúa [1611–1616] 1987).

There are clear similarities between one of Morúa's texts ([1605] 1946) and portions of the illustrated narrative prepared by Felipe Guaman Poma de Ayala ([1615] 1987). Guaman Poma was actively working on his narrative in the same period as Morúa, and the two of them knew each other (Pease García Yrigoyen 1995:264, 293). As will be seen below, when genealogical information contained in the various historical narratives is compared, Morúa and Guaman Poma are markedly discrepant from the other narratives in the information they give about particular generations in the Inca dynastic line but similar to each other at precisely these points. Only Guaman Poma and Morúa create separate chapters for the Coyas. The material Guaman Poma includes about the Coyas is unique and often fantastic. In these chapters Morúa does not follow Guaman Poma; rather, he substitutes material drawn from Mexican sources (Rowe 1987). Neither author appears to have reproduced Inca genres to any degree, although a memory of the painted tradition may have inspired their work.

Other authors have been included in the comparison of genealogical information that follows, but the sources of their information are not readily identified. In some cases — for example, Bartolomé de las Casas and Pedro Gutiérrez de Santa Clara — the author never visited the Andes and probably took his information from a text (Pease García Yrigoyen 1995: 19–20, 31, 55, 71, 82). Some of Las Casas's sources can be identified, but not the source of his Inca history.[7] Jerónimo Román y Zamora is doubly removed from the subject; he never visited the Andes, and he apparently took his information on the Incas from Las Casas (Pease García Yrigoyen 1995: 36, 333, 382). Two authors are native Andeans, although neither is Inca. Guaman Poma de Ayala, through his constant representation of himself in a tunic like the one his father wore, indicated an identification with Yarobamba, a region in the Huánuco area of the northern highlands ([1615]; 1987: 5–6, 366[368]–367[369]). Pachacuti Yamqui Salcamaygua was from Canchis, a province near Cuzco in the area east of modern Urcos ([early seventeenth century]; 1993: fol. 1, p. 183). Garcilaso de la Vega was Inca on his mother's side. Born after the Spanish arrival, he left Peru for Spain at age twenty and did not write about the Inca past until he was an old man (Porras Barrenechea 1986: 391–394). These circumstances alone do not disqualify what he wrote, but he is far removed from the kind of Inca source material Spaniards drew on decades before in Cuzco, and he must be read with care.

One text, known alternatively as the *Discurso* or the *Relación de los quipoca-mayos*, contains a genealogical account that may or may not have been collected in 1542. The document itself was written in the early seventeenth century, between 1602 and 1608, to support claims then being made by Melchor Carlos Inca, the grandson of Paullo Inca (see chapter 2), in the Spanish court. However, the seventeenth-century author refers to an inquiry made in 1542 by Governor Vaca de Castro in consultation with Inca *quipocamayos* and conveys the impression that he is taking information from it (Pease García Yrigoyen 1995: 23, 28). Whether the information was supplied from memory or copied from a text is not at all clear. Like other seventeenth-century texts that relied on memory, it is wrong in matters of fact that can be confirmed by earlier documents. For example, it provides the wrong date for the death of Paullo Inca! By including this document in our comparison, we may learn something about the nature of the sources used by its author.

Our interest here is with unraveling an underlying Inca genealogical genre. Problematic sources like the *Discurso* and Las Casas may still contribute to what we can learn about it or about versions of it that were transmitted during the first decades of Spanish Cuzco. As will be evident from the comparison of the accounts we have selected, similarities in the type of information chosen for inclusion as well as in the information itself seem to reflect the commonly held canons of a genre.[8] One type of information that was consistently chosen was the identification — for each generation — of both the male and female through whom succession passed. Many accounts also give the name of the *panaca* associated with each generation, sometimes in a separate list. Given that some narratives provide little more than a list of the Incas and Coyas through whom the succession passed and the *panaca* information (Las Casas, Gutiérrez, Fernández, the *Discurso*), it may be that an underlying Inca genre included both classes of information.

## DYNASTIC GENEALOGY

First let us look at the genealogical information in the historical narratives with links to Inca sources. For each generation, the information from each source has been selected and edited in tabular form (tables 3.1–3.13). The spellings of names have been preserved exactly as found in the published texts, though some of the texts have obviously been modified by particular transcription rules. The divergent spellings are distracting, but similarities between the names provide clues to relationships between texts. Since the division of names into particular words was arbitrary in the Spanish manuscripts of the sixteenth to seventeenth centuries, the names of individuals have been divided into discrete segments to facilitate comparison. The accounts chosen have been ordered according to the time of their composition (see dates in the key to table 3.1).

With some exceptions, each story begins with an account of the emergence of the Ayar brothers and sisters from the cave of Pacaritambo. In two instances (Pachacuti and Garcilaso), the story of origins is told, and eight siblings are mentioned, but the names of only two sisters are given. Usually, however, the names of four brothers and four sisters are provided. There are differences in the order of the names and in their spellings: no two lists are identical. Nonetheless, some of the lists are quite similar to others.

Two of the earliest authors list six names and not seven. Cieza de León and Las Casas give the names of only three brothers and three sisters. Although Cieza's manuscript was in Spain at the time Las Casas wrote, there are enough differences in the information they gave about Manco Capac's descent group to establish that their genealogies were independent of each other. The other account that lists six Ayar siblings was by Román y Zamora, who followed Las Casas. Cobo's list is somewhat aberrant, as he mentions both Manco Capac and Ayar Manco, skipping Ayar Auca. The differences in the number of Inca siblings given are important; there may have been more than one version of Inca origins (see chapter 8).

TABLE 3.1. *The Ayar siblings*

*Key to Sources*

| | |
|---|---|
| CL | Pedro de Cieza de León [1553]; 1986 |
| B | Juan de Betanzos [1551–57], pt. 1; 1987 |
| CS | Bartolomé de las Casas [1562–64]; 1967 |
| FZ | Diego Fernández [1571], bk. 3; 1963, vol. 165 |
| S | Pedro Sarmiento Gamboa [1572]; 1906 |
| RZ | Jerónimo Román y Zamora [1575]; 1897 |
| GZ | Pedro Gutiérrez de Santa Clara [after 1575]; 1963, vol. 166 |
| CV | Miguel Cabello Valboa [1586]; 1951, pt. 3 |
| P | Juan de Santa Cruz Pachacuti Yamqui Salcamaygua [early seventeenth century]; 1993 |
| D | *Discurso* [1602–8]; 1920 |
| MI | Martín de Morúa [1605], bk. 1; 1946 |
| GP | Felipe Guaman Poma de Ayala [1615]; 1987 |
| M2 | Martín de Murúa [1611–16], bk. 1; 1987 |
| CO | Bernabé Cobo [1653], bk. 12; 1892 |
| G | Garcilaso de la Vega [1609]; 1990 |

| Source | Ayar Brothers | Ayar Sisters |
|---|---|---|
| CL | Ayar Ocho | Mamaco [Mama Ocllo or Mama Guaco?] |
| | Ayar Hache Arauca | Mama Cona |
| | Ayar Mango | Mama Ragua |
| B | Ayar Cache | Mama Guaco |
| | Ayar Oche | Cura |
| | Ayar Auca | Ragua Ocllo |
| | Ayar Mango | Mama Ocllo |
| CS | Ayar Udio | Mama Ragua |
| | Ayar Ancha | Mama Cora |
| | Ayar Mango | Mama Ocllo |
| FZ | Mango Capa Inga | Mama Guaco |
| S | Mango Capac | Mama Ocllo |
| | Ayar Auca | Mama Guaco |
| | Ayar Cache | Mama Ipacura [or Mama Cura] |
| | Ayar Ucho | Mama Raua |
| RZ | Ayar Udio | Ma[ma] Ragua |
| | Ayar Ancia | Mama Cora |
| | Ayar Mango | Mama Ocllo |
| CV | Mango Capac | Mama Guaco |
| | Ayar Cache | Mama Cora |
| | Ayar Auca | Mama Ocllo |
| | Ayar Uchi | Mama Ragua |
| GZ | Mango Inga Zapalla | Mama Ocllo |

| Source | Ayar Brothers | Ayar Sisters |
|--------|---------------|--------------|
| P | [Progenitors: Apo Tambo and Pacha Mama Achi] | |
| | Manco Capac Inca | 4 sisters, only two names given are: |
| | Ayar Cachi | Ypa Mama Uaco |
| | Ayar Uchu | Mama Ocllo |
| | Ayar Aoca | |
| D | Mango Capac | Mama Vaco |
| MI | Guana Cauri | Tupa Vaco |
| | Cuzco Guanca | Mama Coia |
| | Mango Capac | Curi Ocllo |
| | Supa Ayar Cacse | Ipa Baco |
| GP | Uana Cauri Ynga | Tupa Uuaco |
| | Cuzco Uanca Ynga | Mama Cora |
| | Mango Capac Ynga | Curi Ocllo |
| | Tupa Ayar Cachi Ynga | Ypa Uaco |
| M2 | Manco Capac | Mama Huaco |
| | Ayar Cache | Mama Cora |
| | Ayar Auca | Mama Ocllo |
| | Ayar Huchu | Mama Tabua |
| CO | Manco Capac | Mama Huaco |
| | Ayar Cuche | Mama Ocllo |
| | Ayar Uche | Mama Ragua |
| | Ayar Manco | Mama Cura |
| G | Manco Capac | Mama Ocllo Huaco |
| | Ayar Cachi | |
| | Ayar Uchu | |
| | Ayar Sauca | |

*Sources*: CL: chap. 6, pp. 13–14; B: chap. 3, p. 17; CS: bk. 3, chap. 250, p. 573; S: chap. 11, p. 33; FZ, chap. 5, p. 80; RZ: chap. 11, p. 8; GZ: chap. 49, p. 209; CV: chap. 9, p. 161; P: 193–197; D: 12; MI: chap. 2, p. 50; GP: 84; M2: chap. 2, p. 49; CO: chap. 3, p. 62; G: bk. 1, chap. 19, p. 34, chap. 21, p. 38.

Another feature of the Cieza and Las Casas lists is the use of the name Ayar Manco instead of Manco Capac to refer to one of the brothers in the origin story. Betanzos, also an early writer, joins them. After the story of origins, in all three accounts this person is called Manco Capac, the name that all of the other authors consistently use.

There are interesting aberrations in the accounts of later authors. For example, Pachacuti is the only author who names the parents of the Ayar siblings: Apo Tambo and Pacha Mama Achi. For all of the other authors, the apical ancestors of the dynastic descent group are a sibling pair from among the set of Ayar siblings. Both Guaman Poma and Morúa give similar aberrant versions. Here, the later Morúa manuscript (M2) (Murúa [1611–1615] 1987) provides names similar to those found in other accounts of the Pacaritambo story. His earlier manuscript (MI) (Morúa [1605] 1946) gives virtually the same names as those given by Guaman Poma.

Not all of the authors include the story about the Ayar siblings. It is absent from Fernández, Gutiérrez de Santa Clara, and the *Discurso*. Gutiérrez de Santa Clara borrowed from Fernández, but there are differences in their accounts of the Inca past that suggest the possibility that Gutiérrez had other sources at his disposal. Fernández says nothing at all about the origins of the first Inca pair. Gutiérrez locates the events associated with the Inca progenitors in the Lake Titicaca basin. The *Discurso* tells the "shining mantle" story, in which Manco Capac puts on a shirt with shining spangles and fools the local people in Pacaritambo into believing his claims to be "son of the Sun." This story is told in several late-sixteenth-century accounts and gives reason to doubt that the *Discurso* was pristinely transmitted from an account taken from *quipocamayos* in the time of Vaca de Castro.[9]

All of the accounts name Manco Capac as the male progenitor of the Inca dynastic descent group (see table 3.2). The accounts nearly always agree on the name of the male member of the dynastic pair, disagreeing more often on the name of the woman through whom succession passed. There is notable disagreement about who Manco Capac's spouse was: either Mama Ocllo or Mama Huaco, and in the case of Garcilaso, Mama Ocllo Huaco was named. Mama Ocllo was named most frequently. Morúa (MIa) and Cabello Valboa name Mama Huaco; Morúa contains several retellings of the genealogical account, but one (MIa) regularly parallels the information contained in Cabello Valboa and, therefore, in the underlying account of Molina as well. Fernández and Cobo also name Mama Huaco. Cobo appears to list four brothers and four sisters, but he really only lists the names of three brothers; he gives both Manco Capac and Ayar Manco. Cieza does not give a name for the female progenitor of the dynastic line.

The information we have is sufficient to indicate that there were two competing stories about who was the female progenitor of the dynastic descent group. Morúa (MIb and M2a) noted that there was a competing version. The question will be taken up in chapter 8.

There are very interesting differences in what was recorded for the second generation (table 3.3). If we look first for agreement, we find the story that Sinchi Roca and a woman named Mama Coca, daughter of a lord named Sutic Guaman of the town of Saño in the Cuzco Valley, is told by Sarmiento and by both Cabello Valboa and Morúa (M2a), indicating that the Molina account named her as well. Betanzos provides the same information but does not sup-

TABLE 3.2. *First pair*

| Source | First Pair |
|---|---|
| CL | Manco Capac and a sister have 3 sons and 1 daughter. One son is Cinche Roca Ynga, and the daughter is Achi Ocllo. |
| B | Manco Capac and Mama Ocllo have Sinche Roca. |
| CS | Manco Capac and Mama Ocllo have Sinchi Roca. |
| FZ | Mango Capa Inga and Mama Guaco have Siche Roca Inga. |
| S | Manco Capac and Mama Ocllo have Cinchi Roca; Chima Panaca Ayllo. |
| RZ | Ayar Manco and Mama Ocllo have Cinchi Roca. |
| GZ | Mango Inga Zapalla and Mama Ocllo, daughter of an important lord, have Sinchi Roca Inga. |
| CV | Manco Capac and Mama Ocllo have Cinchi Ruca. |
| P | Manco Capac and Mama Ocllo have Çinchi Ruca; Chima Panaca Ayllo. |
| D | Mango Capac and Mama Vaco have Chinche Roca and Topa Auca Ylli; Chima Panaca. |
| M1 | a) Mango Capac and Mama Baco have Sinchiroca, Chimpo, and Pachacuti (bastard). |
| | b) Manco Capac and Mama Vaco [or Mama Ocllo] have Cinchi Roca, Chimbo, and Pachacuti (bastard). |
| GP | a) Mango Capac Inga fathers Cinche Roca Ynga, Ynca Yupanqui, Pachacuti Ynga, and Chinbo Urma. |
| | b) Mama Uaco is mother of Mango Capac Ynga (unknown father); they have Sinchi Roca, Ynga Yupangui, Pachakuti, and Chimbo Urma. |
| M2 | a) Manco Capac and Mama Ocllo (others say Mama Huaco) have Cinchi Roca. |
| | b) Mama Huaco and Manco Capac have Sinchi Roca and Chimpo Coya. |
| CO | Manco Capac and Mama Huaco have Sinchi Roca; Chima Panaca. |
| G | Manco Capac and Mama Ocllo Huaco have Sinchi Roca. |

*Sources*: CL: chap. 8, p. 22; B: chap. 5, p. 21; CS: bk. 3, chap. 250, pp. 574–575; FZ, chap. 5, p. 80; S: chap. 12, p. 35; RZ: chap. 11, p. 10; GZ: chap. 49, p. 209; CV: chap. 9, p. 261; P: 197, 199; D: p. 12; M1: chap. 3, p. 53, chap. 16, p. 81; GP: p. 87, 121; M2: chap. 2, p. 49, chap. 4, p. 59; CO: chap. 4, p. 128; G: bk. 1, chap. 25, p. 43.

ply the name of the lord of Saño (cf. M1a). Cobo gives the same account, except that he gives the woman's name as Mama Chura. His account is not the same as that of Fernández this time, although Fernández names the woman as Mama Cura, a name only slightly different from what Cobo gives. Coca and Cura (and even Coya, given by Gutiérrez) could be divergent transcriptions of the same name. Fernández and Gutiérrez give an odd spelling of the name Lloque Yupanqui, the son born to the second pair. Fernández gives "Llocuco," and Gutiérrez follows him. Las Casas has "Lluchi" Yupanqui. Cieza tells a different story from all the others. Sinchi Roca marries a sister, but then the lord of Saño begged him to take a daughter for his son, which he did (see third pair, table 3.4). Morúa (M2b, M2c, M1b) and Guaman Poma (GPa and GPb) give similar but odd versions. They name Chimbo Coya or Chimbo Urma Coya. For Morúa (M1b), she is sister to Sinchi Roca. That the Incas marry their sisters is the story consistently told in Guaman Poma and one Morúa account (M1b).

TABLE 3.3. *Second pair*

| Source | Second Pair |
|---|---|
| CL | Sinche Roca Ynga and sister have Quelloque Yupangue [elsewhere Lloque Yupangue]. A lord from Çaño begged Sinchi Roca to take his daughter for his son, which he did. |
| B | Sinche Roca and Mama Coca of Zaño have Lloque Yupanque. |
| CS | Cinchi Roca and Mama Coca, daughter of a lord from half a league from Cuzco, have Lluchi Yupangi. |
| FZ | Sinche Roca Inga and Mama Cura have Cuxi Guanan Chiri and Llocuco Pangue Inga. |
| S | Sinchi Roca and Mama Coca, daughter of Sutic Guaman of Saño, have Lloqui Yupanqui; Raura Panaca Ayllo. |
| RZ | Cinchi Roca and Mama Coca, daughter of a lord from near Cuzco, have Lluchi Impangi. |
| GZ | Sinchi Roca and Mama Coya have Llocuco Yupangue Inga and Cuxi Guanan Chiri. |
| CV | Cinchi Ruca and Mama Coca, only daughter of Suti Guaman, lord of Saño, have Mango Sapaca and Lluqui Yupangui. |
| P | Sinchi Roca fathers Ynga Lluqui Yupangui. |
| D | Chinche Roca and Mama Coca have Lloque Yupanqui Inga and Mango Capac; Raorao Panaca. |
| MI | a) Sinchi Roca and Mama Coca, the daughter of "su tía Huamán" [*sic*: Sutic Huaman] of Saño, have Mango Sapaca. |
|  | b) Sinchi Roca and Chimpo Coya, his sister, have Lloque Yupangui, among others. |
|  | c) Sinchi Roca and Chimpo Coya, his sister, have Lloque Yupangui and Cusi Huanan Chiri, among others. |
| GP | a) Cinchi Roca Inga and Chinbo Urma Coya have Mama Cora Ocllo Coya and Lloqui Yupanqui Ynga, Uari Tito Ynga, Topa Amaro Ynga. |
|  | b) Cinche Roca and Chinbo Urma Coya have Lloqui Yupanqui Ynga, Mama Cora Ocllo, Capac Uari Titu Ynga, and Topa Amaro Ynga. |
| M2 | a) Cinchi Roca and Mama Coca of Sano have Lloqui Yupangui; Raura Panaca Ayllo. |
|  | b) Sinchi Roca and Chimbo Ollo (daughter of Mama Vaco) have Cuxi Guanan Chiri, Lloque Yupangui Inga, and Mama Cura. |
| CO | Cinchi Roca and Mama Chura, daughter of Sutic Guaman of Sañoc, have Lloque Yupanqui; Raurahua Panaca. |
| G | Sinchi Roca and Mama Ocllo or Mama Cora (sister) have Lloque Yupanqui. |

*Sources*: CL: chap. 31, p. 95; B: chap. 5, p. 21; CS: bk. 3, chap. 250, p. 575; FZ: chap. 5, p. 80; S: chap. 15, p. 43; RZ: chap. 11, pp. 10–11; GZ: chap. 49, pp. 209–210; CV: chap. 10, p. 268, chap. 11, p. 280; P: 204; D: p. 13; MI: chap. 4, p. 54, chap. 17, pp. 83–84; GP: 89, 123; M2: chap. 3, pp. 54–55, chap. 4, p. 59, chap. 6, p. 60; CO: chap. 4, p. 129, chap. 5, p. 133; G: bk. 1, chap. 16, p. 76.

In the case of the third pair (table 3.4), the accounts of Sarmiento and Cabello Valboa/Morúa (MIa) are again similar. Lloque Yupangui and Mama Caua, daughter of the lord of Oma, produce Mayta Capac. This time they are joined by Cobo. Las Casas tells the same story but calls her Mama Cahua Pata. He is echoed by Román y Zamora, who followed him in just about everything, and also by Gutiérrez. In this generation, Gutiérrez names the female

TABLE 3.4. *Third pair*

| Source | Third Pair |
|---|---|
| CL | Lloque Yupangue and woman from Çaño have Mayta Capa. |
| B | Lloque Yupangue fathers Capac Yupangui. |
| CS | Lluchi Yupangi and Mama Cagua Pata, daughter of the lord of Oma, have Indi Maitha Capac. |
| FZ | Llocuco Pangue Inga and Mama Ana Uarque have Maita Capa Inga. |
| S | Lloqui Yupangui and Mama Caua of Oma have Mayta Capac; Avayni Panaca Ayllo. |
| RZ | Lluchi Impangui and Mama Cagua Pata, daughter of a lord from 3 leagues [15 km] away from Cuzco, have Indi Maytha Capac. |
| GZ | Llocuco Yupangue and Mama Cagua Pata have Indi Mayta Capac Inga. |
| CV | Lluqui Yupangui and Mama Caua, daughter of the lord of Oma, have Mayta Capac. |
| P | Ynga Lluque Yupangui and Mama Tancarry Yachi Chimpo Urma Cuca, daughter of the lord of Tancar, have Mayta Capac. |
| D | Lluque Yupangue Inga and Mama Caba have Mayta Capac Inga, Apo Conde Mayta, and Apo Taca; Ayllo Chiguayuin. |
| MI | a) Lloqui Yupangui and Mama Caua of Oma have Mayta Capac; Avayni Panaca Ayllo. |
|  | b) Lloque Yupangui and Mama Cura [or Anac Varqui] (his first cousin) have Mayta Capac and Chimbo Orma Coya [or Mama Yacche]. |
| GP | a) Lloqui Yupanqui Ynga and Mama Cora Ocllo Coya have Ynga Cuci Uanan Chiri, Mayta Capac Ynga, Chinbo Urma Mama Yachi Coya, Curi Auqui Ynga, Runto Auqui Ynga, Cuci Chinbo Coya. |
|  | b) Lloque Yupanqui and Mama Cora Ocllo Coya have Mayta Capac Ynga, Cusi Chinbo, Mama Yachi Urma, and others. |
| M2 | a) Lloque Yupanqui and Mama Cura (his sister), also known as Ana Chuarque, have Maita Capac and maybe others. |
|  | b) Lloque Yupangui and Mama Cura (his first cousin), also known as Ana Chuarque, have Maita Capac, their only child. |
| CO | Lloque Yupanqui and Mama Cachua of Oma have Mayta Capac; Ahucani Ayllu. |
| G | Lloque Yupanqui and Mama Cahua have Maita Capac. |

*Sources:* CL: chap. 32, pp. 97–98; B: chap. 5, pp. 21–22; CS: bk. 3, chap. 250, p. 575; FZ: chap. 5, p. 80; S: chap. 16, p. 45; RZ: chap. 11, p. 11; GZ: chap. 49, p. 210; CV: chap. 12, p. 283; P: 205; D: p. 13; MI: chap. 5, p. 57, chap. 18, pp. 85–86; GP: 97, 125; M2: chap. 7, p. 60, chap. 8, p. 62; CO: chap. 6, p. 137; G: bk. 2, chap. 20, p. 82.

member of the Inca pair as Mama Cahua Pata. He may be following Las Casas or Las Casas's source, since both name Indi Maita Capac as the scion of this pair. Fernández gives a wildly divergent name for the female member: Mama Ana Uarque. Morúa (M2a, M2b, M1b) and Guaman Poma (GPa and GPb) name Mama Cura as the spouse. Where any information is given about her origins, she is said to be a close female relative, either a sister or a first cousin (M2a, M2b). The author Pachacuti names Mama Tancarry Yachi Chimpo Urma Cuca, the daughter of the lord of Tancar, as the female member of the Inca pair. There is a place known as Tancar in the Urubamba Valley. Pachacuti supplies a very similar name for this woman, without giving her origins, in the fourth generation. Perhaps he had difficulty in coming up with a name for the third woman. From this point until the tenth generation, Betanzos gives no information about the female member of the dynastic pair.

Sarmiento and Cabello Valboa/Morúa (M1a) tell a very similar story about the fourth pair (table 3.5). Maita Capac and Mama Tacucaray of Tacucaray have Capac Yupanqui. Morúa here follows Sarmiento exactly; the names of the sons born to this pair are the same and are listed in the same order as given by Sarmiento. The author Pachacuti appears to give the same information, including the names of two sons that match two on the lists of Sarmiento and Morúa (M1a), but he calls the woman Mama Tancaray Yacchi, repeating the name he gave for the woman of the third pair. Cobo appears to follow a similar version and provides the additional information that the woman is the daughter of a Collaguas lord. Cieza gives an account of the female member of the Inca pair and her origins that is very like the story given by Las Casas about the woman of the third generation. Perhaps by inserting a sister in the second generation and moving the daughter of the lord of Saño to the third, he had displaced the woman of the third pair to the fourth. Other authors cannot be reconciled. The Las Casas story is odd. He names Mama Diancha of Saño as the female member of the fourth Inca pair. Betanzos switches Maita Capac and Capac Yupanqui in his ordering of the genealogy. Guaman Poma and several of the Morúa versions again diverge from the other accounts but are similar to each other.

Sarmiento and Cabello Valboa again tell a similar story about the fifth pair: Capac Yupanqui and Curi Hilpay bear Inca Roca Inca (table 3.6). Sarmiento says the woman is either the daughter of an Ayarmaca lord, a woman from Cuzco, or both. Cabello Valboa says she is from Cuzco. This time, Morúa does not give a parallel account in any part of his texts. Cobo names Curi Hilpay as the female member, calling her "Cori Ilpay Cahua." Pachacuti tells the same story and provides a similar name. Cieza does not name her. The *Discurso* calls her Chuqui Hilpay. Las Casas calls her Inti Chiquia; however, he agrees with Sarmiento that she is the daughter of the lord of Ayarmaca. Gutiérrez may follow him. Fernández calls her Mama Cagua. Mama Cagua is also the name given by Morúa (M2b) as an alternate for Chimpu Ocllo and as part of the name Chimpu Ocllo Mama Caua by Guaman Poma. Everywhere those two authors give Chimpo Ocllo or a name composed of the parts Chimpo, Ocllo, Mama, or Cahua.

The story told by Sarmiento and Cabello about the sixth pair is similar: Inca Roca Inca and Mama Micay, daughter of the lord of Guayllacan, bear Yahuar Huaca (table 3.7). Sarmiento names the place as Pataguayllacan, while Cabello

TABLE 3.5. *Fourth pair*

| Source | Fourth Pair |
|---|---|
| CL | Mayta Capac, who had no sisters, and Mama Cagua Pata, daughter of the lord of Oma, have Capa Yupangue. |
| B | Capac Yupangue fathers Mayta Capac. |
| CS | Indi Maitha Capac and Mama Diancha of Sañe have Capac Yupangi. |
| FZ | Maita Capa Inga and Mama Yacchi have Capac Yupangue Inca and others. |
| S | Mayta Capac and Mama Tacucaray of Tacucaray have Capac Yupangui and four others: Tarco Guaman, Apo Conde Mayta, Queco Avcaylli, and Roca Yupangi; Usca Mayta Panaca Ayllo. |
| RZ | Indi Maytha Capac and Mama Chiancha, daughter of the lord of Sañe, a league from Cuzco, have Capac Yupangi. |
| GZ | Yndi Mayta Capac Inga and Mama Chianta have Capac Yupangue Inga. |
| CV | Mayta Capac and Mama Coca Taucaraz of Taucaraz have Capa Yupangui and Tarco Guaman. |
| P | Mayta Capac and Mama Tancaray Yacchi have Capac Yupangui, Apo Tarco Guaman, Inti Conti Mayta, and Orco Guaranga; Usca Mayta Ayllo and Hauayñin Ayllo. |
| D | Mayta Capac and Mama Taocaray have Capac Yupangui Inga and Apo Tarco Guaman; Ayllo Usca Maita. |
| MI | a) Maita Capac and Chimpo Urma (first cousin) have eight sons and three daughters, including Capac Yupanqui (the eldest), Faico Huamán, and Chimpo Ocllo (a daughter). |
| | b) Maita Capac and Chimpu Urma (first cousin) have many children, among them Capac Yupanqui and Cimpo Ocllo. |
| GP | a) Mayta Capac and Chimbo Urma Mama Yachi have Chinbo Ucllo Mama Caua, Apo Maytac Ynga, Uilcac Ynga, Uiza Topa Ynga, Capac Yupanqui Ynga, and Curi Ucllo. |
| | b) Mayta Capac Ynga and Chinbo Mama Yachi Urma Coya have Chimbo Ocllo Mama Caua, Cuci Chinbo Mama Micay, Capac Yupanqui Ynga, Apo Maytac Ynga, and Bilcac Ynga. |
| M2 | a) Mayta Capac and Mama Tacucaray of Tacucaray have Capac Yupangui, Tarco Guaman, Apo Conde Mayta, Queco Aucaylli, and Roca Yupangui. |
| | b) Mayta Capac and Chimpu Urma (sister) have Capac Yupangui and Chimpo Ocllo. |
| CO | Mayta Capac and Mama Tancaray Yacchi, daughter of Collaguas lord, have Capac Yupanqui and Tarco Huaman; Usca Mayta Ayllo. |
| G | Maita Capac and Mama Cuca (sister) have Capac Yupanqui. |

*Sources*: CL: chap. 33, pp. 100–101; B: chap. 5, p. 22; CS: bk. 3, chap. 250, p. 575; FZ: chap. 5, p. 80; S: chap. 17, p. 47; RZ: chap. 11, p. 11; GZ: chap. 49, p. 210; CV: chap. 12, p. 286; P: 209; D: p. 13; MI: chap. 6, p. 60, chap. 19, pp. 87–89; GP: 99, 127; M2: chap. 9, p. 64, chap. 10, p. 66; CO: chap. 7, p. 140; G: bk. 3, chap. 9, p. 111.

uses Nicaz for the woman's name, although this difference may have resulted from a copying error. Cobo tells the same story but says that the woman herself is lord of Guayllacan. Others who use some form of Nicay or Micay as the woman's name are Cieza, Las Casas, Fernández, Román y Zamora, Gutiérrez, the author Pachacuti, the *Discurso*, Guaman Poma (GPa), Morúa (MIb), and

TABLE 3.6. *Fifth pair*

| Source | Fifth Pair |
|--------|------------|
| CL | Capac Yupangue and the Coya have Ynga Roque Ynga. |
| B | Mayta Capac fathers Ynga Roca Ynga. |
| CS | Capac Yupangi and Indi Chigia, daughter of the lord of Ayarmacha, have Inga Roca Inga. |
| FZ | Capac Yupangue Inga and Mama Cagua have Inga Roca Inga and others. |
| S | Capac Yupangui and Curi Hilpay, daughter of an Ayarmaca lord from Cuzco, or both, have Inga Roca Inga; five other children, born to other women; Apo Mayta Panaca Ayllo. |
| RZ | Capac Yupangi and Indi Chigia, daugher of the lord of Yarmacha, have Inga Roca Inga. |
| GZ | Capac Yupangue Inga and Mama Yndi Chiquia have Inga Roca Inga. |
| CV | Capac Yupangui and Curi Illpay of Cuzco have Ynga Ruca Ynga and Apoc Mayta. |
| P | Capac Yupangui and Mama Cori Illpay Cahua have Ynga Ruca. |
| D | Capac Yupangui and Mama Chuqui Yllpay have Inga Roca, Apo Calla Humpiri, Apo Saca Inga, and Chima Chabin; Ayllo Apo Maita. |
| MI | a) Capac Yupangui was killed by a sister who took Inga Roca, a "serrano" [*sobrino?*] of Maita Capac, for her husband. |
| GP | a) Capac Yupanqui Ynga marries Chinbo Ucllo Mama Caua; he later marries Cuci Chinbo Mama Micay Coya Curi Ocllo; he fathers Auqui Topa Ynga, Ynga Yupanqui, Cuci Chinbo Mama Micay Coya, Ynga Roca, Ynti Auqui Ynga, Capac Yupanqui, and Ynga Yllapa. |
|  | b) Capac Yupanque and Chinbo Mama Caua had a child, and she ate it; Capac Yupanqui marries younger sister Cuci Chinbo Mama Micay (see 6th pair). |
|  | b) Capac Yupangui and Chimpu Ollo [or Mama Caua] have Cusi Chimpu. |
| M2 | a) Capac Yupanqui and Chimpo Ocllo (sister) have Inga Roca, Apo Naita, and Cusi Chimpo (a daughter). He was killed by his sister, Cusi Chimpo. |
|  | b) Capac Yupanqui and Chimpu Ocllo (or Mama Cahua) have Cusi Chimpu. |
| CO | Capac Yupanqui and Cori Ilpay Cahua have Inca Roca Inca and Apo Mayta; Apu Mayta Ayllo. |
| G | Capac Yupanqui and Coya Maca Curi Ilpay (sister) have Inca Roca. |

*Sources*: CL: chap. 34, p. 104; B: chap. 5, p. 22; CS: bk. 3, chap. 250, p. 575; FZ: chap. 5, p. 80; S: chap. 18, p. 48; RZ: chap. 11, p. 12; GZ: chap. 49, p. 210; CV: chap. 13, p. 289; P: 211; D: pp. 13–14; MI: chap. 7, p. 63, chap. 20, pp. 90–91; GP: 101, 129; M2: chap. 11, p. 67, chap. 12, pp. 67–68; CO: chap. 8, pp. 143–144; G: bk. 3, chap. 19, p. 129.

Garcilaso. Only Las Casas and Román y Zamora (who had Las Casas) echo Sarmiento, Cabello, and Cobo about her origins in Guayllacan. Guaman Poma and Morúa usually call her Cusi Chimbo or combine the name with Mama Micay. Morúa also gives "Cusi Quicgsu" (MIa).

Sarmiento and Cabello Valboa both give Mama Chiquia (or Chicya), daughter of Tocay Capac, who was the lord of Ayarmaca, as the woman of the seventh pair (table 3.8). Similar stories are told by Cieza, Las Casas, and Román y Zamora. Cobo calls her Mama Choque Chiclla Yupay and does not

TABLE 3.7. *Sixth pair*

| Source | Sixth Pair |
|--------|-----------|
| CL | Ynga Roca and Nicay Coca, his sister, had Ynga Yupangue but no daughters. |
| B | Ynga Roca fathers Yaguar Guaca Ynga Yupangue. |
| CS | Inga Roca Inga and Mama Micay, daughter of the lord of Guallaca[n], have Yaguar Guacac Inga. |
| FZ | Inga Ruca Inga and Mama Micay have Yaguar Guac[a] Inga Yupangue, Apo Maita, and Vilca Quiri. |
| S | Inga Roca Inga and Mama Micay of Pataguayllacan, daughter of Soma Inca, have Tito Cusi Gualpa [Yaguar Guaca] and four others, including Vica Quirao Inga; Vica Quira[o] Panaca Ayllo. |
| RZ | Inga Roca Inga and Mama Micay, daughter of the lord of Guayllaca[n], have Yaguar Guacaci Inga Yupangi. |
| GZ | Inga Roca Inga and Mama Micay have [Ya]guar Guac[ac] Inga Yupangui, Appo Mayta, and Vilca Quiri. |
| CV | Ynga Ruca Ynga and Mama Nicaz, daughter of the lord of Guayllacan, have Yaguar Guaca and Veca Quiroa; Veca Queroa [Ayllo]. |
| P | Ynga Ruca and Mama Micay Chimpo have Yabar Uacac Ynga Yupangui. |
| D | Inga Roca and Mama Micay have Yavar Uacac Inga (earlier Maita Yupangue), Mayta Capac Inga, Yuman Tarsi, Vica Quirao Inga, and Cuzco Urco Guaranga; Ayllo Vica Quirao. |
| MI | a) Inga Roca and Cusi Quicgsu have Yaguar Guacac Inga. |
| | b) Inga Roca and Cusi Chimpo [or Mama Macai] have Yaguar Guacar, Apo Maita, Vilcaquiri, and daughter Ipa Guaco [or Mama Chiqui]. |
| GP | a) Inga Roca and Cici Chinbo Mama Micay Coya have Yauar Uacac Ynga, Ypa Uaco Mama Machi, Apo Camac Ynga. |
| | b) Ynga Roca and Cuci Chinbo Mama Micay Coya have Ypa Uaco Mama Machi Coya, Yauar Uacac Ynga, Apo Camac Ynga, Maytac Ynga. |
| M2 | a) Ynga Roca and Cusi Chimpo have Yahuar Huacac, Paucar Hinga, Huamantassi Inga, Vica Quirao Inga, Cacachicha Vica Quizao, Apo Maita, and Ypa Huaco (daughter), also known as Mama Chiqui. |
| | b) Ynga Roca and Coya Cusi Chimpo [or Mama Micay] have Yahuar Huacac and others, as well as daughter Ypa Huaco, who was also known as Mama Chiquia. |
| CO | Inca Roca and Mama Michay [or Micay], who is *cacica* of Guayllacan, have Yahuar Huacac, Vica Quirao, and Apo Mayta; Vica Quirao Ayllo. |
| G | Inca Roca and Mama Micay have Yahuar Huacac; in a later chapter (20, p. 163), brother Apo Maita is mentioned. |

*Sources*: CL: chap. 35, pp. 105–107; B: chap. 5, p. 22; CS: bk. 3, chap. 250, p. 575; FZ: chap. 5, p. 80; S: chap. 19, pp. 49–50; RZ: chap. 11, p. 12; GZ: chap. 49, p. 210; CV: chap. 13, pp. 293–294; P: 214; D: p. 14; MI: chap. 8, p. 65, chap. 21, pp. 92–93; GP: 103, 131; M2: chap. 13, p. 69, chap. 14, p. 70; CO: chap. 9, pp. 145–146; G: bk. 4, chap. 28, p. 161.

TABLE 3.8. *Seventh pair*

| Source | Seventh Pair |
|--------|--------------|
| CL | Ynga Yupangue and Mama Chiquia of Ayarmaca had no children. Elsewhere he notes that Viracocha is a nephew of this Inca (chap. 38). |
| B | Yaguar Guaca fathers Viracocha Ynga. |
| CS | Yaguar Guacac Inga and Mama Chiguia, daughter of lord of Ayarmacha, have Viracocha Inga. |
| FZ | Yaguar Guac[a] Inga Yupangue and Mama Chiquia have Viracocha Inga, Apo Cama, Apu Maroti, Inga Maita, Paguac Guallica Maica, and Chima Chauic. |
| S | Yaguar Guaca and Mama Chicya, daughter of Tocay Capac, have three sons: Paucar Ayllo, Pahuac Gualpa Mayta, and Viracocha; Aucaylli Panaca. |
| RZ | Yaguar Guacaci Inga Yupangi and Mama Chiguia, daughter of the lord of Ayarmacha, have Viracocha Inga. |
| GZ | Yaguar Guac[a] Ynga and Mama Chiguia have Viracocha Inca (and six others). |
| CV | Yaguar Guaca and Mama Chiquia, daughter of the lord of Ayarcama [Ayarmaca], have Viracocha Inga. |
| P | Yabar Uacac Ynga Yupangui and Mama Chuqui Chicya Illpay, from Ayarmaca, great-granddaughter of Tocay Capac, have Uiracochampa Incan Yupangui. |
| D | Yavar Uacac Inga and Mama Chicquia have Viracocha Inga, Paucar Yalli, Pauac Vallpa Mayta, Marca Yuto, Topa Ynga Paucar, and Inga Roca; Ayllo Aucayllo Panaca. |
| MI | a) Yaguar Guacac and Cuche Impuino had no children. <br> b) Yaguar Vacac and Ipa Vaco [or Mama Chiquia] have Mama Yunto Cayan. |
| GP | a) Yauar Uacac Ynga and Ypa Uaco Mama Machi Coya have Ynga Maytac, Mama Yunto Cayan Coya, Ynga Urcon Ranga, Uira Cocha Ynga. <br> b) Yauar Uacac Ynga and Ypa Huaco Mama Machi Coya had Mama Yunto Cayan Coya, Uiracocha Ynga, Apo Maytac Ynga, and Bilcac Ynga. |
| M2 | a) Yahuar Guacac and Ypa Guaco Coya [or Mama Chiquia] have Viracocha Ynga and Mama Yunto Coya. <br> b) Yahuar Huacac and Coya Hipa [or Mama Chiquia] have Mama Yunto Coya. |
| CO | Yaguar Huacac Inca Yupanqui and Mama Choque Chiclla Yupay have Viracocha; Aucayllo Panaca. |
| G | Yahuar Huacac and Coya Mama Chicya have two sons: an unnamed son who has been officially forgotten and Viracocha. |

*Sources:* CL: chap. 35, p. 107; B: chap. 5, p. 22; CS: bk. 3, chap. 250, p. 575; FZ: chap. 5, p. 81; S: chap. 23, p. 54, chap. 24, p. 55; RZ: chap. 11, p. 12; GZ: chap. 19, p. 210; CV: chap. 13, p. 295; P: 216; D: p. 14; MI: chap. 9, p. 67, chap. 22, pp. 94–96; GP: 105, 132; M2: chap. 15, p. 71, chap. 16, p. 72; CO: chap. 10, pp. 148, 151; G: bk. 4, chap. 21, p. 163, bk. 5, chap. 20, p. 200.

note her origins. The author Pachacuti notes exactly the same name but supplies her origin; again, she is Ayarmaca. Those who give some version of the name Chiquia are Fernández, Gutiérrez, and Garcilaso. Guaman Poma and Morúa name Ipa Huaco or some version of it most frequently (M2a, M2b, GPa, GPb); Morúa names Mama Chiqua as an alternate three times (M2a, M2b, and MIb). He also provides a wildly variant name: Cuche Impuino (MIa).

The story told by Sarmiento, Cabello Valboa, the author Pachacuti, and Las Casas is that Viracocha and Mama Ronto Caya of Anta produce the next generation (table 3.9). Cabello gets the place-name wrong, but it is identifiable as Anta. Cobo provides essentially the same information but calls her "Mama Roncay," perhaps a composition from the two names. The most common spelling of her name is with an *r*, but a number of authors give the first part of her name as "Yunto," including Fernández, Gutiérrez, Morúa (M2a, M2b, M1a), and Guaman Poma (GPa, GPb).

Whenever the woman of the ninth pair is named, she is called Mama Ana Huarque or some variant of that name (table 3.10). Sarmiento says that she was from Choco, but later on in his account, he says she was Pachacuti's sister. Las Casas, Cabello Valboa, and Cobo say merely that she is from Choco. Given that so much information is provided about this Inca and that he was said to have organized the preservation of information about the past, it is odd that Cieza, Betanzos, the author Pachacuti, and Morúa (M1a) do not name her. The versions of Guaman Poma and Morúa that usually vary from other accounts this time concur with the name Anahuarqui.

There is even more uniformity in the naming of Mama Ocllo as the sister-wife of Topa Inca in the tenth generation (table 3.11). Some authors do not say she is a sister, but no one suggests she has origins outside of Cuzco. At this point, Garcilaso introduces an extra Inca pair named Inca Yupanqui and Coya Chimpu Ocllo. When other authors name the progenitors of the eleventh generation, Garcilaso gives the names of Topa Inca and Mama Ocllo. He is off by a generation after that.

For the eleventh pair, divergent accounts again appear (table 3.12). Sarmiento and Cabello Valboa again parallel each other: Huayna Capac and Cusi Rimay Coya have no sons. Sarmiento does not say she is a sister, but he gives no outside origins for her. Others who mention Cusi Rimay are the author Pachacuti, Morúa (M2a), and Cobo. For both the author Pachacuti and Cobo, Huayna Capac and Cusi Rimay father a son: Ninan Coyoche. The other author to mention the parentage of Ninan Coyoche is Sarmiento, who says he is a son of Rahua Ocllo. Pillco Huaco was named as the principal wife of Huayna Capac by Fernández and Gutiérrez, who says she is the daughter of a lord of Urcos. Both note that she had no children.

Most authors note that Huascar was the son of Rahua Ocllo, including Betanzos, Fernández, Sarmiento, and Cabello Valboa. Accounts of who she was diverge wildly. Betanzos said she was from Hurin Cuzco and a distant relative of Pachacuti. For Cabello Valboa, the *Discurso*, and Morúa (M2a), she

TABLE 3.9. *Eighth pair*

| Source | Eighth Pair |
|---|---|
| CL | Viracocha Inga marries Rondo Caya, a principal lady. Presumably, Inca Urcon and Ynga Yupangue are her sons. |
| B | Viracocha fathers Inga Urco and Ynga Yupangue (seven in all). |
| CS | Viracocha Inga and Mama Runto Caya, daughter of the lord of Antha of the Valley of Jachijaguana, have Pachacuti Inga Yupangi. |
| FZ | Viracocha Inga and Mama Yunto Cayan have Pachacoti Inga, Inga Urcon Inga, Inga Maita, Cuna Yurachali Curopangue, and Capac Yupangue. |
| S | Viracocha and Mama Rondo Caya of Anta have four sons: Inga Roca Inga, Topa Yupangui, Inga Yupangui, and Capac Yupangui. With Curi Chulpa, an Ayavila of the Cuzco Valley, he had two sons: Inga Urcon and Inga Çocço; Çocço Panaca Ayllo. |
| RZ | Viracocha Inga and Miama Runto Caya, daughter of the lord of Ancha in the Valley of Xachixaguana, have Pachacuti Capac Inga Yupangi. |
| GZ | Viracocha Inga and Mama Yunto Cayan have Inga Urcon, four others, and Pachacote Capac Inga Yupangue (the youngest). |
| CV | Viracocha Inga and Mama Rundu Caya of Canto [Anta] have Ynga Yupangui. Viracocha fathers Inga Urco and Topa Guara Chiri (mother not named). |
| P | Uiracochampa Yncan Yupangui and Mama Rontocay of Anta have Ynca Yupangui (later Pachacuti Ynga Yupangui). |
| D | Viracocha Inga and Mama Rondo Cayan have Inga Yupangue, Inga Urcun, and Inga Maita; Ayllo Sucsu Panaca. |
| MI | a) Viracocha and Mama Yunto Cuyan had Pachacuti Inga [or Ynga Yupangui], Urcon Inga, Inga Mayta, Cuna Yura Chali Coropangui, and Capac Yupangui. <br> b) No account. |
| GP | a) Uira Cocha Ynga and Mama Yunto Cayan Coya have Pachacuti Ynga Yupanqui, Mama Ana Uarque Coya, Urcon Ynga, Apo Maytac Ynga, Bilcac Ynga. <br> b) Uira Cocha Ynga and Mama Yunto Cayan Coya had Ynga Yupanqui, Urcon Ynga, Apo Maytac Ynga, Bilcac Guaman Ynga, Mama Ana Uarque Coya, Curi Urma, Quispi Quipi, and Cuci Ynquillay. |
| M2 | a) Viracocha Ynga and Mama Yunto Coya had five children, including Pachacuti Ynga Yupangui [or Ynga Yupanqui], Urcu Ynga, Ynga Mayta, Coropanqui, and Capac Yupanki; or he was not married, and after his death a brother named Ynga Yupanqui took his place. <br> b) Viracocha Ynga and Mama Yunto Coya had sons and Mama Anahuarque Coya (daughter). |
| CO | Viracocha and Mama Roncay, daughter of the lord of Anta, have Pachacuti Inca Yupanqui, Inca Roca, Topa Yupanqui, and Capac Yupanqui; Socsoc Panaca. |
| G | Viracocha and Coya Mama Runto (sister) have Titu Manco Capac [later Pachacutec]; later (bk. 6, chap. 10, p. 233), a brother, Capac Yupanqui, is mentioned. |

*Sources*: CL: chap. 38, p. 113, chap. 43, p. 128; B: chap. 6, pp. 25–26; CS: bk. 3, chap. 250, p. 575; FZ: chap. 5, p. 81; S: chap. 24, pp. 56–57; RZ: chap. 11, pp. 12–13; GZ: chap. 49, pp. 210–211; CV: chap. 14, pp. 297–298; P: 216, 218, 221; D: p. 19; MI: chap. 10, p. 68, chap. 33, p. 96; GP: 107, 135; M2: chap. 17, p. 72, chap. 18, p. 73; CO: chap. 11, pp. 153–155, chap. 12, p. 156; G: bk. 5, chap. 28, p. 213.

TABLE 3.10. *Ninth pair*

| Source | Ninth Pair |
|---|---|
| CL | Ynga Urcon's sister and wife, who had had no children by him, marries Ynga Yupangui when the latter becomes ruler. Ynga Yupangui and this sister presumably have Topa Inga. |
| B | Pachacuti fathers Yamque Yupangue and Topa Ynga Yupangue; Capac Yupangue born to another wife. |
| CS | Pachacuti Inga Yupangi and Mama Hana Guarqui, daughter of the lord of Chuco, have Apo Yanqui Yupangui, Tillca Yupanqui, Amaro Topa Inga, and Topa Inga Yupangui; Capac Ayllo. |
| FZ | Pachacoti Inga and Mama Ana Barque have Topa Inga Yupangue, Amaro Topa Inga, Capac Guairi, Sinche Roca Inga, and Guaillipa Tupa. |
| S | Pachacuti and Mama Aña Guarqui, from Choco or Pachacuti's sister, had four sons: Amaro Topa and Topa Inga Yupangui are named; Hatun Ayllo [also Inaca Panaca Ayllo]. |
| RZ | Pachacuti Capac Inga Yupangi and Mama Hana Guarqui, daughter of the lord of Chuco, have Topa Inga. |
| GZ | Pachacoti Capac Inga Yupangue and Mama Ana Guarque Micay have five sons: Topa Inga Yupangue, Amaro Topa, Capac Guayiri, Sinchi Roca, and Guallipa. |
| CV | Ynga Yupangui and Mama Anahuarqui of Choco have Topa Ynga Yupangui. Later, Amaro Topa Ynga is described as a brother of Topa Ynga. |
| P | Pachacuti Ynga Yupangui fathers Amaro Ttopa Ynga and Ttopa Ynga Yupangui; Capac Ayllos. |
| D | Inga Yupangue (or Pachacuti Inga) and Mama Aana Barque have Topa Inga Yupangue, Topa Yupangue, and Amaro Topa Inca; Ayllo Innaca Panaca. |
| MI | a) Pachacuti dies in Quito; son Tupa Inga Yupangui succeeds him. <br> b) Inga Yupangui and Mama Anahuarqui [or Ipa Vaco] have Mama Ollo Coya. |
| GP | a) Pachacuti Ynga Yupanqui and Mama Ana Uarque have Mama Ocllo, Topa Ynga Yupanqui, Cuci Uanan Chire Ynga, Mango Ynga, Topa Amaro Ynga, Maytac Ynga. <br> b) Pachacuti and Mama Ana Uarque Coya have Ynca Maytac, Topa Ynga Yupanque, Tupa Amaro Ynga, Mama Ocllo Coya, Ynga Urcon, Apo Camasca Ynga. |
| M2 | a) Ynga Yupanqui [or Pachakuti Ynga] and Mama Anahuarqui [or Hipa Huaco] have Tupa Inga Yupangui, Amaro Tupa Ynga, Tupa Yupanqui, and Mama Ocllo. <br> b) Ynga Yupanqui and Coya Mama Anahuarqui [or Hipa Huaco] have sons and daughter Mama Ocllo. |
| CO | Pachacutic Inca Yupanqui and Mama Anahuarqui of Choco have Tupa Inga Yupanqui, Amaro Tupa Inca, and Tupa Inca; Yñaca *panaca*. |
| G | Pachacutec and Coya Anahuarqui (sister) have Inca Yupanqui. |

*Sources*: CL: chap. 46, p. 135; B: chap. 20, p. 99; CS: bk. 3, chap. 250, p. 575, chap. 259, p. 613; FZ: chap. 5, p. 81; S: chap. 34, p. 72, chap. 47, pp. 93–94; RZ: chap. 11, p. 20; GZ: chap. 49, pp. 211–212; CV: chap. 15, p. 303, chap. 18, p. 334; P: 223–224, 228, 230; D: p. 20; MI: chap. 11, pp. 71–72, chap. 24, pp. 97–98; GP: 109, 137; M2: chap. 21, p. 80, chap. 22, pp. 84–85, chap. 23, p. 86; CO: chap. 12, p. 156, chap. 14, p. 167; G: bk. 6, chap. 34, pp. 273–274.

TABLE 3.11. *Tenth pair*

| Source | Tenth Pair |
|---|---|
| CL | Topa Ynga and Mama Ocllo, sister, have Guayna Capac. |
| B | Topa Ynga and Mama Ocllo, younger sister, have Guayna Capac. |
| CS | Topa Inga and Mama Ocllo, full sister, have Pidi Topa Yupangui Guaina Topa Inga and Guaina Capac. |
| FZ | Topa Inga Yupangue and Mama Ocllo have Guaina Capa Inga, Auci Topa Inga, and Auqui Toma. |
| S | Topa Inga Yupangui and Mama Ocllo, sister, have Tito Cusi Gualpa (or Guayna Capac) and Auqui Topa Inga; Capac Ayllo. |
| RZ | Topa Inga is succeeded by Guayna Capac. |
| GZ | Topa Inga Yupangue and Mama Ocllo have Guayna Cappa, Topa Inga, Anci Topa Inga, and Anqui Topa. |
| CV | Topa Ynga Yupangui and Mama Ocllo, first cousin, have Guayna Capac. Later, Mama Cusi Rimay and Mama Ragua Ocllo are described as sisters of Guayna Capac. |
| P | Ttopa Ynga Yupangui and Coya Mama Ana Guarque have Guayna Capac Ynga. |
| D | Topa Inga Yupangue and Mama Ocllo (sister; he was the first to marry his sister), have Inti Cusi Vallpa (later Guaina Capac Inga) and Auqui Topa Inga; Capac Ayllo. |
| MI | a) Tupa Inga Yupangui and Mama Ocllo have Guana Capac. |
|  | b) No account. |
| GP | a) Topa Ynga Yupanqui and Mama Ocllo have Apo Camac Ynga, Ynga Urcon, Auqui Topa Ynga, Uiza Topa Ynga, Amaro Ynga, Otorongo Achachi Ynga, Tupa Guallpa, Mama Uaco, Cuci Chinbo, Ana Uarque, Raua Ocllo, Guayna Capac, and Juana Curi Ocllo. |
|  | b) Topa Ynga Yupanqui and Mama Ocllo Coya have Uiza Topa Ynga, Topa Ynga Yupanqui, Raua Ocllo, Curi Ocllo, Ana Uarque, Amaro Ynga, Otorongo Achachi Ynga, Tunpa Guallpa, Guallpa Ynga, and Guayna Capac Ynga. |
| M2 | a) Tupa Ynga Yupanqui marries Mama Ocllo. |
|  | b) Tupa Ynga Yupanqui and Mama Ocllo [or Tocta Cuca] have Huayna Capac, Ausi Topa, Yauqui Toma [Cusi Topa and Auqui Toma, see p. 112 for Auqui Toma], and daughter Rahua Ocllo [or Pilli Coaco Coya]. |
| CO | Tupa Inca and Mama Ocllo, full sister, have Guayna Capac and Coya Cusi Rimay; Capac Ayllo. |
| G | Inca Yupanqui and Coya Chimpu Ocllo (sister) have Tupac Inca Yupanqui. |

*Sources*: CL: chap. 56, p. 160, chap. 57, p. 164; B: chap. 26, pp. 27–29; CS: bk. 3, chap. 261, p. 622; FZ: chap. 5, pp. 81–82; S: chap. 56, p. 103, chap. 57, p. 103; RZ: chap. 11, p. 20; GZ: chap. L, p. 215; CV: chap. 16, p. 320, chap. 21, p. 364; P: 230; D: p. 21; MI: chap. 24, p. 87, chap. 27, pp. 100–101; GP: pp. 111, 139; M2: chap. 12, p. 74, chap. 25, p. 99; CO: chap. 14, pp. 167–168; G: bk. 7, chap. 26, p. 323.

was a sister. For Morúa (M2b, MIa) and Guaman Poma (GPa, GPb), she was Huayna Capac's principal wife. For the author Pachacuti she had a son, Topa Cusi Huallpa (later Huascar), before Huayna Capac took his principal wife. Only Cieza names someone else as the mother of Huascar (Chimbo Ocllo).

The mother of Atahuallpa also generated some controversy. For Cieza, she is either Tuta Palla, a Quilaco woman from the Quito area, or a woman from

TABLE 3.12. *Eleventh pair*

| Source | Eleventh Pair |
|---|---|
| CL | Guayna Capac and Chimbo Ocllo had Huascar; Atahualipa is son of either Tuta Palla of Quilaco or a woman of Hurin Cuzco. |
| B | Huayna Capac and Palla Coca, second cousin and great-granddaughter of Pachacuti through the male line, have Atahualpa; he has Huascar with Ragua Ocllo, a woman of Hurin Cuzco and a distant relative of Pachacuti; Ragua Ocllo also has daughter Chuqui Huipa. |
| CS | Guayna Capac fathered two sons, Guascar and Atapalipa. |
| FZ | Guayna Capa Inga and Coya Pilico Vaco have no sons; with Raua Ocllo he has Guascar; with Mama Runto Coya he has Mango Inga Yupangue; list of sixteen more (no mothers named). |
| S | Guayna Capac and Cusi Rimay Coya have no children; with Aragua Ocllo he has Topa Cusi Gualpa [Guascar] and Tito Atauchi; Ninan Cuyoche and Atagualpa are bastards, the latter born to Tocto Coca, cousin, of the lineage of Pachacuti; Tumibamba Ayllo. |
| RZ | Guayna Capac is succeeded by Guascar and Atapalipa. |
| GZ | Guayna Capa Inga and Mama Coya Pilico Vaco, daughter of the lord of Urcos, have no children; he has Guascr Inga, Mango Inga Zapalla, Paulo Inga, Guanca Auqui, Titio Antaychi, and Ingil Topa with other women; sons born in Quito include Atahualpa, born to the daughter of an important lord there. |
| CV | Guayna Capac and sister Mama Cusi Rimay had no sons; Guayna Capac married sister Mama Ragua Ocllo and had Topa Cusi Gualpa [Guascar]. Later, Mama Chuqui Uzpai is said to be his full sister. |
| P | Guayna Capac and his sister Mama Cuçi Rimay have Ninan Cuyochi; Guayna Capac and Raua Ocllo had Inti Topa Cussi Guallpa before his marriage; Guayna Capac and Tocto Ocllo Coca have Ttopa Ataguallpa. |
| D | Guaina Capac Inga and Coaia Rava Ocllo (sister) have Topa Cusi Vallpa (or Guascar Inga); mentions Atao Vallpa but does not give mother's name (p. 22). |
| MI | a) Guaina Capac and Raua Allo have Tito Cussi Gualpa [or Guascar Inga]; Atagualipa is the son of a woman from Chincha. |
|  | b) No account. |
| GP | a) Guayna Capac Ynga and Raua Ocllo Coya have Uascar Ynga; illegitimate ones are Atagualpa Ynga, Mango Ynga, Ninan Cuyochi, Yllescas Ynga, Paullo Topa, Titu Atauchi, Uari Tito, Ynquil Topa, Uanca Auqui, Quizo Yupanqui. |
|  | b) Guayna Capac and Raua Ocllo Coya had Tupa Cusi Gualpa Uascar Ynga, Chuqui Llanto, Atagualpa Ynga, Mango Ynga, Yllescas Inga, Ynga Paullo Topa, and others. |
| M2 | a) Huayna Capac marries Mama Cusi Rimay (full sister), then Rahua Ocllo [or Pilco Huaco] (also a sister), and they have Tupa Cusi Hualpa [of Huascar Ynga]. |
|  | b) Huayna Capac and Coya Rahua Ocllo have Huascar Ynga and Mama Huarcay [also Chuqui Llanto or Chuqui Huipa]. |
| CO | Huayna Capac and Mama Cusi Rimay have Ninan Cuyuchi; he has Huascar [or Tupa |

(*continued on page 78*)

TABLE 3.12 (*continued*)

| Source | Eleventh Pair |
|---|---|
| | Cusi Gualpa] with Rahua Ocllo; Antau Hualpa [elsewhere Atau Hualpa] with Tocto Ocllo. |
| G | Tupac Inca Yupanqui and Mama Ocllo (sister) have Huaina Capac; other sons are Auqui Amaru Tupac Inca, Quehuar Tupac, Huallpa Tupac Inca Yupanqui (Garcilaso's maternal grandfather); Titu Inca Rimachi and Auqui Maita. |

*Sources*: CL: chap. 62, p. 181, chap. 63, p. 184; B: chap. 46, pp. 193–194; CS: chap. 261, p. 623; FZ: chap. 5, p. 82; S: chap. 60, pp. 105–106, chap. 63, p. 112, chap. 65, p. 120; RZ: chap. 11, p. 20; GZ: chap. 50, p. 215; CV: chap. 21, p. 364, chap. 25, p. 399; P: 243, 246–247; MI: chap. 29, p. 107, chap. 31, pp. 111–112, D: p. 23; MI: chap. 8, p. 76, chap. 26, p. 99; GP: 114, 141; M2: chap. 38, p. 137; CO: chap. 17, pp. 189–190, chap. 18, p. 190; G: bk. 8, chap. 7, pp. 341–342, chap. 8, p. 345.

Hurin Cuzco. For Betanzos, she is Palla Coca, Huayna Capac's second cousin and great-granddaughter of Pachacuti through the male line.

When the divergent stories about Huascar's and Atahuallpa's mothers are considered in light of the logic of *capac* status developed in chapter 2, the divergence in the accounts can be interpreted. Betanzos, when he said that Rahua Ocllo was from Hurin Cuzco and only a distant relative of Pachacuti, presents her as a relatively low status woman. Cieza is presenting Atahuallpa's mother in the worst possible light when he says that she was from Quito or from Hurin Cuzco. Because of the fratricidal civil war between these two brothers, and because we understand the importance of the lineage of the woman in each Inca generation, we can see here how discrepancies in information on the parentage of this woman indicate a particular bias.

The genealogical account effectively ends with Huayna Capac for Cieza, Las Casas, Román y Zamora, and Gutiérrez (table 3.13). The others merely tell us who Huascar's principal wife was. She may have produced sons, but if so, they were killed by Atahuallpa's generals, and no one provides names for them. Almost all authors name Huascar's principal wife as Chuqui Huipa, although Guaman Poma (GPa, GPb) and Morúa (MIa, MIb) name Chuqui Llanto. Cobo calls this woman Choque Yupa. Several authors say she is a sister. Fernández, Morúa (MIa, MIb), and Garcilaso say the pair had a daughter, Cusi Huarcay. Garcilaso adds a generation between the ninth and tenth pairs; all the other authors name the same list of Incas in the same order, except for Betanzos, who reverses Mayta Capac and Capac Yupanqui (fourth and fifth rulers). Since descent was determined through the male line, the consistency reflects a general consensus on the sequence. Disagreement is found in the identification of the female member of the dynastic pair, providing us with a means of identifying relationships between accounts.

TABLE 3.13. *Twelfth pair*

| Source | Twelfth Pair |
|---|---|
| B | Guascar marries Chuqui Huipa, his sister; Atagualpa receives Cusi Rimay Ocllo, daughter of Yamque Yupangue, as *piviguarmi*. |
| FZ | Guascar and Mama Varcay have Coya Cuxi Varcay. |
| S | Tito Cusi Gualpa Indi Illapa [Guascar] and Chucuy Huypa have no male descendants; Guascar Ayllo. |
| CV | Topa Cusi Guallpa [Guascar] marries Mama Chuqui Uzpai. |
| P | Inti Cuçi Uallpa Guascar Ynga and Coya Mama Chuqui Huypa Chuquipay have one or two sons. |
| D | Topa Cusi Vallpa (or Guascar Inga) and Chuqui Huipa Coia (or Coca) (sister) have two children who were killed in front of his eyes and their mother right after them; some say Cusi Varcay was a daughter, but she was a daughter of Manco Inca. |
| MI | a) Guascar Ynga and Chuqui Llauto [or Mama Varita Cayo] have daughter Cussi Varcay Coya. <br> b) Guascar and Chuqui Llauto [or Mama Guarqui] have Cusi Varcay Coya. |
| GP | a) Topa Cuci Gualpa [or Guascar Ynga] marries Chuqui Llanto Coya. <br> b) Guascar Ynga marries Chuqui Llanto Coya. |
| M2 | Huascar marries Chuqui Huipa. |
| CO | Huascar marries Coya Choque Yupa. |
| G | Huaina Capac and Pillcu Huaco (sister) have no children; with Raua Ocllo (also sister) he has Inti Cusi Huallpa (or Huascar); with Mama Runto (first cousin) he has Manco Inca; Huascar has daughter Cusi Huarque. |

*Sources*: B: chap. 47, pp. 197–198, chap. 48, p. 199; FZ: chap. 5, p. 82; S: chap. 68, p. 125; CV: chap. 25, p. 399; P: 254, 266; D: p. 23; MI: chap. 14, p. 78, chap. 27, pp. 100–101; GP: 116, 143; M2: chap. 43, p. 152; CO: chap. 19, p. 202; G: bk. 8, chap. 8, pp. 344–345, bk. 9, chap. 37, p. 432.

One general observation that results from our comparison is that Cabello Valboa and Sarmiento are in general agreement about the genealogy of the dynastic descent group. The lost historical narrative of Molina would have been similar to Sarmiento in its genealogical content. Cobo, on the other hand, differs from Sarmiento and Cabello Valboa in a number of specific details. An underlying Polo account would have included the same list of Incas but would have differed from Sarmiento in the names given for some of the women in the dynastic line.

Since it is the identification of the woman in each generation which is a source of difference between accounts, let us look again at the accounts with this in mind. To simplify comparison, table 3.14 has been compiled from the materials of the various parts of tables 3.1–3.13. When authors use what appear to be variants of the same name, the variants are noted. In some cases, where a name has an additional part but the part itself may be the equivalent of one of the names listed, I have set it apart. I have also listed names separately that may simply be mistranscriptions. For example, in the case of the eighth pair,

TABLE 3.14. *Female member of the Inca pair named in short accounts*

| Generation | Woman Named | | |
|---|---|---|---|
| 1 | *Mama Ocllo*<br>Las Casas<br>Gutiérrez | *Mama Huaco*<br>Fernández<br>*Discurso*<br>Cobo | |
| 2 | *Mama Coca*<br>Las Casas<br>*Discurso* | *Mama Cura/Chura*<br>Fernández<br>Gutierrez<br>Cobo | |
| 3 | *Mama Cagua Pata*<br>Las Casas<br>Gutiérrez | *Cachua/Caua*<br>*Discurso*<br>Cobo | *Anahuarqui*<br>Fernández |
| 4 | *Mama Chianta/Dianta*<br>Las Casas<br>Gutiérrez | *Taocaray*<br>*Discurso*<br>Cobo | *Yacchi*<br>Fernández |
| 5 | *Indi Chigia*<br>Las Casas<br>Gutiérrez | *Chuqui/Cori Ilpay*<br>*Discurso*<br>Cobo | *Cagua*<br>Fernández |
| 6 | *Mama Micay*<br>Las Casas<br>Gutiérrez<br>Fernández<br>*Discurso*<br>Cobo | | |

Cobo's use of Roncay may reflect a transcription error rather than the use of a different name for this woman. The names Chuqui and Cori Ilpay may also refer to the same person. Chuqui is Aymara for "gold"; Cori is the Inca word for the same metal.

Sometimes the accounts reflect general agreement on who the woman of the dynastic pair was (the sixth, seventh, possibly eighth and ninth, and tenth pairs) (table 3.14). The differences are evident primarily in the early generations (first, second, third, fourth, and fifth pairs). Where there are differences, Cobo and the *Discurso* generally reflect one choice of names while Las Casas and Gutiérrez reflect another. Fernández does not follow either consistently. This general statement holds, except for the second and eighth pairs. Here, Cura may have been a mistranscription of Cuca, but both Cora and Coca are good names for Inca women, so they have been listed separately in the table. Gutiérrez supplies Mama Coya, further confusing the analysis. In the case of the eighth pair, Cobo is the odd one, and Las Casas and the *Discurso* use dif-

| Generation | Woman Named | | |
|---|---|---|---|
| 7 | *Mama Chiguia*<br>Las Casas<br>Fernández<br>Gutiérrez<br>*Discurso*<br>Cobo | | |
| 8 | *Runto Caya*<br>Las Casas<br>*Discurso* | *Yunto Caya*<br>Fernández<br>Gutiérrez | *Roncay*<br>Cobo |
| 9 | *Anahuarqui*<br>Las Casas<br>Fernández<br>*Discurso*<br>Cobo | *Anahuarqui Micay*<br>Gutiérrez | |
| 10 | *Mama Ocllo*<br>Las Casas<br>Fernández<br>Gutiérrez<br>*Discurso*<br>Cobo | | |
| 11 | *Pillco Huaco*<br>Gutiérrez<br>Fernández | *Cusi Rimay*<br>Cobo | |
| 12 | *Mama Huarcay*<br>Fernández | *Chuqui Huypa*<br>*Discurso*<br>Cobo | |

ferent spellings. Errors in transcription or understanding may account for different spellings of what, essentially, was the same name.

What the results of this comparison suggest is that Cobo and the *Discurso* relied on the same source to structure their narratives, while Las Casas and Gutiérrez relied on another. Cobo may have taken the genealogical structure of his account from a text by Polo de Ondegardo. The *Discurso* probably relied on a source with the same underlying genealogical structure. Polo collected his information from Inca sources in Cuzco. The *Discurso* makes the same claim about the origins of the material it contains. On the other hand, neither Las Casas nor Gutiérrez was ever in Peru. Their accounts may have drawn from a manuscript source that was available to them in Spain, one that was structured differently from the source used by Cobo and the *Discurso*.

When we take Spanish historical narratives that include a great deal more material than genealogy into account, other differences appear. For example, it is hard to reconcile Cieza de León with either of the two genealogical structures. Sarmiento, the author Pachacuti, Morúa (M2), and Cabello Valboa (who used Molina's lost historical narrative) reflect the same genealogical structure as Cobo and the *Discurso*. Guaman Poma and Morúa (M1) reflect a variant genealogical structure, one that cannot be tied to the first decades of the Spanish presence in Cuzco. This latter point is important. The genealogical accounts that underlie Cobo and the *Discurso*, on the one hand, and Las Casas and Gutiérrez, on the other, can be linked to the period before 1560, when it is much more likely that people who had a firsthand acquaintance with Inca genres could transmit a version of them. What is most important, a version of dynastic genealogy similar to what was recorded in Cobo and the *Discurso* was collected from Inca sources in Cuzco during a period of at least several decades.

## PANACA LISTS

Nine authors incorporate the names of *panacas*, or descent group segments. Since we have already established a pattern of relationships among sources structured by genealogy, we might expect to find that these sources show the same pattern of relationships in their presentation of information about the *panacas*. They do. Because of this linkage, we can infer that these accounts rely on a source that incorporated this information.

As might be expected, Cobo and the *Discurso* are similar in their presentation of information about the *panacas* and quite different from Las Casas and Gutiérrez. First of all, Las Casas and Gutiérrez list the *panacas*, inserting the list into the narrative when the subject is Pachacuti and organizing the *panacas* according to their affiliation with either Hanan or Hurin Cuzco.[10] In the case of Cobo and the *Discurso*, the information about the *panacas* is distributed throughout the historical narrative, each *panaca* linked with the name of the Inca associated with it. There are other differences in the *panaca* lists, however, which do not have to do with how they are integrated into the narrative. These differences may be important to what we can learn about an underlying Inca source, so we will examine the *panaca* information included in each account, beginning with Cobo and the *Discurso*. In the tables which follow, variations in the spelling of names have been preserved.

Both Cobo and the *Discurso* associate *panaca* names with the name of an Inca (tables 3.15, 3.16). Since the information was presented in genealogical order, we can derive an order for a list of *panacas*. Cobo also assigns *panacas*

TABLE 3.15. Panacas *from Cobo*

*Not included in Hanan/Hurin*

| Manco Capac | Chima Panaca Ayllo |
|---|---|

*Hurin Cuzco*

| Cinchi Roca | Raurahua Panaca |
|---|---|
| Lluqui Yupangui | Ahucani Ayllu |
| Mayta Capac | Usca Mayta |
| Capac Yupanqui | Apu Mayta |

*Hanan Cuzco*

| Inca Roca | Vica Quirao |
|---|---|
| Yahuar Huacac | Aucayllo Panaca |
| Viracocha Inca | Socsoc Panaca |
| Pachacútic | Yñaca Panaca |
| Tupa Inca | Capac Ayllo |
| Guayna Capac | Tumibamba |

*Sources*: [1653]; bk. 12, chap. 4; 1892:132; bk. 12, chap. 5; 1892:135; bk. 12, chap. 6; 1892:138; bk. 12, chap. 8; 1892:144; bk. 12, chap. 9; 1892:147; bk. 12, chap. 10; 1892:55; bk. 12, chap. 12; 1892:156; bk. 12, chap. 14; 1892:168; bk. 12, chap. 17; 1892:189–190.

TABLE 3.16. Panacas *from the* Discurso

| Mango Capac | Chima Panaca |
|---|---|
| Chinche Roca | Raorao Panaca |
| Lluque Yupanqui | Ayllo Guguayuin |
| Mayta Capac | Ayllo Usca Mayta |
| Capac Yupangui | Ayllo Apo Maita |
| Inga Roca | Ayllo Vica Quirao |
| Yavar Yuacac | Aucayllo Panaca |
| Viracocha Inca | Ayllo Sucsu Panaca |
| Inga Yupangue | Ayllo Innaca Panaca |
| Topa Inga Yupangue | Capac Ayllo |
| Inti Cusi Vallpa (Guayna Capac Inga) | no mention of descent group |

*Source*: [1602–1608]; 1920:12–23.

to the Hanan/Hurin Cuzco division. He interrupts his narrative after his treatment of Capac Yupanqui, the fifth Inca, to describe the division of Cuzco into Hanan or Hurin and to affiliate particular Incas with each division. This point is appropriate because he associates the first four generations descended from Manco Capac with Hurin Cuzco and those following with Hanan Cuzco. He also notes that Manco Capac "as head and trunk of both divisions" was neither. Elsewhere in his manuscript, where he describes the shrines tended by the *panacas*, he associates the *panaca* of Manco Capac with a *ceque* in

TABLE 3.17. Panacas *from Fernández*

| | |
|---|---|
| Mango Capa Inga | Chima Panaca Aillo |
| Siche Roca Inga | Piauragua Aillo |
| Llocuco Pangua Inga | Uzca Mayta Aillo |
| Mayta Capa Inga | Apo Mayta Aillo |
| Capac Yupangue Inga | Aguanin Aillo |
| Inga Rupa Inga | Vica Cupa Aillo |
| Yaguar Guac[ac] Inga | Aoca Aillo |
| Viracocha Inga | Cococ Panaca Aillo |
| Pachacoti Inga Yupangue | Hatren Aillo |
| Topa Inga Yupangue | Capac Aillo |
| Guaina Capa Inga | Tome Bamba Ayllo |

*Source*: [1571], bk. 3, chap. 7; 1963, vol. 165:84

Condesuyo, part of Hurin Cuzco (Cobo [1653], bk. 13, chaps. 12–16; 1893: 5–47). Some of the buildings where Manco Capac and his sisters lived when they came to Cuzco were also shrines in Condesuyo. Whether or not the *panaca* was assigned to care for these shrines or localized in Condesuyo, Cobo and others note the special status of this *panaca* (Sarmiento [1572], chap. 14; 1906:42). Perhaps Cobo is telling us something important about the division between Hanan and Hurin Cuzco: what united them was descent from Manco Capac and little else. The *Discurso*, on the other hand, does not mention the Hanan/Hurin Cuzco division, let alone associate *panacas* with it. It also indicates the names of a younger brother or brothers of each ruler who would form that ruler's *panaca*. Cobo names an eleventh *panaca*, but the *Discurso* does not.

Before examining Las Casas and Gutiérrez de Santa Clara, we will look at how the same information is presented in the accounts of Diego Fernández (table 3.17), Sarmiento de Gamboa (table 3.18), and Morúa (MI) (table 3.19). Remember that Fernández sometimes follows the Las Casas/Gutiérrez version and sometimes the Cobo/*Discurso* one in his genealogical account. In the case of *panaca* information, Fernández, like Cobo and the *Discurso*, follows a genealogical order in listing the *panacas*, but he does not distribute the *panacas* to the point in his narrative when he talks about a particular ruler. Instead he inserts a chapter on the *panacas* after finishing his narrative of the Inca past (Fernández [1571], pt. 2, bk. 3, chap. 7; 1963, vol. 165:84).

What is also noteworthy in Fernández is that, as in the *Discurso*, there is no attempt to affiliate the *panacas* with either Hanan or Hurin Cuzco. Moreover, like Cobo, Fernández includes the *panaca* of Huayna Capac. Unlike anyone

TABLE 3.18. Panacas *from Sarmiento*

Hurin Cuzco

| | |
|---|---|
| Mango Capac | Chima Panaca Ayllo |
| Cinchi Roca | Raura Panaca |
| Lloqui Yupangui | Avayni Panaca Ayllo |
| Mayta Capac | Usca Mayta Panaca Ayllo |
| Capac Yupangui | Apo Mayta Panaca Ayllo |

Hanan Cuzco

| | |
|---|---|
| Inga Roca | Vicaquira Panaca Ayllo |
| Tito Cusi Gualpa or | |
| Yaguar Guaca | Aucaylli Panaca |
| Viracocha | Çocço Panaca Ayllo |
| Inga Yupangui or | |
| Pachacuti Inga Yupangui | Inaca Panaca Ayllo |
| Topa Inga Yupangui | Capac Ayllo |
| Guayna Capac | Tumibamba Ayllo |

*Sources*: [1572], chap. 14; 1906:42–43; chap. 15; 1906:44; chap. 16; 1906:45; chap. 17; 1906:47–48; chap. 18; 1906:48–49; chap. 19; 1906:50; chap. 23; 1906:55; chap. 25; 1906:59; chap. 47; 1906:93; chap. 54; 1906:02; chap. 62; 1906:111–112.

TABLE 3.19. Panacas *from Morúa (M1)*

Urin Cuzco

| | |
|---|---|
| Mango Capac Inga | Chima Panaca Ayllo |
| Sinchi Roca Inga | Piauragua Ayllo |
| Lloque Yupangui Inga | Esca Mayta Ayllo |
| Maita Capac Inga | Apo Maita Ayllo |
| Capac Yupangui Inga | Aguami Ayllo |

Anan Cuzco

| | |
|---|---|
| Inga Roca Inga | Vaca Capac Ayllo |
| Yavar Vacac Inga Yupangui | Aoca Ayllo |
| Viracocha Inga | Cococ Pacana Ayllo |
| Inga Yupangui [or Pachacuti] | Hatren Ayllo |
| Topa Ynga Yupangui | Capac Ayllo |
| Guanacac Inga | Tomebamba |

*Source*: [1605], bk. 1, chap. 15; 1946:79–80.

else, Fernández lists three "lineages" after the lineage of Huayna Capac (those of Huascar, Manco Inca, and Saire Topa) but does not provide *panaca* names for them. He also lists Ahuayni Ayllo (the third *panaca* on the Cobo and *Discurso* lists) in fifth place, changing the association of Inca to *panaca* in the case of three Incas: Lloque Yupanqui, Mayta Capac, and Capac Yupanqui.

Sarmiento presents essentially the same list as Cobo, except that the Hanan/Hurin Cuzco affiliation of each *panaca* is clear because he notes in each case whether they are "Hanancuzcos" or "Hurincuzcos." Unlike Cobo, he does not set Manco Capac's *panaca* outside the Hanan/Hurin Cuzco division; its members are "Hurincuzcos" (Sarmiento [1572], chap. 14; 1906:43).

Morúa's list is like Fernández's, except that he sorts the list into Hanan and Hurin Cuzco categories. Like Fernández, he presents a list rather than distributing the information to the appropriate points in his narrative. Like Fernández, he lists Ahuayni Ayllo as the *panaca* of the fifth Inca rather than the third, changing the association between *panaca* and Inca for the third, fourth, and fifth Incas. Morúa may have been following Fernández; there are other indications of dependency between the two manuscripts.[11] He includes this list in his later manuscript (M2), the one which reflects a dependency on the lost historical narrative of Cristóbal de Molina. Neither the earlier Morúa (M1) nor Cabello Valboa includes *panaca* information, except in one instance where Cabello Valboa mentions Vica Quirao Panaca as the descent group of Inca Roca ([1586], pt. 3, chap. 13; 1951:294).

Las Casas and Gutiérrez provided information about the *panacas* in a separate list (tables 3.20, 3.21). Although they assign *panacas* to Hanan and Hurin Cuzco like other authors, they change the ordering of both the Hanan/Hurin division and the *panacas*: they list Hanan Cuzco first, then Hurin Cuzco; then they list the *panacas* of Hanan Cuzco in the reverse of genealogical order, giving Capac Ayllo, the *panaca* of Topa Inca, first and Vica Quirao Panaca, the *panaca* of Inca Roca, last. Gutiérrez may have copied Las Casas, but "Cuma *panaca*" appears instead of Vica Quirao Panaca in the same slot in Gutiérrez's list. What is most unusual about the order of their lists is that they reverse the association between Inca and *panaca* in Hurin Cuzco; that is, Chima Panaca is the *panaca* of the fifth Inca, not the first one (compare with Sarmiento, table 3.18). Las Casas and Gutiérrez appear to have used a common source. That source included a genealogical account of the Inca dynasty and a *panaca* list. It was different from the source that underlies Cobo and the *Discurso*. If it was a written source, it was probably formatted as a list, as in Las Casas and Gutiérrez. Another possibility is a graphic representation, using symbols for the *panacas*. Such a representation could be "read" as a list. Either way, Hanan Cuzco occupied a superior position. The ordering of the *panacas* in either case was not strictly genealogical.[12]

There is another case that should be considered here because of its importance to arguments about dynastic succession. Joseph de Acosta cited material

TABLE 3.20. Panacas *from Las Casas*

Hanan Cuzco
    Capac Aillo, Pachacuti's eldest son who had been chosen to succeed him
    Iñaca Panaca and Zuczo Panaca, his father's and [his own] descendants in the transverse line
    Aycailli Panaca, his grandfather's descendants in the transverse line
    Vicaquirau Panaca, his great-grandfather's descendants in the transverse line
Rurincuzco
    Uzcamaita, second son of the first Inca
    Apomaitha, second son of the second Inca
    Haguaini, second son of the third Inca
    Raurau Panaca, second son of the fourth Inca
    Chima Panaca, second son of the fifth Inca
*Source*: [1562–64], bk. 3, chap. 251; 1967:581.

TABLE 3.21. Panacas *from Gutiérrez de Santa Clara*

Annan Cuzco
    Ayllo Cappa, Pachacuti's eldest son who had been chosen to succeed him
    Yñaca Panaca and Cucco Panaca, his descendants in the transverse line
    Ylli Panaca, his grandfather's descendants in the transverse line
    Cuma Panaca, his great-grandfather's [descendants in the transverse line]
Hurin Cuzco
    Uzca Mayta, second son of the first Inca
    Appo Mayta, second son of the second Inca
    [second sons of the third, fourth, and fifth Incas]
*Source*: [after 1575], chap. 49; 1963:214.

from a text written by Polo de Ondegardo. As noted above, he used material from Polo in the *Confesionario*, a document prepared for the Third Church Council in Lima (Polo de Ondegardo 1585) and again in his own historical narrative (1590) (tables 3.22, 3.23). Acosta's list of rulers is similar and yet fundamentally different from the lists found in other Spanish narratives. He adds not one but two later rulers to the Hanan Cuzco list: Huayna Capac and Huascar. When he removes Manco Capac from the Hanan/Hurin division and lists Sinchi Roca as the first ruler in Hurin Cuzco, he parallels Cobo. However, when he lists Tarco Huaman as the ruler who follows Mayta Capac in the *Confesionario* (Polo de Ondegardo 1585:8), he departs radically from Cobo. In his own historical narrative, he further extends the list to include an unnamed son of Tarco Huaman and don Juan Tambo Maytapanaca, who was alive in Polo's day.[13] Could Acosta have used a *panaca* list for his genealogy, editing

TABLE 3.22. *Inca rulers from the* Confesionario

Hanan Cuzco
    Ynga Roca
    Yahuarhuaqui
    Viracocha Ynca
    Pachaccuti Ynca
    Topa Ynca Yupanqui
    Huayna Capac
    Huascar Ynca
Vrin Cuzco
    Cinchiroca
    Capac Yupanqui
    Lluqui Yupanqui
    Mayto Capac
    Tarco Huaman
*Source*: Polo de Ondegardo 1585:8.

TABLE 3.23. *Inca rulers from Acosta*

    Ingaroca
    Yaguarguaque
    Viracocha Inga
    Pachacuti Inga Yupangui
    Topa Inga Yupangui
    Guaynacapa
    Tito Cussi Gualpa [Guascar Inga]
Urincuzco
    Cinchiroca
    Capac Yupangui
    Lluqui Yupangui
    Maytacapa
    Tarco Guaman
    un hijo suyo
    D. Juan Tambo Maytapanaca
*Source*: [1590], bk. 6, chaps. 20–23; 1940:306–311.

the names of the *panacas* to produce a list of rulers? For one thing, Acosta puts the *panacas* of Hanan Cuzco first, like the Las Casas/Gutiérrez source. In his account of Hanan Cuzco he appears to distribute the *panaca* information throughout a historical narrative, although the narrative is exceedingly thin on material. His Hurin Cuzco account is no more than a listing of *panaca* information, with genealogical links. In later chapters, when we look at sources that appear to have had access to a genealogical genre (Cobo among them), the paucity of material in Acosta, especially for Hurin Cuzco, will become clear. Acosta may have based his historical account on a source that was little more than a *panaca* list.

## A GENEALOGICAL GENRE

From the outset we have been asking if the Incas preserved a formal record of dynastic genealogy. There need have been no formal means of preserving or transmitting genealogical information. The number of generations since the time of origins was only twelve. The remains of Inca rulers or images that substituted for them were assembled periodically in Cuzco. The public appearance of these cult objects and their placement in a genealogical sequence several times a year would have been sufficient to preserve a memory of the dynastic line. The genealogy of the line of Manco Capac and his sister could have been represented through processions or other public performance long into the colonial period. A purpose was served, however, by keeping an official record. It was possible to lie with genealogy. Angelina Yupanqui's efforts to rewrite the dynastic past to highlight her own forebears is an example of how claims to status — even untruthful ones — were argued from genealogy (see chapter 2).

We know that a record of the Inca past was privately kept. Painted on wooden tablets were the lives of the Incas and the lands they conquered, as well as the origin myth. If the *paños* sent to Spain by Viceroy Toledo with Sarmiento's manuscript are a further indication of their subject matter, the tablets also included images of the Coyas and information about the *panacas*. Having a private record served to protect the dynastic line against a manipulation of the dynastic past. It is not possible to conclusively link the genre we have reconstructed from the historical narratives with a physical record or, specifically, with the painted tablets, but the possibility that the wooden tablets were the medium for preserving the genealogical genre is a strong one. Molina, cited above, noted that what was painted on the tablets included "the life of each one of the Incas and the lands he conquered." If we can link the genre reflected in the historical narratives to the painted tablets, it may also have included a graphic representation of the *panacas*. The genealogical genre was about dynastic origins, but it was also about how each Inca generation gave rise to a *panaca*. An account like the *Discurso* provides all of the essential information — genealogy, the names of the *panacas*, and a brief mention of the deeds of particular Incas — in a narrative format that is little more than a list. The genealogical genre may have been no more than that.

Some accounts are brief, but others include considerable narrative material about the lifetimes of particular Incas. They drew from other Inca genres. Now that we have identified one genre, we can begin to distinguish others that were incorporated in the Spanish historical narratives.

# 4 Life History

Although the genealogical genre may have included information about the conquests of particular rulers, some of the longer narratives (for example, Betanzos, Sarmiento, Morúa [M2], Cabello Valboa) incorporate voluminous accounts of particular lifetimes, especially in the case of later rulers. Are there other Inca genres underlying these "long accounts"? In this chapter we will explore what these might be. A life history genre can be defined with a fair degree of certainty, and others can be identified. Some of the argument for these other genres is advanced in chapter 5, so the focus here will be on the life history.

In the preceding section, a painted genre was described that was a medium for representing the genealogy of the dynastic descent group. The authors who were selected for comparison all reproduced what appears to have been the essential feature of a genealogical account: the names of the pair through whom the dynastic succession passed in each of eleven generations. One — the narrative of Juan de Betanzos — did not reproduce this genre. After a story about Inca origins, told in four chapters, Betanzos summarizes in a single chapter the names of the rulers prior to the time of the Chanca invasion, which occurred — according to Betanzos — in the time of Viracocha Inca. In this brief treatment, Betanzos entirely omits the names of the women through whom succession passed. He also reverses two rulers in his sequence of Inca rulers, the sort of error no one else makes. When the subject becomes Pachacuti, Betanzos's narrative fills twenty-seven chapters. The events of the two subsequent rulers were presented in some detail but occupy only fifteen chapters. What Betanzos appears to have used as the cornerstone of his work was a life history of Pachacuti.

Pachacuti's life, as represented by Betanzos, might have been composed by Betanzos himself, but it is more likely that he took the structure of his narrative from an oral genre (Hamilton in Betanzos [1551–1557]; 1996:xi; Niles 1999: 10–11). Support for this possibility can be found through a careful comparison between the structure of Betanzos's narrative and that of the other "long accounts." All of the accounts are structured by a sequence of events. When the narratives are compared, similarities between the event structures of certain narratives are manifest. Of course, an author could borrow the structure of events from another text, and in the case of Cabello Valboa and Morúa (M2), we know that one of the authors based his text on the lost historical narrative of Cristóbal de Molina and can hypothesize that both were based on it. More to the point, however, accounts that do not appear to have a common textual source exhibit similarities in the nature and sequencing of events.

In the discussion that follows, a group of "long accounts" will be compared for the information they contain about events in the life of Pachacuti. Two authors — Betanzos and Sarmiento — are crucial to the argument for a life history genre. Cobo has been included so that the event-structure of his text can be compared with that of other accounts; whether his text follows theirs or not is important to the question of whether he based his account on a historical narrative written by Polo de Ondegardo (see chapter 3, p. xx; note 3 to chapter 3; and table 4.3). No conclusions can be reached, but the question will be explored here.

In the process of teasing out a life history genre, we will also begin to explore what else the authors of the Spanish historical narratives chose to incorporate in their histories. Sarmiento incorporates a story about an incident in the life of Pachacuti that is repeated by other authors but not by Betanzos. The Ulti story may represent another Inca genre — a story about a discrete incident in the Inca past. The story is about an attempt on the life of Pachacuti. A potter, urged by someone else who wanted to kill the young Inca, threw a lime container at Pachacuti's head, cracking his skull. Various authors describe this incident, though who was involved changes, and the story may be sequenced differently in their accounts. That the story was sequenced differently by different authors is an indication that authors were compiling material from different Inca sources.

Compiling material from different Inca sources is characteristic of Sarmiento, and he appears to have incorporated material from a *quipo* that recorded the conquests of Topa Inca. Some of these conquests occurred during the lifetime of Pachacuti, so this material overlaps with Pachacuti's life history. In this chapter we will also begin to excavate a life history of Topa Inca. Once we widen our analytical frame to include the life of Topa Inca, we can begin to ask not just what the structure of the life history genre was but how it was kept and, even, how it was performed. Our focus is on the content of genres, so our discussion of these aspects of transmission is limited to a brief mention at the end of this chapter (but see Niles 1999: 28–44).

A comparison of event structures is an important tool for uncovering underlying oral sources. Even when an author deliberately writes a work of fiction, as in the case of the historical novel, the background is usually composed of historical events that are familiar to the reader and give the story a recognizable structure. In the case of narratives written by Spaniards, the problem of translation from a foreign language and into a story that reads more like European history may result in radically different interpretations of the underlying story line. If military events are the stuff of European political history, then the recorder may choose to privilege these events, suppressing other information that seems irrelevant. The process of selection is based on an understanding of what a historical narrative should be. Still, to represent the past some kind of structure is needed. We have seen that genealogy can provide an overarching sequence. Events are another means of introducing sequence. Lifetime events like marriage, the production of children, the arrival of those children at maturity — all of these events and the arrangement of other events in a particular order around such markers — introduce a sense of historical process into a narrative. It is possible that Spanish authors may have developed a sense of historical process to a greater degree in their narratives than that found in underlying Inca genres. However, these authors selected from Inca sources; they found the events, the individuals, the places, and even the relative sequence there. Whether there was a sense of process in Inca source material is an open question, and one we will return to in chapter 6 and in the conclusions.

The similarities and the differences between the narratives of Sarmiento and Betanzos suggest that each author drew from the same underlying source on the life of Pachacuti. Their accounts exhibit a fundamentally similar event structure, though the two accounts have very different emphases. Our interest is first in how they are similar.

## THE LIFE OF PACHACUTI

To compare accounts, a list of events, organized by categories, has been prepared from close readings of Betanzos and Sarmiento (table 4.1). Each event has been given a number that indicates both a general subject matter and a specific event. The tables that follow are coded so that they can be read for the representation of events from a particular category as well as for the inclusion of specific events. Two additional tables compare the narratives according to

TABLE 4.1. *Events in the life history of Pachacuti*

| Event | Related Detail |
|---|---|
| I. Chanca invasion | Ia. Vision |
| | Ib. First attack |
| | Ic. Dealings with Viracocha Inca |
| | Id. Second attack |
| | Ie. Dealings with Viracocha Inca |
| II. Pachakuti's accession | IIa. Definitive accession |
| | IIb. Marriage |
| III. Reorganization of Cuzco | IIIa. Land distribution/regional projects |
| | IIIb. Pacaritambo |
| | IIIc. Historical tradition |
| | IIId. Coricancha |
| | IIIe. Inca forebears |
| | IIIf. Cult objects |
| | IIIg. Endowment of *huacas* |
| | IIIh. Moroy Urco |
| | IIIi. Dedication of Coricancha |
| | IIIj. Initiation |
| | IIIk. Builds palaces |
| | IIIl. Initiates fortress construction |
| | IIIm. Calendar |
| | IIIn. Rebuilds and repopulates Cuzco |
| IV. Death of Inca Urcon | |
| V. Death of Viracocha | |
| VI. Military campaigns | VIa. Ayarmacas |
| | VIb. Cuyos and/or Vitcos and Vilcabamba |
| | VIc. Ollantaytambo |

different criteria. One (table 4.2) lists the events in the order of table 4.1, making possible a quick comparison of whether or not an event is represented in a particular account. The second (table 4.3) includes the same events but sequences them following the order in which they are presented in the narrative. In cases where the same event or action is repeated, the code for that event appears more than once. The Ulti story and others are listed by name.

From an examination of the tables, it is evident that the accounts most similar in structure are the narratives of Cabello Valboa and Morúa (M2). The similarity can be explained by textual borrowing from the lost historical narrative of Cristóbal de Molina. What is evident from a comparison of the event structures of these two narratives is that each author virtually duplicates the events covered by the other. Although both authors added (or deleted) a small amount of material, they relied very heavily on the same source for their Inca history. At the same time, a number of differences in sequence are apparent. If

| Event | Related Detail |
|---|---|
| | vid. Cugma and Guata |
| | vie. Guancara |
| | vif. Toguaro |
| | vig. Chancas and/or Soras and Lucanas |
| | vih. Acos |
| | vii. First Condesuyo |
| | vij. First Collasuyo |
| | vik. First Chinchasuyo |
| | vil. Second Collasuyo |
| | vim. Second Chinchasuyo |
| | vin. Third Chinchasuyo |
| | vio. Third Collasuyo |
| | vip. First Andesuyo |
| | viq. Second Condesuyo |
| | vir. Second Andesuyo |
| VII. First Colla revolt | |
| VIII. Territorial organization | viiia. Administrators |
| | viiib. Huaca cults |
| | viiic. Resettlement |
| | viiid. Ordinances |
| IX. Descent group | ixa. Legitimate sons produced |
| | ixb. Successor named |
| X. Thupa Inca | xa. Coronation |
| | xb. Marriage |
| XI. Topa Inca's descent group | xia. Legitimate sons produced |
| | xib. Successor named |
| XII. Pachacuti's death | |
| XIII. Andes revolt | |
| XIV. Second Colla revolt | |

TABLE 4.2. *Events in numerical order*

| Sarmiento | Betanzos | Cabello Valboa | Morúa (M2) | Cobo |
|---|---|---|---|---|
| Ia | Ia | | | Ia |
| Ib | Ib | Ib | Ib | |
| Ic | Ic | Id | Id | |
| Id | | | | |
| Ie | | | | |
| IIa | IIa | IIa | IIa | IIa |
| IIb | IIb | IIb | IIb | IIb |
| IIIa | IIIa | | | |
| IIIb | | | | |
| IIIc | IIIc | | | |
| IIId | IIId | IIId | IIId | |
| IIIe | IIIe | | | |
| IIIf | IIIf | IIIf | IIIf | |

(*continued on page 96*)

TABLE 4.2 (*continued*)

| Sarmiento | Betanzos | Cabello Valboa | Morúa (M2) | Cobo |
|---|---|---|---|---|
| IIIg | IIIg | IIIg | IIIg | |
| IIIh | | | | |
| | IIIi | | | |
| | IIIj | | | |
| | | IIIl | [IIIl] | |
| IV | | IV | IV | IV |
| V | V | V | V | |
| VIa | | VIa | VIa | |
| VIb | | VIb | VIb | VIb |
| VIc | | | VIc | |
| VId | | | | |
| VIe | | | | |
| VIf | | | | |
| VIg | VIg | VIg | VIg | VIg |
| VIh | | | | |
| VIi | | | | VII |
| VIj | VIj | VIj | VIj | VIj |
| VIk | VIk | VIk | VIk | VIk |
| VIl | VIl | | | |
| VIm | VIm | VIm | VIm | |
| VIn | | | VIn | |
| VIo | VIo | | | |
| VIp | VIp | VIp | VIp | VIp |
| VII | | | | VII |
| VIIIa | | VIIIa | VIIIa | |
| VIIIb | | | VIIIb | |
| VIIIc | VIIIc | VIIIc | | |
| | VIIId | VIIId | VIIId | |
| IXa | IXa | | | |
| IXb | IXb | | IXb | |
| Xa | Xa | Xa | Xa | [Xa] |
| Xb | Xb | Xb | Xb | [Xb] |
| XIa | XIa | XIa | | |
| | XIb | | | |
| XII | XII | XII | XII | [XII] |
| XIII | XIII | | | |
| XIV | XIV | XIV | XIV | |
| Ulti | | Ulti | Ulti | |
| Visita | | | Amaybamba | |

TABLE 4.3. *Events sequenced as in accounts*

| Sarmiento | Betanzos | Cabello Valboa | Morúa (M2) | Cobo |
|---|---|---|---|---|
| | Ia | VIa | VIa | IIa–b |
| | Ib | VIb | VIb | Ia |

| Sarmiento | Betanzos | Cabello Valboa | Morúa (M2) | Cobo |
|---|---|---|---|---|
| Ic | Ic | Ib | IIa-1 | VIb |
| Id | IIId | Id | IIb | IV |
| Ie | IIIg | Ulti | Ulti | VIg, k |
| IIa | IIIi | IIa | VIc | VIi |
| IIIa-1 | IIIf | IV | Ib | VIj |
| IIIb | IIIa | V | Id | [XII] |
| IIIc | IIIj | IIb | IIa-2 | Xa−b |
| IIId | IIa | VIg | IV | VIp |
| IIIe | IIb | IIId-1 | V | VII |
| IIIf | V | VIj | VIg-1 | |
| IIIg | IIIe | IIId-2 | VIIIa | |
| IIIh | IIIg | IIIg | VIg-2 | |
| IIIa-2 | IIIc | VIIId | IIId-1 | |
| IV | VIg | VIk | VIj | |
| V | VIj-1 | VIm | IIId-2 | |
| VIa | IXa-1 | XIa | IIIg | |
| IIb | VIj-2 | IIIf | VIIId | |
| Ulti | VIIId | IIId | VIIIb | |
| VIb | IXa-2 | Xa | VIk | |
| VIc | VIo | VIp | [IXb] | |
| VId | VIk | XIV | VIm−n-1 | |
| VIe | VIIIc | XII | Amaybamba | |
| VIf | VIl | IIIl | VIm−n-2 | |
| VIg | IXb-1 | Xb | IIIf | |
| VIh | VIm | VIIIc | IIId | |
| VIIIa | Xb | VIIIa | Xa | |
| IIId | IXb-2 | | XII | |
| VIi | XIa | | [IIIl] | |
| VIj | X | | Xb | |
| VIIIb | Xa−b | | VIp | |
| VIk | XIb-2 | | XIV | |
| VIIIc | VIp | | | |
| VII-1 | XII | | | |
| IXa | XIV | | | |
| VII-2 | XIII | | | |
| VIl | | | | |
| IXb | | | | |
| Xa | | | | |
| Xb | | | | |
| VIm | | | | |
| *Visita* | | | | |
| VIn-1 | | | | |
| XIa | | | | |
| VIn-2 | | | | |
| XII | | | | |
| XIII | | | | |
| XIV | | | | |

Molina was indeed the common source of these accounts, then one author may have been more faithful to the original order than the other.

The similarities between the Sarmiento and Betanzos accounts are not as immediately apparent, but they are there. Sarmiento includes more material than Betanzos, but frequently, and especially when events other than military campaigns are described, Sarmiento includes what is found in Betanzos but missing in the other accounts. The similarities in the sequencing of events are also striking. Of course, our list was based on these two accounts, so the order of the categories better reflects their structures than the structures of the other narratives. However, this observation itself supports a conclusion that Betanzos and Sarmiento are more similar to each other and less similar to Cabello Valboa and Morúa (M2).

Perhaps the most striking difference between the two accounts is that Sarmiento splits the accession to power and marriage of Pachacuti, putting a long list of military campaigns in between, while Betanzos links the two and locates them on the eve of the death of Pachacuti's father. Sarmiento may have been trying to bolster the claim Viceroy Toledo was trying to make that Pachacuti tyrannically took power instead of following customary practice, which linked marriage and accession. Betanzos's account may reflect the Inca ideal of the joint accession of a brother-sister pair.

Finally, Cobo's history is a much more parsimonious account of the life of Pachacuti and one substantially different in structure from either Betanzos or Sarmiento, on the one hand, and Morúa (M2) or Cabello Valboa, on the other. If Cobo took his Inca history from Polo de Ondegardo (a question only), then what Polo wrote was not the basis for either Sarmiento's or Molina's later works.

### Sarmiento and Betanzos

Polo's manuscript might have been available to Sarmiento. A more important question, however, is whether Sarmiento consulted Betanzos's manuscript, utilizing it for material on the life of Pachacuti. Sarmiento specifically said he relied on *memoriales* he collected from dynastic sources, however. In the case of Betanzos, we can hypothesize that Betanzos drew from an oral genre preserved by Pachacuti's *panaca* because of the overwhelming amount of information about this ruler in his narrative. If both authors collected material from Inca sources, then the similarities are not because of textual borrowing at all; they derive from borrowing from a similar oral source. Beyond the presence or absence of a particular event, other features of their texts may tell us about an underlying oral source and their different interpretation of it. A comparison of their texts follows in which their accounts have been paraphrased.

Both stories begin with a vision — or a dream — that Pachacuti had on the eve of the Chanca invasion. Somewhere near Cuzco (Sarmiento identifies the place as Susurpuquio), Pachacuti encounters a supernatural being. Betanzos identifies him as Virachocha Pacha Yachachic, a Creator. Sarmiento is unclear about the identity of this being: he is "like the Sun." Later in the same segment of the story he mentions Ticci Viracocha Pachayachi as a Creator and as the being to whom Cuzco was dedicated. The Sarmiento story has more detail on the Chanca battle than the Betanzos one does.

*Sarmiento*

1a. The story begins on the eve of the invasion of Cuzco by the Chancas, a local power whose seat was west of Cuzco. Two Inca captains who did not like the successor chosen by Viracocha, the eighth ruler, determined to have another son, Cusi Inca Yupanqui, succeed. The captains enticed Viracocha to go to his estate at Caquia Xaquixaguana and deal with the Chancas from there. By leaving, Viracocha would appear to have abandoned Cuzco. If, on the other hand, their candidate for the succession were able to defend Cuzco from a Chanca attack, the ground would be laid for his accession (chap. 26, pp. 60–61). Before the attack, Cusi Inca Yupanqui, later known as Pachacuti, fasted and prayed to Viracocha, the Creator, and the Sun to protect Cuzco. He was at Susurpuquio when a supernatural being, "like the Sun," appeared before him and showed him a mirror that revealed the provinces he was to conquer. Pachacuti kept the mirror with him always (chap. 27, p. 62). His victories were credited to help from the Sun (chap. 27, p. 64), although Sarmiento quotes an oration of Pacha-

*Betanzos*

1a. Before Uscovilca's attack on Cuzco, Pachacuti sought solitude just outside the city and entreated his father, Viracocha Pacha Yachachic, for help. Pachacuti had been left in Cuzco by his father and brother, whom he had entreated for help with no success. Pachacuti delivered his oration and fell asleep. In a dream, Viracocha, the Creator, appeared to him in the shape of a man. Viracocha promised to send him help and to give him victory. Pachacuti returned each night and delivered the same oration, and on the night before the Chanca attack, while Pachacuti was delivering his oration, Viracocha appeared before him and made the same promise (chap. 8, p. 32).

cuti in which he refers to himself as son
of the Sun and to Cuzco as dedicated to
the Creator, here called Ticci Viracocha
Pachayachi. The identity of the being
who appeared to Pachacuti is unclear.
1b. Pachacuti was directly informed of
the Chanca attack and immediately departed to do battle. He was successful
and the next day defeated Uscovilca. Uscovilca had been an important Chanca
captain and had created a division of the
Chancas called Hananchanca. A man
named Ancovilca created Hurinchanca.
Both had long since died but still led
their divisions to war. The Incas won the
first encounter. What Pachacuti got was
a statue (chap. 26, p. 60, and chap. 27,
p. 63).

1b. The Incas won the first encounter.

The story then turns to the relationship between Pachacuti and his father,
Viracocha. In the Sarmiento narrative, a captain is sent. In Betanzos, Pachacuti goes himself, accompanied by three captains.

*Sarmiento*

1c. Pachacuti sent one of his captains,
Quilliscachi Urco Guaranga, with the
things that had been captured from the
Chancas during battle to his father, who
was in Chita, a plain near Cuzco. The
captain entreated Viracocha to step on
the spoils of battle, thus claiming the victory. Viracocha wanted his other son,
Inca Urcon, to perform this act. The captain would not allow it, saying that it
was not right for cowards to triumph
from the deeds of Pachacuti. He took the
spoils and returned to Cuzco (chap. 27,
pp. 63–64).

*Betanzos*

1c. Pachacuti, in the company of his three
captains, Vicaquirao, Apoymayta, and
Quilescache Urco Guaranga, departed to
take the defeated Uscovilca's insignia,
weapons, and clothing to Viracocha. The
spoils also included several of Uscovilca's
captains. Viracocha, when asked to claim
the victory by stepping on the spoils, de-
ferred to his son, Inca Urcon. Pachacuti
refused. Viracocha resorted to treachery,
maintaining amiable relations with
Pachacuti but plotting all the while to
capture and kill him. Pachacuti's captains
detected the plot, and Pachacuti, after

defeating a quantity of his father's troops who were waiting in ambush, returned to Cuzco with the captives and other prizes to claim the victory himself. Meanwhile, Viracocha decided to remain in his estate at Caquia Xaquixaguana for the rest of his days. Pachacuti took many of the people who were in his father's company back to Cuzco, where they returned to their homes, which had not been touched in their absence (chap. 9, pp. 35–41). Pachacuti sacrificed the best of the spoils and gave the rest away to the people who had served him.

The next topic is a second Chanca attack. The Incas are victorious. In the Betanzos account, what happens after the battle is more important than the battle itself. Again, as soon as the battle is over, the story turns to Pachacuti's relation with his father. This time there is a different outcome. In the Sarmiento story Viracocha did what Pachacuti asked but secretly favored his other son. In the Betanzos version there is no hint of any hesitance on Viracocha's part to recognize Pachacuti as his successor. In both stories, when the spoils of the battle are offered to Viracocha, he refuses to step on them and names a son, Inca Urcon, to perform this act. Pachacuti (Betanzos) or the captain sent by Pachacuti (Sarmiento) refuses this substitution.

*Sarmiento*

1d. Then a second Chanca attack occurred. Pachacuti captured two Chanca captains in battle, cut off their heads, and put the heads at the tips of lances. At the sight, the Chanca troops fled. The Incas followed and killed a great number of them. The spoils from this battle were even greater than the spoils from the first.

*Betanzos*

1d. Meanwhile, four other Chanca captains had reformed an army with people from the Caquia Xaquixaguana area. Pachacuti and his three captains formed squadrons. As he went into battle, he turned and saw that a great number of people had taken up arms and joined his troops. The battle took place, and Pachacuti's troops were victorious. The people from Caquia Xaquixaguana who had fought the Incas were forgiven. Their hair, braided for battle, was cut short, Inca style, and all returned to their homes without penalty. Pachacuti was merciless with the Chanca captives, saying that since their captain, Uscovilca, had been captured, they should have seen that the war was over. He hung them from stakes, cut off their heads and put those on stakes, and burned the remaining bodies. The bones were left as testimony. He was generous in rewarding the people who had spontaneously joined his ranks, and their captains offered to serve him and pleaded with him to wear the fringe which signified kingship. Pachacuti politely declined, saying that his father was still alive, but asked them to go to his father and do whatever Viracocha commanded. The captains went to Viracocha.

1e. Pachacuti decided to seek his father in person. Viracocha again wanted Inca Urcon to claim the victory but decided not to anger Pachacuti and did as he asked (chap. 28, pp. 65–66).

1e. After drinking and sharing coca together, Viracocha delivered an oration in which he recognized Pachacuti as his successor and offered to place the fringe on his head. In return, he asked them for help to build his palaces in Caquia Xaquixaguana (chap. 20, pp. 43–47).

Only Sarmiento places Pachacuti's accession immediately after the Chanca war. He does not link accession with marriage; that occurs later. Betanzos locates Pachacuti's accession and marriage after the death of Viracocha (see below).

*Sarmiento*

11a. The scene then returns to Cuzco. To celebrate Pachacuti's victory, a large sacrifice was made in Inticancha, the "House of the Sun." The victorious captains went to the statue of the Sun, made of gold and about the size of a man, to ask who should be Inca. The oracle, possibly the statue itself, named Pachacuti. All assembled called him "capa Inca intip

*Betanzos*

churin," glossed in the text as "only lord, son of the Sun" (chap. 29, p. 66). On another day, Pachacuti returned to Inticancha, where the statue held out the fringe which the Inca ruler wore at the center of the forehead. After sacrifices, the priest of the Sun, called "intip apu," took the fringe and placed it on Pachacuti's head, and all named him "intip churin Inca Pachacuti," glossed in the text as "son of the Sun, lord, cataclysm" (chap. 29, p. 66).

The story of the organization of Cuzco is interrupted at this point by Betanzos, who inserts the accession of Pachacuti and the death of Viracocha into the story. For Sarmiento, these events are followed by military campaigns outside of the Cuzco Valley. Betanzos returns to the story of the organization of Cuzco.

*Sarmiento*

111a. Then Pachacuti began the reorganization of Cuzco by retracing its plan and by constructing agricultural terraces near it.

*Betanzos*

111d. Pachacuti began to refashion Cuzco and the area around it long before he was legitimized. He began by building a temple and dedicating it to the Creator, Viracocha Pacha Yachachic. This Viracocha created the Sun and everything in the sky and on the earth. Betanzos notes that this attribution was not constant, that sometimes Viracocha was held to be the Creator and at other times the Sun. Elsewhere, other deities had this property. Pachacuti wanted to commemorate the figure who had appeared to him before the battle with Uscovilca. The figure had shone, and so perhaps it had been the Sun. Further, it had told him that he would go down in history as a son of the Sun. For these reasons, Pachacuti built a house of the Sun. When it was built, he staffed it with 500 young women who were to serve the Sun. *Yanaconas*, who were young married men, were assigned to serve the temple as well.

111b. Then, he visited Pacaritambo, the site of the Inca origin myth. There, he adorned Capac Toco, the central window of three windows that were held to be mythical origin places by three Cuzco groups, and the one the Incas claimed as their own. He then organized a cult at the site, and from that time onward, people consulted an oracle and made sacrifices there (chap. 30, p. 68).

111c. His next step was to inquire into the history of the Cuzco area by inviting the oldest and wisest people, principally those who knew about the earliest Incas, his antecedents. A painted record was made (chap. 30, p. 69).

111i. Large sacrifices were made, including the sacrifice of young boys and girls called *capac ucha*. They were buried alive in the temple. With the blood of sacrificed animals, he and his three captains, all barefoot, anointed the walls of the temple. They also anointed the young women. Then they ordered all of the people of the city, men and women, to come to the temple to make sacrifices. For the common people, the sacrifice consisted of maize and coca. They came and burned their offerings in a fire, all barefoot and looking downward. As they left, they were also anointed with the blood of sacrificed animals. All were enjoined to fast from that day until the time the image of the Sun, to be fashioned of gold, was finished. Anyone who broke the fast would be sacrificed and burned in the same fire. The fire was kept burning day and night.

111d. Then he turned to rebuilding Coricancha, the house of the Sun. It was still a rustic structure, and no one had made any significant additions to it since the time of Manco Capac. Sarmiento notes here that the embellishment was intended to awe and terrify ignorant people who would, so entranced, follow

111f. A small child was fashioned to resemble the figure that had come to Pachacuti. After a month, when it was finished, it was dressed in a fine shirt decorated with gold, a headdress like the fringe the Inca king wore, and given a scepter and golden sandals. Pachacuti came to visit the statue, barefoot. He

him off to the conquests he was already planning. Again, the program involved more than remodeling.

paid it the proper respect and then took it by hand to the place in the temple where it was to be. He put a golden brazier in front of it and began the ritual feeding of the Sun that would be done by the steward of the Sun thenceforward. Only the most principal people were allowed to see this statue. They had to approach barefoot and with lowered heads. During the feeding, no one was to enter. A stone was erected in the main square of Cuzco for the common people to worship. Pachacuti announced that the stone was to be erected on the same day that he ordered the golden image to be made, and the stone was placed in the plaza on the same day the image was placed in the temple. A golden litter had been made. The image was to be paraded through Cuzco on the litter, announcing that the Sun blessed Cuzco and his children and that everywhere they went they were to be adored as sons of the Sun. They made a sacrifice to him known as *arpa*. Then, before the stone was erected, they dug a large hole, and the people placed offerings of gold in it. The hole was closed, and a trough was placed over it. Then, in the earth inside the trough and near its walls, they buried little golden figures representing all of the lineages of Cuzco and the most principal person in each lineage. These figures were an offering to the Sun from the lineages of Cuzco since the time of Manco Capac. Then the stone that symbolized the Sun was erected on top. Many sacrifices of animals were made to this stone, never less than 500 (chap. 11, pp. 49–53).

111e. Pachacuti had the bodies of his seven forebears disinterred. They were

111a. Then Pachacuti undertook the reorganization of the lands around Cuzco,

dressed and adorned appropriately. Then a celebration, called *purucaya*, was held, during which the life of each Inca was represented. Sacrifices were made to each mummy, and so they were transformed into gods for those who were not from Cuzco to worship (chap. 31, p. 68).

including the lands belonging to the neighboring lords who had offered to serve him. It was necessary to rationalize the provisioning of Cuzco because, when they were at war, it would be impossible to take care of their lands the way they had. A census was carried out, lands were assigned on a permanent basis, and boundary markers were erected. Storage facilities were constructed. The lords from neighboring areas who had voluntarily assented to serve Cuzco went back home in the company of Inca nobles to tell their subjects what was to be provided to Cuzco and where storage houses were to be built. The neighboring lords were given many gifts, including wives from Pachacuti's lineage whose children were to become the lords' heirs (chap. 12, pp. 55–58). After a year, the lords returned. They greeted Pachacuti with an oration that identified him as a son of the Sun and then gave him all the produce that they had brought to be put into the storage houses. A celebration followed. These same lords were then enjoined to help Pachacuti channel the water that flowed through the Cuzco Valley. The lords divided up the work, and each carried out the part that fell to him. At this time, Pachacuti also told them that he wanted to create stores of clothing, and that to effect this plan, a large celebration was to take place. They met in the main plaza of Cuzco, the Inca with his women and the lords with theirs. A large banquet was held, and afterward a great quantity of beer was drunk. Then Pachacuti had four golden drums brought out, and the singing began. The women, who were seated be-

hind the men, began the singing. The
song related the defeat of Uscovilca.
More beer was drunk during the festivi-
ties, which lasted six days, and toward
the end Pachacuti told them there would
be storage houses in Cuzco for both
cotton and woollen clothing. Mantles
would be made with cords in the corner
for tying. Those who had worked on the
canal project would make them. The
mantles would be used for carrying earth
and stone for this type of project, and
no one would have to use their own.
He also ordered that, back in their own
lands, women were to be assembled and
given fine wool in many colors in order
to make, along with the men, clothing to
his measurements. The clothes were to
be brought to Cuzco. These projects
took four years, and afterward a celebration of thirty days took place. He also
inquired into the number of young unmarried men and women in their lands.
With this knowledge, his three friends
went to visit them and married the
young women of one province to the
young men of another. His purpose was
to encourage them to multiply and create
perpetual friendship and kin ties among
them. The lords, still at the celebration,
were given many gifts and then went
home to carry out Pachacuti's instructions. Remaining in Cuzco, Pachacuti
himself married the young unmarried
men and women of Cuzco and a few
small nearby villages, giving to each man
and woman two costumes and a mantle
to use at work and in construction projects. He gave them food and dishes and
everything they needed for a household.
From this time on, every four months

111f. He made two golden statues at that time, one called Viracocha Pacha Yachi, who represented the Creator, and the other called Chuqui Ylla, who represented the Thunder. The first was placed at the right hand of the Sun image and the second at the left hand. The image of the Sun was held by Pachacuti to be his *huaoque*, a word that meant brother or lineage member older than oneself. It was more sacred than the other two images.

111g. Pachacuti then endowed each of these supernatural beings with land, livestock, and people to serve them, especially the women who lived in the house of the Sun. Sarmiento notes that Pachacuti had access to these women, and they bore many of his children. These activities were accompanied by a round of sacrifices, including the sacrifice of children, or *capac ucha*, at other sacred places near Cuzco (chap. 31, p. 69).

111h. He also had the Moroy Urco made. This was a cord, some 150 *brazas* long, made of many colors of wool and decorated with golden sequins and two tas-

the people of Cuzco received what they needed from the storehouses (chap. 13, pp. 59–63).

111j. Pachacuti's next concern was the organization of the initiation ceremony whereby the young men of Cuzco became nobles. He consulted his three friends, and among them the rite was designed. The young men had to have a noble father. If his father was not living, the relatives of his father had to make a special request that the young man be initiated. There follows a long description of the rite (chap. 14, pp. 65–70). He also organized the remainder of the ritual calendar (chap. 15, pp. 71–74) and rebuilt Cuzco and resettled the lineages so that the descendants of his three friends lived in Hurincuzco, the neighborhood below the house of the Sun, and his descendants lived in Hanancuzco, the upper neighborhood (chap. 16, pp. 75–79). Pachacuti gave it the name "body of the feline," because the residents of Cuzco were to be its body while he was to be its head (chap. 17, p. 81).

sels at the end. It was used in the four
principal celebrations held in Cuzco, and
he names three of them: *raymi* or *capac
raymi*, *situa*, and *inti raymi* or *aymoray*.
The Moroy Urco would be taken out
of Coricancha by the most important
people, all beautifully dressed and in a
particular order, and carried to the principal plaza of Cuzco, where the cord
reached all the way around it.
111a cont. Following Pachacuti's succession and the reorganization of Cuzco
itself, he returns briefly to the task of
reorganizing the agricultural land near
Cuzco. He resettled all of the people
living nearby so that the land around
Cuzco could be devoted to the support
of the people living there.

Betanzos makes clear the reasons why the accession story is so late: Pachacuti does not want to replace his father until after his father's death. He does
accede before Viracocha's death, but only because Viracocha comes out of re-
tirement and personally places the fringe on Pachacuti's head. Viracocha still
has to atone for some act, whether for the abandonment of Cuzco or treachery toward Pachacuti, and Pachacuti makes him drink from a dirty vessel. The
story of the relation between father and son, in this detail as well as others, is
more prominent in Betanzos than in Sarmiento.

*Sarmiento*

*Betanzos*

11a. At this point, the question of Pachacuti's legitimacy arises among the lords
of Cuzco. They are determined to give
him the fringe of rulership. Of course,
Pachacuti laughed and said they had gotten ahead of themselves. His father was
still alive, and besides that, the fringe was
to be given to his brother, Inca Urcon.
When his brother wore the fringe, he
would personally take the fringe off of
his brother's head, and his brother's head

off as well. He promised them he would
not wear the fringe during his father's
lifetime unless his father came to Cuzco
and put it on his head.

So the lords went to Viracocha and entreated him to give the fringe to Pachacuti as well as to visit the new Cuzco.
Viracocha came and was impressed.
When he met his son, he declared him to
be truly a son of the Sun and took the
fringe and put it on his head. Viracocha
gave him his new name: Pachacuti Inca
Yupanqui, king and son of the Sun.
Pachacuti then brought out a dirty pot
and, without washing it, made his father
drink beer from it. Then Viracocha
begged his pardon. After this insult,
Viracocha was taken to his sumptuous
new palaces where he and Pachacuti had
a meal. Then the rites which conferred
the succession began.

11b. The ceremony involved Pachacuti's
marriage, but Betanzos does not provide
the name of the woman or any detail
about her place of origin or family.

IV. Betanzos does not mention the fate
of Inca Urcon.

IV. At this time, he went to meet his
older brother, Inca Urcon, who was
waiting to do battle with him. Urcon
was the brother favored by Viracocha,
who was still supporting his choice. Inca
Urcon was killed, and Pachacuti went to
visit his father, who did not want to
speak with him. Pachacuti returned to
Cuzco to celebrate the victory over his
brother in the same manner as other victories came to be celebrated: there were
songs and dances, the battles were re-
enacted, and the captives were placed
on the ground and, in a symbol of their
submission, were stepped upon by the
victors.

v. Soon after, Viracocha died (chap. 32, p. 71).

v. Viracocha returned to his palaces in Caquia Xaquixaguana, where ten years later he died. After his death, Pachacuti brought his body, well adorned and riding on a litter, back to Cuzco, where great sacrifices were made to him as a "son of the Sun."

In Betanzos, Pachacuti continues to be occupied with the reorganization of Cuzco after the death of Viracocha. The subject then turns to military campaigns.

*Sarmiento*

*Betanzos*
111e. Then Pachacuti made up bundles to represent all of the Incas from Manco Capac to his father and organized a cult to them. At the temple, visitors first honored the Sun, then the bundles, and finally were allowed into the presence of the Inca.
111g. Each of the bundles was given lands and livestock and servants. Each had a steward, and great care was taken to see that they were continuously fed.
111c. Songs about each were composed, and the servants performed them in order during celebrations (chap. 17, pp. 81–86).

Betanzos does not even mention local campaigns. For him, Pachacuti effectively begins with the campaign against the Soras (see below). Sarmiento relates the organization of Cuzco into two *sayas* (Hanan Cuzco and Hurin Cuzco) to the beginning of military campaigning. Betanzos places the *saya* division in the context of the reorganization of Cuzco (see Betanzos 111j, above). This is the last topic he discusses in that context, and since he does not even mention local campaigns, the difference may be owed to a difference in context, rather than a structural difference.

*Sarmiento*

VIa. The first military foray was really
the campaign against Inca Urcon. Afterward Pachacuti campaigned successfully
against a number of local powers both
east of Cuzco, in the Urubamba Valley,
and in the west in tandem with his older
brother, Inca Roca. To launch these
campaigns, he organized the people of
Cuzco into two groups, later known as
Hanan Cuzco and Hurin Cuzco, to
create a whole that no one could defeat. Pachacuti consulted them, and all
agreed that their neighbors should be
conquered. The first campaign against a
non-Inca enemy was against the hereditary ruler of the Ayarmacas, whose title
was Tocay Capac.
11b. Then Pachacuti married Mama
Anahuarqui, a woman from Choco, near
Cuzco.

*Betanzos*

Sarmiento tells about a sequence of campaigns, naming the Soras campaign
among the others. For Betanzos, the Soras campaign was the main event, and
the story about it included a great deal of detail about what happened after the
Incas won. At this point Sarmiento digresses to tell the Ulti story. Several
other authors (Cabello Valboa, Morúa [M2], and the author Pachacuti) tell a
version of this story. It is absolutely missing in Betanzos, an indication that it
was material from another genre that Sarmiento compiled in his narrative. We
will return to it below.

*Sarmiento*

The Ulti story.
VIb–f. Local campaigns. The later ones,
undertaken with his brother Inca Roca,
gained control of a section of the
Urubamba Valley, northeast of Cuzco, as
well as the area just west of Cuzco.
VIg. One of the campaigns undertaken
with Inca Roca was waged against the
Soras.

*Betanzos*

VIg. Pachacuti makes preparations to go
to war. He heads first to the Apurimac
Valley, where he must build a bridge to

cross the river. Once across, he went to Curahuasi, where a number of local powers submitted to him peacefully. He met armed resistance in Soras and Lucanas. He then divided his army in three parts under the command of Cuzco nobles and sent some to the conquest of what is now known as Condesuyo. Another group was sent to Andesuyo. Pachacuti would return with the third group to Cuzco (chap. 18, pp. 87–91). But first, he had some long red shirts made for the captives to wear. Their hair was bathed in *chicha* and coated with maize flour. The people of Cuzco that were with him dressed in their battle clothes and, with the prisoners among them, began to celebrate. This initial victory celebration, held in Soras, lasted a month. The three armies were to arrive in Cuzco at the same time and met at Xaquixaguana some distance from the town. While there, the Condesuyo army, which had arrived first, made a fire in front of Pachacuti and sacrificed animals, fine clothing, and other things captured in their campaign. Then Pachacuti was asked to step on the arms and other insignias they had captured, which he did. Their captives were then dressed in the same type of garb as the Soras captives. The round of activities was repeated by the Andesuyo army, who had brought him a number of wild animals and some very large snakes, called *amaru*. Then, with the captives in front of his litter, Pachacuti arrived in Cuzco, where the spoils were distributed. First he took what he wanted, then his captains were given their share, and then the common soldiers were given the remainder. Pachacuti then turned to matters of administering the newly won territories. Inca nobles were sent to reside in the provinces who were to act on his behalf. Their duties were to organize the use of agricultural lands, to marry the young men and women each year, to send the tribute for the provisioning of Cuzco every four months, and to have another class of tribute sent each year (chap. 19, pp. 93–97).

vIh–i. A campaign was undertaken at Acos; at this time, some of the peoples of Condesuyo submitted out of fear that the Incas would destroy them (chaps. 34–35, pp. 71–74).

Sarmiento begins his story about how Pachacuti organized the territory he conquered. He also continues the story of how Pachacuti reorganized Cuzco. In Betanzos, a long lapse occurs. Betanzos quantifies the amount of time that passes. Sarmiento does not indicate a break, but both authors can be correlated by their mention of a campaign in the Lake Titicaca region that followed. Betanzos inserts information about the succession at the point where he mentions this campaign.

*Sarmiento*
vIIIa. Pachacuti installed his own authorities, removing control from those he had defeated (chaps. 34–35, pp. 71–74).
IIId. On his return to Cuzco, he observed the ceremony that the women of Coricancha observed in making offerings to the Sun. They used vessels made of ceramic. Pachacuti thought that these vessels were too poor for this purpose and substituted vessels of silver and gold. He also installed other ornaments of gold in the temple (chap. 36, pp. 74–75).
vIj. Pachacuti's next military foray was against Chuchi or Colla Capac, the title of a hereditary who lived in the northern

*Betanzos*

vIj. Pachacuti's next campaign was in Collasuyo twenty years later.

Lake Titicaca basin. He captured this king in battle and returned with him to Cuzco, where the victory ritual was performed. He brought many things back from this campaign which thenceforward were used in the service of the house of the Sun.

ixa. Two legitimate sons, Yamque Yupanque and Topa Inca Yupanque, and another son, Capac Yupanqui, born to another of his women, were old enough to participate. In an aside, Betanzos notes that, at the birth of each of these sons, great celebrations and sacrifices were made. At about the same time, Pachacuti took twenty wives from Hanansaya and twenty from Hurinsaya, all daughters of important lords (chap. 20, pp. 99–102).

vij cont. The campaign in Collasuyo was specifically directed at Ruqui Capana, the lord of Hatuncolla, who had declared himself to be "capac çapa apo inti churi," which means "only king, son of the Sun." One hundred thousand men died in the battle to take this king. A large quantity of loot was taken. Pachacuti returned to Cuzco and staged a victory celebration and distribution of the spoils similar to what was done after the conquest of Soras.

Betanzos adds another time lapse. Although Sarmiento and Betanzos each mention Amaro Topa and Yamqui Yupanqui as adults, the context of each reference is different. Betanzos puts a second Collasuyo campaign here. In Sarmiento, this campaign may be the one that follows the Colla revolt (VII).

*Sarmiento*
viiib. Pachacuti also sent his eldest legitimate son, Amaro Topa Inca, to visit

*Betanzos*
viiid. Then Pachacuti remained in Cuzco for another twenty years

the territories he had conquered. He was charged with deposing the provincial *huacas* that the Incas held for false and installing a cult to the Cuzco *huacas*. The people were also to be taught to perform the sacrifices that he ordered. Another son, Huayna Yamqui Yupanqui, went along with Amaro Topa (chap. 37, pp. 75–77).

(chap. 20, pp. 99–102), devoting himself to organizational matters, particularly to a series of ordinances (chaps. 21–22, pp. 103–117).

ixa cont. Pachacuti was seventy by now. His innumerable women had borne him 300 children, 200 boys and 100 girls. Three were adults, Yamqui Yupanqui, Amaro Topa, and Paucar Usno. vii. He sent the latter two on a campaign to Collasuyo with six other captains and an army composed of 50,000 troops from Collasuyo and 50,000 troops from elsewhere. Paucar Usno died in a fire in Chichas province. Amaro Topa brought his body back as well as the usual captives dressed in red. Pachacuti sent the body back to Chichas with some Inca nobles and women, where it was venerated and treated as if it were alive.

Another campaign was launched in the north. Both Betanzos and Sarmiento are in agreement that a son, Yamqui Yupanqui, went. Betanzos says the son Pachacuti had chosen to succeed him also went, accompanied by a brother whose name appears to be Capac Yupanqui. In the Sarmiento story, Capac Yupanqui is a brother of Pachacuti, who, with a Chanca ally, conquered northward of the limits Pachacuti had set for the campaign. Both Betanzos and Sarmiento mention *mitimas* at this point.

*Sarmiento*
vik. Another round of conquests was planned, this time north of Cuzco, but Pachacuti delegated his command to two of his brothers, one named Capac Yupanqui, and a son, named Apo Yamqui

*Betanzos*
VIk. Pachacuti then sent Yamqui Yupanqui, his eldest son and the son he wanted to be his successor, on a campaign to Chinchasuyo. This son chose one of his brothers, Capa[c] Yupanqui, to accom-

Yupanqui. The campaign was undertaken with the Chancas, who were under the command of a Chanca captain, Anco Ayllo, who had developed a relationship of trust in Cuzco. The campaign won a considerable territory but was a disaster from another perspective: one of his brothers went beyond the limits Pachacuti had set for this campaign as well as provoked the enmity of the kingdom of Chimor, probably the most important political entity in the Central Andes at the time. Pachacuti had both of his brothers put to death as they returned to Cuzco from the north (chap. 38, pp. 77–80).

pany him. After this campaign, Yamqui Yupanqui returned to Cuzco and celebrated with his father for three years.

VIIIc. Given more territory to administer, Pachacuti began to develop appropriate means. He began the resettlement of people from one area to another, removing the local people from defensible places and introducing settlers from the Cuzco region as a security measure (chap. 39, pp. 80–81).

VIIIc. The resettlement of people, known as *mitimas*, began at this time (chap. 24, p. 123).

Then the story of the first Colla revolt is told. Pachacuti himself goes to put it down. He returns home and finds that Anahuarqui has borne him a son, whom he names Topa Inca. Betanzos says nothing about the Colla revolt and, in what may be the strangest omission in his account, never mentions Ana Huarque or the circumstances of the birth of Topa Inca.

*Sarmiento*

VII. At about this time, the sons of the Colla Capac that Pachacuti had executed in Cuzco organized a revolt against Inca rule. Pachacuti himself, with two of his sons, Topa Ayar Manco and Apo Paucar Usno, headed south and extinguished the revolt. More loot was taken, and Pachacuti returned to Cuzco to celebrate

*Betanzos*

the triumph. His two sons continued
campaigning farther south (chap. 40,
pp. 81–82).

ixa. On his return to Cuzco, Pachacuti
found that Anahuarqui had given birth
to a son, whom he named Topa Inca Yupanqui. He made elaborate gifts of gold
and silver to the Sun and other oracles
and *huacas* well as *capac ucha* sacrifices.
He determined that this son would succeed him, although he had several older,
legitimate sons born to him and to
Anahuarqui, here described as his sister
(chap. 40, pp. 82–83).

vii cont. Meanwhile, his sons Amaro
Topa Inca and Apo Paucar Usno continued the campaign against the Collas in
the south. This campaign is clearly a continuation of the reconquest mentioned
above, so Sarmiento may have erred in
the names he gives for the sons who
served as captains in this campaign. The
captains campaigned far to the south of
the Lake Titicaca region, during which
time Pachacuti devoted himself to building quite a number of palaces for himself. His sons returned from their campaign in triumph, great celebrations
were held, and Pachacuti gave them
many gifts (chap. 41, pp. 83–84).

Meanwhile, in Betanzos, Yamqui Yupanqui is sent on a second campaign to
Chinchasuyo with his brother Topa Inca.

| *Sarmiento* | *Betanzos* |
|---|---|
| | vim. Then Yamqui Yupanqui went on a second campaign to Chinchasuyo, this time with his brother Topa Inca Yupanqui. After campaigning all the way to Cañar territory, the brothers returned to Cuzco to celebrate their victories. |

Sarmiento and Betanzos tell completely different stories about Topa Inca from beginning to end. When the story turned, as it inevitably would, to the question of Pachacuti's successor, Betanzos casts Yamqui Yupanqui as Pachacuti's first choice. Sarmiento identifies another son, Amaro Topa, as first choice. The story of how a second choice was made is perhaps the point where the two stories are most divergent. Sarmiento narrates the steps that Pachacuti took to get Amaro Topa to peacefully acquiesce to the naming of his younger brother as the next Inca. Betanzos casts Yamqui Yupanqui in the decisive role. Yamqui had been named as the successor but was too old. Yamqui advises Pachacuti that his own son, also named Yamqui, is too young. At this point, Pachacuti meets another grandson, Huayna Capac, and fixes the succession so that this child will eventually inherit. The outcome is the same as in Sarmiento, that is, the succession passes from Pachacuti to Topa Inca to Huayna Capac, but the Betanzos story is slanted to show Betanzos's wife's forebear as having been the son chosen by Pachacuti to succeed.

| *Sarmiento* | *Betanzos* |
|---|---|
| 1xb. Pachacuti, recognizing his age, then showed his concern about the succession. Sarmiento cites an oration, addressed to Hanan and Hurin Cuzco, in which Pachacuti counters their expectations that his eldest son, Amaro Topa, would be chosen to succeed him and offers them instead Topa Inca Yupanqui, now about fifteen years old. The boy, kept virtually hidden until then, appeared. The older and most important nobles took him to the place where the image of the Sun was and took the fringe which had been placed on the image's arm and placed it on Topa Inca's head in the position which indicated that he was king. He was seated on a golden stool and given the other insignia of rulership. Then he remained in the temple, preparing for his initiation ceremony (chap. 42, pp. 84–85, chap. 43, p. 85). Pachacuti ordered that no one visit Topa Inca without bearing a gift to offer him and that | 1xb. Pachacuti gave Yamqui Yupanqui a warm welcome when he returned and placed the Inca fringe on his son's head. Three years went by (chap. 25, pp. 125–126). |

his descendants should be treated likewise. In anticipation of the initiation
ceremony, called *huarachico*, Pachacuti
had four temples built that were to be
dedicated to the Sun (chap. 43, p. 85).
Amaro Topa's reaction to this turn of
events is also considered. Instead of playing foul, he requests to see his brother,
and when taken into the house of the
Sun where his brother was fasting in
preparation for the initiation ceremony,
he was so impressed with the majesty of
his wealth and service that he fell down
on his face in worship. Topa Inca, knowing that this was his brother, helped him
rise and greeted him in peace (chap. 43,
pp. 85–86).

VIII. Yamqui Yupanqui leaves on a third
campaign to Chinchasuyo with his
brother Topa Inca Yupanqui.
xb. As they left Cuzco, Yamqui gave
Topa Inca a wife, one of their sisters
named Mama Ocllo. Pachacuti had
given Mama Ocllo to him as a wife at
the time he received the fringe. The campaign reached as far north as Quito before Yamqui Yupanqui headed back to
Cuzco.
IXb cont. Pachacuti suggested to Yamqui
Yupanqui, who was also growing old,
that his son, also named Yamqui Yupanqui, be chosen to succeed. Yamqui, the
father, thought his son was too young
and named his brother Topa Inca Yupanqui instead.
XIa. Topa Inca was still in Tumebamba,
where Mama Ocllo had borne him a son
(chap. 26, pp. 127–129). When they returned to Cuzco, Mama Ocllo went back
to live with her sisters, where she had
lived before.

xib. Pachacuti saw the child, named
Huayna Capac, and determined that this
grandchild would succeed Topa Inca. At
this point Topa Inca and his sister Mama
Ocllo are prepared for the succession
ceremonies.

Sarmiento may or may not separate the succession from the marriage ceremony. They are more clearly one and the same in Betanzos. The succession of
Huayna Capac preoccupies Pachacuti until the time of his death. Little is said
about Topa Inca.

*Sarmiento*
xa. For his initiation, Topa Inca was
brought from the temple of the Sun with
the images of the Sun, Viracocha, the
other *huacas*, the bodies of the Incas and
the *moroy urco*, all placed in order and
taken to the main plaza with never-
before-seen pomp. Many animals were
sacrificed, and all assembled offered Topa
Inca, the new Inca, lavish gifts, following
the example set by his father. His ears
were pierced to wear the ear spools de-
noting noble rank, and he was then taken
to the four new temples and given the
weapons and other insignias of warfare.
xb. At this time, he was given his sister,
Mama Ocllo, in marriage (chap. 43,
p. 86).

*Betanzos*
Xa and Xb cont. Then the succession ceremony was held, and Mama Ocllo was
presented to Topa Inca Yupanqui as if
she had not been married before.

Betanzos says nothing about northern campaigns, but Sarmiento describes
two campaigns by Topa Inca in the north before the death of Pachacuti. On
the second one, Huayna Capac is born. Both Sarmiento and Betanzos end the
life of Pachacuti with a song. The versions are similar. While Betanzos mentions that Topa Inca went campaigning in Andesuyo just prior to Pachacuti's
death, Sarmiento tells the story of an Andesuyo rebellion just afterward. He
refers to the conquest of that region (vip) in the time of Pachacuti (table 4.1),
although he had made no prior reference to it.

*Sarmiento*

VIm. Because as successor and now as a
warrior, Topa Inca should make a name
for himself, he was sent on a campaign
to the north. As he traveled, he was
treated as a divinity. No one looked at
his face, and the people viewed his passage from the hills above. They pulled
out their lashes and eyebrows and blew
them in his direction as a sign of offering. They also offered fistfuls of coca to
him. When he arrived in a town, he
would wear their clothing. The people
would put a brazier in front of him
where he sat and would sacrifice animals
and birds there in the same way that offerings were given to the Sun. Topa Inca
traveled among people who had been defeated but who were armed and ready to
rebel. His person gave such an impression of power and pomp that not only
did these dreams fade, but he usurped
the veneration they gave to their own
gods (chap. 44, pp. 86–87).

VIn. Topa Inca campaigns again in Chinchasuyo, this time reaching as far north
as Quito (chap. 44, pp. 86–88).

XIa. During this campaign a son was
born to Topa Inca's wife and sister. He
was named Tito Cusi Yupanqui and later
renamed Huayna Capac.

VIn cont. Topa Inca returned in the company of two of his brothers, Tilca Yupanqui and Auqui Yupanqui. Pachacuti had
one or both of the brothers killed, blam-
ing them for taking longer to conduct
the campaign than the time allotted for it
(chap. 46, pp. 89–92).

*Betanzos*

XIb cont. Pachacuti also wanted to name
Topa Inca's successor. He had the child
brought to him, and he placed a miniature of the Inca fringe on the baby's
head. Yamqui Yupanqui gave him the
name Huayna Capac. Then Pachacuti retired and spent the rest of his days caring
for his grandson (chap. 27, pp. 131–132).

VIp. Topa Inca went on a campaign to
Andesuyo, and his brother Yamqui Yupanqui remained in Cuzco to govern in
his place, making sure that no one tried
to usurp Topa Inca's rule while he was
gone from Cuzco. When Topa Inca returned, he brought more felines and
snakes with him. From the gold he
brought with him, a band of gold two
and a half palms wide was fashioned. It
was placed around the exterior of the

temple, above the stonework and below the roofline.

XII. Pachacuti was happy to see his grandson and kept the child with him at his residence. Happier than he had ever been in his life, he took gravely ill. Before he died, he counseled Topa Inca and other Inca nobles to take care of what had been his life's work. No one was to "raise his two eyes against you" and live, even if it was a brother. He left instructions about the ceremony that was to take place after his death. He then sang a song in low and sad tones that stated simply that he had been born like a lily in a garden, he had been raised, and when age came, he grew old, dried up, and died. Then he expired (chap. 47, pp. 92–93).

XII. Pachacuti then assembled the lords of Cuzco and all his children to inform them of some plans he had made and to enjoin them to look after Topa Inca Yupanqui and Huayna Capac, who was in the care of Yamque Yupanqui. He anticipated rebellions following his death, and he knew that Topa Inca would be involved in military campaigns. He also foresaw the arrival of tall, white, bearded men (chap. 29, pp. 137–139). Then he described the rites that were to be performed after his death (chaps. 30–31, pp. 141–148). Then he died. After he died, a song was sung through the town: I flowered like a flower in the garden, I gave order and reason to the best of my ability, and now I am dust (chap. 32, p. 149).

XIII. After Pachacuti's death, Andesuyo, which had been conquered by Pachacuti, rebelled.

One of the most notable differences between the two accounts of Pachacuti's life has to do with military campaigns. Sarmiento records many more campaigns than Betanzos, and what was written about those they each record is quite different. For example, although both authors mention the Soras campaign (VIg), Sarmiento describes the campaign in a straightforward military manner, while Betanzos hardly mentions the campaign at all and is preoccupied instead with ritual activities afterward, for example, with the preparation of captives for the victory march into Cuzco.

A special circumstance allows us to understand where some of the material Sarmiento included about campaigns was obtained. In 1569, the "grandsons" (*nietos*) of Topa Inca presented a memorial in Cuzco in which they provided a list of their forebear's conquests. The list names provinces, fortresses, and rulers conquered by Topa Inca. John Rowe (1985b) located this important document and systematically compared it with the accounts of Sarmiento, Cabello Valboa, and Morúa (M2). Rowe argued that the pattern of borrowing evidenced by Cabello Valboa and Morúa (M2) was due to the use of a common source, probably Molina. He also suggested that the original information had been stored on a *quipo*. Sarmiento and Molina both wrote in Cuzco in the early 1570s, and both appear to have made use of this *quipo* (or of those who kept it). Some of the conquests of Topa Inca occurred during the lifetime of Pachacuti, so this information was incorporated by Sarmiento into his account of Pachacuti. Because the events are also important when we consider what a life history of Topa Inca included, we will return to this *quipo* below.

What else did Sarmiento add? From Sarmiento's perspective, adding additional material made his history more complete. However, he was creating a text that would be submitted to members of the Inca dynastic descent group for their verification. It had to be recognizable to them as their past. Perhaps he could add materials from different Inca sources, and this compilation would still be recognizable to them as a representation of their own past, even if different in format and presentation.

One addition to the Sarmiento text is material from Polo de Ondegardo about the location of Inca mummies. This material is uniformly included at the end of each lifetime in the Sarmiento account. Polo arrived in Cuzco from Charcas at some point between June and August 1571. Sarmiento could have gotten the information from Polo himself or from a written report. Alternatively, he could have been told by his Inca informants about where the mummies had been found. At the end of each lifetime Sarmiento also mentions the *panaca* of the Inca in question; some of the living members of each *panaca*; and his *huaoque*, a sacred object associated with each ruler. In our discussion of the painted genre, we noted that some of the short accounts present the information about the *panacas* as a unit, while others note each *panaca* name in their accounts of a particular Inca, usually together with information about the Coya and heirs. Sarmiento puts the information about the Coya and heirs at an appropriate point in the narrative, naming the *panaca* at the end. Thus, he appears to be both adding to and rearranging the genealogical account.

A second addition is the Ulti story, about an attempt made on Pachacuti's life by the servant of a local lord. The other authors who repeat this incident are Cabello Valboa, Morúa (M2), and the author Pachacuti. Sarmiento places it after the marriage of Pachacuti, after both the Chanca invasion and Pachacuti's accession to rulership ([1572], chap. 34; 1906:72). It occurs in the Cuyos province during a continuation of the celebration of Pachacuti's marriage. The lord of Cuyos and two other lords were behind the plot. Because of this treachery, Pachacuti exterminates the people of Cuyos and annexes a great deal of territory on a subsequent rampage down the Urubamba Valley. In the other accounts, the story is similar, although the culprit behind the attempt may be different, and the story can be placed elsewhere in the narrative. For example, Cabello Valboa places the incident after the Chanca invasion but before Pachacuti becomes Inca ([1586], pt. 3, chap. 14; 1951:300). In Murúa (M2) it occurs before the Chanca invasion but after Pachacuti's marriage (Murúa [1611–1616], bk. 1, chap. 19; 1987:74–75). In the author Pachacuti, the incident occurs much later in the lifetime of Pachacuti ([early seventeenth century]; 1993:226–227). The story is completely absent from Betanzos. Its absence is an indication to us that it was not part of a life history genre but, rather, was a story about an event that occurred while Pachacuti was young that was incorporated by authors who were compiling material from more than one Inca source.

By the same token, what did Betanzos add? Some of what Betanzos included seems like an interruption in his historical narrative. For example, two chapters in Betanzos are devoted to a series of ordinances (1551–1557], pt. 1, chaps. 21–22; 1987:103–117), a substantial interruption of his story line. He also includes a great deal of information about the reorganization of Cuzco which has a narrative line that is completely missing from Sarmiento (see chapter 7). Were these topics part of an Inca genre about the life of Pachacuti, or were they additions to it?

If the difference between Sarmiento's and Betanzos's life history was simply a matter of stripping away what each author added, then we would expect to find an underlying story common to both accounts. That simply is not the case. What remains differs in subtle yet important ways. The story told by Betanzos reflects a process of deformation that can be attributed to the pretensions of Betanzos's wife (Niles 1999:19). What parts of the life history are affected by this process of deformation? One clear result is the total subordination of Topa Inca to an older brother who, coincidentally, is the forebear of Betanzos's wife, Angelina. Topa Inca's role in the dynastic past can be subordinated — although his role in dynastic succession is included in its essentials — to a person whose importance serves the interests of the author.

The Sarmiento and Betanzos accounts are also different in style and emphasis. Even where they describe the same event, their treatment is entirely different. What they have in common is that they cover many of the same events in a somewhat similar order. Some of the differences may be due to the way each worked. Betanzos, who was translating, may have stayed closer to the story he was told. Sarmiento collected material via a translator and may have suppressed what seemed less like history to him, giving prominence to aspects of the story that came closer to the historical canons he knew.

Betanzos appears to have collected his Inca history in 1551. Sarmiento

worked in 1571 but could still find a version of it. He explicitly states that he collected material from different "lineages," presumably the *panacas*:

> And so, examining the most prudent and aged people from every condi-
> tion and estate, those whose stories are most highly regarded, I gathered
> and recorded the present history, referring the declarations and statements
> of some to their enemies, because they are organized in factions, and ask-
> ing for an account from each lineage of its own history and the history of
> their opponents. And from these accounts, which are all in my possession,
> reading them and correcting them with their opponents and, finally, rati-
> fying them in the public presence of all the *ayllos* and factions, following
> the administration of an oath by a judge, and with expert general inter-
> preters, and very inquisitive and good ones, also sworn, what has been
> written here was refined.

> Y así examinando de toda condición de estados de las más prudentes y an-
> cianos, de quien se tiene más credito saqué y recopilé la presente historia,
> refiriendo las declaraciones y dichos de unos á sus enemigos, digo del
> bando contrario, porque se acaudillan por bandos, y pidiendo á cada uno
> memorial por sí de su linaje y dél de su contrario. Y estos memoriales que
> todos están en mi poder, refiriéndolos y corrigiéndolos con sus contrarios,
> y ultimamente ratificándolos en presencia de todos los bandos y ayllos en
> público, con juramento por autoridad de juez, y con lenguas expertas ge-
> nerales, y muy curiosos y fieles intérpretes, también juramentados, se ha
> afinado lo que aquí va escripto. (Sarmiento de Gamboa [1572], chap. 9;
> 1906 : 31–32)

The "*ayllos* and factions" who publicly ratified Sarmiento's Inca history were
the *panacas* ([1572]; 1906 : 130–134).

That the *panacas* still kept life history material at the time Sarmiento wrote
was mentioned by others. In 1572, after Sarmiento had finished, the *cabildo* of
Cuzco wrote to the Spanish crown about Toledo's collection efforts. Polo de
Ondegardo, who had just finished a term of office as *corregidor* of Cuzco, is one
of the signatories. The letter begins with a preface on how the Incas kept a formal memory of the past, mentioning the use of *quipos* as a recording device:

> Dear Sir. If the care and diligence of placing the origin and foundations,
> events and deeds of those who founded or won them in all republics is
> praised by all the Greek and Latin historians and commonly admitted in

all nations of the world, both in order to conserve the memory of men and to animate their descendants and successors to do heroic and exemplary works and deeds as their forebears did — which has been used not only by people of Christian doctrine and order in their political life, and letters and other means of easily conserving it, but also by barbarians, who, lacking both, through a natural instinct have looked for the means of doing so, some with pictures and signs, and all over this kingdom with strings and knots and registers, having particular individuals who were not employed in anything else, the fathers teaching the sons their meaning with such care that from three hundred years ago to the present, or perhaps a little less, we find a general conformity in their memories, both of the succession of persons and in their deeds, works, buildings, wars, and events that occurred in this time — something certainly admirable and difficult to believe for those who have not seen or examined their methods.

Exçelentisimo señor. Si el cuidado y diligençia de poner en las rrepublicas el origen y fundamento dellos, hechos y haçañas de los que las fundaron y ganaron, está tan aprouado por todos los ystoriadores griegos y latinos, y admitido comunmente en todas las naçiones del mundo, ansi para conservar la memoria de los honbres como para animar a los deçendientes y subçesores para hazer obras y hechos eroycos señalados como lo hizieron sus antepassados — lo qual no solamente a vsado la gente que a tenido dotrina y poliçia vmana, letras y medios faciles para ello, pero todos los barbaros a quien les faltó lo vno y lo otro por ynstinto natural los an buscado, vnos con pinturas y señales, y todo este rreino con hilos y nudos y rregistros, tiniendo señaladas personas que no entendian en otra cossa, enseñando los padres a los hijos la significaçion dello con tanto cuidado que de treçientos años a esta parte o poco menos hallamos conformidad en las memorias, ansi de la subçesion de las personas como de los hechos obras y edefiçios y guerras y subçesos que tuvieron en este tienpo, cossa çierto de admiraçion y dificultossa de creer para quien no lo a uisto ni exsaminado. (Archivo General de Indias, Lima 110, fol. 1)

Later in the same letter, reference is made to the collection of information from *quipo* sources by the Toledo project:

By the confession of the elders and by the succession of those who were rulers, and by the life that each one lived from Viracocha Inca to Huascar, it is evident that little more than eighty years had gone by since the Incas possessed no more than the Cuzco Valley, as small a territory as all of the other little groups and valleys who had no natural lords, each one in their own land. And the Incas became rulers through force of arms, and they never had the territory completely pacified. In the inquiry about this, in addition to the notable service that the King has received from discovering the truth from its very origins, all of this land and its inhabitants remain particularly obligated to serve Your Excellency [Viceroy Toledo] all of our lives, because, with only the motive of learning the truth and without any supplication or request from us, you undertook a great deal of work, which we saw and understood, inquiring about it from the same *quipos* — knots and registers — with which they had conserved the memory of their deeds and genealogies, and with the same mummified remains of those who had carried out that conquest with the cruelties and notable and terrifying punishments that they carried out in order to put the people under their dominion and lordship.

Por la misma confision de los viejos y por las subçesiones de los que se hizieron señores, y por la uida que cada vno biuio dende Viracocha Ynga hasta Guascar, consta poco mas de ochenta años que los ingas no poseian mas deste valle del Cuzco, tan poco como las demas behetrias y valles cada vna su tierra; y ellos los señorearon por fuerça de armas y nunca lo tuuieron del todo paçifico; en cuya averiguaçion, allende del notable seruiçio que su magestad a rreçiuido en sacar de Raiz el hecho uerdadero, toda esta tierra y los moradores della quedamos en particular obligaçion de seruir toda nuestra uida a vuestra excelencia, porque, con solo zelo de sauer la uerdad sin suplicaçion ni pedimiento de nuestra parte tomo tanto trauajo, qual todos vimos y entendimos, aberiguandola por sus mismos quipos nudos y rregistros con que tenian conseruada la memoria de sus hechos y genelogias, y con los mismos cuerpos enbalsamados de los que auian hecho la dicha conquista con las crueldades y castigos notables y espantosos que hizieron para meter la gente debaxo de su dominio y señorio. (Archivo General de Indias, Lima 110, fol. 3v)

Nowhere in Sarmiento or other Toledo documentation does a similar reference to the mummified remains of the Inca rulers appear. The connection between the remains of the Inca rulers and an Inca historical genre is not accidental. Polo de Ondegardo, when he went out to collect the mummified remains of the Inca rulers in 1559, found *quipos* with the body of Pachacuti: "And

I found the mummified body of the Inca Pachacuti, held in grand veneration, and the strings and account of his deeds, and celebrations and idolatries" [Y yo hallé el cuerpo del inga Yupangui enbalsamado, en gran veneraçión, y los hilos y quenta de sus hazañas, e fiestas e ydolatrías que estatuyó] ([1561]; 1940:154). However, both the *quipos* and mummies had been kept by the *panacas*. Following the initial creation and editing of a life history around the time of a ruler's death, a version of this genre became the responsibility of the *panaca*.[1]

That a life history was a separate genre and not just part of the genealogical genre is evident not only by these references to its keeping and transmission but also from certain artistic devices manifested in the Betanzos and Sarmiento versions of it. The story has a definite beginning and end. It begins with a vision. On the eve of the Chanca invasion a being appears to Pachacuti and presages the victory of the young man over the Chancas, who are about to attack the city. His father is awaiting the attack elsewhere, but the Chancas attack the city, and Pachacuti bravely defends it with the help of some of the local lords and many of the stones on the landscape that turn into warriors to defend Cuzco. Both Sarmiento and Betanzos chronicle the efforts the young Pachacuti made to reconcile with his father in more detail than elsewhere. Although the battle is a prominent event and marks not just the survival of Cuzco but the birth of a warrior society, the focus of the Inca story is on the rupture between father and son, and the vision is the dramatic device which explains and justifies what follows.

Although the story begins not with Pachacuti's birth but with his dramatic role in the defense of Cuzco and his subsequent rise to power, the story ends with his death. Another artistic device is used to close the narrative: a song Pachacuti sang just before he died. What Sarmiento tells about this moment is the following:

> And this [instructing Topa Inca] done, they say he began to sing in a low and sad tone in the words of his language, which in Spanish are
>> I was born like a lily in the garden, and thus it was raised;
>> and when age came, I became old;
>> and since I had to die, I dried up and died.
> These words spoken, he reclined his head on a pillow and expired, releasing his soul to the devil.

> Y esto acabado dizen que començo a cantar en vn baxo y triste tono en palabras de su lengua, que en castellano suenan naçi como un lirio en el jardin y ansi fue criado y como vino mi edad evejeçi y como avia de morir

asi me seque y morí y acabadas estas palabres recosto la cabeça sobre vna
almohada y espiro dando el animo al diablo (Sarmiento de Gamboa n.d.
[1572], chap. 47, fol. 91; 1906:93)

Betanzos reproduces a somewhat different version of the same song, which he
noted that members of Pachacuti's lineage still sang:

> And speaking and giving orders about what was to happen after his death,
> he began to sing a song in high voice that those of his *panaca* still sing to-
> day in his memory, which goes like this:
>> From the time I flourished like a garden flower until now
>> I have ordered things in this life and world as far as my strength
>>     allowed
>> and now I am turned to earth.
>> And saying these words in his song Inca Yupanqui Pachacuti expired,
>> leaving the land ordered in the way already mentioned.

> Y estando ansi hablando y mandando Ynga Yupangue lo que se auia de
> hazer despues que falleciese alço en alta voz vn cantar el cual cantar el dia
> de oy cantan los de su generaçion en su memoria el cual cantar deçia en
> esta manera desde que floreçia como la flor del guerto hasta aqui he dado
> horden y razon en esta vida y mundo hasta que mis fuerças bastaron y
> ya soy tornado tierra y diziendo estas palabras en su cantar espiro Ynga
> Yupangue Pachacuti dejando toda la tierra y razon y en la horden y razon
> ya dicha. (Betanzos n.d. [1551–1557], pt. 1, chap. 32; 1987:149)

Certainly there are notable differences between the two versions of Pachacuti's
song, but they are the same song. The incorporation of a song at this point in
the narrative marks a dramatic closure. Neither Sarmiento nor Betanzos ends
his historical narrative at this point, but they both may have preserved for us
the ending of a life history drawn from an Inca genre.

## THE LIFE OF TOPA INCA

What Sarmiento and Betanzos transmitted was not a pristine version of
an earlier historical genre. To illustrate this point and to put some of the
more outstanding differences between the Sarmiento and Betanzos accounts

of Pachacuti's life into perspective, let us examine what was written about Topa Inca.

There should have been a formally composed account of the life of Topa Inca. As mentioned in the preceding chapter, a collection of *quipos* was recovered by Polo with the mummy of Pachacuti. Cobo mentions *quipos* associated with Topa Inca, as well as people who recited an oral account drawn from them: "And, as it appeared from the *quipos* and registers of the time of this Inca and by the speech of the old men in whose power they were, he [Topa Inca] made a law that only the kings could marry their full sisters" [Y según pareció por los quipos y registros del tiempo deste Inca y por el dicho de los viejos en cuyo poder estaban, hizo ley que solos los reyes se pudiesen casar con sus hermanas de padre y madre] ([1653], bk. 12, chap. 14; 1892:167). When Cobo mentions *quipos* and the old men who kept them, he may be citing Polo de Ondegardo, since these *quipos* were still in *panaca* hands in Polo's time.

Even if an account of the life of Topa Inca survived into the period when the Spaniards began to use material from Inca genres, it will still be more difficult to tease a life history out of the existing source materials than the life of Pachacuti. Special circumstances allowed us to identify a version of Pachacuti's life that was arguably the truest transmission of an Inca life history that we have. Betanzos could translate an oral version directly. Only when his account is compared with Sarmiento's is it possible to detect features of a life history genre in Sarmiento. When the subject is Topa Inca, we cannot be so certain of the material in Betanzos. His alteration of the story line to foreground the pretensions of his wife may have affected the account of Topa Inca in other ways that are not so obvious.

An account of Topa Inca may have been deformed for other reasons. For example, even though we can assume that a life history was formally composed and preserved for transmission, the nearness in time of the life of Topa Inca makes the use of material drawn from memory rather than from a generic source more likely than would be the case for earlier rulers. Another, more destructive force is the attempt to exterminate the *panaca* of Topa Inca that was carried out by Atahuallpa's generals on the eve of the Spanish arrival. If the *panaca* was the guardian of the life history, then these events may have affected what was preserved about this Inca. Topa Inca's mummy was burned; *quipos* kept by the *panaca* may not have survived (Sarmiento de Gamboa [1572], chap. 66; 1906:23; Niles 1999:19).

There are other problems. If, as may well be the case, the "long accounts" incorporate material from the life history genre as well as the genealogical one, integrating the two genres to produce a continuous historical narrative requires a complex manipulation of the subject matter of both. Events which occurred during the overlap between lifetimes would be particularly subject to manipulation. By all accounts, Topa Inca did a great deal of campaigning during the lifetime of Pachacuti and may have succeeded his father well before Pachacuti's death. If what was wanted was a seamless narrative, then Spanish authors might have obscured clues that would help us identify material from different genres. Those who wrote in the decades following the Spanish arrival in Cuzco were not interested in transmitting Inca genres but in composing their own "histories" following very different canons. Compilation from different source materials was not shunned; indeed, it appears to have been a common practice.

Still, we can try to use our extractive process on the account of Topa Inca. We have already noted that Sarmiento includes a great deal of information on military campaigns toward the end of Pachacuti's life and identified the probable source for it. That source may have been a list of the provinces conquered by Topa Inca recorded on a *quipo*, as mentioned above (Rowe 1985b). Like the complete Betanzos manuscript published in 1987, it is one of the new sources which allow us to penetrate the complex relationship between the Spanish historical narratives and their underlying sources. A first step in trying to identify material from a life history of Topa Inca is to extract material from the *quipo* source on Topa Inca's campaigns.

### Campaigns

The *quipo* source, which we will refer to as the *Memorial*, is organized by the four *suyos*: Chinchasuyo, Andesuyo, Collasuyo, and Condesuyo (table 4.4). The names of the *suyos* appear in this, their canonical order, at the beginning of the document, though Rowe has supplied the names of the *suyos* in brackets in the text at the appropriate places. As Rowe has observed, the verbs used in the document establish a narrative of the conquests that occurred in each *suyo*; for example, the first campaign listed in Chinchasuyo is temporally prior to the second, and so on. The conquests also appear to follow a geographical order, as if all of the conquests in a particular *suyo* were undertaken during a single expedition.

Rowe also provides a correspondence between the new source and the narratives of Sarmiento, Cabello Valboa, and Morúa (M2), following the order of the *Memorial*. In table 4.4, the names of provinces, fortresses, and captains have been excerpted, preserving the names as established by Rowe. The entries occur in the same order as in the *Memorial*. The *suyo* names are those

TABLE 4.4. *The campaigns of Topa Inca from the* Memorial

[Chinchasuyo]

| | |
|---|---|
| 1 | province of Quichuas, fortress of [Ca]yara [and] Tuara Mar[ca], fortress of Curamba |
| 2 | province of Angaraes, which is in Guamanga, Vrcolla, and Guailla Pucara, king Chuquis Guaman |
| 3 | province of Xauxa, Taya, and Siquilla Pucara |
| 4 | Tarma and Atavillos |
| 5 | province of Guaillas Guanuco, Chunco, and Pillau |
| 6 | province of Caxamarca, Guamachuco, Chachapoyas, and Guayacondos |
| 7 | province of Pal[tas], Pa[casmayo], and Chimo |
| 8 | province of the Cañars and Quito, captured Piçar Capac, Cañar Capac, and Chica Capac and other kings |
| 9 | Puerto Viejo and Guancavilca, Guayaquil and Manta, and Vapo and Guamo Curba Turuca Quisin and Aba Chumbi Nina Chumbi; provinces toward the sea |
| 10 | set the frontier in Quinchicaxa, put *mitimas*, and returned to this city |

[Andesuyo]

| | |
|---|---|
| 11 | province of the Andes, province of Paucarmayo, as far as Iscayssingas |
| 12 | province of Opatari and Manari |
| 13 | province of [Ca]yanpussi, province of Paucarguambo, Aulapi, Manupampa, Chicoria, where they captured the kings called Santa Guancuiro Vinchincayna [Nutan]uari |

[Collasuyo]

| | |
|---|---|
| 14 | province of Collao, from the markers of Uilcanota, [provinces] of Capahanco and Pocopoco, fortress of Lallagua Arapa Pucara, where the whole province had defended itself; he went in person and captured the kings called Coaquiri Pachacuti, Carapuri, and Chucachuca before passing onward |
| 15 | Asillo and Asangaro to the province of Carabaya before returning to Pucara |
| 16 | province of Lupaca Pacaxa and Pucarani and the Poxa Carangas to Paria |
| 17 | province of Charcas, both Uila Charca and Hanco Charca |
| 18 | province of Chichas and Moyomoyos and Amparais and Aquitas Copayapo, Churomatas, and Caracos; up to the Chiriguanas, up to Tucuman, and there he made a fortress and put many *mitimas* |
| 19 | province of Chile, toward the sea, then through Tarapaca, where they did not campaign |
| 20 | province of Chiriguanas, coming out at Pocona; they made many fortresses in Pocona and Sabaypata, which is in the Chiriguanas and in Cuzcotuiro, putting Indians from all over to guard the said fortress and frontier |
| 21 | they found a fortress in the province of Chuis and Chichas called Huruncuta; after taking it, they settled it with Incas |

[Condesuyo]

| | |
|---|---|
| 22 | province of Condesuyo, some fortified themselves in the fortress of Omaguasgua |
| 23 | they went on to Camana and Camanchaca and Chilpaca and Pomatambos and then returned to Cuzco |

*Source*: Rowe 1985b: 224–226.

attributed by Rowe. The entries have been numbered consecutively for use in the comparison of written narratives that follows.

Here, our question is whether or not information from a source like the *Memorial* was used by Sarmiento or other authors in their narratives. If, as seems likely, Cabello Valboa and Morúa drew from the lost historical narrative of Cristóbal de Molina, then Molina may have had access to the same class of material. He composed his historical narrative in Cuzco the year after Sarmiento composed his. It may be no coincidence that detailed information about military campaigns is incorporated into historical narratives after the *Memorial* was brought to the attention of Spanish authorities in Cuzco.

In the following comparison of Sarmiento and Cabello Valboa, information about military campaigns has been foregrounded. Where the subject matter is related to the list of campaigns in the *Memorial*, the enumeration from table 4.4 has been added in the left margin, and the text has been italicized. Other events are summarized only to contextualize the campaigns. Given the possibility that Sarmiento had access to a life history of Topa Inca, the first appearance of Topa Inca in his account has been chosen as a starting point. Again, the material has been paraphrased.

Sarmiento is the only author to say anything about the sequestration of Topa Inca in the house of the Sun and the reception of the news by his older brother, Amaro Topa, that Pachacuti had designated Topa Inca as successor instead of himself. Like the negotiations between Pachacuti and Viracocha over the defense of Cuzco against the Chancas, this story also has a familial orientation. It may have opened an Inca narrative on the life of Topa Inca.

*Sarmiento*

Chap. 43. Pachacuti had raised his son Topa Inca in the house of the Sun, hidden from view. It was time for his initiation. For it, Pachacuti invented new rites and built four additional houses of the Sun to be used in his son's initiation rites.

Years before, Pachacuti had named Amaro Topa as his successor. Pachacuti had to get him to accept the change. One means of convincing him was to take him to where his brother was fasting and preparing. Amaro Topa saw the great

*Cabello Valboa*

treasure and the lords surrounding him. He was impressed and fell on his face in worship.

The initiation was carried out, with the *moroy urco* and *huacas* in attendance, in never-before-seen pomp.

Pachacuti himself offered him a gift and everyone followed suit.

Chap. 44. Pachacuti sent his son to campaign in Chinchasuyo at the head of the army. The particular object was Chuqui Sota, a lord in Chachapoyas. Pachacuti named Auqui Yupanqui and Tilca Yupanqui to go with him.

Chap. 16. Pachacuti decided to return to Cajamarca. At this time his son and heir, Topa Inca, had reached the age to go to war.

Pachacuti named Topa Capac, Auqui Yupanqui, and Tillca Yupanqui to go with him.

At the same time, Apoc Auqui was sent out on campaign, under commission from Topa Inca, as far as Amaybamba. He campaigned successfully as far as Pillasuni (Don Juan Yupanqui, a descendant who is alive "today," is mentioned).

Topa Inca was worshiped as if he were a *huaca*.

In the next segment of the Sarmiento and Cabello Valboa stories, the subject is military campaigning. Both authors have access to information about Chinchasuyo campaigns that is closely similar to the list in the *Memorial*. There are several reasons to think that they had another common source, and not the *Memorial*. For one thing, when an item from the list in the *Memorial* is missing in one (for example, the fourth entry on the list, concerning Tarma and Atavillos), it is missing in the other. For another, the two accounts preserve the same order of campaigns, an order different from the order in the *Memorial*. Finally, both accounts — but especially Cabello Valboa's — preserve additional detail about campaigns listed in the *Memorial* or similarly detailed information about campaigns entirely absent from the *Memorial*. For example, when the subject is Chile (in a segment cited below), both Sarmiento and Cabello Valboa list the names of the captains who were defeated. This information is missing from the *Memorial*. Cabello Valboa also describes a campaign in the area south of Pachacamac in some detail (also cited in a segment below). The *Memorial* does not mention a campaign in that region.

The two accounts are very similar, but there is one notable difference: Sarmiento describes two campaigns to Chinchasuyo in which Topa Inca participated; Cabello Valboa mentions only one. Sarmiento's first campaign includes all of the items on the list except the conquest of the area of Puerto Viejo, which both he and Cabello Valboa describe as taking place after the farthest boundary marker was set in Quinchicaxa (see next section). Betanzos describes three campaigns to Chinchasuyo which extended at least as far as Cajamarca during the lifetime of Pachacuti, so multiplication of campaigns may be a narrative device. What is interesting to note is that the sense conveyed by the *Memorial* that all of the places conquered in Chinchasuyo were conquered during a single expedition has been preserved in Cabello Valboa and Sarmiento.

*Sarmiento*

[1] *In the province of Quichuas he conquered the fortress of Tohara and Cayara and the fortress of Curamba.*

[2] *In the Angaraes he took the fortress of Urcocolla and Guayllapucara and captured their captain named Chuquis Guaman.*

[3] *In the province of Jauja he took Siciquilla Pucara.*

[5] *In the province of Guayllas he took Chungomarca and Pillaguamarca.*

[6?] *In Chachapoyas he took the fortress of Piajajalca and captured their rich captain named Chuqui Sota.*

[7] *And the province of Palta and the valleys of Pacasmayo and Chimo, which he destroyed, Chimo Capac being his object.*

[8] *And the Cañar province, where he took their captains named Pisar Capac and Cañar Capac and Chica Capac.*

[10] *And built an impenetrable fortress in Quinchicaxa.*

*Cabello Valboa*

[1] *In the province of Quichuas he took the fortresses of Toara and Cayara and then the fortress of Curamba.*

[2] *In the province of Angaraes he took the fortresses of Orcolla and Guaila Tucara, capturing their captain Chuquis Guaman.*

[3] *From there he went to Jauja, where they took Siquilla Pucara.*

[5] *Then they arrived at the valley of Huaylas, where they took the fortress and land of Chuncomarca and Pillaguamarca.*

[6?] *Then they went on to Caxamarca, from which Topa Inca sent a large part of his army on to Chimo. This army went down through Huamachucos.*

[7] *Arriving on the coast, the army fought many times with those of Chimo and were successful. Then they went on to the Pacasmayo River, upsetting those valleys. They returned to Cajamarca via Nepos.*

[6?] *Then they went to Chachapoyas, walking to Raymibamba. And they passed Chaz-*

*mal, Jalca, Apia, and Javanto before re-*
*turning to Cajamarca with many stories*
*and prisoners for Topa Inca.*

Then he returned to Cuzco, where he
was well received by his father.
Chap. 45. Pachacuti orders a *visita* to be
carried out by sixteen *visitadores*. They
return to Cuzco with painted mantles
showing the provinces they visited. Then
Pachacuti sends Inca nobles out to make
roads and road stations.
Chap. 46. Topa Inca is sent off to Chinchasuyo again. He is again accompanied
by Tilca Yupanqui and Anqui Yupanqui.

The whole army went to Guambos and
conquered Llaucanes, Chotas, Cutervos,
and Guambos; from there they went to
Guancabamba and fought a little; then
they went to Cusibamba and defeated
the Paltas, who had fortified themselves
in Zaraguro. At that place the Cañars
came to swear obedience.

When they arrived at Tomebamba, they
found that the captain, Pisar Capac, had
confederated with Pillaguaso of Quito.
They (Cañars and Quitos) refused to negotiate, and a battle was fought in which
the outcome was very uncertain for a
time. The Incas won, and Pillaguaso
was captured.

[8] *Without fighting they arrived in*
*Cañaribamba and Tumibamba, where*
*there was trouble with the Cañars, whom*
*Topa Inca punished, capturing Pisar Capac,*
*Cañar Capac, and Chica Capac, the lords*
*of that nation.*
*The rebels were required to build him a*
*fortress in Quichicaxa, where Topa Inca left*
*a great number of people.*
Another fortress was built in Azuay,
palaces in Tiocaxas to serve as the frontier with Puruaes and Chimbos. Another
fortress was built in Pomallacta, whose
captains were Apoc Chauan Callo and
Apocanto.
At Tumibamba Mama Ocllo bore him a
son named Huayna Capac.

They camped at what is now Quito.
From there they went to Tumibamba,
where Mama Ocllo bore him a son called
Tito Cusi Hualpa and, later, Huayna
Capac.

After this, Topa Inca decided to enter
Quito — for the first time.
Chap. 17. At this point there is a battle in
which the Incas win. The captain of the
province of Quilacos, called Pillaguaso,
was captured, and the province was
organized.

Both Sarmiento and Cabello Valboa include similar details about campaigning on the coast in the region of Puerto Viejo. Sarmiento provides additional material about Topa Inca's voyage to the islands of Hauachumbi and Ni-
nachumbi that may come from another source, perhaps a story. Cabello
Valboa adds material about the Inca looting of Chimor. In the next section
he incorporates a digression about the earlier history of the same region; he
clearly had a separate source for this material which may have provided him
with other details about Inca activities in the north.

| Sarmiento | Cabello Valboa |
|---|---|
| [9] *Afterward he decided to conquer the im-* | [9] *Once the important area of Quito was* |
| *portant province of Guancavilicas. Above* | *organized Topa Inca decided to explore the* |
| *them, he built the fortress of Guachalla, then* | *region from Quito to the coast. First he* |
| *he went down to Guancavilicas. Dividing* | *entered the province of Chimbos, then the* |
| *his army in three groups, he conquered them* | *province of Guancavillcas, then the valley of* |
| *even though they fought on land and at* | *Xipixapa, then Apelope. He set up camps in* |
| *sea in* balsas *from Tumbez to Guañape,* | *Manta, Charapoto, and Piquaza because he* |
| *Guamo, Manta, Turuca, and Quisin.* | *had a great number of people with him.* |
| *Topa Inca entered the ocean and visited the* | *Topa Inca set off on a* balsa *to explore the* |
| *islands of Puna and Tumbez, where he* | *sea, discovering the islands of Hagua* |
| *learned about the islands Ava Chumbi and* | *Chumbi and Nina Chumbi.* |
| *Niña Chumbi from some merchants.* He | |
| did not believe them, but he had a sor- | |
| cerer with him named Antarqui who was | |
| capable of flying through the air. Antar- | |
| qui used his talents to go to these islands | |
| and reported back to Topa Inca that they | |
| did indeed exist. So Topa Inca built a | |
| great number of *balsas* and took some | |
| 20,000 men with him. He took as cap- | |
| tains Guaman Achachi, Conde Yupan- | |
| qui, Quigual Topa (all Hanan Cuzco), | |

Yancan Mayta, Quiço Mayta, Cachima-
paca Macus Yupanqui, Llimpita Usca
Mayta (all Hurin Cuzco). For general he
took Tilca Yupanqui, leaving the rest
with Apo Yupanqui.

After the voyage, which took nine
months, he returned to Tumebamba. On
the way he sent people down the coast to
Chimo. They recovered a great deal of
treasure and brought it up to Cajamarca.

Afterward they subjected the Guanca-
villcas and Chonos and then went on
to Tumbez, where they built a fortress.
Then they went to Pohechos, where they
rested. Topa Inca went back to the highlands, sending two uncles to explore the
coast.

Then Cabello begins a digression on the
earlier history of the Peruvian coast.

Chap. 18. While Tilca Yupanqui and
Auqui Yupanqui, his uncles, went south,
Topa Inca and his bastard brother Topa
Capac returned with the other half of the
army via the province of Guayacundos,
arriving at the high cordillera in the area
of Guancabamba. There they could see
the land of the Pacamoros. Thinking
they would take it the next year, they
built a fortress. Then they went to Cajamarca to encounter the captains who
had been sent down the coast. They had
had some problems with the cacique of
Jayanca. They had also looted Chimo,
after which they took the loot up to
Cajamarca.

Topa Inca entered Cuzco with all the
treasure. Pachacuti was jealous, and because of this, he ordered the deaths of
Tilca Yupanqui and Anqui Yupanqui.

Topa Inca entered Cuzco with all the
treasure. Pachacuti had Tillca Yupanqui
and Auqui Yupanqui killed for having
taken Topa Inca to such remote parts.
He also had his bastard son Topa Capac
killed.

From all of the loot, Pachacuti had a
number of important statues fashioned.

At the end of the last segment Pachacuti was still alive. In the Sarmiento
story he dies at this point. Sarmiento then devotes two chapters to Pachacuti.

In the Cabello Valboa version Topa Inca succeeds during the lifetime of his father.

The next campaign is a major expedition into the lowlands of Andesuyo. In the Sarmiento version, reference is made to an earlier campaign in the same region by Pachacuti, although the account of Pachacuti made no mention of it. The expedition was undertaken to punish people who had been requested to bring lance shafts from their territory to Cuzco but who refused to do so. In the Cabello Valboa version the expedition appears to be a new conquest. Sarmiento provides some additional detail, but both authors supply the information contained in the *Memorial* about the provinces conquered and captains defeated in Andesuyo. Both Sarmiento and Cabello Valboa include detail about the Inca captains chosen to participate in the Andesuyo campaigns that is simply not a topic in the *Memorial*. Whereas, in the coverage given by Sarmiento and Cabello Valboa of the Chinchasuyo campaign, the items of the list in the *Memorial* could be clearly distinguished, it is impossible to segregate the items listed in the *Memorial* in their Andesuyo coverage.

| *Sarmiento* | *Cabello Valboa* |
|---|---|
| Chap. 47. Pachacuti gives orders for what is to happen after his death, sings his song, and dies. | |
| Chap. 48. After Pachacuti's death Topa Inca is crowned again. Then he carries out all of what his father had asked him to do on his deathbed. | Pachacuti renounced rule in favor of Topa Inca, who receives all the royal insignia. |
| Chap. 49. Topa Inca ordered all the conquered people to come to Cuzco to show their obedience to the new ruler. He requested the people of Andesuyo to bring him some lance shafts made of palmwood for the house of the Sun. To them this was a sign of their subordination to him. They had been conquered in the time of Pachacuti but had never served freely. They fled Cuzco and asserted their independence.<br>Topa Inca was greatly offended and raised a large army. He divided it into three parts. He would lead one and enter the Andes through Aguatona; another | Groups of people from the newly annexed regions of the coast arrive, and Topa Inca requires them to send a certain number of soldiers to him for his Andesuyo campaign.<br>He leaves his brother Amaro Topa as governor, because he wants his brother Topa Yupanqui and Atorongo Achachi and Apoc Chalco Yupanqui, his cousins, to accompany him. |

was given to Otorongo Achachi, who
would enter through a town or valley
called Amaro; the third he gave to
Chalco Yupanqui, who was to enter
through a town called Pilcopata. These
entries were near each other.

After entering, they joined up at
Opatari, where the settlement of the
Andes begins. Chalco Yupanqui had the
image of the Sun with him.

They had a very difficult time traveling.
The lord of a great part of this region
was Condin Xabana, who they believed
could take various forms.

Many of the soldiers got sick and died.
Even Topa Inca was lost a good part of
the time until he encountered Otorongo
Achachi.

[12–13] *He conquered four great nations:*
*Opataries, Manosuyo, and Manaries or*
*Yanaximes, which means "black mouths,"*
*and the province of the Chunchos. Taking*
*the river below Tono, they traveled a great*
*distance until arriving at Chiponauas. And*
*on the road, which is now called the Camata*
*road, he sent another great captain called*
*Apo Curimache, who went all the way to the*
*river, which we have just had news about,*
*called Paytiti, where Topa Inca had markers*
*put. And in these conquests Topa Inca and*
*his captains captured the following lords:*
*Vincin Cayna, Canta Guancuru, and*
*Nutanguari.*

[12–13] *During the campaign he annexed*
*four provinces: Opatarisuyo, Mamansuyo,*
*Chunchos, and Chipomaguas. They arrived*
*where the Manobambas lived, where they*
*chew something that makes their teeth black.*
*He took their caciques captive, including*
*Vinchi Cayna and Santa Guanmiro. Topa*
*Yupanqui, his brother, personally captured a*
*cacique named Nutanguari who was very*
*famous.*

While Topa Inca campaigned in person in the lowlands, a revolt broke out
in the Lake Titicaca region. Sarmiento and Cabello Valboa tell the same story,
incorporating information about fortresses and captains that parallels what
was included in the *Memorial*. They give the names of the captains chosen by
Topa Inca to remain in Andesuyo and those who were to accompany him in
the reconquest of the Collao. The Colla revolt is the first item on the list of
conquests in Collasuyo in the *Memorial*. The fortresses listed are described as

"where the whole province had defended itself," thus conveying the same sense of an extended siege as in the Cabello Valboa and Sarmiento accounts, although nowhere is the event identified as a revolt rather than a new conquest.

| *Sarmiento* | *Cabello Valboa* |
|---|---|
| During this campaign, an Indian from the Lake Titicaca region named Coaquiri fled the army and returned home, spreading the news that Topa Inca was dead and telling them to rise up, that there was no more Inca, and that he would lead them. He called himself Pachacuti Inca. The Collas rebelled and took him for their captain. Topa Inca heard this news while he was in the Andes. He went to reconquer and punish the Collas himself, leaving Otorongo Achachi to continue the Andes campaign. | During this campaign, a Colla who had gone with them returns to the Lake Titicaca area and spreads the word that Topa Inca had been killed by the eastern lowlanders, who had also defeated and captured most of his army. With this news, the Collas took up arms to assert their independence. Amaro Topa heard about this and got word to Topa Inca about it, begging him to punish this daring rebellion. Topa Inca left Otorongo Achache in charge and took a direct route to the Lake Titicaca area. He left half the army with his brother and told him to keep conquering and that, when he was done, he should come out of the lowlands near Pilco and wait for him at Paucartambo. He was not to return to Cuzco without Topa Inca. |
| Chap. 50. Topa Inca named as captains Larico, son of Capac Yupanqui, his cousin, and Achache, his brother, and Conde Yupanqui and Quigual Topa. With this army he marched to the Lake Titicaca area. | Topa Inca took as captains Gualpac and a son of Capac Yupanqui named Alarico. He also took Cuyuchi and Achachi, the brother of his father. |
| [14] *The Collas had fortified themselves in Llallaua, Asilli, Arapa, and Pucara. He captured their captains, Chucachuca and Pachacuti Coaquiri. The war took years, but the Incas were successful.* | [14] *It took him some time, but he reached the Lake Titicaca area and found the Collas fortified in Pucara, Asillo, Arapa, and Lana. Although it cost him some of his people, he took them and captured their lords, Chuca Chuca and Chasuti Coaquiri, whom he later had made into drums.* |

Unlike the coverage for Chinchasuyo, the narrative of the Collasuyo campaign in both Sarmiento and Cabello Valboa omits the detail from the list in the *Memorial* except for the campaign in the far south. Both authors are concerned with describing the placement of the marker at the farthest southern boundary of the territory ruled by the Incas. This information is not in the *Memorial*, although setting the farthest boundary marker was a topic in its Chinchasuyo coverage. The sequencing was a bit different. The *Memorial* puts the setting of the northern boundary at the very end of the Chinchasuyo campaign, while both Sarmiento and Cabello Valboa locate it before the Inca expedition to the Puerto Viejo region. When the subject is Collasuyo, the campaign in Chile is not the last campaign listed in the *Memorial*: afterward, and presumably on his return from Chile, Topa Inca built fortresses on the frontier with the Chiriguanaes and then campaigned against the fortress of Oroncota. Neither Sarmiento nor Cabello Valboa describe these activities, although Cobo and Betanzos describe the taking of Oroncota (see below). What is important to note is that both these activities could be accomplished on Topa Inca's return from Chile; that is, the *Memorial* appears to reproduce the events, in sequence, of a single major expedition to Collasuyo.

| Sarmiento | Cabello Valboa |
|---|---|
| [19?] *And since he has followed his enemy all the way to Charcas, he decided to continue onward, conquering everything in his path. And so he went all the way to Chile, where he defeated the great captain Michimalongo and Tangalongo, captain of the Chileños, from this side of the Maule River to the north. And he reached Coquimbo and the Maule River, where he put his columns or, as others say, a wall as the limit and marker of his conquest.* | [19?] *Topa Inca decided to go on ahead and conquer new lands. He arrived at Coquinbo and built a fortress and left a garrison. Then he went on to Chile, where he put a marker to mark the farthest southern boundary of his empire.* |
| He brought back gold from Chile, and having discovered gold and silver mines in many parts, he returned to Cuzco. He united his spoils with those of Otorongo Achachi, who was waiting for his brother in Paucartambo, and returned together to Cuzco. At this time, the Chumbivilcas decided to submit to the Incas. After this he went to the Chachapoyas and took care of problems. | On this trip he found very rich mines, like those at Porco, Tarapaca, Chuquiabo, Carabaya, and others. With a great deal of treasure he returned to Cuzco after first meeting up with Otorongo in Paucartambo. |
| | While he was gone, Pachacuti died. |

Sarmiento turns his attention entirely away from military campaigns at this point and describes the innovations introduced by Topa Inca, including the initiation of construction at the fortress above Cuzco. Cabello Valboa mentions the *visita*, the building of the fortress, and "other worthy things" Topa Inca did in Cuzco before launching into a description of a campaign on the coast south of Pachacamac that is entirely absent from Sarmiento and from the *Memorial*. Cabello has more to say about Topa Inca the organizer following his description of this final campaign, but first he describes the fortification of the people of Lunahuaná at Huarco. Above, it is listed as a separate episode. The entire coastal campaign may have been part of this episode.

| *Sarmiento* | *Cabello Valboa* |
|---|---|
| Back in Cuzco he made laws, added to the *mitimas* his father had created, ordered a *visita* of the land from Quito to Chile, and set tribute. | Topa Inca stayed in Cuzco to take care of the mourning rituals. |
| | He was able to rest and spend his time making laws, conduct a *visita*, and other worthy things. |
| | In this period he also built the fortress of that city. |
| | Then Topa Inca decided to go to the coast. And so he went to Huamanga, and he had the very difficult Parcos road built. Then he went to Jauja, where he examined some very old buildings that the natives told him had been built by some valiant foreigners. |
| | From here he wanted to go to the coast to see a famous temple that had been built near the valley of Lima. He took the Huarochiri road, and, arriving at some dry dunes, he was very pleased with the service at that temple, although it was not administered according to the rules given by his father. He decided to build a new one, and the natives agreed, provided he did not destroy the old one. He built a very large temple to honor Pachacamac, and so the valley took its name. |
| | From there he decided to go to some nearby valleys which had refused to serve |

the Incas. These were Mara, Runaguana, and Chincha. To conquer these people with order and dispatch, he sent for an army to come to the coast via the valley of Ocoña. This army passed quietly through Acarí, Nasca, and Ica to Chincha, where the people had organized a defense. So had the Runaguanaes and Maras. The events that took place would require an entire book. What happened was that, at a famous fortress built by Topa Inca, many people were hung from the walls. The fortress got the name Guarco, meaning "hanging place." When done, he decided to travel. Arriving in Cajamarca, he took a turn down to Chachapoyas to newly require them to preserve the peace.

He then returned to Cuzco, where he issued more laws and ordinances. He also celebrated marriage to a sister called Mama Ocllo with whom, as we said, he had a son, Huayna Capac, born in Tumibamba.

Here Cabello explains that they also give him the name Pachacuti because of his ability to organize.

He describes *mitimas*, *tucuricos*, and *michoc*.

Chap. 19. The Yanayaco story.

Then Cabello describes resettlement, then how local officials were chosen, then the *acllas* (naming three classes: Mama Aclla, Guayor Aclla, and Sayapayas), then the order that merchants were to report on where precious items came from. He also organized the calendar, naming the months (Cabello lists them).

Chap. 20. Cabello continues his description of the innovations of Topa Inca, including the building of prisons.

In addition to the *tucuricos*, he put *michos* in the provinces who would oversee the collection of tribute. He also introduced the decimal form of administration and the *curacas*.

Chap. 51. The Yanayaco story.

Chap. 52. Then he orders a second *visita*. The one carried out by Topa Capac did not please him, so he sent his brother Apo Achachi. He told this brother not to include the *yanayacos*. This *visita* involved resettlement.

He changed the practice of naming *curacas*. Sons did not automatically inherit; the Inca had to approve. If something displeased the Inca, he would remove the *curaca*. The Inca personally gave the *curacas* servants, women, and

fields, and this was the only means of
access to them. In every province the
people made one large field to raise food
to be paid as tribute to the Inca. Over
all was a *tucorico apo*, the lieutenant of
the Inca there. The first Inca to exact
tribute was Pachacuti, but Topa Inca imposed the assignment of what was to be
paid. Topa Inca also distributed lands
throughout the empire, measured in
*topo*. He also scheduled the labor that
was owed. The people only got three
months to plant their own fields. The
rest had to be spent in service to the Sun,
the Incas, and the *huacas*.

He also organized the merchants. Any
time some precious item would turn up,
he would find out where it came from,
thus discovering many rich mines.

He had two governors called *suyoyoc apo*,
one in Jauja and one in Tiahuanaco.

He also ordered the enclosure of certain
women, maidens of age twelve and up,
called *aclla*. The *tucorico apo* could give
them in marriage. He would give them
to captains and soldiers and other servants as a reward. As some left, others
were added. Any man who took one for
himself or was found inside the enclosure was punished with death.

Chap. 53. Topa Inca knew about his father's planning of Cuzco in the shape of
a puma. It still lacked the head, so Topa
Inca decided to build the fortress. He ordered the provinces to send a great number of people. He assigned labor gangs.
Some quarried stone, others worked it,
others carried it, and others set it in
place. In relatively few years, the large,
sumptuous, and very strong fortress was
done. The fortress was of rough stone,
but the interior buildings were of very

fine stone. When he was done, Topa Inca
ordered the construction of many storehouses for the things needed in times of
necessity and war.

Chap. 54. At Chinchero, where he had
fine palaces, he became ill and died. He
named Tito Cusi Gualpa (Huayna
Capac) as his successor.

Topa Inca dies in Cuzco.

Clearly there are similarities between Sarmiento and Cabello Valboa that
derive from having a source like the *Memorial*. What is important to note is
that the material taken from it carries the narrative except for brief excursions
into family matters or organizational activities. Topa Inca's military campaigns, the names of the captains who participated, the lords who were defeated, and the fortresses that were taken figure prominently in his "history."

If Sarmiento wove material from this type of Inca source — a *quipo* account
of the campaigns of a particular ruler — into his history, perhaps we should
reflect once more on his account of Pachacuti. What differentiates Sarmiento's
account of Pachacuti from Betanzos's is the amount of information Sarmiento
includes on campaigns (table 4.2). In some cases, Sarmiento names the captains who were sent, specific fortresses or towns taken, and the lords who were
defeated ([1572], chap. 35; 1906 : 72–73). When the subject is Viracocha, Sarmiento has some information of this type ([1572], chap. 26; 1906 : 57–58). That
such information may have drawn not from the life history genre but from another kind of source is a matter that only arises because of the relationship between Sarmiento's text and the *Memorial*.

Given that we can document a probable source for this type of information,
once we extract it from the account of Topa Inca we can see that little is left.
The availability of sources on military campaigns was obviously a great temp-
tation to Spanish authors for whom narratives of military events were the stuff
of history. As we have seen in our comparison of the life histories of Pachacuti
recorded by Sarmiento and Betanzos, the accounts differ not only in how
much was written about military campaigns but also in what was chosen for
emphasis. Sarmiento included a great deal of detail on campaigns that is entirely absent from Betanzos; he focuses on conquest, while Betanzos focuses
on ritual. However, their accounts follow a similar event structure and are
opened and closed by similar narrative devices. We have some clues about their
common source.

But how to get at a life history of Topa Inca? Not just Sarmiento but Morúa

(M2) and Cabello Valboa reproduce material about Inca campaigns in their narratives. Since these accounts are late, one approach might be to compare early accounts. These accounts do not include the kind of detail on campaigns that would suggest reliance on sources like the *Memorial*. Perhaps by comparing Betanzos with long accounts that do not rely on such sources we might learn something about a life history of Topa Inca.

### Cieza de León, Betanzos, and Cobo

The two earliest "long accounts" we have are Betanzos and Cieza de León. Cieza attributed parts of his work to particular Inca informants, both in Cuzco and the provinces. His account may draw less from Inca genres than other authors/compilers who narrowed their collecting efforts to *panaca* members. Cieza is also problematic because we could not reconcile his account with the two versions of dynastic descent (Cobo/*Discurso* and Las Casas/Gutiérrez) that we have identified (chapter 3). Cieza may have drawn from informants who were very knowledgeable about the Inca past but who were not transmitting generic material. Cieza, working with the memory of particular individuals, may have constructed a narrative of his own to a much greater degree than those who worked with Inca genres or with underlying texts. Cobo's account has also been included in the analysis (see tables 4.1–4.3). If Cobo used a manuscript by Polo de Ondegardo, then his material is from the late 1550s, more than a decade before Sarmiento wrote. We will include Cobo, *caveat lector*.

In all three sources, military campaigns are treated in far less detail than in Sarmiento or Cabello Valboa/Morúa (M2). However, we must ask, Do the accounts incorporate some of the same campaigns, and if they do, how does their presentation differ from what we have identified as material from a separate, *quipo* source? Since what was remembered about these campaigns could have been totally transformed at any point after first composition, we will cite any references to Inca activity in the areas where Topa Inca led campaigns or sent captains under his authority, beginning in the time of his father's rule, since there would have been considerable overlap between the two lives. An awareness of how each author presented campaigning activity is required, so each will be discussed before any comparison is attempted.

In the case of the Betanzos account we already know that Yamqui Yupanqui overshadows his brother Topa Inca. Both Sarmiento and Morúa represent three Collasuyo campaigns during the lifetime of Pachacuti (table 4.1), the first headed by Capac Yupanqui (Sarmiento de Gamboa [1572], chap. 38; 1906:77; Morúa [1611–1616], bk. 1, chap. 20; 1987:77–78) and the other two by Topa Inca (Sarmiento de Gamboa [1572], chap. 44; 1906:86; chap. 46; 1906:89;

Murúa [1611–1616], bk. 1, chaps. 21–22; 1987:80–82; chap. 25; 1987:93–94). Betanzos also records three campaigns, but all are headed by Yamqui Yupanqui; Topa Inca participates only in the last one. There is no specific information about provinces or fortresses conquered; in each case, the only place mentioned is the farthest point from Cuzco reached during the campaign. It should be remembered that Betanzos said almost nothing about the campaigns of Pachacuti. He described only the campaign against the Soras before turning to the victory march back to Cuzco. If Betanzos is our guide to the life history genre, there was no inclusive treatment of the military campaigns of a particular Inca in the life history genre.

Cieza and Cobo incorporate substantially more information about campaigning into their narratives than does Betanzos. Both also feature Pachacuti, or Inca Yupanqui, as Cieza calls him. The Chinchasuyo campaign is problematic. In Cieza's narrative, the conquest of Chinchasuyo is distributed between Pachacuti and Topa Inca. Pachacuti or his captains conquer as far as Tarma. Topa Inca, after his father's death, extends the empire to the Quito region. Cobo, on the other hand, appears to put all of the action in the region between Cuzco and Quito in the reign of Pachacuti, without mentioning participation by Topa Inca in any campaigns undertaken during his father's lifetime. There is only scant mention of a campaign in Chinchasuyo in which there is fighting in Quito as well as in Cañar and Chachapoyas territory. Most of the action carried out in Topa Inca's name is in Andesuyo and Collasuyo.

| *Betanzos* | *Cieza* | *Cobo* |
|---|---|---|
| Chap. 24. Pachacuti sent Yamqui Yupanqui with his brother Capa Yupanqui on a campaign [6?] to Chinchasuyo. He conquered as far as *Caja-marca*. They returned to Cuzco via the *yungas*. | Chap. 49. Inca Yupanqui raised another army to go against the Huancas and Yauyos. His brother Lloque Yupanqui went as general. Copa Yupanqui also went. So did Anco Allo, a Chanca captain. They were well received in Huamanga, Azangaro, Parcos, Picoy, Acos, and others. [3] *The people of Jauja were afraid and made great sacrifices in their temple at Guarabilca. There was a* | Chap. 13. Pachacuti conquered the provinces of Vilcas and Soras and Lucanas with very little trouble. In Huamanga he met with more resistance. There he took a well-defended fortress. He did not meet resistance in Chocorbos, Angaraes, or Parinacochas. The Huancas of the Jauja Valley, on the other hand, fought valiantly. |

*great battle, but the Huan-cas were treated gently af-terward.* The lands were not reorganized until the time of Huayna Capac. Chap. 50. Those of Bombon fortified themselves on an island. The Incas went on and met the people of [4] *Tarama* in battle.

At this point there was a problem with the Chanca captain. He broke with the Incas and marched off to Chachapoyas and Huánuco into the lowlands, where the descendants of his army remain. Since there was a Chanca captain with the army in the Collao, Inca Yupanqui tried to keep news about the Chanca defection in the north from him. When the Chancas got back to Cuzco they learned what had happened but were unable to do anything about it, so they asked leave to return to their province.

Chap. 51. Inca Yupanqui builds the house of the Sun and begins the fortress.

Chap. 52. Inca Yupanqui decides to campaign in person in the Collao. Leaving a governor in Cuzco, he got as far as Ayavire, where he found

Pachacuti did not put down his arms until he reached Tumebamba, incorporating Guarocheri, Canta, Tarama, Chinchacocha, Cajatambo, Bombon, Conchucos, and Caxamarca as he went. On a second expedition he went as far as the upper limits of the coast and sent a brother with an army to annex the coast itself. On this campaign all of Arequipa from Tarapaca to Hacari was annexed. Nasca, Ica, and Pisco submitted without a fight, but Chincha, Huarco, and Lunaguana resisted for considerable time. Once they were defeated, Mala, Chilca, Pachacama, Lima, Chancay, Guaura, La Barranca, and other areas on the coast below Chimo submitted peacefully.

resistance. He killed all of them and those of Copacopa as well. Since he had already invented *mitimas*, he repopulated the area with them and built buildings.

Some of his captains had gone to Andesuyo.

Inca Yupanqui continued on to Omasuyo. He passed through the towns of Horuro, Asillo, and Asángaro, where there was some resistance. In the main, however, he attracted them through gifts and negotiation. He attracted many other peoples in the Lake Titicaca region to Inca sovereignty at this time. He also paid a visit to the temple of the Sun on the island of Titicaca, ordering palaces built. Then he returned to Cuzco.

Chap. 25. Pachacuti sent Yamqui Yupanqui out again with Capa Yupanqui, this time as far as Cañaripampa. After this campaign, Pachacuti put the *borla* on Yamqui's head.

Chap. 26. Yamqui went out again, this time with his brother Topa Inca. They went to Tumebamba. Yamqui gives him Mama Ocllo as a bride. [In chap. 27 mention is made of the birth of Huayna Capac during this campaign.] They continued their conquest as far as Yaguarcocha, beyond Quito. Yamqui founded a city there, sending a large number of people from there and from Cañar territory to Cuzco as *mitimas*.

Chap. 28. *Topa Inca left* [11–13] *for the Andes*. He arrived in Caxaroma, 200 km from Cuzco, a place his father had conquered. Betanzos describes the area. When he returned to Cuzco he brought treasure and lowland animals. The gold was used to adorn Cuzco. Chaps. 29–32. Pachacuti prepares for his death, knowing that Collasuyo and Andesuyo will rebel after he dies.

Chap. 33. After Pachacuti died, one of the Incas who had been left in the Andes returned to Cuzco to tell Topa Inca that the Andes had rebelled. Topa Inca sent Ynga Achache and Gualpa Rimache to reconquer them. Topa Inca went in person. Betanzos describes the actions of Ynga Achache in some detail. After Topa Inca returned to Cuzco he received word that Collasuyo had rebelled.

Chap. 53. *Inca Yupanqui wanted to go in person* [11–13] *to campaign in the Andes*. He took a large army. Many came to him and accepted Inca rule; others simply fled farther into the interior. Pachacuti, in Marcapata, heard that there was some kind of problem in Cuzco, so he returned.

Because Inca Yupanqui had gone to the Andes, the people of the Collao, thinking he would be killed or defeated, rebelled. They gathered in Hatuncolla and Chucuito under the captains Cari, Çapana [Zapana], Umalla, the lord of Açangaro [Azángaro], and others. They killed the Inca governors and other Incas that were settled there.

Chap. 14. Pachacuti renounced rule in favor of Topa Inca. Then Cobo tells about Topa Inca's marriage to his full sister, Mama Ocllo. [11–13] *Topa Inca decided to campaign in Andesuyo. He went in person, taking a large army. He fought with the Chunchos and Mojos.*

During this campaign, a captain from the Collao returned to his homeland, spreading word that the Inca was dead. Two Inca governors were killed. The governor who had remained in Cuzco got word to Topa Inca.

What anchors all three narratives is the Colla revolt. Even Betanzos, who has the lightest treatment of Inca campaign activity, locates a reconquest of the Colla region at about the time of Pachacuti's death or renunciation, the same temporal placement as in Cieza, Cobo, and other accounts. The presentation of the circumstances surrounding the event is different in each case, however. For Cobo, Topa Inca is in full command. While he is campaigning in Andesuyo, a Colla returns to his homeland and declares that the Inca is dead, germinating a revolt in the northern Lake Titicaca basin. Topa Inca leaves part of the army in Andesuyo and takes the rest with him to put down the rebellion. He does not return to Cuzco but takes a route that appears to gain him both time and the element of surprise. The Collas are fortified in the area of Pucara, Arapa, and/or Asillo. The same scenario is repeated by other authors, including Sarmiento. For Betanzos, Pachacuti is expecting both Andesuyo and Collasuyo to rebel at the time of his death. He is right, and Topa Inca has to put down both rebellions. Cieza is more complex. The story line of an Andes campaign at approximately the same time as a military campaign in the Asillo area is there, but it is present in the reigns of both Pachacuti and Topa Inca. The distribution of the Chinchasuyo campaign between the two rulers and the echo of events may reflect an effort to compose a single historical narrative from material which focused on more than one lifetime. There are problems precisely in areas of overlap.

All three authors describe Topa Inca's reconquest of the Collas and further campaigns "as far as the Maule River" in Chile, but Cieza and Cobo locate them after a return to Cuzco (see the next segment of the comparison). What is interesting to note is that the farthest point reached in the south is not mentioned in the *Memorial*, while the setting of a marker at the farthest point north is noted. Given the emphasis in Betanzos on describing campaigns in terms of the farthest point reached, this may have been a succinct way of presenting a campaign in the life history genre about which a great deal of additional detail was on record in another format. Only really major military events — the Chanca invasion, the conquest of Soras by Pachacuti, the reconquest of the northern Lake Titicaca region by Topa Inca, and so on — were elaborated to any extent in the life history genre.

| *Betanzos* | *Cieza* | *Cobo* |
|---|---|---|
| Chap. 34. Topa Inca dispatched various captains to different *suyos*: Ynga Achache, now called Utu- | Chap. 54. Pachacuti was very old, so he persuaded Cuzco to give Topa Inca the *borla*. Topa Inca had | [14] *Topa Inca went in person to reconquer the Collas. Topa Inca left the Andes via Paucartambo without re-* |

rungo Achache, was sent to Andesuyo; Topa Inca went in person to Colla-suyo; Sopono Yupanqui, a brother, was named governor of Chinchasuyo after Yamqui Yupanqui died, and three captains — Tambo Topa, Gualpache, and Guaina Yupanqui — were sent to campaign there; two other brothers were sent to govern Condesuyo.

[14] *Topa Inca went with 100,000 soldiers from Chin-chasuyo. They fought at Asillo and then chased the Collas to Pucarane, then Arapa.*

Then they went on to the province of Chuquiyapo, to the town of *Surucoto,* where they fought again.

Chap. 35. *Topa Inca fol-lowed his enemies to* [18] *the province of Mayos-mayos, where they were fortified at Tongoche.*

Topa Inca captured them and killed them all.

*He decided to undertake a campaign against the*

already proved himself in war.

Chap. 55. The Canas greeted Topa Inca and his army with gifts. Mean-while, the Collas tried to get their neighbors to join their cause. Topa Inca sent messengers to the Collas to tell them that he did not want to be their enemy and would not punish them for the killing of the governors if they would come and swear obedience.

[14] *The Collas were not in-terested and advanced to-ward the Inca army. They met in the pueblo of Pucara in a fortress they made there.*

Cari was taken captive and sent to Cuzco.

Chap. 56. The Collas, who were now beyond the Desaguadero, sued for peace. They came to an agreement in Chucuito. Topa Inca reorganized the area, removing many *miti-mas* and settling *mitimas* from other areas there.

*turning to Cuzco. He ar-rived in Chungara and took the Colla army from the rear.* Many battles were fought. He was victorious and destroyed the towns that had rebelled. He had drums made out of two important caciques, and with them, and with the heads of others and many captives, he returned to Cuzco.

[20] *Chiriguanaes, which Betanzos describes as a "province," and the province of Zuries.*
*From there they went on to the province of Chile. They explored as far as the Maule River before returning to the pueblo of Chile.*

Chap. 36. After organizing Chile and Copayapo, Topa Inca returned to Cuzco via Atacama. He divided the army: one part returned to Cuzco via the coast of Arequipa; another, via Carangas and Aullagas; the third, on the right hand, left via Casavindo and through Chichas; one part went with him. They would reunite in the Collao. He arrived in the province of Llipi, then Chuquisaca, then he visited the mines of Porco (province of Charcas), then to Paria, where he built a *tambo*, then Chuquiabo, where he heard about gold mines. Then he went to Chucuito, then Hatuncolla, where he reunited with the captains who had taken the coastal route and those who had come via Carangas. They had to wait for the captains who had been sent via Chichas.

For both Cobo and Cieza, Topa Inca undertook a campaign in Chincha-suyo before completing the activities Betanzos records in the south. This campaign may be equated with the third campaign of Yamqui Yupanqui, as reported by Betanzos, before the Colla revolt. In the Betanzos account, it was on this campaign that Yamqui gives Mama Ocllo to brother Topa Inca as sister-wife ([1551–1557], pt. 1, chap. 26; 1987:127). In the same chapter he notes that Mama Ocllo bore Topa Inca a son in Tomebamba (1987:129), in Cañar territory. Cobo does not provide information about the birth of Huayna Capac, but the campaign immediately following his account of the Colla revolt takes Topa Inca to Cañar territory where there is military activity.

| *Betanzos* | *Cieza* | *Cobo* |
|---|---|---|
| Chap. 37. Topa Inca built the fortress of Cuzco. | Topa Inca returned to Cuzco and continued building the fortress begun by his father. | |
| | Chap. 57. Topa Inca left for Chinchasuyo with a big army and with his uncle Capa Yupanqui as general. | Soon after, Topa Inca went on campaign to Chinchasuyo. He took a large army and went all the way to Quito. |
| | [3–6] *They went through Vilcas and Jauja and were well received. In Bonbon and Tarama the reception was the same. There was fighting in some spots between Jauja and Caja-marca.* | |
| | *The Incas were successful in these battles and in Caja-marca. Then Topa Inca went to Huánuco and built palaces. Then he went to Chachapoyas, where he met with resistance.* | |
| | Afterward he went to Bracamoros but retreated rapidly because it was very bad *montaña.* | |

[7] *In the Paltas and in Guancavanbo, Caxas, Ayavaca, and surrounding regions he had a great deal of work to subdue the local people. He was finally able to annex them.*

[8] *Then he went on to Cañar territory. There was more fighting, but he won. In Tumebamba he built large buildings.*

Then Topa Inca went on to Tiçicanbe and Cayanbe, the Puraures [Puruaes], and other places. In Latacunga he had a pitched battle with the locals but was able to come to terms with them. He built a number of buildings there.

[8] *From there he went to Quito*, where he built a town, settled numerous *mitimas*, and built a number of buildings. Quito was to be the second city after Cuzco.

He established a garrison in Carangui.

Huayna Capac was born in the Cañar province.

[8] The king of *Quito* consulted an oracle that told him he would be successful in battle. He fought, but the Incas won. Topa Inca decided to return to Cuzco via the sierra, because he had gone north via the coast. When he got to Cañar territory, some submitted peacefully, while others resisted. When he defeated the rebellious ones, many were sent to Cuzco as *mitimas*. At this time, he headed east to Chachapoyas, where he fought a number of battles. He was

successful and took many prisoners back to Cuzco.

Chap. 58. *He sent some Incas to the provinces we* [9] *call Puerto Viejo, where the people agreed to be ruled by Cuzco.* He also sent Incas to other parts of the coast with gifts for the chief lords asking to be treated as their equal when he would travel through their territory. The response was good, so Topa Inca headed toward the coast.

Chap. 59. *He arrived* [9] *first at Tumbez, where he was well received. He did battle in Chimo. Then he went on to Paramonguilla, where he built a fortress still standing in Cieza's time. Then he went to Pachacamac, where there was an important* yunga *shrine. He wanted to replace it with a temple of the Sun, but he did not dare, so he built a house of the Sun near it. Many Indians say he spoke with Pachacamac. Then he returned to Cuzco via Jauja.*

Chap. 60. The province of Chincha had been important in earlier times. Pachacuti had wanted to send a captain to Chincha to negotiate its annexation, but Chincha was not annexed until the time of

Topa Inca. He left Cuzco via Huaytara. The people of Nazca were assembled to do battle with him, but peace was negotiated. The same happened in Ica. The same happened in Chincha, according to the Incas and the people of Chincha, but others say there were great battles. The Guarco story.

Chap. 61. *Topa Inca* [14–16?] *decided to campaign in Collasuyo*, leaving Huayna Capac as governor of Cuzco. He arrived in Chucuito, where the locals greated him with fiestas and offered to go with him. At this time, he visited Titicaca.

[17–18] *Afterward he sent messengers to Charcas, Carangues, and others. Some of them submitted peacefully, and others resisted. In Paria and elsewhere he built buildings.*

[19] *From Charcas he traveled onward to Chile, where he conquered those lands. He went as far as the Maule River. Then he returned to Cuzco.*

[14–16?] *After a number of years he decided to campaign in Collasuyo.* With a large army he entered the province of Chucuito, where they received him solemnly. He thanked them for their good will. Then he prepared to make the trip to the temple of Titicaca. There, he erected a palace and other buildings.

[17–18] *Then he went on to Tiahuanaco, from which he launched a military campaign against the Carangas, Paria, Cochabamba, and Amparaes.*

[21] *Many fled and fortified themselves at Oroncota. Topa Inca conquered this fortress.*

[19] *Then he went south, opening roads through Lipes. He defeated those of Guasco and Coquimbo and other coastal valleys to the Mapocho, where many Chilenos and some Arau-*

*canos had gathered. There was a bloody battle, but the Inca was victorious. The Araucanos fled. There was a pitched battle at an* angostura *that the Incas won. The Incas wanted to conquer on the other side of the Maule River, but they were unable to. The Araucanos were allied with their neighbors from Tucapel and Puren.*

[11?] To find out about the east, he sent out people disguised as merchants. He then campaigned there, conquering some peoples and ordering the planting of coca fields. Upon returning to Cuzco, he died.

Chap. 38. Topa Inca built Chinchero.

The Guayro story.

Chap. 39. Topa Inca named Huayna Capac to succeed him and died.

The Yanayaco story.

Cieza clearly includes more detail about military campaigns than either Cobo or Betanzos. Betanzos includes less, and if Betanzos mentions a campaign, the others do, too. What is particularly noteworthy about Betanzos, and what does not show up in the paraphrasing of accounts, are details that would seem to express an Inca interest in ritual rather than in military engagement itself. For example, Betanzos pays particular attention to the marching formation of Inca armies, describing their marches in terms that refer to a very different system of orientation.

In his account of Topa Inca, this interest is manifest in Betanzos's description of troop formation on Topa Inca's march from Collasuyo back to Cuzco, but to analyze it we need to look first at other material in his narrative. At one point in Betanzos's narrative of the life of Pachacuti he notes the division of

Inca armies. After the defeat of Soras, while Pachacuti is still there, he sends an army to campaign in Andesuyo and another to campaign in Condesuyo (Betanzos [1551–1557], pt. 1, chap. 18; 1987:90–91). He will return to Cuzco with the Soras captives, elaborately dressed and ornamented. The captains rejoin Pachacuti before he arrives in Cuzco, and the armies return together. From what we know of the boundaries of the *suyos*, if Pachacuti sent captains out from Soras, they would have to travel some distance before they entered either territory (Julien 1991: map 1; Pärssinen 1992: map 15, p. 242). However, Betanzos refers to Condesuyo and Andesuyo elsewhere in his narrative in a way that suggests that they could be defined with reference to another center besides Cuzco.

At the beginning of Betanzos's narrative, he describes the course traced by Contiti Viracocha and his assistants through the Andes. From Tiahuanaco, and with their backs toward the place where the sun rose, one assistant traveled to Condesuyo, "on the left hand" of Contiti Viracocha; the other traveled to Andesuyo "on the right hand." Contiti Viracocha followed a middle course (Betanzos [1551–1557], pt. 1, chap. 2; 1987:13). Unless Tiahuanaco is taken as the reference point in this system of orientation, what Betanzos describes makes no sense.

Another system of orientation that makes reference both to the human body and to the *suyo* division is found in Guaman Poma. Where he draws his map of the world, he describes the *suyos* in these terms:

> You should know that the whole kingdom had four kings, four parts: Chinchasuyo, on the right hand [when facing] the sunset; above to the mountains toward the North Sea, Andesuyo; [with one's back to] the sunrise, on the left hand toward Chile, Collasuyo; toward the South Sea, Condesuyo. These four parts were divided again in two: Incas of Hanan Cuzco [when facing] west, Chinchasuyo [on the right hand]; Lurin Cuzco [with one's back to the] east, Collasuyo, on the left hand. And so the head and court of the kingdom, the great city of Cuzco, falls in the middle.

> As de sauer que todo el rreyno tenía quatro rreys, quatro partes: Chinchay Suyo a la mano derecha al poniente del sol; arriua a la montaña hacia la mar del Norte Ande Suyo; da donde naze el sol a la mano esquierda hacia Chile Colla Suyo; hacia la mar de Sur Conde Suyo. Estos dichos quatro partes tornó a partir a dos partes: Yngas Hanan Cuzco al poniente Chin-

chay Suyo [a la mano derecha], Lurin Cuzco al saliente del sol, Collasuyo
a la mano esquierda. Y ací cae en medio la cauesa y corte del rreyno, la
gran ciudad del Cuzco. (Guaman Poma 1987 [1615]: 982 [1000])

Although Guaman Poma's description is not without certain ambiguities, it
can be interpreted. The axis of the system is the path of the sun. Guaman Poma
refers to the sunrise and sunset, which he can translate easily into east and west.
From this axis and with one's back to the sunrise, the *suyos* and the Hanan/
Hurin division can be defined as "on the right hand" or "on the left hand."[2]

When Betanzos describes Contiti Viracocha's march, he uses Condesuyo
and Andesuyo as directional references. They are "on the left hand" and "on
the right hand" with reference to a center: either Tiahuanaco or Contiti Viracocha. When Pachacuti sends captains to Condesuyo and Andesuyo, they are
again directional references, and again the center is where Pachacuti is. Similar
terms are used to describe Topa Inca's armies on their march from Collasuyo
back to Cuzco. The army was divided into four parts. One returned to Cuzco
by way of the coast of Arequipa; another went via Carangas and Aullagas; a
third followed the "right hand" and traced a course through Casavindo and
Chichas. Directional references to Condesuyo and Andesuyo are not given,
but the bodily notation just mentioned indicates that one of the armies was
on Topa Inca's "right hand" and the others on his left. All of the parts met in
Hatuncolla for the return to Cuzco (Betanzos [1551–1557], pt. 1, chap. 36;
1987:164–165).

Our argument that Betanzos includes some material from a life history of
Topa Inca is not a strong one. There are no obvious motifs to mark the beginning and end of an account of Topa Inca. Still, similarities in what Betanzos
tells about Pachacuti and what he tells about Topa Inca indicate that life history material for Topa Inca may have survived. A study of the accounts of the
lives of Pachacuti and Topa Inca can only start us on the path of unraveling the
contents of an Inca life history genre.

THE CONTEXT OF LIFE HISTORY

Whereas the painted history appears to have been a unique record, kept at
a single location, the life history materials were not kept in a single place, nor
can we assume they were unique. The association between the remains of the
rulers and the "strings and accounts of their deeds" was noted above; at least
one version was held by the ruler's *panaca*. Betanzos drew from the life history

genre because he was close to *panaca* sources. When the remains of Inca rulers were collected in 1559, at least some of the materials — for example, the *quipos* related to Pachacuti — were taken by the Spaniards. These materials had been kept by individuals trained to read them, and this training was said to have been handed down from father to son. Just how this was done is still far from clear, but what concerns us here is the context of this genre. What purpose did it serve?

In this case we have some information about a performance tradition. The first Spaniards to arrive in Cuzco were witness to events during which songs with historical content were sung about the deeds of earlier Inca rulers. A narrative written by one of the Spaniards who arrived with Pizarro describes the victory celebration held after the defeat of the remains of Atahuallpa's armies near Cuzco. The deceased Incas, accompanied by retainers, were carried into the square in a procession. A victory song was sung in accompaniment. Once in the plaza an extended drinking bout began which lasted over a month. Part of this celebration involved songs that extolled the deeds of each Inca:

> The songs dealt with the conquests of each of those lords and of his good qualities and bravery, thanking the Sun, who had allowed them to see this day. And a priest rose up, admonishing the Inca on the part of the Sun that he look to what his forebears had done, and that he would do the same himself.

> En los cantares trataban de lo que cada uno de aquellos señores había conquistado y de las gracias y valor de su persona, dando gracias al Sol que les había dejado ver aquel día, y levantándose un sacerdote amonestaba de parte del Sol a Inga, como a su hijo, que mirase lo que sus pasados habían hecho y que así lo hiciese él.[3]

There were other occasions to perform songs that extolled the deeds of the Incas. Cieza de León noted that songs, or *cantares*, were performed at their principal celebrations, when their *taquis*, or drinking bouts, were held. Cieza is clearly describing a formally transmitted genre that was kept by the *panaca*. At the end of his description, he mentions that the Spaniards witnessed such an event when Manco Inca took the *borla*, or royal fringe ([1553], chap. 11; 1986:28–29). Accession was one time when the life history may have been performed. It was closely tied to male initiation, an event that occurred annually during Capac Raymi. The life history may have been associated with Capac Raymi itself. Toward the end of the succession of events that were part of initiation, the dead rulers were brought to the main plaza of Cuzco, and again a drinking bout was held. The young men were to ask the former rulers to make them as fortunate and valiant as the rulers had been (Molina [1576]; 1989:107–108). Another time when the performance of this historical genre may have occurred was following the death of a ruler. Cieza himself was present in Cuzco for the funeral, or *purucaya*, rite of Paullo Inca in 1550, although he does not mention the performance of *cantares* at this rite ([1553], chap. 32; 1986:98–99).[4]

Betanzos describes the performance of what may be the life history genre following the death of Pachacuti. The events associated with his life were related in public more than once. First, in the days immediately following his death, after the ritual cleansing of members of his lineage in a particular spring and the sacrifice of a number of his wives and servants, all of the nobles of Cuzco were to gather for public mourning during which would be recited "with voices raised, his famous exploits, both in remaking the city and in conquering and acquiring lands and provinces, as well as in governing and organizing the city and the rest of the territory" (Betanzos [1551–1557], pt. 1, chap. 30; 1987:142). Then, a year later, another public performance relating the events of his life was to be held in a month-long event in celebration and mourning of his death known as *purucaya*. Amidst an elaborate round of ceremonies and a reenactment of the wars that had taken place under his command, the nobles of Cuzco would again tell about the Inca's victories and grand deeds "with voices raised" (Betanzos [1551–1557], pt. 1, chap. 31; 1987:145). In the years after, when mummified remains of a ruler were taken out during public celebrations, songs were to be sung about "the things he did during his lifetime, both at war and in his city" (Betanzos [1551–1557], pt. 1, chap. 32; 1987:150).

Betanzos may have drawn from a life history account that was still in *panaca* hands, so we should give particular attention to what he said about the genre. Betanzos describes Pachacuti's composition of the accounts of earlier rulers in the period right after the death of his father, Viracocha. Betanzos clearly describes the composition of songs about individual Incas. First, Pachacuti organized a cult of sacrifice around each former ruler, endowing his *bulto* — either a representation of each ruler or his actual physical remains — with lands, animals, retainers, and women and naming a majordomo to take charge of these resources. Then he ordered the majordomos to compose *cantares*:

> And so he ordered that these majordomos — and each one individually —
> should compose songs which the women and retainers of each Inca would

sing, with the praise of the deeds of each one of these lords in their days; and so it was done, and ordinarily, every time there were fiestas, the servants [of the rulers] would sing them in order, those of Manco Capac beginning first with his *cantar* and praise; and so the women and servants would tell how the rulers had succeeded up to that time; and that would be the order they would follow from that time on so that they would preserve some memory of [the Inca rulers] and their past.

E ansimismo mando a estos mayordomos e a cada vno por si que luego hiziesen cantares los cuales cantasen estas mamaconas y yanaconas en los lores de [*sic*: en loor de] los hechos de cada vno destos señores en sus dias ansi hizo los quales cantares hordinariamente todo tiempo que fiestas vuiese cantasen cada seruiçio de aquellos por su horden y conçierto começando primero el tal cantar e ystoria e loa los de Mango Capac e que ansi fuesen deçindiendo los tales mamaconas e seruiçio como los señores auian suçedido hasta alli y que aquella fuese la horden que se tuuiesse desde alli adelante para que de aquella manera vuiesse memoria dellos y sus antiguedades. (Betanzos n.d. [1551–1557], pt. 1, chap. 17 f. 41; 1987:86)

Sarmiento tells a similar story, though he does not give specific details about who composed or performed the *cantares* ([1572], chap. 31; 1906:68–69).

We might test the written narratives that have survived to see if we can detect that such a composition occurred following the end of Huayna Capac's life, though that task would be a very complex undertaking. What is perhaps a more productive enterprise in this initial stage of exploration is to examine the accounts of the early Incas. Do the accounts themselves reflect a composition process like the one Betanzos relates?

# 5 Composition

Our ability to see a life history in Betanzos's narrative on Pachacuti is supported by the structural similarities between his account and Sarmiento's. Like Betanzos, Sarmiento goes into particular detail about the life of Pachacuti. A comparison of the two texts yields a rough image of the underlying source. The similarities between these two texts and the contrast between them and the other accounts that drew from Inca genres (tables 4.2–4.3) add further support to the hypothesis that their narratives incorporate this Inca source. Drawing out a life history of Topa Inca is a more difficult prospect, but it can and should be attempted. The length of Sarmiento's treatment of this Inca, even after the information about his conquests from the *quipo* source is removed, and the similarities between the motifs used by Betanzos to describe the campaigns of both Pachacuti and Topa Inca provoke a conclusion that there is life history material in both Spanish narratives. Now we turn to an examination of the narrative treatment of rulers before Pachacuti, a task that presents new obstacles to the identification of life history material.

So far we have made a distinction between Spanish historical narratives that were little more than genealogies and others that incorporated substantially more material: the "long accounts." We have hypothesized that the genealogical genre was what was painted on tablets kept privately by the dynastic line and that it included at least a genealogy of the direct descendants of Manco Capac and a mention of the *panacas* associated with each generation, possibly classified into Hanan and Hurin. Molina noted that the painted history also incorporated material on dynastic origins, on the life of each ruler, and on the lands he conquered. Since that is what the life history was also about to some extent, significant potential for overlap between the genealogical genre and the life history exists. The difference between the accounts of Pachacuti in Sarmiento/Betanzos and what we find in Cabello Valboa/Morúa (M2) may be a reflection of a reliance on the genealogical genre in the latter case and on the life history in the former. If, as Betanzos and Sarmiento both state, the accounts of the earlier Incas were composed during the time of Pachacuti, the potential for overlap is even greater. There may have been no really notable

difference in subject matter between the two genres. What if the major difference was that one was kept on *quipos* by the *panaca* and the other was painted
on tablets and kept by the ruler?

Moreover, there is no reason to assume that the genealogical genre was a
single narrative, temporally ordered. What if it was no more than a series of
lifetimes, presented sequentially? Life history materials would have presented
some obstacles to the construction of a seamless narrative of the Inca past, particularly when the lives of rulers overlapped. If both the painted history and
life history were structured around lifetimes, then there had been no seamless narrative of the Inca past until Spanish historical practice produced one.
What may have characterized the painted history was the sequencing of life
histories in a genealogical order, not the synchronization of events into a single
narrative.

Let us examine these questions with the circumstances surrounding the
composition of the accounts of the early rulers in mind. The life histories were
said to have been composed after the death of a ruler, except in the case of the
accounts of the rulers from Manco Capac to Yahuar Huacac. Both Betanzos
and Sarmiento tell us that Pachacuti organized a cult to the memory of the
earlier Incas. Betanzos locates this incident after the death of Viracocha Inca,
Pachacuti's father, while Sarmiento locates it before Viracocha's death. Sarmiento specifically notes that Pachacuti had the bodies of the first seven Incas,
from Manco Capac to Yahuar Huacac, "disinterred" and brought to Coricancha. They were adorned and placed on a bench, then a *purucaya* ceremony was
held for each one, and stories were composed about their lives. Pachacuti created a public cult to his forebears (Sarmiento de Gamboa [1572], chap. 30;
1906:68–69).

The invention of a cult to the Inca forebears is situated within the historical
narrative. Sarmiento's description of the painted history, however, was incorporated into his narrative in the chapter before he narrates Inca origins, that is,
as something set apart from the historical narrative itself ([1572], chap. 9;
1906:31). Here he specifically notes the hand of Pachacuti in the painting of
tablets that were kept in a large room in the "houses of the Sun."

Because Betanzos and Sarmiento tell us about Pachacuti's involvement in
the composition of material about earlier Incas, we can orient our analysis
with this knowledge in mind. In the historical narratives we examine, then,
there are at least two composition events involved. The most recent is the composition of a Spanish narrative from sources—oral and/or written—with material on the Inca past. If a written source underlies the text (as we have argued
in the case of Cabello Valboa and Morúa) then the composition process is

more complex. Each composition process should reflect a perspective on the past situated in that moment. Before we begin to read the historical narratives based on Inca sources (as we do in the next three chapters), we need to know something about the nature of the underlying sources they drew from and the history of composition of these sources. In this chapter our interest is in the account or accounts of the early Incas. Can we determine from their content that they were composed at a specific point in time and for specific dynastic purposes?

There are several other tasks related to this endeavor. The problem of sequencing and overlap between the narratives is something we can discuss more fully after examining the accounts of the early Inca rulers. One important concern is with the story of Inca origins. Can we detect where it ends and where the lifetime of Manco Capac begins? What if more than one story of origins is told? What story began the Inca genealogical genre? Another question, best addressed here, is whether the dates given by two of the narratives—Sarmiento and Cabello Valboa—for the lifespans of particular Incas are their own invention or have some basis in local knowledge. Also, Betanzos and Sarmiento tell us that Pachacuti composed the life histories of earlier rulers, but Betanzos places this event after the death of Viracocha Inca, while Sarmiento puts it before. Was there a history of Viracocha Inca that was composed as a separate event from the composition event that produced the accounts of the first seven rulers?

To answer some of these questions it is important to know something about the lost historical narrative of Cristóbal de Molina. Although we appear to digress at this point to compare the accounts of Miguel Cabello Valboa and Martín de Morúa, we need to know about Molina's account, particularly if, as we suspect, it may have drawn largely from a genealogical genre.

## CABELLO VALBOA AND MORÚA

Molina's text is important to us. He collected his material in Cuzco at approximately the same time as Sarmiento. Cabello Valboa said he took his material from Molina, and we have already seen that, in the event structure of the life of Pachacuti, there are structural similarities between Cabello Valboa's narrative and one of the Morúa accounts (M2) (tables 4.1–4.3). But how similar are they?

The stories Cabello Valboa and Morúa tell about Inca origins are very similar. One notable difference is that Morúa introduces a chapter heading where the story appears to shift from origins to the life of Manco Capac, although he does not give it a number. The lack of coincidence between chapter headings supplied by the two authors indicates that chapter structure was not borrowed from an underlying text. Molina, then, appears not to have used one. In the following comparison, the texts are paraphrased. Spellings have been Hispanicized, but different renderings of what may be the same place-name have been preserved.

Other differences are relatively minor: Morúa tells us that Ayar Auca was sent back to Pacaritambo from a place called Chasquito and calls the cups he was sent to fetch *topacusi*; both authors give wildly divergent spellings of Tamboquiro; Cabello Valboa names the rite in which the Incas received ear spools (*tocochicui*); and Morúa puts an additional entry on his list of rites (*raimis*). Perhaps the most striking difference is that Morúa incorporates direct speech into his text (Niles 1999 : 32 – 37). Direct speech is sometimes incorporated in other accounts, and Titu Cusi makes it a functional part of his narrative (1988), so it is not beyond possibility that direct speech was used in the Molina text.

The event which signals the beginning of Manco Capac's story in Morúa — marked by the insertion of an unnumbered chapter heading — is the founding of Cuzco. Immediately after that heading, the narrative backtracks to Matagua to tell about Mama Huaco and the golden rods and about the initiation of Sinchi Roca (see below). This sequencing parallels what is found in Cobo. Cobo begins his story of Manco Capac with the founding of Cuzco but then returns to Matagua to talk about the initiation of Sinchi Roca (see the comparison of Cobo and Cabello Valboa later in this chapter). If we can mark the point where the origin story ends and the account of Manco Capac proper begins, it is here.

| *Cabello Valboa* | *Morúa* |
|---|---|
| Chap. 9. The Ayar siblings leave Pacaritambo or Tambotoco. | Chap. 2. The Ayar siblings leave Pacaritambo at night. |
| They arrive at Pachete but don't like it. | They arrive at Pachete but don't like it. |
| They go on to Huaman Cancha, where Mama Ocllo gets pregnant. | They go on to Huayna Cancha, where Mama Ocllo gets pregnant. Some say it was Mama Huaco. |
| Then they go to Tambo Oir [Tamboquiro], where Sinchi Roca is born. | Then they go to Tambuqui [Tamboquiro], where Sinchi Roca is born. |
| Ayar Auca was disgusted and could not disguise his hatred. He was sent back to | Then they went on to Chasquito. From there, Ayar Auca was sent back to Pacari- |

Tambotoco for some golden cups and some seed with a servant named Tambo Chacay. The latter walled him up inside the cave.

Ayar Auca was troublesome because he was able to create landslides by throwing rocks.

They get to Huanacauri and see a rainbow, which they interpret as a sign that the world would not be destroyed by flood.

Near the top they see a certain wizard from Saño making sacrifices to a *huaca* called [Chimboycagua]. They send Ayar Cache to capture him. He turns Ayar Cache to stone. Ayar Cache tells them to sacrifice to him when they perform *huarachico*.

They go to the foot of the hill to a place called Matagua. Here is where Sinchi Roca is initiated and given ear spools. He was the first to be initiated in the ceremony of *tocochicui*. The name of Ayar Cache was invoked many times. A reference to "father Sun."

This is also the origin of Inca mourning and other rites (*quicochico, guarachico, rutuchico,* and *auyscay,* which is to celebrate a birth with drinking and dancing for four days).

tambo to get some golden cups, called *topacusi*. He did not want to go, but Mama Huaco talked him into it. A servant, Tambo Chacai, went with him and sealed him into the cave with a large boulder. [Direct speech incorporated in the story.] Tambo Chacay remained outside the cave, turned to stone.

Ayar Auca was troublesome because he would throw stones and bring down mountains.

They get to Huanacauri and see a rainbow, which they interpret as a sign that the world would not be destroyed by flood.

From a distance they see a *huaca* in the shape of a seated person at which the rainbow ended. This was the *huaca* of Saño, about 5 km from there, called Chimpo y Cahua. They decided to take it. Ayar Cachi addresses it and climbs on it. He turns to stone. He tells them to sacrifice to them when they perform *huarachico*. [Direct speech incorporated.] They go to the foot of the hill to a place called Matagua. Here is where Sinchi Roca is initiated and given ear spools.

This is also the origin of Inca mourning and other rites (*raimis, quicochico, huarachico, rutuchico,* and *ayuscai*).

Chapter heading, no chapter number. Manco Capac history begins. Manco Capac creates Cuzco in what had been open fields before. He divides it into two districts, making Sinchi Roca

head of one of them. He distributed the
rest among his descendants and gave out
many orders.
[Here follow two plates showing Manco
Capac and Sinchi Roca.]

The event structure in Cabello Valboa and Morúa through the life of Manco
Capac is virtually the same, with the exception of material that Cabello Valboa
repeats and the founding of Cuzco. Cabello Valboa describes the organization
of Cuzco just after the settlement of the remaining Ayar siblings at Coricancha. He incorporates exactly the same information about the four neighborhoods of Cuzco as Sarmiento, though this material is missing from Morúa.
Again, Morúa incorporates direct speech at one point in the text.

A major difference between Morúa and Cabello Valboa is Morúa's development of separate chapters for the Coyas and the provision of two different
names for each one, one of which is the name provided by Cabello Valboa and,
hence, may derive from Molina. Morúa's manuscript also includes full-length
portraits of each Inca and Coya to accompany the text. The effort to present
visual material as accompaniment to the narrative may be an attempt to restore
aspects of the genealogical genre. Guaman Poma, whose text and Morúa's
exhibit certain dependencies, are alike in their inclusion of portraits and separate accounts for Incas and Coyas (Guaman Poma [1615] 1987). As noted in
chapter 3, what they say about the Coyas is unique to their accounts, and
Morúa used material from a source on ancient Mexico in his (Rowe 1987).
Both authors wrote in the late sixteenth to early seventeenth century. Although this format may well have been developed with the earlier genre in
mind, what we have been able to learn about the earlier genre suggests that the
development of a visual history at the end of the century would have been a
substantial innovation.

| *Cabello Valboa* | *Morúa* |
|---|---|
| Chap. 10. They occupied some aban-<br>doned houses [in Matagua]. The town<br>was a marketplace. They got all dressed<br>up and tried to convince the people there<br>that they had come from the heavens and<br>that they were sons of the Sun. People<br>were impressed.<br>[Then he retells some of what he has al-<br>ready told with some different details.] | |

Mama Ocllo becomes pregnant. Ayar Auca is sent back to Tambotoco to retrieve cups, etc., Tambo Chacay walls him up, etc. The story is circulated that Mama Ocllo is bearing a child of the Sun. Sinchi Roca is born.

Ayar Cache is killed by a sorcerer with poison. A new manner of mourning is invented. They spend twenty years in Matagua.

Neither Ayar Ucho nor Mama Ragua left descendants.

Then the story about Mama Huaco and the two golden rods is told. One lands in Colcabamba and the other in Huanaipata, a place near the gateway on the road that goes to San Sebastián.

Chap. 3. They are in Matagua. The story about Mama Huaco and the two golden rods is told. One lands in Colcabamba and the other in Huanaipata, a place near the gateway on the road that goes to San Sebastian.

Sinchi Roca is initiated. At three years of age they perform *tocochicui*, which is when they pierce the ears. At four they perform *rutuchicuy*, which is when they cut the hair. At fifteen they perform *huarachicui*, which is when a boy wears a breechcloth.

Sinchi Roca is initiated.

Sinchi Roca is old enough for a wife. She is Mama Coca, only daughter of Sutic Huaman, the lord of Saño. They have Manco Sapaca in Matagua.

Sinchi Roca engenders Manco Sapaca in Mama Coca, daughter of "su tía Huaman" [Sutic Huaman], lord of Saño.

Then they move on to Colcabamba. They test the land there.

Then they move on to Colcabamba, where the first golden rod had fallen. They test the land there and find it not good for planting.

They go on to Huamantianca.

They go on to Huamantianca and Huanaypata, where the second rod fell. The soil is better and they plant. They found Cuzco, called Acamama, here. The people in this place are Lares, Poques, and Huallas.

In this place Mama Huaco kills one of the Huayllas with a knife and removes

Then they killed some of them and blew into their lungs. With bloody mouths,

his lungs and entrails, anointing the others with his blood.

Copalimayta, the natural lord of Cuzco, gathered as large a group as possible and came out to meet them.
The Incas defended themselves at a small arroyo and had to retreat to Huanaypata, where they remained until after harvest.
The harvest was good, and they went back on the attack. They won and took Copalimayta captive.
He turned over his family and possessions to Mama Huaco and departed.

The Incas settled at Coricancha, where Santo Domingo is now. They built a temple dedicated to the Sun.
They established four neighborhoods, calling them Quinti Cancha, Chumbi Cancha, Aranbui Cancha, and Sayri Cancha. Manco Capac founds Cuzco in Chumbi Cancha.

Age at death, length of rule, calendar year of death.

they went to attack the Huallas. The Huallas fled, thinking they were cannibals.
Copalimayta, the lord of Cuzco, went out to meet them.

The Incas returned to Huanaypata, where they remained until after the harvest.
The harvest was good, and they went back on the attack. They won and took Copalimayta captive. He turned over his lands and possessions to Mama Huaco and departed. [Direct speech incorporated.]
The Incas settled at Coricancha, where Santo Domingo is now. They built a temple of the Sun.
Manco Capac dies, leaving Sinchi Roca as his successor.
Mentions again that Mama Huaco is his mother.
They also have a daughter, Chimpo Ocllo, and a bastard son, Pachacuti.

Chap. 4. Mama Huaco's history begins. [Nothing in it is in Cabello Valboa.] [Reference to a plate showing this Coya.]

Neither author had much to say about Sinchi Roca. Morúa reiterates the names of Sinchi Roca's parents and notes that this Inca was interested in warfare and expansion. Sarmiento often begins his accounts of particular Incas this way (see the comparison later in the chapter). The material included in Cabello Valboa about insignia (here) and ritual (in later lives) does not appear in Morúa, indicating to us that this digression may have been an innovation by Cabello Valboa.

Both Cabello Valboa and Morúa noted that Sinchi Roca produced a son named Manco Sapaca with the daughter of the lord of Saño. Morúa tells us that the next ruler, Lloque Yupanqui, was the son of Sinchi Roca and a sister named Chimpo Coya. From this point onward, Morúa consistently adopts a theory of sister-marriage. In the account of each ruler, he names a sister who becomes Coya in the next generation. Cabello Valboa does not identify the mother of Lloque Yupanqui.

| Cabello Valboa | Morúa |
|---|---|
| Chap. 11. Sinchi Roca history begins. | Chap. 5. Sinchi Roca history begins. Mentions that Manco Capac and Mama Huaco are his parents. He was valiant and inclined to go to war. He was the first to order the Incas to pierce their ears. |
| Sinchi Roca and Mama Coca have Manco Sapaca. | Sinchi Roca and Chimpo Coya, his sister, have Lloque Yupanqui. [Reference to a plate showing this Inca.] |
| He was the first to use the *borla* called Masca Paycha, the Suntur Paucar, and the Capac Ongo, Tarco Gualca. Mentions Lloque Yupanqui. Age at death, calendar year of death. | Chap. 6. Chimpo Coya history begins. [Nothing in it is in Cabello Valboa.] [Reference to a plate showing this Coya.] |

The accounts are closely parallel except for Morúa's naming of a different Coya and inclusion of a chapter on her.

| Cabello Valboa | Morúa |
|---|---|
| Lloque Yupanqui history begins. | Chap. 7. Lloque Yupanqui history begins. Mentions again he is son of Sinchi Roca and Chimpo Coya. He marries Mama Cora, by another name, Mama Anahuarque, his sister. |
| Chap. 12. Many lords come to serve Lloque Yupanqui, the first and most important being Guaman Samo (of Guaro), Pachachulla Viracocha, the Ayarcamas, Tambo Vincais, and Quiliscochas. | Many lords come to serve Lloque Yupanqui, such as Huamac Samo, Pachachulla Viracocha, and the Ayarmacas and the Quilescaches. |
| He had fathered no children. The Sun appeared to him in human form to console him, saying that he would be a great | One day, the Sun appeared to him in human form and told him he would be a great lord and would yet father a son. |

lord and would father a son. Manco Sapaca had told Pachachulla Viracocha of this business, who took it to hand and found Lloque Yupanqui a wife.

He marries Mama Cahua in an elaborate ceremony.

A servant or a bastard brother named Manco Capaca took him to where the Coya was one day and made him have intercourse with her. She got pregnant, and the child that was born was Mayta Capac.
Certain practices originated with him. [Reference to a plate showing this Inca.]

Chap. 8. Mama Cora history begins. [Nothing in it is in Cabello Valboa.] [Reference to a plate showing this Coya.]

Morúa ends the history of Lloque Yupanqui and tells the story of Mayta Capac's deeds as a boy in the next chapter, when the subject is Mayta Capac. Cabello Valboa places this material in the lifetime of Lloque Yupanqui. Except for this, the stories are closely parallel. Morúa includes a second Alcabiza attack on Coricancha, bringing the total number of encounters to three. The last encounter is away from Coricancha and involves supernatural intervention, as in the final encounter described in Cabello Valboa. Morúa adds the invention of a victory celebration that he calls *huarichico*. The royal insignia are also a topic, one that Cabello Valboa includes in his discussion of Sinchi Roca and returns to when the subject is Capac Yupanqui.

*Cabello Valboa*
[Here, Cabello Valboa tells about Mayta Capac as a boy, although he has not ended the history of Lloque Yupanqui.]

As a boy Mayta Capac fought with other boys, injuring them and even killing some. He fought with the sons of some Alcabizas [Allcayvillas] and Culunchima [Culluim Chima] lords, and they came to hate the Incas.
They decided secretly to kill Lloque Yupanqui and his son, choosing ten men to

*Morúa*
Chap. 9. Maita Capac history begins. Mentions again that Mamacora is his mother.
Describes his appearance and disposition.
As a boy Maita Capac fought with other boys from Cuzco, called Alcabizas [Alcayvisas] and Culunchima [Cullumchima], killing some.
The Alcabizas came to hate the Incas.

They decided secretly to kill Lloque Yupanqui and his son, choosing ten men ambush them at Coricancha. Mayta Capac was there with his cousins Apoc Conde Mayta and Taca Chungay playing with a certain kind of bolas called Cuchu, accompanied by two dogs. Mayta Capac could tell that the men who had entered meant harm, and with one bola he killed two of them. Lloque Yupanqui, Mayta Capac, and others pursued the other eight, killing all but three.

to ambush them at Coricancha. Maita Capac was there with other boys, playing with a certain kind of bolas called Cuchu.

Since he saw them come in with arms, with one bola, he killed two of them. Those who were with him went to tell Lloque Yupanqui, who came out with others and dogs and pursued them, killing five. The others escaped to tell it to Culunchima and Alcabizas, their caciques. [Oration incorporated.]

The Alcavizas gathered a large number of people. Lloque Yupanqui was upset about the trouble his son caused, but the elders and religious specialists of the Incas told him not to be, and Mayta Capac was allowed to lead them out to battle. The Incas managed to chase the Alcabizas back to their enclosures.

They got help from their neighbors. Lloque Yupanqui was upset about the trouble and called his son in to see him. [Oration incorporated.] His captains told him to leave the boy alone. Maita Capac, seeing that the Alcabizas were coming to attack, led them out to battle and won.

The Alcabizas returned and entered Coricancha on three sides. Maita Capac and only a few others went out the door to fight them and won.

He invented *huarichico*, which is a victory celebration.

A second battle was fought. When they were fighting, a black cloud came and separated them, keeping the Incas from defeating them.

The Alcabizas attacked a third time. He went out to meet them. This time it hailed, and that is what defeated them.

A lot of peoples, learning of this victory, swore obedience to the Incas.

Describes Inca insignia.

He was married to Chimpo Urma, first cousin.

Length of rule, calendar year of death of Lloque Yupanqui.

The stories about Mayta Capac's youth told, neither author has much to say about his adulthood. Cabello Valboa digresses to talk about religious specialists.

*Cabello Valboa*
Mayta Capac history begins.
Mayta Capac marries Mama Coca
Taucaraz.
Mentions Capac Yupanqui (successor)
and Tarco Huaman.

*Morúa*

Mentions Capac Yupanqui (successor)
and Faico Huaman [Tarco Huaman] and
a daughter, Chimpo Ocllo.
[Reference to a plate showing this Inca.]

A long description of different kinds of
religious specialists which have their
origin at about this time.
Length of rule, calendar year of death (at
beginning of chap. 13).
Mentions Capac Yupanqui.

Chap. 10. Chimpo Urma, also called
Mama Yacche, history begins.
[Nothing in it is in Cabello Valboa.]
[Reference to a plate showing this
Coya.]

Again, there appears to be little to say about the ruler. Cabello Valboa describes the royal insignia, and Morúa introduces a theological debate. The only
event worthy of mention is some kind of military action in Andesuyo.

*Cabello Valboa*
Chap. 13. Capac Yupanqui history
begins.

Describes the royal insignia (Topa Yauri,
Tarco Gualca, Marca Pacha, Suntur Paucar).
Capac Yupanqui marries Curi Hilpay.
Mentions Inca Roca (successor) and Apo
Mayta.
When his sons are old enough to campaign, they campaign against the Cuyos,
who, because they lived in the mountainous Andes, imagined themselves to be
free of Inca rule. Capac Yupanqui was
offended and armed himself and his sons

*Morúa*
Chap. 11. Capac Yupanqui history
begins.
He is valiant and bellicose.

He conquered the Cuyos [Suyos], which
is the province of Andesuyo.

and brought them back to obedience.
Their neighbors and confederates also
submitted.

He makes sophisticated arguments about
how the Sun cannot be the Creator because a cloud can cover it. He sends
envoys to Pachacamac.
[Oration incorporated.]
A miracle occurred at Cacha in Canas
and Canchis at this time.
Marries a sister named Cusi Chimpo
who kills him with poison. She is the
mother of Inca Roca.
[Reference to a plate of this Inca.]

Age at death, calendar year of death.

Chap. 12. Chimpo Ocllo (also called
Mama Cahua) history begins.
[Nothing in it is in Cabello Valboa.]
[Reference to a plate showing this
Coya.]

When Inca Roca is the topic, Cabello Valboa and Morúa include fairly similar information about efforts to expand the authority of Cuzco but sequence
it differently. Cabello Valboa puts marriage at the beginning of the account;
Morúa, at the end. Both describe building the canals of Hananchaca and
Hurinchaca, but for Cabello Valboa, a campaign against Wimpilla, Quisalla,
and Caytomarca is mentioned first; for Morúa, the campaign is sequenced
afterward. Wimpilla and Quisalla are both places in the Cuzco Valley on the
south side of the Huatanay River after the confluence with the Tullumayo.
Caytomarca, according to Sarmiento, is 20 km away.

There are other differences between the two authors. Morúa includes information about making a series of statues of the Incas. This topic is connected
to the division of Cuzco into Hanan and Hurin, since Morúa specifies which
Incas were Hanan and which Hurin. Cobo and several of the "short accounts"
also clarify which Incas were Hanan and which Hurin. The insertion of the
topic here may have some tie to the genealogical genre. Morúa also describes
a battle at Ocongate, a place to the east of Cuzco, that no one else mentions.
He also asserts that Inca Roca died of a poisoned arrow wound. Cabello Valboa introduces a unique account of a problem in the Mascas territory, south

of Cuzco. Cabello Valboa inserts the story about the young Yahuar Huacac at about midpoint in his account of Inca Roca. Morúa puts it early in his account of Yahuar Huacac.

| *Cabello Valboa* | *Morúa* |
|---|---|
| Inca Roca history begins. | Chap. 13. Inca Roca history begins. |
| A group of families called Mascas had exempted themselves [from the Inca confederation]. Inca Roca's brother Apo Mayta wanted to campaign against them and asked for permission. He made war against them, saying how, when they had been remiss and late in their confederation with the Incas, they had been badly advised. He defeated them, capturing their captain, Guari Guaca. He marries Mama Nicaz [Micay], daughter of the lord of Guayllacan. | |
| Mentions Yahuar Huacac (successor) and Vica Quirao (Veca Quiroa). | |
| His son Vica Quirao conquers Moyna and its surrounding area, capturing its lords, Moynapongo and Guamantopa. | |
| When Yahuar Huacac was very young, some lords from Andesuyo tried to steal him from his cradle. When they got him to their land, he cried tears of blood. After a divination ceremony, they returned him to the place they had taken him from. | |
| The sons of Inca Roca win more lands in the area, including Wimpilla [Bimbilla], Quisalla, and Caytomarca. | |
| Inca Roca built the canals called Hananchaca and Hurinchaca. | Inca Roca discovers the waters of Hurinchaca and Hananchaca. |
| Inca Roca divided Cuzco into Hanan Cuzco and Hurin Cuzco. | He also divided Cuzco into Hanan Cuzco and Hurin Cuzco. |
| | He was generous and magnificent and ordered that drinking parties be held in public. |

He also had a number of statues made of the Incas. When they were found, the first was the statue of Inca Roca, head of Hanan Cuzco. The others, in order, were Yahuar Huacac, Viracocha Inca, Topa Inca Yupanqui, Huayna Capac, Huascar Inca, and Manco Inca.

The statue was feared, and when it was addressed, the speaker looked at the ground. [There follows a description of how they spoke to the statue and how it responded.]

He conquers Wimpilla [Pimpila] and Quisalla, near Cuzco, and Caytomarca. He marries Cusi Chimpo. They have Yahuar Huacac (successor), Paucar Hinga, Hamantassi, Incas; Vica Quirao, Inca; Cacachicha Vica Quirao, and Apo Maita, and a daughter named Ypa Huaco, by another name, Mama Chiqui. After a battle with people near Cuzco who were fortified at Ocongate, he was injured by an arrow. An herbalist from Hualla cured him, but he died several days later of a fever.

Age at death, calendar year of death.

[Reference to a plate showing this Inca.]

Chap. 14. Cusi Chimpo, also called Mama Micay, history begins.
[Nothing in it is in Cabello Valboa.]
[Reference to a plate showing this Coya.]

Shorn of the story of his youth, the accounts include little about Yahuar Huacac. Cabello Valboa indicates a proclivity for sexual experimentation, something that is not even remotely a topic in the other accounts for any Inca. Morúa includes some unusual information about three children this Inca had with a non-Inca woman. He also talks about taking the *huacas* of conquered people hostage. Since there are no references to any conquests whatever during the time of Yahuar Huacac, this comment seems out of place.

| *Cabello Valboa* | *Morúa* |
|---|---|
| Yahuar Huacac history begins. | Chap. 15. Yahuar Huacac history begins. |
| His rule is brief, and there is not much to say. | As a boy, he had a sickness of the blood, and it came out his nose. |
| | Some say that his enemies stole him when he was a boy and took him to Vilcabamba, where they wanted to kill him. He cried tears of blood. He had three children with a *yunga* woman. |
| | When he conquered a people, he took their *huaca* hostage so they would not rebel. The people also had to contribute people and wealth for sacrifice. |
| Yahuar Huacac marries Mama Chiquia. | He married Ypa Huaco, also called Mama Chiquia. |
| Mentions Viracocha Inca. | Mentions son, Viracocha Inca, and a daughter, Mama Yunto Coya. [Reference to a plate showing this Inca.] |
| He was given to venereal delights, which shortened his life by a number of years. | |
| | Chap. 16. Ipa Huaco Coya, also called Mama Chiquia, history begins. [Nothing in it is in Cabello Valboa.] [Reference to a plate showing this Coya.] |

Morúa names Inca Urco as the second son of Viracocha Inca and Mama Rondocaya, born after Pachacuti. Pachacuti is also the eldest in Cabello Valboa's account. Neither one agrees with Sarmiento that Inca Urco and another son were born to a different woman ([1572], chap. 24; 1906:57). Morúa also notes that "some say" that Viracocha Inca never married and that a brother, Inca Yupanqui, succeeded.

| *Cabello Valboa* | *Morúa* |
|---|---|
| Chap. 14. Viracocha Inca history begins. Mentions again that Mama Chiquia is his mother. | Chap. 17. Viracocha Inca history begins. He is valiant and full of energy; some say he is bearded. |
| Some say the name Viracocha means "sea foam," but *vira* means lard and foam is called *puczu*, so they are wrong. | He conquers many towns and disappears. |

Viracocha Inca marries Mama Rondo-caya of Canto [*sic*: Anta].

Mentions Inca Yupanqui (successor). In the following story about campaigns at Caytomarca and Calca, he mentions sons Topa Huari and Inca Urco.

Viracocha Inca conquers Caytomarca and Calca [Callca]; he conquers Tocay Capac and Suayparmaca [Guaypar-marca]. He also brings Maras [Mallas] and Mollaca [Mullucan] to obedience, although some say that these victories were won by Topa Guarachiri and Ynga Urco, accompanied by their uncles Inca Sucsu and Inca Roca.

Viracocha Inca names Ynga Urco to succeed him, although by rights it should have been the oldest brother, Ynga Yupanqui.

At this time the Chancas had attacked some Cuzco people who were working lands that belonged to the Incas and the Sun. Viracocha Inca names Ynga Yupanqui as general. He campaigns against people who had been exempt, including Pinao Capac, Cuyo Capac Chaguar Chuchuca, and others of lesser name. Then they approached the Chancas, who had fortified themselves in the lands of Quiachilli (to the rear of Ayavira). The Incas beat them, and the Chancas retreated to Ychubamba (to the rear of

Viracocha Inca marries Mama Yunto Coya and has five sons: Pachacuti Inca Yupanqui, also called Inca Yupanqui, Urcu Inca, Inca Mayta, Coropanqui, and Capac Yupanqui.

Some say he never married, and after his death, a brother named Inca Yupanqui succeeded.

He was given to witchcraft and had an infinity of sorcerers and diviners dedicated to the cult to the *huacas*; they wore their hair long and, by order of the Inca, wore a long white shirt with a mantle knotted at the shoulder. [More about them.]

Viracocha Inca conquers Marca Piña, Ocapa, and Caquiamarca in Calca; he conquers Tocay Capac and Huaypor-marca, Maras and Mollaca [Mullaca], although some say that these victories were won by Inca Urco, his son. [Reference to a plate showing this Inca.]

Xacxaguana), where they regrouped. The
Incas reinforced their army, and the
Chancas fled in shame back to Anda-
guayllas. Their captains, Tomayguaraca
and Astoguaraca, had been taken captive
by Ynga Yupanqui, who made cups out
of their heads.
The Ulti story.
Pachacuti conquers the Urubamba Valley
and puts the *borla* on his own head.
Pachacuti plots the murder of his brother
Inca Urco in a town called Canche.
Viracocha Inca dies of sadness.
Length of rule, calendar year of death.

Chap. 18. Mama Yunto Coya history
begins.
[Nothing in it is in Cabello Valboa.]
[Reference to a plate showing this Coya.]
Chap. 19. Pachacuti history begins. He
was married to Mama Anahuarqui.
He conquered the Cuzco area and the
Cuyos, destroying all of them. That
province of Cuyo Capac Chahuar Chuchuca was very large. The lords were
Cuyo Capac, Yanqui Lalama, and Pu-
canataqui. They gave him a wife.
The Ulti story.
Pachacuti conquers the Urubamba Valley
down to Vitcos and Vilcabamba.
Then the Chancas come to attack Cuzco,
as they had in the time of his father.
Pachacuti fought them in two battles,
one at Quialtichi, behind Yavira, and the
other at Sichupampa (behind Sacsa-
huana). The Incas were successful and
took Jumay Huaraca and Asto Huaraca
captive. Drinking cups were made from
their heads.
Pachacuti plots the murder of his brother
Ynga Urco at Cache. Viracocha Inca dies
of sadness.

We have seen sequencing problems before in our comparison of these two historical narratives, but the problem is much more pronounced when the topic is Viracocha Inca. The information they give about campaigns in Calca and against Tocay Capac seem similar, although different place-names appear in their coverage of these events. That Inca Urco participated in these campaigns is mentioned by both; what is different is the sequencing of campaigns against the Cuyos and the Chancas. Cabello Valboa puts both campaigns after the naming of Inca Urco as Viracocha Inca's successor. Then he tells the Ulti story. Finally, he describes Pachacuti's usurpation of his father's authority and the murder of his brother, followed by the death of Viracocha Inca. Morúa locates all of these events early in the rule of Pachacuti, and he sequences the Ulti story between a campaign in Cuyos and the battles with the Chancas. The events which follow—the murder of Inca Urco and the death of Viracocha Inca—are given in the same order as by Cabello Valboa.

What do these differences tell us about an underlying text? In our comparison of the events of the life of Pachacuti, clear similarities between the structuring of Morúa and Cabello Valboa indicate a common, underlying text (see tables 4.1–4.3). Both Morúa and Cabello Valboa register the conquests of Topa Inca in a similar way, and we can assume that the underlying text drew from a source like the *quipo* that was read into the *Memorial*. When we examine their accounts of the earlier rulers, the most noteworthy difference between them is in the sequencing of certain events. For example, stories about the childhood of Mayta Capac and Yahuar Huacac are sequenced during the life of their fathers in Cabello Valboa and at the beginning of the accounts of these rulers in Morúa. We have already examined differences in how the Ulti story was sequenced. Since both authors appear to have imposed their own chapter structure on what they wrote, some of the sequencing differences may simply be due to their choice of where to end a chapter. The construction of a single narrative from a series of life histories, choosing how to deal with events that occurred before the death of an Inca but that were part of a life history of the son, may have been features of Molina. In one instance—the place where the story of origins ended and the story of Manco Capac proper began—the narrative backtracks, indicating that no effort was made to impose a chronological order on the underlying material. Both authors incorporate information about Inca insignia and rites, but not in a consistent way. Cabello Valboa, especially, seems to elaborate on a subject matter that was present in an underlying account but not treated with the same amount of detail.

We now have a guide to what the historical account of Molina was like. Cabello Valboa and Morúa are so like each other and so different from either

Sarmiento or Cobo that we can use them to give us a rough idea of how Molina would have differed from Sarmiento and Cobo.

## SARMIENTO, CABELLO VALBOA, AND COBO

We will compare the material on earlier rulers from the accounts of Sarmiento, Cabello Valboa, and Cobo. Since Cabello Valboa said he followed Molina, and we have already established the similarities between his text and Morúa's, Cabello Valboa will stand in for Molina ([1586], pt. 3, chap. 9; 1951:259–260). Molina wrote just after the time Sarmiento composed his historical narrative. In roughly the same period, then, Sarmiento and Molina collected somewhat different accounts of the Inca past from native sources.

Cobo has been selected because he may have drawn his material from a narrative by Polo de Ondegardo. If so, Polo wrote a narrative that was noticeably shorter and less detailed than the accounts of Sarmiento and Cabello Valboa. We cannot control for Cobo's editing, and he certainly behaved more like a modern historian than other authors of his time. One gets a sense, when reading him, that he injected a fair degree of his own interpretation of the materials he had at his disposal. When he says he could have gotten the same material from Inca sources in the Cuzco of his own day, he is telling us that he was comparing material from more than half a century earlier with what he was hearing. It is hard to imagine that an active mind like Cobo's would not be influenced by what he heard or the voices in his other manuscripts. Perhaps the biggest danger is that he may have reordered or suppressed events to bring a text that he used for the basis of his account into line with what he "knew" from other sources. When we put Cobo into our comparison, however, we see enough similarities between his narrative and the other two to confirm that his underlying source drew from some of the same fonts as Sarmiento and Cabello Valboa/Molina.

Since the origin myth is the subject of a later chapter, and here we are primarily interested in comparing the event structure of the lives of the early rulers, we have chosen the departure of the Ayar siblings from Pacaritambo as the starting point for our comparison. If we are right about where the origin story ends (see the above comparison of Morúa and Cabello Valboa), we have included a large part of it in our comparison. Since the account of Inca origins has an event structure just like the lives of particular Incas, we should look at its structure in the context of the account(s) of the early rulers.

Both Sarmiento and Cabello Valboa provide information in years (such as age at death, age at succession, length of rule, and/or calendar year of death) at the end of their accounts of each ruler. (The numerical material has been gathered together in tabular form in a separate section in this chapter where it is given full consideration.) Sarmiento and Cobo provide information about the location of the body and the *huaoque*, a sacred object associated with each ruler, at the end of their accounts. Both authors had information about where these objects were when Polo found them (or did not find them) in Cuzco more than a decade earlier (Hampe Martínez 1982). Whether information about the location of the mummy of an Inca ruler had anything to do with an Inca genre or not, it appears at the end of a life in some Spanish narratives and thus is part of what ends each life history. Finally, spellings have been normalized in the following comparisons, except where a variant is transparent. If a spelling diverges to any great degree from the normalized version, the actual spelling of a name in the text is enclosed in brackets the first time the name appears. Again, the accounts have been paraphrased.

Sarmiento and Cabello Valboa give accounts of the Ayar siblings' journey to Cuzco that are broadly similar as well as similar in many details. For example, the itinerary the Incas followed in their gradual move from Pacaritambo to Cuzco is roughly the same, as are the details about what happened in these places. Sarmiento has a bit more detail; for example, he names the place at the foot of Huanacauri where the Incas stopped. In Cabello Valboa, the Ayar siblings speak to the sorcerer from Saño who was offering to their *huaca*. In Sarmiento they speak to the *huaca* itself. Cabello Valboa and Sarmiento do not agree on which brother was walled up at Tambotoco or on which brother became a *huaca* at Huanacauri. Sarmiento says that Ayar Cache was walled up at Tambotoco and Ayar Uchu became a *huaca* at Huanacauri. Later on in Sarmiento's narrative (see a later segment in the comparison), Ayar Auca becomes a *huaca* in Cuzco. Cabello Valboa, in contrast, says Ayar Auca was walled up at Tambotoco, and Ayar Cache became a *huaca* at Huanacauri. Interestingly enough, both are in agreement that the servant Tambo Chacay walled up one of their brothers in Tambotoco.

Cobo only notes that "some say" a brother returned to the cave at Pacaritambo and never emerged again. He also notes that one brother became a stone at Huanacauri, and another turned into a stone "not far from there," but "others say" all the brothers and sisters arrived in Cuzco, and only afterward did a brother turn to stone there. Cobo gives no names. The confusion over what became of the Ayar siblings is something that will be considered in the chapter on the origin myth (chapter 8).

Both Cabello Valboa and Sarmiento account for the marriage of Manco

Capac to a sister, and they agree on Mama Ocllo. She bears Sinchi Roca, and he is born in Tamboquiro. The itinerary is largely missing from Cobo, who only mentions that the Incas went to Huanacauri, where they solemnly took possession of Tawantinsuyo. He mentions the production of the next Inca after he describes other versions of Inca origins, mentioning in passing that the child was born to Manco Capac and Mama Huaco in Matagua.

Another difference between Cabello Valboa and Sarmiento is that the former attributes Ayar Auca's hatred to disgust at the marriage of brother and sister. This kind of interpretation of motive may well have been supplied by Cabello Valboa. There are some narrative digressions in the text which are clearly statements by the author and others, like this one, that cannot be identified as his voice with any certainty. Sarmiento is always quick to call the Incas tyrants or to spotlight political violence, but he is less apt to give the Incas Christian consciences than Cabello.

| *Sarmiento* | *Cabello Valboa* | *Cobo* |
|---|---|---|
| Chap. 12. The Ayar siblings leave Tambo Toco. Manco takes Inti, an object shaped like a bird, with him. | Chap. 9. The Ayar siblings leave Pacaritambo or Tambotoco. They arrive at Pachete but don't like it. | Chap. 3. The eight Ayar siblings leave Pacaritambo for a large hill called Huanacauri. From there the eldest brother throws four stones with his sling to the four parts of the world and takes possession of them. |
| At Guanacancha Manco Capac gets Mama Ocllo pregnant. They go to Tamboquiro, where Sinchi Roca is born. Then they go to Pallata, nearby. Still not content, they go on to Haysquisrro. | They go on to Guamancancha, where Mama Ocllo gets pregnant. Then they go to Tambo Oir [Tamboquiro], where Sinchi Roca is born. | |
| They make a plan to get rid of Ayar Cache. Manco Capac sends him back for golden cups, a golden llama, and some seed. | Ayar Auca is disgusted and cannot disguise his hatred. He is sent back to Tambotoco for some golden cups and some | Some say that one of the brothers returned to Pacaritambo, reentered the cave, and never again emerged. |

Someone who had come with them, Tambo Chacay, goes back with him and walls him up.

seed with a servant named Tambo Chacay. The latter walls him up inside the cave.

Ayar Cache was famous for creating *quebradas* with his sling.

Ayar Auca was troublesome because he was able to create landslides by throwing rocks.

They arrive at Quirirmanta, at the foot of the hill that was later called Huanacauri.

It was decided that Ayar Uchu should remain there as a *huaca* and that Ayar Auca should go take possession of the lands where they would settle.

They see a rainbow, which they interpret it as a sign that the world would never again be destroyed by flood.

They go to Huanacauri and see a rainbow, which they interpret as a sign that the world would not be destroyed by flood.

Near the top, where the rainbow was, there is a *huaca* in the figure of a person. They decide to remove it. Ayar Uchu sits on it and begins to converse with it. He finds he cannot move his feet. When his siblings arrive, he asks them to be the first *huaca* to receive offerings when they perform *huarachico*. He was named Ayar Uchu Huanacauri.

Near the top they see a certain wizard from Saño making sacrifices to a *huaca* called Chimbo y Cagua [Chimboycagua]. They send Ayar Cache to capture him. He turns Ayar Cache to stone. Ayar Cache tells them to sacrifice to him when they perform *huarachico*.

Two brothers become stones, one at Huanacauri and the other not far from there.

The next segment of the story is about the sojourn of the Ayar siblings in Matagua. They spend a period of two (Sarmiento) or twenty (Cabello Valboa) years there. Although there is nothing in Cobo about this period, he mentions the birth of Sinchi Roca in Matagua later as a flashback (see a later segment).

In identifying Matagua as Sinchi Roca's birthplace, however, he contradicts both Sarmiento and Cabello Valboa, who say Sinchi Roca was born at Tamboquiro, the first place the Ayar siblings stopped after they left Pacaritambo. As we noted above, Cabello Valboa repeats elements of the story of what happened prior to the Incas' arrival at Tamboquiro, perhaps to fill in the rather long period he has them staying there.

Both Sarmiento and Cabello Valboa include information about the first practice of rites associated with life passages. Cabello Valboa goes into the matter in far more detail than Sarmiento, and the details have not been reproduced here. Cobo is quiet on these matters. The subject is tied to the initiation of Sinchi Roca, and when that subject comes up in Cobo, he notes that *rutuchico* and other practices associated with the succession of the Inca ruler originated in Sinchi Roca's initiation.

Both Sarmiento and Cabello Valboa tell a story about Mama Huaco, who threw two golden rods with the apparent purpose of locating good land for cultivation. One landed at Colcabamba, the name of a settlement where the parish of San Sebastian was later founded (Rowe 1979:37; Julien 1998b:85). Although the story tells us that the Incas settled at Colcabamba briefly, they moved on to the place where the other rod fell, Huanaypata, near the gateway called Arco Punco in the colonial period.[1]

Only Sarmiento tells us that Ayar Auca turned to stone in Cuzco. This event occurred at the time the golden rods were thrown, while the Incas still lived in Matagua, because Sarmiento later notes that only Manco Capac and his four sisters are left while they are still in Matagua (see later segment). Cobo mentions a version of the story of the Ayar siblings where a brother turns to stone in Cuzco after all of the brothers and sisters arrive, that is, only one brother among the four ever becomes a *huaca*. In the Cabello Valboa and Morúa accounts, two brothers become *huacas* before reaching Cuzco. Only Manco Capac is mentioned, however, in the narrative of events following the Inca arrival in Cuzco, except that Cabello Valboa is very careful to note that Ayar Uchu, the one brother of Manco Capac who did not become a *huaca* on the way to Cuzco, did not leave descendants.

| *Sarmiento* | *Cabello Valboa* | *Cobo* |
|---|---|---|
| Chap. 13. They go to the foot of the hill to a place called Matagua. Here is where Sinchi Roca is initi- | They go to the foot of the hill to a place called Matagua. Here is where Sinchi Roca is initiated | |

ated. They give him ear spools. This is called *huarachico*.

This is also when Inca mourning and other rites originated (the dances called *capac raymis*, when they wear long purple robes; *quicochico*, the first menstruation of a girl; *guarachico*, when the ears are pierced; *rutuchico*, the first haircut; and *ayuscay*, to celebrate a birth, when they drink for three to four days).

and given ear spools. He was the first to be initiated in the ceremony of *tocochicui*. The name of Ayar Cache was invoked many times. Cabello refers to "father Sun." This is also when Inca mourning and other rites originated (*quicochico*, *guarachico*, *rutuchico*, and *auyscay*, which is to celebrate a birth, when they drink and dance for four days).

Chap. 10. They occupy some abandoned houses [in Matagua]. The town was a marketplace. They get all dressed up and try to convince people there that they had come from the heavens and are sons of the Sun. People are impressed.
[Then he retells some of the story he has already told with some different details.] Mama Ocllo becomes pregnant. Ayar Auca is sent back to Tambotoco to retrieve cups, and so on. Tambo Chacay walls him up, and so on. The story is circulated that Mama Ocllo is bearing a child of the

After two years, they decide to go to the upper valley and look for good lands.

Mama Huaco throws two golden rods toward the north. One lands at Colcabamba but does not dig in like it should. The other digs itself in well at Huanaypata. Another version is told. Back in Matagua they plot to take the land at Huanaypata away from the people there.

From Matagua they can see a stone marker near what would later be Santo Domingo. Since Ayar Auca had been delegated to take possession of the land, Manco Capac sends him there, where he turns into stone and becomes a

Sun. Sinchi Roca is born.
Ayar Cache is killed by a sorcerer with poison. A new manner of mourning is invented.
They spend twenty years in Matagua.
Neither Ayar Ucho nor Mama Ragua left descendants.
Then the story about Mama Huaco and the two golden rods is told. One lands in Colcabamba and the other in Huanaipata, a place near the gateway on the road that goes to San Sebastián.

[More repeating] Sinchi Roca is initiated. At three years of age they perform *tocochicui*, which is when they pierce the ears. At four they perform *rutu-chicuy* which is when they cut the hair. At fifteen they perform *huarachicui*, which is when a boy first wears a breechcloth.

sign of Inca possession.
The marker, in old
speech, was called *cozco*,
and that is where the
name Cuzco originated.
Another version is told
where Ayar Cache be-
comes the marker and the
name *cozco* is glossed as
"sad and fertile."

In this part of the story the accounts of Sarmiento and Cabello Valboa are closely parallel. Before the Incas leave Matagua, Sinchi Roca receives a wife, who is the daughter of the lord of Saño. Both Sarmiento and Cabello Valboa (and Morúa, too) call her Mama Coca and note that she produced a son named Manco Sapaca first. Cobo calls the wife Mama Chura and—like Cabello Valboa—does not specifically name her as the mother of Lloque Yupanqui.

In the Cabello Valboa account, the Ayar siblings stop first at Colcabamba. They move on to Huamantianca. Sarmiento has Guanaypata. Morúa treats Huamantianca and Huanaypata as if they were the same place. The Incas destroy the people, the Huallas, at this place and also confront the most important lord in the area, Copalimayta. The first round of confrontation is indecisive, but the Incas are able to retreat and plant at Huanaypata, which they then occupy continuously afterward. Here or very near this place, Cuzco is founded. However, the outcome of the conflict situation with Copalimayta must be told before turning to the organization of the new settlement. The distribution of land is part of the story of Manco Capac's organization of the new site, and Copalimayta turned over his land before leaving the valley so that the Incas could occupy these lands as well as the lands of the Huallas.

Embedded in the Sarmiento and Cabello Valboa accounts is a story about the very violent confrontation between the Incas and the Huallas. Mama Huaco has a leading role in both stories, and the underlying story may be the same, but the Spaniards offer different interpretations of Mama Huaco's acts which are not adequately reflected in the paraphrasing of their accounts given above. Sarmiento uses her violent act to demonstrate the inhumanity of the Incas, while Cabello interprets what she did within a ritual framework.

Sarmiento and Cabello Valboa also embed the genealogical information about the next Inca generation in their narratives. Cobo is silent on all counts.

| *Sarmiento* | *Cabello Valboa* | *Cobo* |
|---|---|---|
| Only Manco Capac and the four women are left. At this point Manco Capac gives Sinchi Roca a wife. She is Mama Coca of Saño, daughter of Sutic Huaman. Later, they have Sapaca, who is the inventor of *capac ucha*, which is the sacrifice of two children, a boy and a girl, to Huanacauri at the time of initiation. | Sinchi Roca is old enough for a wife. She is Mama Coca, only daughter of Sutic Huaman, the lord of Saño. They have Manco Sapaca in Matagua. | |
| | Then they move on to Colcabamba. They test the land there. | |
| When they get to Huanaypata, which is near the gateway to the Charcas province, they found the Huallas. Mama Huaco kills one of them and, with his heart and lungs in her mouth, attacks. To cover up this cruelty, they attempted to kill every last Hualla. | They go on to Huamantianca. In this place Mama Huaco kills one of the Huallas with a knife and removes his lungs and entrails, anointing the others with his blood. | Only Manco Capac and his four sisters got to Cuzco. Others say that all eight brothers and sisters arrived in Cuzco. One became a stone there, and the other brothers took up residence. |
| They then encountered Copalimayta, one of the three captains from the area where the Ayar siblings had originated, who was now heading the Sauaseras. | Copalimayta, the natural lord of Cuzco, gathered as large a group as possible and came out to meet them. | |
| The siblings met with a great deal of resistance and had to return to Huanaypata. | The Incas defended themselves at a small arroyo and had to retreat to Huanaypata, where they remained until after harvest. | |
| A few months later, they tried again and captured | The harvest was good, and they went back on the | |

| Copalimayta. He aban- | attack. They won and |
|---|---|
| doned his property and | took Copalimayta captive. |
| fled. | He turned over his family |
| Mama Huaco and Manco | and possessions to Mama |
| Capac took his houses, | Huaco and departed. |
| land, and people. | |

In the description of early Cuzco, the parallels between Sarmiento and Cabello Valboa are remarkable, down to the listing of the four *canchas*. The lists are similar except for the very different spelling of Yarumbuy Cancha and its order on the list. Cobo is concerned with temple building and the organization of space in Cuzco itself, but he does not mention the four neighborhoods and notes only that Manco Capac divided Cuzco into Hanan and Hurin. Cobo is caught in a contradiction when he returns to the subject in his account of Inca Roca, because this Inca was also given credit for dividing Cuzco. Just who was responsible for the *saya* division created confusion in the Spanish narratives, owing perhaps to the contradictory nature of the sources they compiled or to their treating later reform as if it were a first invention.

In Cobo, the chapter heading indicates that the history of Manco Capac begins with the founding of Cuzco. Cobo's narrative is structured so that each chapter contains the history of each ruler, except in the case of some later rulers who merit more than one chapter. The title of chapter 4, for example, is called "On Manco Capac, the First King of the Incas," where the history of this Inca—as a separate matter from origins—begins. Right after, Cobo injects some of the material that other accounts located at a more appropriate point in the sequence, notably the information about Sinchi Roca's birth, the institutions of *rutuchico* and initiation (*huarachico*), and Sinchi Roca's marriage. Cobo locates Sinchi Roca's birthplace at Matagua, rather than Tamboquiro, as noted above. Sinchi Roca's marriage takes place in Cuzco, rather than in Matagua. The placement may reflect the appropriateness of accounting for the production of the next Inca generation in the account of each ruler. For example, both Cabello Valboa and Sarmiento reiterate the information about Sinchi Roca's marriage during their story about his life. Cabello Valboa also provides information about the production of an heir when he mentions marriage. The volatility in the placement of information about this matter and/or duplication probably reflects the problems the authors were having in sequencing material.

Only Sarmiento tells about Manco Capac's dealings with the Alcabizas. This particular interest may relate to his participation in a series of interviews with the non-Incas who lived in Cuzco conducted by Toledo when he arrived in Cuzco (Levillier 1940, vol. 2:182–195). Sarmiento also notes earlier that Copalimayta had served as the leader of the Sauaseras. Again, Sarmiento may have incorporated this information because of Toledo's interview with this group. A comparison of these interviews with what Sarmiento wrote about the initial contacts between the Incas and these groups would be a fruitful exercise but is beyond the scope of the present analysis (but see Sherbondy 1992:53–54).

Once the lifetimes of particular rulers became a tool for structuring the narrative, a certain format is developed to convey a series of details at the end of each life, whether the end is also marked by a chapter ending or not. Both Sarmiento and Cobo supply the name of each ruler's *panaca*. Sarmiento generally tells us if they are Hanan or Hurin Cuzco and gives the names of some living *panaca* members. This information has not been included in the comparison. Sarmiento also tells us if the ruler lived in Inticancha, which is generally the case before Inca Roca. Sarmiento and Cobo also include information about where the body and the *huaoque*, a sacred object that had been the possession of each ruler, were found. Each refers to Polo de Ondegardo's search for these items in 1559, when he was *corregidor* of Cuzco, and there is reason to suspect textual borrowing, although establishing a pattern of borrowing may be impossible. The problem will be taken up at an appropriate point in the discussion below.

One difference between the accounts of Cabello Valboa and Sarmiento is that Sarmiento tells a story about Inti, the stone object that was the *huaoque* of Manco Capac. He tells it in several installments, beginning at the time the Ayar siblings leave Pacaritambo and continuing here and during the time of Mayta Capac. This story is entirely absent from Cabello Valboa and may be an example of Sarmiento's skill in developing a narrative thread to unify what otherwise would have been a disjointed compilation. In this case, he may have taken a story and distributed parts of it to appropriate points in his narrative.

| *Sarmiento* | *Cabello Valboa* | *Cobo* |
|---|---|---|
| There they made a house of the Sun, which they called *inticancha*. The land occupied the spot from Santo Domingo down to the confluence of the rivers. | The Incas settled at Curicancha, where Santo Domingo is now. They built a temple dedicated to the Sun. | Chap. 4. Manco Capac history begins. He divided the population of Cuzco into Hanan Cuzco and Hurin Cuzco. He organized the religion and built the temples. He as- |

sembled all the lords from Carmenca to the Angostura called Ancoyacpuncu, which were the limits of his territory. Then he assigned the lands to himself, the *huacas*, his people, and the residents of the territory. He taught the men what they needed to know. The Coya taught the women. He founded towns.

Cuzco was divided into four *canchas*, like blocks, called Quinti Cancha, Chumbi Cancha, Sayri Cancha, and Yarumbuy Cancha. They divided them among themselves and populated the city, which they called Cuzco.

They established four neighborhoods, calling them Quinti Cancha, Chumbi Cancha, Aranbui Cancha, and Sayri Cancha. Manco Capac populated his city in Chumbi Cancha.

Sinchi Roca, the son of Manco Capac and Mama Huaco, had been born in Matagua before they arrived in Cuzco. So that the people recognize him as successor and respect him, Manco Capac ordered the celebration of *rutuchico*, the first haircut. This rite had never been celebrated before. When Sinchi Roca was initiated, they assembled a greater number of people in Matagua than they had for the *rutuchico*. In this initiation they began to perform the rituals that would be used in later succession rites.

When the prince arrived at the age of marriage, a marriage was arranged with the daughter of Sutic Guaman of Saño, here named Mama Chura. Manco Capac chose the site of Coricancha and began work on it.

Those of Hanan Cuzco and Hurin Cuzco descended from Manco Capac. Cobo describes how *panacas* were created and how the body continued to hold the property that had belonged to that Inca in life.

Chap. 14. At the time Manco Capac defeated Copalimayta, there was another group in Cuzco: the Alcabizas. They were settled near what became Santa Clara. Manco Capac wanted their land. They had given him some, but he wanted it all. Mama Huaco tells him to take their water, and he will get their land. They also wanted the lands of those at Humanamean, between Inticancha and Cayocache, where another captain called Culunchima lived. The attack on these people and the Alcabizas was successful, and they

were forced out and had
to resettle at Cayocache.
After that, the Alcabizas
served the Incas.

Inti was Manco Capac's
*huaoque*. He leaves Inti
enclosed in a little chest.

Mentions Inca insignia
(*topa yauri*, *suntur paucar*,
*napa*).

| | |
|---|---|
| Age at death, length in years of residence in the places between Pacaritambo and Cuzco. | Age at death, length of rule, calendar year of death. |

Describes his appearance
and character.

He turned to stone on his
death. Polo found the
statue.

Describes the *huaoque* and
how Manco Capac instituted this practice.

Manco Capac had ordered
that the ten groups who
had come with him from
Tambotoco and his own
lineage form a single
group to aid his son and
elect a successor.

Gives *panaca* name.

| | |
|---|---|
| The *panaca* of Manco Capac adored only the statue of Manco Capac and not the bodies of the other Incas, while the other *panaca* members universally adored the statue of Manco Capac. The Incas took the statue into battle with them. | The *panaca* of Manco Capac adored only the body and *huaoque* of Manco Capac and not the bodies of the other Incas, while the other *panaca* members universally adored the statue of Manco Capac. |
| | Gives *panaca* name. |

| | |
|---|---|
| No body was ever found, only the statue. Calendar year of death. He lived in Inticancha. | Notes that a statue, not a body, was found by Polo. |

No one has much to say about Sinchi Roca per se. Sarmiento says he was not a warrior, and Cobo explains that his mother specifically advised him not to expand Cuzco. Whether an Inca had expanded Cuzco or not was certainly a topic in the accounts of rulers to come and was a topic here, even if the assessment was negative.

Since all three authors have already noted that Sinchi Roca married the daughter of Sutic Huaman, lord of Saño (though she is Mama Chura in Cobo and Mama Coca in the others), Sarmiento and Cabello Valboa repeat information they have already given. At this point, Cabello Valboa notes that their firstborn was Manco Sapaca. Sarmiento has already given this information. Only Sarmiento states definitely that Lloque Yupanqui is the son of this same pair.

| *Sarmiento* | *Cabello Valboa* | *Cobo* |
|---|---|---|
| Chap. 15. Sinchi Roca history begins. Mentions again that he was son of Manco Capac and Mama Ocllo. He was not a warrior, and neither he nor any captains went out from Cuzco. | Chap. 11. Sinchi Roca history begins.<br><br><br><br><br><br>Sinchi Roca and Mama Coca have Manco Sapaca. | Chap. 5. Sinchi Roca history begins. He visits the towns in the Cuzco Valley. He increases the lands planted to potatoes in the area around Cuzco. They reached as far as Cinga [Senca] at this time.<br><br>After Lloque Yupanqui is born, Mama Huaco advises him not to expand the territory he ruled. When she died, she was greatly mourned. The rites lasted more than two months. Sinchi Roca spent most of his time training his son. Some |

| | He was the first to use the *borla* called Masca Paycha, the Suntur Paucar, and the Capac Ongo, Tarco Gualca. | lords submit to his authority. The word got around that the Incas are children of the Sun, and people send many gifts. This Inca invented the Suntur Paucar. |
|---|---|---|
| Sinchi Roca and Mama Coca of Saño have Lloque Yupanqui. | Mentions Lloque Yupanqui. | |
| Gives *panaca* name. | | Gives *panaca* name. |
| He lived in Inticancha. | | |
| Age at death, age at accession, length of rule, calendar year of death. | Age at death, calendar year of death. | |
| Mentions *huaoque*. He left a stone *huaoque* in the figure of a fish, called Guanachiri Amaro. Polo found the body and *huaoque*. | | Mentions *huaoque*. He left a stone *huaoque* in the figure of a fish, called Huana-chiri-amaro. Polo found the body and *huaoque*. |

The three accounts are strikingly parallel on the subject of Lloque Yupanqui. Although he did not extend the territory of Cuzco by warfare, a number of lords from the area around Cuzco either communicated with the Incas as equals or submitted peacefully to the authority of Cuzco at this time. Essentially the same lords are named by Sarmiento, Cobo, and Cabello Valboa. In all three accounts, the Sun appears to Lloque Yupanqui in human form and tells him about the future greatness of his lineage. All three also represent the agency of others, including the Sun, in finding this Inca a wife.

Sarmiento confirms that Lloque Yupanqui is the son of Sinchi Roca and Mama Coca at the beginning of his account. He is fairly consistent in repeating this information, but it is absent in Cabello Valboa and Cobo.

Cabello Valboa presents the information about Mayta Capac's youth before he closes the account of Lloque Yupanqui. Where to put any significant material about the next Inca's youth is a problem again in the story about Inca Roca and Yahuar Huacac.

| *Sarmiento* | *Cabello Valboa* | *Cobo* |
|---|---|---|
| Chap. 16. Lloque Yupanqui history begins. Mentions again that Lloque Yupanqui is son of Sinchi Roca and Mama Coca. Manco Sapaca should have succeeded because he was older. | Chap. 12. Lloque Yupanqui history begins. | Chap. 6. Lloque Yupanqui history begins. |
| | | The Sun appears to Lloque Yupanqui in the figure of his grandfather to show support. |
| Lloque Yupanqui does not conduct any military campaigns or do anything worthy of note, except to communicate with the provinces of Guaro Guamay Samo, Pachachulla Viracocha, the Ayarmacas of Tambocunca, and the Quilliscaches. | Many lords come to serve Lloque Yupanqui, the first and most important being Guaman Samo (of Guaro), Pachachulla Viracocha, the Ayarcamas, Tambo Vincais, and Quiliscochas. | A number of peoples come to Cuzco to submit peacefully. The first who came were those of Guaro. The most important were Guamasano and Pachachulla Viracocha. Then the Ayarmacas of Tambocunca and the Quilliscaches came. They swore obedience in the temple of Coricancha in front of the Sun and the Moon. |
| The Sun appeared to him in the figure of a person and told him his descendants would be great. At this point Manco Sapaca found a wife for him. | He had fathered no children. The Sun appeared to him in human form to console him, saying that he would be a great lord and would father a son. Manco Sapaca had told Pachachulla Viracocha of this business, who took it to hand and found Lloque Yupanqui a wife. | Lloque Yupanqui was old but still unmarried. Those around him called Pachachulla Viracocha, one of the lords of Guaro, who found him a bride in Oma, about 10 km from Cuzco. |
| Lloque Yupanqui marries Mama Cahua of Oma. Mentions Mayta Capac. | He marries Mama Cahua of Oma in an elaborate ceremony. | He marries Mama Cahua of Oma in an elaborate ceremony. |

Lloque Yupanqui dies
when Mayta Capac is very
young. Before his death
he calls Apu Conde Mayta
and Tacac Huincay, sons
of Sinchi Roca, to serve as
regents.

He lived in Inticancha.
Gives *panaca* name.
His *huaoque* is called Apo
Mayta.
Age at death, age at suc-
cession, length of rule,
calendar year of death.
Polo found the body and
*huaoque*.

Gives *panaca* name.

Polo found the body and
*huaoque*.

A big deal is made of the bravery of Mayta Capac as a boy. All three authors describe the problem with the Alcabizas as owing to the aggressive play of Mayta Capac with boys from that group. Sarmiento and Cabello Valboa involve the Culunchimas as well as the Alcabizas. In their accounts, after the adults get involved, an ambush and two battles take place, with a supernatural intervention (a hailstorm or black cloud) occurring in the last one. Cobo includes only the Alcabizas and but a single battle in which the Incas attack the Alcabizas. Mayta Capac, not Lloque Yupanqui, directs the Inca forces in all of the encounters.

Sarmiento has already told of the Inca defeat of the Alcabizas in the time of Manco Capac. Here, Culunchima is a lord. Manco Capac is successful, and the Incas take the lands held by the Alcabizas away from them. They resettle at Cayocache, a site which may be located at or near Coripata (Rowe 1994). There are no details about location in the stories about an encounter in the time of Mayta Capac, and whether the Incas displaced them again from their lands is unclear.

Cabello Valboa includes a long section on religious specialists. It might be that the additional material on religious practice came from Cristóbal de Molina, but the material is missing from Morúa and may well have been something Cabello Valboa added.

Sarmiento mentions Inti, the *huaoque* of Manco Capac, picking up the thread of a story that is absent in Cabello Valboa. Mayta Capac opens the box containing the bird. His two predecessors were not known for their aggressive behavior, and although there are no campaigns outside of Cuzco associated with Mayta Capac, even later in life his bellicose spirit may reflect the dawn of imperial expansion.

| *Sarmiento* | *Cabello Valboa* | *Cobo* |
|---|---|---|
| Chap. 17. Mayta Capac history begins. | | Chap. 7. Mayta Capac history begins. |
| He was born after only three months' gestation and already had teeth. At a year, he looked like an eight year old. From two years on, he fought with everybody. | As a boy, Mayta Capac fought with other boys, injuring them and even killing some. | He was an aggressive child, and his treatment of the sons of other lords when they played together was getting him into trouble. |
| Still a boy, he was playing with some boys from the Alcabizas and Culunchimas. He hurt them and killed some. Another day he broke the leg of the son of a captain of the Alcabizas and persecuted others so much that they stayed hidden in their houses. | He fought with the sons of some Alcabizas [Allcayvillas] and Culunchimas [Culluim Chima] lords, and they came to hate the Incas. | |
| The Alcabizas chose ten men and went to the house of the Sun to kill Lloque Yupanqui and Mayta Capac. Mayta Capac was playing bolas with some boys when they came. When he saw armed men enter, he attacked them, killing two and causing the others to flee. | They decided secretly to kill Lluque Yupanqui and his son, choosing ten men to ambush them at Coricancha. Mayta Capac was there with his cousins Apoc Conde Mayta and Taca Chungay playing with a certain kind of bolas called Cuchu, accompanied by two dogs. Mayta Capac could tell that the men who had entered meant harm, and | One day, the lords sent armed men after him. He went out to meet them without fear and recognized them as Alcabizas [Alcayviczas]. He killed a couple of them right away, without even asking them their business. Then other people came running out, and the attackers fled. |

with one bola he killed two of them. Lloque Yupanqui, Mayta Capac, and others pursued the other eight, killing all but three. The Alcabizas gathered a large number of people. Lloque Yupanqui was upset about the trouble his son caused, but the elders and religious specialists of the Incas told him not to be, and Mayta Capac was allowed to lead them out to battle. The Incas managed to chase the Alcabizas back to their enclosures.

Out of fear, all of the native residents of the Cuzco Valley united to get rid of the Incas. Lloque Yupanqui was upset, but the groups who were united with the Incas were pleased and told him to let Mayta Capac be. Mayta Capac led them into battle and won after a long fight.

Others decided to join the Alcabizas and kill him, thinking that he was too young to know how to defend himself. Mayta Capac found out about the plan. He sent the messenger to tell the Alcabizas that he wanted to go hunting. Their response was that they did not recognize him as lord, and that they were in their lands and he was in his. He decided to teach them a lesson and, with his uncles and fifty men, attacked them before they could organize to defend themselves.

A second battle was fought. Hail fell on the Alcabizas, and they lost.

A second battle was fought. When they were fighting, a black cloud came and separated them, keeping the Incas from defeating them.

He marries Mama Tancaray Yacchi.
Mayta Capac was a more important lord than his predecessor and used gold and silver dishes.
Mayta Capac sent word to the lords subject to him that he wanted their children to come to Cuzco to serve him.

| | | |
|---|---|---|
| | Length of rule, calendar year of death of Lloque Yupanqui. Mayta Capac history begins. | |
| Mayta Capac marries Mama Tacucaray. Mentions Capac Yupanqui (legitimate), Tarco Huaman, Apo Conde Mayta, Queco Aucaylli, and Roca Yupanqui. | Mayta Capac marries Mama Coca Taucaraz. Mentions Capac Yupanqui (successor) and Tarco Huaman. | Mentions Capac Yupanqui (successor) and Tarco Huaman. |
| | A long description of different kinds of religious specialists which have their origin at about this time. | |
| Mayta Capac was the first to open the straw box in which Inti [the *huaoque* of Manco Capac] was enclosed. He lived in Inticancha. Gives *panaca* name. Age at death, calendar year of death. | Length of rule, calendar year of death (at beginning of chap. 13). Mentions Capac Yupanqui. | Gives *panaca* name. He lived "many years." |
| Polo found the body and *huaoque*. | | Polo found the body and *huaoque*. |

Capac Yupanqui is the first Inca to conduct a campaign outside the Cuzco Valley. Sarmiento names two places that cannot be located but at least gives us an indication that they are at some distance from Cuzco. Both Cabello Valboa and Cobo refer to a campaign against the Cuyos. Capac Yupanqui appears to have gone there in person. No fighting takes place. Cobo says that Capac Yupanqui sends his brother Tarco Huaman there as governor. He also adds that Capac Yupanqui conquered "Condesuyo."

Cabello Valboa again incorporates material not found elsewhere. This time his topic is the royal insignia.

| *Sarmiento* | *Cabello Valboa* | *Cobo* |
|---|---|---|
| Chap. 18. Capac Yupanqui history begins. Mentions again that Mayta Capac and Mama Tacucaray are his parents. Capac Yupanqui wasn't the eldest; that was Conde Mayta. | Chap. 13. Capac Yupanqui history begins. Describes the royal insignia (*topa yauri, tarco gualca, marca pacha, suntur paucar*). | Chap. 8. Capac Yupanqui history begins. Some of his illegitimate brothers have been given towns to govern, and they come to him to ask for certain exemptions. He learns that they are plotting to remove him and give the rule to his brother Tarco Huaman. He assembles everyone and speaks so lovingly of his brothers that they forget the plot. |
| | Capac Yupanqui marries Curi Hilpay. Mentions sons Inca Roca (successor) and Apo Mayta. | |
| Leaves the Cuzco Valley to conquer Cayumarca and Ancasmarca, about 20 km from Cuzco. | When his sons are now old enough to campaign, there is a campaign against the Cuyos [Suyos], who, because they live in the mountainous Andes, imagine themselves free of Inca rule. Capac Yupanqui takes offense and arms himself and his sons to restore them to obedience. Their neighbors and confederates also submit. | When the Inca asks the lord of Cuyos, in the Andes, for certain birds that they raise there in cages, the lord replies that they have no such birds. The Inca is determined to punish him, so he raises an army and goes there. There is no resistance. He takes the lords and their families back to Cuzco and executes the lords. Then he sends his brother Tarco Huaman there to be governor. The brother sends 1,000 cages of birds back to Cuzco. Conquers Condesuyo. |
| Capac Yupanqui marries Curi Hilpay. | | Capac Yupanqui marries Curi Hilpay Cahua. |

Mentions sons Inca Roca
(legitimate), Apo Calla,
Humpiri, Apo Saca, Apo
Chimachaui, and Uchun-
cunascallarando.
Apo Saca has a son called
Apo Mayta who, with
Vica Quirao, becomes fa-
mous in the time of Inca
Roca and Viracocha Inca.
Age at death, length of
rule, calendar year of
death.
Gives *panaca* name.
Polo found the body and
*huaoque*.

Age at death, calendar
year of death.

Mentions sons Inca Roca
(successor) and Apo
Mayta.

Gives *panaca* name.
The *huaoque* has the same
name.
Polo found the body and
*huaoque*.
Cobo discusses Hanan-
cuzco and Hurincuzco
here.

If length denotes importance, Inca Roca was the most important figure before the time of Viracocha Inca. Inca Roca continued to conquer beyond the
Cuzco Valley and developed canals to irrigate lands in Hanan Cuzco. His first
campaign, according to Sarmiento, is in the area of Mohina. The other two authors stage this campaign later in his rule, probably because the leadership was
attributed to his sons. Cabello Valboa is the only author to talk about a problem with the Mascas, who had been part of an Inca confederation but who
wanted to withdraw from it. A brother, Mayta Capac, goes to war against
them and captures their captain.

Inca Roca is given credit both for dividing the waters of Hanan Chacan and
Hurin Chacan and for dividing Cuzco into Hanan and Hurin. Cobo does not
believe the story because the creation of Hanan Cuzco and Hurin Cuzco has
already been attributed to Manco Capac. Just prior to the beginning of this
chapter, at the end of his account of Capac Yupanqui, Cobo described the
Hanan/Hurin division. In some of the accounts which include genealogical
material and little else, a summary of the *panacas* and their division in Hanan
and Hurin is given in list form in the text. Since Cobo has given the *panaca*
names in their appropriate places, what he discusses here is the assignment of

different Incas to Hanan and Hurin. His reiteration of this material together in one place may be a reflection of the genealogical genre.

Sarmiento notes that Inca Roca authored the Hanan/Hurin division and that he was the first Inca who did not live in Inticancha: he and his descendants built their own palaces and "began" the Hanan Cuzco band. Sarmiento also notes that the descendants of Pachacuti also say that their forebear authored the Hanan/Hurin division. Confronted with different stories, Sarmiento explains the apparent contradiction by noting that Pachacuti reformed Cuzco. The creation of Hanan and Hurin, or the redefinition of urban Cuzco, was also linked to a new distribution of water at this time. All three authors mention the creation of the Hanan Chacan and Hurin Chacan canals. In the Cobo account, the idea of bringing water originated with his wife, and the subject comes up immediately after Cobo mentions the marriage. Sarmiento and Cabello Valboa locate the subject after the Caytomarca campaign.

The sequencing may have to do with the proper placement of the story about Yahuar Huacac. Both Cabello Valboa and Sarmiento mention the Yahuar Huacac kidnapping, although Cabello Valboa only gives a brief summary of it. Sarmiento, on the other hand, retells the story in great detail in two chapters inserted between the account of Inca Roca and a chapter on the period of Yahuar Huacac's rule proper. Although we have incorporated the structure of this story into our comparison as if it were part of a longer narrative, it may have been a story that was introduced into the text by Sarmiento in the same manner as the Ulti story. We have already noted in our comparison of Cabello Valboa and Morúa (above) that this story was sequenced differently in those two accounts. Another clue that the kidnapping story was introduced by authors who were compiling material is that Cobo does not include the incident per se in his narrative. He does, however, mention the kidnapping at the beginning of his account of Yahuar Huacac, but only in the context of explaining what the name means.

Cobo places an Inca campaign against the Chancas at the end of his account of Inca Roca. Like the conquest of Condesuyo, no one else discusses anything like it. He also describes a military campaign led by Yahuar Huacac in the Andes. In the Cobo account the Inca expansion began generations before the time of Pachacuti. It involved campaigning in regions adjacent to Cuzco and led, perhaps inevitably, to conflict with the Chancas. The other accounts represent the beginnings of Inca imperial expansion as occurring only after the defense of Cuzco from the Chancas in the time of Pachacuti. This difference between Cobo and the other Cuzco accounts is a very important one and will be discussed again below.

| *Sarmiento* | *Cabello Valboa* | *Cobo* |
|---|---|---|
| Chap. 19. Inca Roca history begins. Mentions again that Capac Yupanqui and Curi Hilpay are his parents. | Inca Roca history begins. | Chap. 9. Inca Roca history begins. He was said to be the first Inca of Hanan Cuzco. Cobo does not believe this, because Manco Capac divided the city into Hanan Cuzco and Hurin Cuzco. |
| Inca Roca conquers Mohina [Muyna] and Pinagua, 20 km from Cuzco, and killed their captains, Muyna Pongo and Vamantopa, although some say the latter fled and was never seen again. | A group of families called Mascas had exempted themselves [from the Inca confederation]. Inca Roca's brother Apo Mayta wants to campaign against them and asks Inca Roca for permission. He goes to war against them, saying that bad advice was to blame for their being remiss and late in their confederation with the Incas. He defeats them, capturing their captain, Guari Guaca. | |
| He marries Mama Micay of Pataguayllacan. Because of this marriage, there were wars with Tocay Capac, as will be told later. | He marries Mama Nicaz [Micay], daughter of the lord of Guayllacan. | He marries Mama Micay, a *cacica* of Guayllacan. She notices that Cuzco lacks sufficient water for the maize lands. Inca Roca brought most of the water to the city that is there today. Because the project originated with him, his family was responsible for the division of water. |
| Mentions sons Yahuar Huacac (successor), Inca Paucar Inca, Guaman Taysi Inca, and Vica Quirao Inca. | Mentions sons Yahuar Huacac (successor) and Vica Quirao [Veca Quiroa]. | Mentions sons Yahuar Huacac (successor), Vica Quirao, and Apo Mayta. |

Vica Quirao does famous
deeds in the time of Viracocha Inca and Pachacuti
with Apo Mayta.
What happened between
Inca Roca and the Ayar-
macas will be told in the
life of Yahuar Huacac.

He also conquers Cayto-
marca, 20 km from
Cuzco.

His son Vica Quirao con-
quers Mohina [Moyna]
and its surrounding area,
capturing its lords,
Moynapongo and
Guamantopa.

This Inca conquers many
provinces; some submit
peacefully. He sends an
army led by his sons to
conquer the road to Col-
lasuyo, beginning at Mo-
hina [Moina]. They cap-
ture the lord of Mohina
and another at Cayto-
marca. Another lord,
named Guaman Topa,
flees and is never heard
from again. It is said that
he disappeared into the la-
goon there. The sons con-
quer as far as Quiquijana,
30 km beyond Mohina.

When Yahuar Huacac was
very young, some lords
from Andesuyo tried to
steal him from his cradle.
When they got him to
their land, he cried tears
of blood. After a divina-
tion ceremony, they re-
turned him to the place
they had taken him
from.
The sons of Inca Roca
win more lands in the
area, including Bim-
billa, Quisalla, and
Caytomarca.

Inca Roca discovers and channels the waters of Hurinchacan and Hananchacan, used ever since to irrigate the lands.
Inca Roca, seeing that his forebears had lived in lower Cuzco and were Hurin Cuzcos, ordered that, from then on, there be a second division called Hanan Cuzco.
Inca Roca and his descendants are Hanan Cuzcos, and they move out of the house of the Sun and build their own residences, leaving the property and servants of their fathers intact. The descendants of Inca Roca were and are Hanan Cuzco, but Pachacuti reformed the organization, and some say he created the division.

Inca Roca built the canals called Hananchaca and Urinchaca.

Inca Roca divided Cuzco into Hanan Cuzco and Hurin Cuzco.

Shortly after, the Inca decides to go to war against the Chancas, some 170 km from Cuzco. The Inca attacks suddenly with a large army and is victorious. He has help from the Canas and Canchis, who were not his subjects. Then he sends his son Yahuar Huacac to war in the provinces of the Andes. He conquers Paucartambo and the towns around it.

Gives *panaca* name.

Age at death, length of rule, calendar year of death.

Polo found the body.

Age at death, calendar year of death.

Gives *panaca* name.

Polo found the body and *huaoque*, which had the same name as the *panaca*.

Creating a concordance for Yahuar Huacac is more difficult than for any other Inca. Cabello Valboa does not appear to have any life history material in his account at all. Morúa puts a brief mention of the kidnapping story here.

When the subject is the adult Yahuar Huacac, Sarmiento describes campaigns that appear to repeat what was told for Inca Roca and Viracocha Inca. The first campaign, led by brother Vica Quirao, is to Mohina and Pinagua, echoing the first campaign of Inca Roca. In the account of Yahuar Huacac, the next campaign in sequence occurs in Mollaca, although no mention is made of Vica Quirao. In Sarmiento's account of Viracocha Inca, Vica Quirao and Apo Mayta lead a campaign to Mohina and Pinagua. They capture the captains named Moynapongo and Guaman Topa, exactly the same captains named in the story about Inca Roca. The two Inca captains are sent out again, and Mollaca figures among the towns taken. Vica Quirao is the common denominator in these stories. Rather than repeated campaigns, we may have a case for repeated mention of a single campaign led by Vica Quirao. Sarmiento includes another round of campaigning without naming captains. He mentions places in the Pisac area that do not appear elsewhere. Cobo had credited Yahuar Huacac with a campaign in the Paucartambo area in the time of his father, but there is no mention of anything like it in the other accounts.

One very remarkable difference between Cobo and the others is that Cobo tells the story of the Chanca invasion in the lifetime of Yahuar Huacac. This story, of course, is what begins the life history of Pachacuti in the accounts of Sarmiento and Betanzos. Cobo begins without identifying the Inca at first, telling the story of the appearance of the supernatural Viracocha to the young prince at Susurpuquio. Viracocha describes himself as the universal Creator. Then Cobo identifies the young prince as Viracocha Inca. Cobo has recast Viracocha Inca as the brave son and defender of Cuzco, incorporating details like the aid given to the Incas by the *pururaucas*, the stones that magically turn into warriors, that echo the story told by Sarmiento. Why does the story appear here? Sarmiento, in an explanation of the meaning of Viracocha's name, describes a vision this Inca beheld at the *huaca* of Viracocha near Urcos.

Cobo—or his Polo source—may have conflated the two supernatural visions and linked a supernatural Viracocha to the young prince. However, Cobo also includes an attack on the Chancas in the time of Inca Roca, so he has laid the narrative groundwork for Chanca retribution in the time of Yahuar Huacac.

There are several thorny problems embedded in this confusion, not the least of which is the tendency of Spanish writers and possibly their Inca informants to identify the supernatural Viracocha as a Prehispanic manifestation of the Catholic God. The subject will be taken up in chapter 8.

| *Sarmiento* | *Cabello Valboa* | *Cobo* |
|---|---|---|
| Chaps. 20–22. Story of Yahuar Huacac's youth begins. Mentions that Yahuar Huacac is the son of Inca Roca and Mama Micay. A long, detailed story is told about the kidnapping of Yahuar Huacac by the Guayllacanes. | Yahuar Huacac history begins. His rule is brief, and there is not much to say. | Chap. 10. Yahuar Huacac history begins. His name means "he who cries blood." He was given this name because once, when he had been captured, he was in so much distress he cried blood. He had a reputation for being a coward. Because of bad omens, he was afraid to go to war. |
| Yahuar Huacac succeeds his father. Before his father's death he marries Mama Chicya, daughter of Tocay Capac; and Tocay Capac marries Curi Ocllo, daughter of Inca Roca. | Yahuar Huacac marries Mama Chiquia. Mentions Viracocha Inca. | Yahuar Huacac marries Mama Choque Chiquia Yupay. She bears Viracocha Inca (successor). |
| Chap. 23. History of Yahuar Huacac's rule begins. Yahuar Huacac pardons the Ayarmacas. Then he sends an army to conquer Mohina and Pinagua, 20 km from Cuzco, naming his brother Vica Quirao as captain. | He was given to venereal delights, which shortened his life by a number of years. | |

He spends a long period
in Cuzco, during which
he conquers Mollaca.
Mentions sons Paucar
Ayllo, Pahuac Hualpa
Mayta (first named suc-
cessor), and Viracocha
Inca.
Yahuar Huacac had
named one of his three legitimate sons as successor.
The Guayllacanes wanted
one of his natural sons to
succeed and attempted to
kill the son Yahuar Hua-
cac had named. They did,
and Yahuar Huacac pun-
ished them by killing
most of them.
Then he went off to con-
quer Pillauya, 15 km from
Cuzco in the Pisac Valley,
then Coyca in the same
area, and Yuco.
Then he took the towns
of Chillincay, Taocamarca,
and the Cabiñas and made
them pay tribute. He con-
quered ten towns, though
some say Viracocha Inca
was captain of some of
the campaigns.

Because his eldest son did
not have the character to
become Inca, he was sent
to Chita, 10 km from
Cuzco, where he was or-
dered to guard the live-
stock belonging to the
Sun.
During this period, the
Chancas rebelled, killing

the governors the Incas
had left. Then the Chan-
cas raised an army of
30,000 and headed for
Cuzco. Yahuar Huaca
fled.

The eldest son decided to
oppose the Chancas, re-
turning to the city to fight
with the few people who
had remained.

To get the people to sup-
port him, he told them a
story about while he was
resting one day in the
shadow of a stone, Vira-
cocha appeared to him as
a white, bearded man in a
long robe, complaining to
him that he was the uni-
versal creator and that he
had created the Sun, the
Thunder, and the Earth,
which had been more
greatly venerated than he
had been. If the prince
would raise an army in his
name, he would help
them.

The prince was Viracocha
Inca. He managed to raise
an army of 30,000. They
fought on a plain near
Cuzco. Because of all the
blood that was spilt, it
was afterward called
Yahuarpampa.

During this campaign, a
large number of bearded
men fought that only
Viracocha Inca could see.
The Chancas later heard

about this and agreed that, without this kind of help, there was no explanation for the Inca victory. They gave the name *pururaucas* to these people. After fighting the *pururaucas* became stones. They were collected and venerated.

Age at death, length of rule.

Gives *panaca* name.
He says Polo did not find the body, and it is probably in the town of Paulo with the *huaoque*, but witnesses correct him and say Polo found it.

Length of rule, calendar year of death.

Gives *panaca* name.
The body and *huaoque* were found in the town of Paullu, near Calca.

Compared with the parallels between accounts of the lives of Lloque Yupanqui or Mayta Capac, for example, there is very little echo that can be heard between the different narrative accounts of Viracocha Inca. If we remember what Sarmiento said about the composition of the earlier lives (that the accounts from Manco Capac to Yahuar Huacac were composed at one time), then the account of Viracocha Inca was a separate, later composition, and we might expect it to be different. By the same logic, the accounts of Pachacuti and Topa Inca were separate, later compositions, but in these cases there are more parallels between our authors.

The volatility in accounts about Viracocha Inca may be due to historical circumstances. If we take the content of the narratives into account, there was an abrupt change in the transmission of power. Pachacuti became ruler long before his father's death and may have defied his father's role in naming a successor. The problematic relationship between Viracocha Inca and Pachacuti can have had an effect on what was transmitted about the former. Where there is bias and interest, the result may be various stories rather than consensus.

Both Sarmiento and Cabello Valboa explain the meaning of the name Viracocha Inca at the beginning of their treatment of this ruler. They place his campaigning activity after his marriage to Mama Rondocaya of Anta. Cobo has already told the story about the Chanca invasion when the subject was Yahuar

Huacac. He has very little to say about Viracocha Inca's campaigns. Sarmiento and Cabello Valboa, and particularly the former, have much more to say. The campaigns, however, are not led by Viracocha Inca but by two captains who had served earlier Incas. As noted before, the early conquests echo what Sarmiento has said about the conquests of the two generations immediately preceding Viracocha Inca. Sarmiento's account of later campaigning, directed by the captain (not the ruler) Inca Roca, contains a great deal of information not repeated in Cabello Valboa. Both Sarmiento and Cabello Valboa note campaigns against Tocay Capac and in Mollaca, Cayto (Caytomarca), and Calca, but the information is conveyed very differently and with an abundance of uncorroborated details. Of the places mentioned by the others, Cobo mentions Calca only.

Cobo, however, notes that Viracocha Inca conquered Canas and Canchis, building a temple in Cacha, in Canas territory. Cieza de León provides information about campaigns in this region by Viracocha Inca and about exploration farther south ([1553], chaps. 41–43; 1986:121–128). Again, Cobo is documenting Inca forays into regions fairly distant from Cuzco in the period before the rule of Pachacuti, although in this instance not before the Chanca invasion.

| *Sarmiento* | *Cabello Valboa* | *Cobo* |
|---|---|---|
| Chap. 24. Viracocha Inca history begins. | Chap. 14. Viracocha Inca history begins. | Chap. 11. Viracocha Inca history begins. |
| The Guayllacanes had killed the son chosen to succeed Yahuar Huacac, so Viracocha Inca was chosen. | Mentions again that Mama Chiquia is his mother. Some say the name Viracocha means "sea foam," but *vira* means lard, and foam is called *puczu*, so they are wrong. | His father had not been a great warrior, but Viracocha Inca was. |
| Viracocha Inca marries Mama Rondocaya of Anta. | Viracocha Inca marries Mama Rondocaya of Canto [*sic*: Anta]. Mentions Inca Yupanqui (successor). In the following story about campaigns at Caytomarca and Calca, he mentions sons Topa Huari and Inca Urco. | |

Once, when Viracocha Inca was in Urcos, where the great *huaca* of Ticci Viracocha was, the supernatural Viracocha appeared to him at night. The next day, Viracocha Inca assembled the nobles, including Gualpa Rimache, governor, and told them that great success was foreseen for the Incas. Gualpa Rimache saluted him, saying, "O Viracocha Inca," and the name stuck.

Until this time, the Incas had done no more than rob and shed blood, but Viracocha Inca began to change all this.

He had the help of Apo Mayta and Vica Quirao.

Until this time the towns near Cuzco were not subject to it but, rather, formed part of a confederation. Viracocha Inca began to change all this. Some say he went to war with them because they did not feel good about his usurping rule from his father and that he was trying to change the religion, preferring Viracocha to the Sun.

Viracocha Inca and Mama Rondocaya have Inca Roca Inca, Topa Yupanqui, Inca Yupanqui, and Capac Yupanqui. With Curi Chulpa of Ayavilla, he had Inca Urcon and Inca Sucsu, whose descendants say this marriage was the legitimate one.

Chap. 25. Viracocha Inca sends Apo Mayta and Vica Quirao to Pacaycacha in the Valley of Pisac. It did not submit, so the people and their captain, Acamaqui, were killed. Then they went after Mohina and Pinagua, Casacancha and Rondocancha, 25 short km from Cuzco. Again the people and their captains, named Muyna Pongo and Guaman Topa, were killed. Viracocha Inca names a son, Inca Roca, to go with the two captains on the next campaign. They also take Inca Yupanqui along. They destroyed the town of Guayparmarca and the Ayarmacas, killing their captains, Tocay Capac and Chiguay Capac, who had their seats near Cuzco. They also annexed Mollaca and ruined the town of Cayto, 20 km from Cuzco, killing their captain, Capac Chani. They defeated the towns of Socma and Chiraques and killed their captains, called Poma Lloque and Illacumbe.
Then Calca and Caquia Xaquixaguana, 15 km from Cuzco, were conquered, then Collocte and Camal. They also conquered the towns from Cuzco to

Viracocha Inca conquers Caytomarca and Callca; he conquers Tocay Capac and Suayparmaca [Guayparmarca]. He also brings Mallas and Mullucan to obedience, although some say that these victories were won by Topa Guarachiri and Ynga Urco, accompanied by their uncles Inca Sucsu and Inca Roca.

Viracocha Inca campaigns in Calca, 20 km from Cuzco, and its environs in the Yucay Valley.

Quiquixana and their sur-
rounding areas, as well as
Papres and other towns in
that area.

Viracocha Inca is old and
names Inca Urco to suc-
ceed him. This choice is
opposed by other sons
and by Apo Mayta and
Vica Quirao. Apo Mayta
wanted to kill Viracocha
Inca because he had had
access to one of Viracocha
Inca's wives. All of this
happens on the eve of the
Chanca invasion. At this
time Viracocha Inca, out
of fear of the Chancas,
flees Cuzco and hides at
Caquia Xaquixaguana.

Viracocha Inca names
Ynga Urco to succeed
him, although by rights
it should have been the
oldest brother, Ynga
Yupanqui.

At this time the Chancas
had attacked some Cuzco
people who were working
lands that belonged to the
Incas and the Sun. Vira-
cocha Inca names Ynga
Yupangui as general. He
campaigns against people
who had been exempt, in-
cluding Pinao Capac,
Cuyo Capac Chaguar
Chuchuca, and others of
lesser name. Then they
approached the Chancas,
who had approached the
lands of Quiachilli (to the
rear of Ayavira) and

Viracocha Inca marries
Mama Ron[do]cay[a] of
Anta.
After his marriage he con-
quers Canas and Canchis.
He builds a temple in
Cacha and places a statue
of Ticci Viracocha there.

fortified themselves there. The Incas beat them, and the Chancas retreated to Ychubamba (to the rear of Xacxaguana), where they regrouped. The Incas reinforced their army, and the Chancas fled in shame back to Andaguayllas. Their captains, Tomayguaraca and Astoguaraca, had been taken captive by Ynga Yupanqui, who made cups out of their heads.
Ulti story.
Pachacuti conquers the Urubamba Valley and puts the *borla* on his own head.

Viracocha Inca lives many years after his son takes possession of Cuzco.

Pachacuti plots the murder of his brother Inca Urco in a town called Canchi.
Viracocha Inca dies of sadness.

Age at death, length of rule, calendar year of death left blank.
Supplies *panaca* name.
Inventor of *viracochato-capu*, a kind of clothing.
Body was burned by Gonzalo Pizarro; Polo recovered ashes and the *huaoque*, named Inca Amaro. [Wording nearly identical to Cobo.]

Length of rule, calendar year of death.

Supplies *panaca* name.

Body was burned by Gonzalo Pizarro; Polo recovered ashes and the *huaoque*, named Inca Amaro.

Cobo incorporates information about his descendants at the beginning of

chap. 12. Viracocha Inca
and Mama Chiquia have
Pachacuti Inca Yupanqui
(successor), Inca Roca,
Topa Yupanqui, and Ca-
pac Yupanqui. He does
not mention Inca Urco
until he describes his murder by Pachacuti.

The Chanca invasion provokes a crisis in dynastic authority in both the
Betanzos and Sarmiento accounts. It precedes the imperial expansion, and it
catapults the young Pachacuti into power. How does it play in the other accounts? As noted above, Cobo tells the story of the Chanca invasion during
the time of Yahuar Huacac, casting him in the role of the father who abandoned Cuzco and Viracocha Inca as the son who remained to defeat the enemy. There is no trace of the Chanca invasion or dealings with the Chancas in
Cobo's account of Viracocha Inca or, subsequently, in his account of Pachacuti, although he does reiterate the vision at Susurpuquio. Cabello Valboa, on
the other hand, describes Inca involvement with the Chancas during the rule
of Viracocha Inca in some detail. What he tells involves a battle very near
Cuzco and a Chanca retreat. Inca Yupanqui—Pachacuti—was the captain who
defeated the Chancas. When Cabello Valboa begins the narration of Pachacuti,
there is no story about the Chanca invasion. He tells the story as if it were an
unproblematic episode in the life of Viracocha Inca and not an abrupt turn in
the course of dynastic history. Sarmiento drew from a life history of Pachacuti
where the Chanca invasion is a highly dramatic event. Did the Molina and
other versions draw from the genealogical account, in which more information about Inca-Chanca relations was included and each event was noted without the dramatization of the defense of Cuzco given in the life history of
Pachacuti?

Another thread in the same story is Viracocha Inca's choice of another
son—not Pachacuti—as his successor. Sarmiento notes that Viracocha Inca
and Mama Rondocaya have four sons, including Pachacuti. Viracocha Inca
and Curi Chulpa of "Ayavilla" have Inca Urco and Inca Sucsu. Their descendants, named at the end of Sarmiento's account, tell him that the sons of Curi
Chulpa are legitimate. Cabello Valboa provides information about Inca Urco's
involvement in military campaigns in the time of his father, noting only at the
end of his account that Viracocha Inca had named this son to succeed him

when he should have named the eldest, Pachacuti. Cobo mentions Inca Urco only during the account of Pachacuti's life and, specifically, when Pachacuti has him murdered. If, as Sarmiento indicates, the sons of Viracocha Inca by Curi Chulpa are members of his *panaca*, and life history material was transmitted by it, then we might expect that there would be differing stories about Inca Urco and that, rather than being suppressed, his story might be told. Effectively, it was.

In cases like this one, trying to pin down when and under what circumstances a story changed may be a fruitless exercise. Disturbance in the transmission of accounts of Viracocha Inca's life is evident, however, especially when compared to the life history material on Pachacuti in the Betanzos and Sarmiento accounts and the briefer accounts of the lives of Lloque Yupanqui and Mayta Capac, outlined above.

## DATES IN SARMIENTO AND CABELLO VALBOA

Sarmiento and Cabello Valboa incorporate several kinds of measurements in years into the texts of their narratives. For each Inca, Sarmiento generally supplies figures for lifespan, age at accession, length of rule, and calendar year of death; Cabello chooses either lifespan or length of rule and calendar year of death (tables 5.1 and 5.2).[2]

Both authors had to have calculated a calendar year of death. Cabello Valboa specifically notes, when he supplies the date of death of Capac Yupanqui, that he has arrived at it "by our reckoning" [a nuestra cuenta] ([1586], pt. 3, chap. 12; 1951:291). There are a number of inconsistencies in the numbers each author supplied. Sarmiento did a very poor job of calculating the calendar year of death, since we can assume that he used the length of rule he supplies in making his calculation. Recalculating the year of death back to the rule of Mayta Capac, for whom the data are not provided, the new figures are still out of line with those supplied by Cabello Valboa (table 5.3). The calendric sequences are out of synch by about three hundred years over a five-generation span. Sarmiento's estimates are the most outlandish, given that the lifespans for all but the last two rulers are more than one hundred years.

From a comparison of their figures, it is clear that Sarmiento and Cabello Valboa were working with different information. Moreover, since Morúa did not provide any estimates in years, it is unlikely that Molina is the source of Cabello Valboa's calculations. Sarmiento and Cabello Valboa were working on their own. In the case of the latter—and, to a less noticeable degree, the

TABLE 5.1. *Years in Sarmiento [1572]*

| Inca | Lifespan | Age at Accession | Length of Rule | Year of Death |
|---|---|---|---|---|
| Manco Capac | 144 | 44 | | 665 |
| Sinchi Roca | 127 | 108 | 19 | 675 |
| Lloque Yupanqui | 132 | 21 | 111 | 786 |
| Mayta Capac | 112 | | | 896 |
| Capac Yupanqui | 104 | 15 | 89 | 985 |
| Ynga Roca | 123 | 20 | 103 | 1088 |
| Yahuar Huacac | 115 | 19 | 96 | |
| Viracocha Inca | 110 | 18 | 101 | [blank] |
| Pachacuti | 125 | 22 | 103 | 1191 |
| Topa Inca | 85 | 18 | 67 | 1258 |
| Huayna Capac | 80 | 20 | 60 | 1524 |

TABLE 5.2. *Years in Cabello Valboa [1586]*

| Inca | Lifespan | Age at Accession | Length of Rule | Year of Death |
|---|---|---|---|---|
| Manco Capac | 91 | | 60+ | 1006 |
| Sinchi Roca | 77 | | | 1083 |
| Lloque Yupanqui | 78 | | | 1161 |
| Mayta Capac | | | 65 | 1226 |
| Capac Yupanqui | 80 | | | 1306 |
| Ynga Roca | 50+ | | | 1356 |
| Yahuar Huacac | | | 30 | 1386 |
| Viracocha Inca | | | 50 | 1438 |
| Pachacuti | | | 36 | 1473 |
| Topa Inca | | | 22 | 1493 |
| Huayna Capac | | | 33 | 1525 |

TABLE 5.3. *Comparison of Sarmiento (Corrected) with Cabello Valboa*

| Inca | Rule | Death | Corrected | Cabello Valboa |
|---|---|---|---|---|
| Manco Capac | | 665 | | 1006 |
| Sinchi Roca | 19 | 675 | | 1083 |
| Lloque Yupanqui | 111 | 786 | | 1161 |
| Mayta Capac | | 896 | | 1226 |
| Capac Yupanqui | 89 | 985 | 1008 | 1306 |
| Ynga Roca | 103 | 1088 | 1097 | 1356 |
| Yahuar Huacac | 96 | | 1200 | 1386 |
| Viracocha Inca | 101 | [blank] | 1296 | 1438 |
| Pachacuti | 103 | 1191 | 1397 | 1473 |
| Topa Inca | 67 | 1258 | 1464 | 1493 |
| Huayna Capac | 60 | 1524 | 1524 | 1525 |

former—the reason for calculating the calendar year of death was to synchro-
nize Inca history with what was happening in Europe at the same time. This
concern is overwhelming in Cabello Valboa, who provides more material
about the European past than about the Incas.

Was the obvious interest of these authors in creating equivalent time scales
between the New World and the Old a reason for them to wholly invent information about the lifespan or length of rule of the Inca rulers? Or were their
calculations based in some way on underlying Inca source material? As a way
of moving toward an answer, let us pose a further question: if the calculations
were based on Inca knowledge, then what kind of knowledge?

During the time Sarmiento was collecting material for his narrative, Viceroy Toledo was also querying the Incas on a variety of matters. He used a
questionnaire designed to elicit information about burial practice, sacred objects (*huacas*), and "other customs" (dated Yucay, 2 June 1571; Levillier 1940,
vol. 2:122–125). Question 16 asked:

16. If they know how many years Huayna Capac, Topa Inca, and his father, Pachacuti, lived, and if they died as old or young men, more or less.

XVI. Si saben cuántos años vivió Guaynacapac y el Topainga Yupangui y
su padre Pachacuti Ynga Yupangui y si murieron viejos o mozos poco más
o menos. (Levillier 1940, vol. 2:125)

Only one group of respondents was able to provide an answer to this question.
It included several *panaca* members, among them Alonso Tito Atauchi and
Diego Cayo. They were interviewed in Cuzco on September 5, 1571.

Alonso Tito Atauchi was the son of another Tito Atauchi and a grandson of
Huayna Capac (Sariemento de Gamboa [1572], chap. 60; 1906:105; chap. 63;
1906:114; chap. 68; 1906:125; chap. 69; 1906:128). He was said to be forty
years old at the time of the interview (Levillier 1940, vol. 2:167). He had been
in charge of service to Huayna Capac's mummy in the years before 1559 when
it was removed from *panaca* hands by Polo de Ondegardo. He appears listed
as a member of the *panaca* of Huascar in the list of Incas who authenticated
the Sarmiento manuscript in February 1572 (Sarmiento de Gamboa [1572];
1906:132) either because he was Huascar's full brother or because he had been
accorded that status. In the short statement identifying him in the text before
the questions appear, he noted that his father "had at times been in charge of
governing the kingdom." Diego Cayo was a descendant of Pachacuti; he was

seventy (Levillier 1940, vol. 2:168). He also authenticated the Sarmiento text (Sariento de Gamboa [1572]; 1906:132). In the statement identifying him before the questionnaire he noted that his father had been "second person" of Huayna Capac. I will read their answer to question 16:

16. [In answer] to the sixteenth question the said don Diego Cayo and don Alonso Tito Atauche said that they saw a tablet [or board] and *quipos* where the ages of the said Pachacuti; Topa Inca, his son; and Huayna Capac, son of Topa Inca, were recorded. From the said tablet and *quipo* they saw that Pachacuti had lived one hundred years; Topa Inca, to fifty-eight or sixty; and Huayna Capac, to seventy. The others said that they knew nothing about the matter addressed in the question.

XVI. A las diez y seis preguntas dijeron los dichos don Diego Cayo y don Alonso Tito Atauche, que ellos vieron una tabla y quipos donde estaban sentadas las edades que hubieron los dichos Pachacuti Inga y Topa Inga Yupangui su hijo, y Guayna Capac, hijo del dicho Topa Inga, y que por la dicha tabla y quipo vieron que vivió Pachacuti Inga Yupangui cien años, y Topa Inga Yupangui hasta cincuenta y ocho o sesenta años y Guayna Capac hasta setenta años, y los demás dijeron que no saben de lo contenido en la pregunta cosa alguna. (Levillier 1940, vol. 2:173)

How do we interpret the "tabla y quipo" on which the ages of the Incas were recorded? Gary Urton describes the "reading" of tribute figures from a *quipo* in sixteenth-century Bolivia. In order to arrive at the amount of tribute that was to be paid, a calculation was made using stones. The *quipo*, concluded Urton, encoded the list of what was paid and some multiplier. To answer the question—how much was paid?—a calculation had to be made (1998:413–421). Was the tablet a calculation device? Was the manner of storing information similar to what Urton describes?

There is also reference to using *quipos* for recording information about the length of time an Inca ruled. Cabello Valboa establishes a concordance between the years registered in *quipo* accounts and calendar dates at points in his text where he records when the reigns of Manco Capac and Sinchi Roca began. First he establishes a concordance for Manco Capac:

Finding a concordance between our accounts and those the natives have on their *quipos* and knots of their kings and ancient lords, and using these accounts and their principles, it seems that around the year 945 of Christ our Lord, with Pope Stephen, eighth of those of this name, having the apostolic seat of Saint Peter in Rome [Manco Inca began his rule].

> Concordadas las cuentas nuestras con las que estos naturales tienen por sus Quipos, y ñudos de sus Reyes, y Señores antiguos y de la realidad y principios de ellos parece resultar que cerca de los años de el nacimiento de Christo nro. Redemptor de 945 teniendo la Apostolica Silla de Sant Pedro en Roma el Papa Estefano octauo de los de este nombre. (Cabello Valboa [1586], pt. 3, chap. 10; 1951:264)

Cabello can be obtuse, but he clearly intends for his reader to assume that a concordance had been established between *quipo* records and the papal chronology. His account of Sinchi Roca also begins with a similar statement.

> And according to the *quipos* of the Indians and the conformity of the ages and times with our history that has been found in the matters that we have been talking about, which should be about 1006, more or less, Pope John—the seventeenth of this name—had the holy apostolic see in Rome.

> Y segun la cuenta de los Quipos de los Yndios, y la conformidad que con nras. historias los han allado por la edades, y tiempos en este de que vamos ablando que deue (ser el de mil y seys poco mas o menos) tenia la Silla apostolica en Roma el Papa Juan decimo septimo de este nombre. (Cabello Valboa [1586], pt. 3, chap. 10; 1951:274–275)

Let us suppose, for the sake of argument, that the ages of the Incas had been recorded on a *quipo*. If there was a knowledge of the lifespan of the Inca rulers (even if it was vaguely remembered by people like Diego Cayo and Alonso Tito Atauchi), then this information may have been what Sarmiento and Cabello used as the basis for their calculations. The issue is not whether the information was correctly remembered. Nor does it matter whether or not the numbers recorded on a *quipo* were true measures of the lifespans of particular individuals. The ages recorded can have been ridiculously long; remember that Methuselah was said to have lived more than nine hundred years. The point is that Diego Cayo and Alonso Tito Atauchi described a method of recording ages that had nothing to do with European practice, and Cabello Valboa mentions using them in his calculations.

There is another estimate for the lifespan of Pachacuti that we should look at. Betanzos, too, gives a figure for Pachacuti's life (see table 5.4). However, it

TABLE 5.4 *Lifespan of last three Incas*

| Inca | Cayo and Atauchi | Sarmiento | Betanzos |
|---|---|---|---|
| Pachacuti | 100 | 125 | 120 |
| Topa Inca | 58–60 | 85 | |
| Huayna Capac | up to 70 | 80 | |

*Source*: Betanzos [1551–57], pt. 1, chap. 32; 1987: 150.

is closer to the figure given by Sarmiento than to the hundred years mentioned by Tito Atauchi and Cayo. Since Betanzos appears to have relied on a life history of Pachacuti, we should seriously consider whether or not there was local knowledge about the lifespan of the Incas.

If some kind of information could be gleaned from Inca informants about lifespan, then, in order to derive a series of calendar dates for the dynastic succession, either a figure for the age of each Inca at accession or for the length of rule was also required. Sarmiento routinely supplies both, except for Mayta Capac. What can be noted from the ages he gives for the succession of each ruler is that, with the exception of the first two, all of the Incas succeeded as young men, age fifteen to twenty. If Sarmiento had asked how old the Incas were at the time of succession and was told they were young men, he could have supplied the figure for their age at accession so that he could calculate length of rule. Cabello Valboa gives lifespan information for five of the first six Incas and length of rule for the next five. However, when you examine his calculations, it is immediately apparent that he is using lifespan as if it were length of rule. It is unfortunate that he does not supply lifespan figures for the last three Incas. These figures might have been more in line with the ages given by Alonso Tito Atauchi and Diego Cayo.

## COMPOSITION

Despite the latitude available to Spanish authors to impose their own order on material drawn from Inca sources and to suppress, editorialize, and invent, there are enough similarities between the narratives they composed to substantiate a claim that they drew from Inca genres. The only other acceptable hypothesis is that these authors copied from each other, and the similarities are due to textual borrowings. While there is no reason not to continue to look for textual borrowing, comparison of the texts for their Inca content is long overdue. Since we have seen the results of textual borrowing in the case of Morúa's and Cabello Valboa's use of Molina, we can also hypothesize that textual borrowing may tend to reproduce the structure of an underlying text to a greater degree than would borrowing from an oral source. The differences between a presumed Cobo/Polo source and Sarmiento, for example, will have more to do with what these authors took from their Inca informants and, in the case of generic material, from which genres. The same kind of archaeological methods that we use to uncover dependencies on written sources can be used to excavate oral sources, although the results are an approximation.

Our focus has been on two genres that were principal vehicles for a representation of the Inca past, if we judge by what was incorporated in Spanish historical narratives. They were certainly what the Incas of Cuzco responded with when Spaniards began to be interested in what the Incas knew about their own past. Moreover, the explicit statements that Spaniards like Betanzos and Sarmiento make about the preservation and transmission of Inca genres fit fairly well with the evidence from Spanish historical narratives about them.

Our entree into the subject was an Inca interest in genealogy. Genealogy is a kind of history itself. There is another form of history which we know as biography. The Incas, too, had a kind of biography that had as its subject the life history of Inca rulers. To unravel the subject matter of an Inca genre we have examined what our sources said about Pachacuti and Topa Inca. The sheer length of the accounts of these two Incas would suggest that they drew from life history sources, even if we had no other way of making that argument. Since we can extract a fairly clear picture of the life history of Pachacuti from the account of Betanzos, we can begin to see the traces of a life history in the much murkier material recorded in the Spanish narratives about Topa Inca.

Since these rulers were actively involved in expanding the authority of Cuzco over distant regions, it stands to reason that their lives were fertile sources for the production of detailed life histories, stories, and long lists of the Andean lords, fortresses, and territories annexed to what had become an empire. When the subject is earlier rulers, identifying life history material is a different sort of problem. It may overlap to a greater degree with the genealogical genre, expecially if the two genres were composed at the same time.

Perhaps the accounts that drew from the life history sources are those which contain evidence of underlying narratives, assuming, as we do, that the life history has a narrative basis. For example, the Lloque Yupanqui story has narrative features. The Sun appears and talks with Lloque Yupanqui. There is a story about how the problem of his marriage was solved. That Sarmiento, Cabello Valboa, and Cobo drew from a similar underlying source is evident not simply from the parallels between events but also from the list of local lords who came to talk with Lloque Yupanqui. Are these features of a life history? Likewise, the Mayta Capac story incorporates a narrative about a war with the Alcabizas in which Mayta Capac shows his bellicose spirit. The young Inca leads the Incas into battle. The narrative structure includes events leading up to conflict, two battles, and a supernatural intervention. Is this the stuff of life history? Whether there is an underlying narrative is less obvious in the case of Capac Yupanqui. There are some parallels in the accounts of Cabello Valboa and Cobo. Is it possible that they reflect life history material while Sarmiento does not?

The problems multiply in the accounts of Inca Roca and later Incas. Cabello Valboa has very little to say about Inca Roca. Sarmiento may be repeating what he has included on other Incas. Cobo sequences his material differently and includes information about the conquests of the rulers from Capac Yupanqui onward that appears nowhere else, for example, Capac Yupanqui's campaign in Cuyos and his conquest of Condesuyo, Inca Roca's alliance with the Canas and Canchis and his campaign in Paucartambo, and Viracocha Inca's conquest of Canas and Canchis. Both Cabello Valboa and Cobo contextualize the Chanca attack on Pachacuti in a very different manner than Betanzos and Sarmiento, who appear to have drawn from a life history. Perhaps at some point we are dealing with differences between the life history and genealogical genre, but how are we to know when this is the case, or when the difference is due to how the Spanish authors dealt with generic material?

Although we have been able to identify two genres, it is only possible in certain cases to tell where the narratives drew from one or the other. We can be fairly certain that Betanzos drew from a source within a particular *panaca*: the life history. Other authors, like Sarmiento, had material from the genealogical genre, including the story of Inca origins. The genealogical genre may have had an event structure like the life histories. If the story of origins headed the genealogical genre, it certainly did.

Sarmiento and Betanzos present problems, but we can feel more certain about what they included. But what about Polo, if we can use Cobo as a guide to a historical account. Could he have drawn from both the genealogical and the life history? Polo was well acquainted with the *panacas* and found some of the *quipos* said to be recordings of the deeds of Pachacuti. Would these have been his principal sources, or is he rather the first author to marry the genealogical genre with the life history material? What about Molina? Will a comparison between Cobo, on the one hand, and Cabello Valboa/Morúa (after the material from the *quipo* of the conquests of Topa Inca is removed), on the other, produce a sharper image of the text of the genealogical genre?

We have noted in passing a number of specific cases where the sequencing of events in the period of overlap between two lifetimes caused problems in the narrative. The problems with sequencing explain one of the anomalies of the corpus of historical narratives that has long bothered scholars interested in the Incas: the repetition of events, particularly military campaigns. We can explain this repetition. If the Inca genre or genres that supplied them with material followed a life history format, then the sequencing of events near the accession or death of a ruler was done by the authors of Spanish narratives in the creation of a seamless, temporally ordered narrative. We would thus expect there to be problems in sequencing events that occurred during the overlap in lifetimes between one ruler and the next. When, as in the case of Topa Inca, the successor reached adulthood many years before the father died, a great deal of repetition might be the result.

What is interesting to note is that sequencing was also a problem in the accounts of the Incas prior to Pachacuti. The problems with sequencing are all the more evident because of the interest shown in the early years of the future ruler. A precocious interest in warfare or a demonstration of bravery was a topic that seems more often than not to have outshown the deeds of the mature person, at least in the period before the Incas campaigned outside their political neighborhood. For example, the most important events related about Yahuar Huacac and Mayta Capac occurred during their youth and long before the transfer of power. In the case of Sarmiento's treatment of Yahuar Huacac's kidnapping, the account may have been a separate story, like the Ulti story. However, other authors who do not tell this story in any detail at least mention it (Cieza de León [1553], chap. 37; 1986 : 100), sequencing it in their narratives differently from other authors.

So far, our concern with sequence has been with how Spanish authors worked. If they were constructing a narrative from life histories, they would have had to fuse the accounts for the period of overlap between lifetimes. But what of the genealogical genre, especially the accounts of the first seven rulers? Was it a single narrative or a sequence of life histories? We have argued that Sarmiento and Cabello Valboa/Morúa (M2) had access to it. If the underlying genre was a single narrative, temporally ordered, we would not expect the sequencing problems that we have seen. The genealogical genre may have been a composite of life histories. Within a life history format, life events were used to structure Inca accounts, so a sense of historical process may have been a feature even of the genealogical genre.

More comparative study can sharpen what we know about underlying Inca genres, and questions certainly remain. Now we have some idea of what the underlying Inca genres were like. Nonetheless, other issues only begin to emerge as we read the Spanish historical narratives. As will become clear when we start to read them, an awareness of the nature of Inca source materials guides how we understand the themes and messages conveyed in them. Since there are various voices in our texts, we want to try to distinguish between themes and messages communicated by the Spaniards and those of their sources.

# 6 Emergence

Heretofore we have spoken of historical narratives in Spanish and what we have called Inca genres. The texts we have are the former. In them are the hazy reflections of the latter. So far we have treated the underlying Inca sources like texts, but can we? The Inca genres we have identified were very different from the written narratives which drew from them. Some were unique products. A performance tradition was associated with them, and to the extent that aspects of their content were linked to performance, we will never fully know them. Still, like the plays that are performed on our stages, there was a recorded version that could be transmitted independently. Recorded genres do not have to be performed to be transmitted. What we are "reading" is not a performance tradition but an underlying text. Like texts, we can assume there was a certain stability in the content of recorded genres that would not characterize the products of memory alone. Texts can also be changed, and whether these texts reflect the form they had when first composed is an open question. When they were transmitted to Spaniards and translated into Spanish, they evolved in other ways.

However, so long as the transmission process was in native hands, we can consider these sources to be Inca genres. Certain events affected the keeping of these genres: at some point the painted wooden tablets were removed from their setting; Polo de Ondegardo collected the bodies of the Inca rulers in 1559 and perhaps removed the *quipo* records from the hands of the individuals who kept them; individuals who had learned oral versions of a story or other generic material at some point failed to transmit it. However, even when records were destroyed or removed from context, there was still memory. As long as there was some benefit to be gained from genealogical calculation to the line of descent from Manco Capac, the genealogy was transmitted. When Cobo wrote in the mid–seventeenth century, he said he could still collect an account from the Incas of Cuzco like the one told in his manuscript sources.

In our study of Inca genres we have privileged historical narratives that drew from Inca sources in Cuzco. Some Spaniards, like Sarmiento and Betanzos, transmitted or compiled Inca generic material, subordinating their own voices to a degree. However, we do not know who their informants were or how they had learned what they knew. When Betanzos wrote, the *quipos* of the life history of Pachacuti were still held by his *panaca*. When Sarmiento came to Cuzco twenty years later, he collected a version of this account that was similar in general outline. That he could collect something similar in outline is evidence for some kind of formal transmission process. Here we are speaking of a specific life history, but what of the content of the painted history? If the physical record had been destroyed, were its contents preserved in another format so that later accounts drew from some type of record, or was a knowledge of it preserved through memory alone?

There are other questions as well. Sarmiento's text is a compilation of Inca source materials. We have assumed that the processing of Inca source material into a new form of narrative was done by Sarmiento, but the compilation or reconciliation of Inca source material may have been done to some extent by those who kept and transmitted Inca genres, particularly as they learned about European forms of scholarship. In the process of translating and recording this material in Spanish, the stories may have been retold in answer to queries that resulted in explanation. As will be seen, Sarmiento embodies an explanation of the rise to power of the descent group of Manco Capac. He may have understood what he heard as an explanation, the underlying account may have already incorporated an explanation, or the explanation was supplied by his informants in the process of transmission. We cannot know how the explanation was inserted into the text. Furthermore, we need to ask as well about how changes in values or beliefs may have affected the transmission of generic material. Such changes may affect the content of the narratives in subtle ways. When we read, we have to read with these questions in mind.

There are messages embedded in the historical narratives, some of which seem to transcend both the genealogical and the life history formats. At times the authorial voice seems to have expert knowledge of the Inca past, a knowledge which the Spanish author could not have had. For example, Sarmiento gives voice to an overarching narrative about the Inca expansion that he does not seem to understand. At other times, one part of his story cannot be squared with another, and each sends messages about the organization of Cuzco that would seem to reflect a rationale that was not Sarmiento's own. Sarmiento's narrative accomplishes a number of tasks, aside from its essential purpose in documenting the shallow time depth of the Inca empire, structured by a string of only twelve rulers. It is a story about the emergence of the Incas. It identifies the people descended from Manco Capac as well as the peoples who inhabited Cuzco who were not Inca. In short, it answers the questions,

Who are the inhabitants of Cuzco, and how did they come to be there? Sarmiento also describes the expansion of Cuzco. Through the story of Inti, he describes the emergence of Inca aggression in largely symbolic terms. The symbols are not European, so he is giving voice to another interpretive system. Finally, he describes a political landscape populated by other peoples recognized as *capac* who, as the story is told, constituted obstacles to Inca hegemony. Sarmiento himself does not seem to understand the significance of the term *capac*, so the narrator's voice in this story is not his.

At the same time, the basic Inca sources he drew from — if we have correctly grasped their nature — are insufficient as vehicles for these messages. Sarmiento had access to an Inca genealogical genre. He also had other materials, for example, the life history of Pachacuti and a *quipo* recording the conquests of Topa Inca. He compiled a narrative from native sources, adding what was known about the collection of the mummies and idols of particular rulers and their descendants then alive. We cannot be certain of all the sources he used, but — based on our understanding of the genealogical genre and life history genres — they do not permit the incorporation of threads of narrative that span the sequence of rulers or explain the transformation of Cuzco and the growth of Inca power. Nonetheless, the knowledge that would permit the incorporation of such features into the narrative did not come from Sarmiento. In fact, Sarmiento knew very little about the Incas. He had only recently arrived in Cuzco. What he writes when he is not representing Inca history is very different in tone from what he wrote about the Incas: his compositions — even his letters — display an erudition that creates a very different impression on the reader than his narration of Inca history.[1]

In this chapter we will examine one of the messages embedded in Sarmiento's text. We will look at what he says about the emergence of the Incas and the expansion of Inca power. Our interest in the first half of the book was to detect the Inca sources available to Spanish authors when they composed their narratives. From this point on, we are beginning the task of reading Inca history.

## THE EMERGENCE OF THE INCAS

The story is essentially local history until near the time of the Inca expansion. Although we know that the Cuzco region had been inhabited for thousands of years, the story only spans the time covered by eleven generations. Even some of the Spaniards who transmitted the dynastic history, for example, Cieza de León and Bernabé Cobo, were aware that there were ruins of buildings from earlier times, times that the dynastic story did not reach (Cieza de León [1550], chap. 102; 1984:278; chap. 105; 1984:282–284; Cobo [1653], bk. 12, chap. 1; 1892:111–112).

The most universally repeated story about Inca origins describes the emergence of four brothers and four sisters, two of whom were the progenitors of the Inca dynastic descent group, from the central of three windows at a place called Tambotoco or Pacaritambo (map 1). Sarmiento and Molina add an earlier phase of creation, where a Creator god organizes the emergence of not just the Incas but other Andean peoples (Molina [1576]; 1989:50–55). An account of this earlier, universal creation phase is absent from the *Discurso* and Las Casas. Cobo tells it after telling several other origin stories: the first about the arrival of Manco Capac from the Lake Titicaca area; the second, the Pacaritambo origin story; and the third, the story of a universal creation by a Creator god. Gutiérrez tells the first of Cobo's versions, extending the time that the dynasty spent in the Lake Titicaca area.

Clearly, what was told about origins was in a state of flux. Some versions may reflect the penetration of Christianity, which involved a belief that the world was created all at once by a single Creator deity. There may have always been competing versions in the earlier period, but the Inca genealogical genre began with the Pacaritambo story. All of the accounts we have compared include it except Gutiérrez. Of course, the story of the Ayar brothers and sisters is the logical starting point of an account of the descent group of Manco Capac.

The origin myth as myth will be analyzed in chapter 8. Here we will read the story of the arrival of the Ayar siblings in Cuzco. Although versions of the genealogical genre that have been transmitted through Spanish narratives differ in important details, the story — however it is told — incorporates a landscape that is real. Gary Urton, in a study of Pacaritambo that looks toward the present and interprets the story in light of ethnographic research in Pacaritambo, reads it against the background of contemporary ethnography. In his reading, he sees a reflection of the world as viewed from Pacaritambo. He also relates the story to concrete places on the landscape in the Pacaritambo region (1990:37–39, map 2). The story is about a journey from Pacaritambo to Cuzco. Although the identity of some places is tentative (i.e., Matagua, but see Rowe 1944: fig. 1 and p. 43), Urton is clearly able to trace the itinerary of the Ayar brothers and sisters from the area near Pacaritambo to Cuzco (1990:37–41). Moreover, the story of origins has an event structure like the life histories of particular rulers and would be impossible to separate from the material related to Manco Capac were it not for textual clues (see chapter 5). Although there are other versions of origins, we will analyze the Pacaritambo story here.

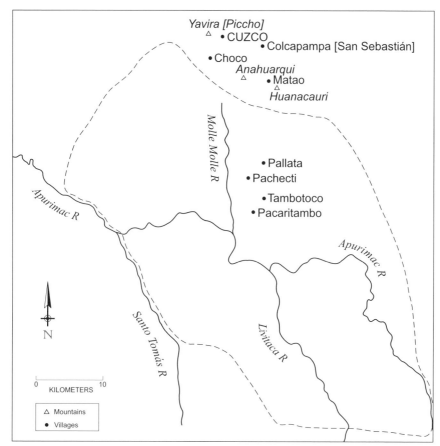

Map 1. Places associated with the story of Inca origins.

The painted history was said to have begun with a story of origins. If this story was the Pacaritambo story, then we can apply the same theory of composition to it as we have done in the case of the genealogical genre and as the life histories of the early rulers; that is, if we accept as a hypothesis that both were composed by Pachacuti after the Inca expansion began, then this material was composed in one or two specific composition episodes at approximately the same time. The life history material recorded after the death of Viracocha, Pachacuti, Topa Inca, and, possibly, Huayna Capac was composed in separate, later episodes. Moreover, the later material may have been more strongly influenced by memory at the time Inca historical traditions were being transmitted to Spaniards. What Pachacuti recorded about earlier generations in the Inca dynastic line may have involved working with memory alone, but we cannot discount the possibility that some kind of formal record had been kept. Regardless, Pachacuti could easily reshape these materials into a story that foreshadowed the Inca imperial project in his own time. When we read the accounts of the earlier rulers, we should not read these accounts as a pristine transmission of a remote Inca past but as a story told after Inca power was a fact.

As we read the story of the emergence of the Incas we will keep this compositional history in mind, treating it as a hypothesis. First we will read the story of origins for the image it contains of a historical landscape. Sarmiento is our principal source and point of departure, so we will take the narrative line from him, considering other sources when they confirm Sarmiento or present other possibilities.

Sarmiento does not begin with Ayar origins but rather with a chapter on the peoples who resided in the Cuzco Valley before the Incas came and then another on the absence of natural lords in the Andean region. The second chapter is clearly an addition motivated by the Toledo campaign to prove that the Incas were not natural lords and that there had been none in the Andes. The first may be as well. Near the time Sarmiento finished his work and prior to the assembly of *panaca* members to authenticate it, Toledo collected testimony from various groups of people from the *ayllos* which, as noted in Sarmiento's text, had resided in the Cuzco Valley at the time of Manco Capac's arrival. A standard questionnaire was administered to each of four groups, named the Ayllo Sahuasiray, Quisco (or Ayllo Antasayac), the *ayllo* of Ayarucho (or the Alcabizas), and the Huallas (spellings as in the original; Levillier 1940, vol. 2:182–195). Sarmiento may have used some of the same people who appeared before Toledo, but there are differences between what he narrated and what the witnesses answered in their interviews. First, let us look at the story Sarmiento told.

Sarmiento writes that the Incas emerged from the central window of Tambotoco and that two other lineages, called Maras and Sutic, emerged from the windows on either side of it. People descended from these two lineages still lived in Cuzco when Sarmiento wrote. People from other lineages in the Tambotoco area also accompanied the Ayar siblings to Cuzco. Sarmiento lists ten such groups, including the descendants of two of Manco Capac's brothers as well as the Maras and Sutic groups ([1572], chap. 11; 1906:34):

*Hanan Cuzco*
   Chauin Cuzco Ayllo, the lineage of Ayar Cache
   Arayraca Ayllo Cuzco Callan, the lineage of Ayar Uchu
   Tarpuntay Ayllo
   Huacaytaqui Ayllo
   Saño Ayllo

*Hurin Cuzco*

    Sutic Toco Ayllo, those who emerged from Sutic Toco

    Maras Ayllo, those who emerged from Maras Toco

    Cuycusa Ayllo

    Masca Ayllo

    Oro Ayllo

When the scene shifts to Cuzco, Sarmiento describes a number of groups that were already settled near what would become the Inca city. Two had been there for a long time, while three others had arrived in the more recent past from the same area from which the Incas had come and were led by three captains. The first two groups were the Sauaseras and the Huallas. The Huallas were settled near Arco Punco, the gate on the road to the Lake Titicaca region (map 2). The Sauaseras were settled at the site of modern Santo Domingo. Obviously, these were small groups. They were agriculturalists, and their fields were adjacent to their houses. The Incas attacked the Huallas first, killing everyone. They then threatened the Sauaseras, who had chosen one of the three captains, named Copalimayta, to defend them. The Incas defeated Copalimayta and took what had belonged to him. They settled permanently on Copalimayta's site, where the temple of Coricancha was later built. From this time forward, the Incas held the land between the Huatanay and Tullumayo Rivers, where Cuzco was to develop (Sarmiento de Gamboa [1572], chap. 11; 1906:30; chap. 13; 1906:39–40).

There are details in the testimony collected by Toledo that tell a different story. For one thing, the witnesses from the *ayllo* of Sauasiray said they were descended from Sauasiray, a captain from Sutic Toco. When this captain arrived in the Cuzco Valley, he found only the Huallas. In Sarmiento's story, the "Sauaseras" are represented as non-Inca, or at least they are not identified as having originated in Pacaritambo. According to the witnesses, the captain Sauasiray settled at Quinticancha and Chumbicancha, later renamed Coricancha by Pachacuti. Manco Capac displaced Sauasiray and his family, but Pachacuti later organized a descent group of his descendants (Levillier 1940, vol. 2:185).

Two groups remained, referred to as Alcabizas and Culunchimas in the Sarmiento story, after the captains who had led them to the Cuzco area. Both groups occupied lands on the other side of the Huatanay, the Alcabizas near modern Santa Clara and the Culunchimas in the area northeast of Belén at its first location in Coripata (map 2). The Incas took lands away from the Alcabizas by taking their source of irrigation water away. The Culunchimas were

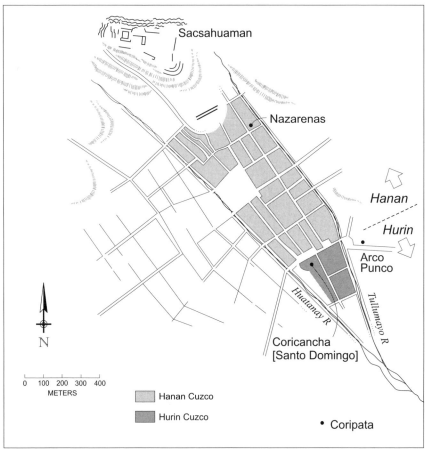

Map 2. Imperial Cuzco (after Niles 1999: fig. 3.5).

made to pay tribute (Sarmiento de Gamboa [1572], chap. 14; 1906:41–42; Rowe 1994:173–184).

Again, the Sarmiento story does not agree with the information given to Toledo. The group of people identified as the *ayllo* of Ayar Ucho said they were now called Alcabizas (Levillier 1940, vol. 2:186–187). In Sarmiento's list, the descendants of Ayar Ucho belonged to the *ayllo* named Arayraca Ayllo Cuzco Callan, a group that arrived in Cuzco with Manco Capac ([1572], chap. 11; 1906:34), while the Alcabizas were already present in the Cuzco Valley at the time the Ayar siblings arrived.

Rather than try to reconcile these discrepancies, it is more productive to ask why they exist, particularly since information about early Cuzco was collected by both Sarmiento and Toledo at nearly the same time. Perhaps the best answer is that Sarmiento took his information from the descendants of Manco

Capac, since it was their story he was trying to tell, whereas Toledo interviewed people from the other groups. Where the stories differ, the Inca version portrays a group as being essentially foreign, whereas in the group's own testimony, a relationship to the Incas is evident. There is a bias in these stories, although we do not have very sophisticated methods for interpreting it.

If we follow the account of the witnesses who belonged to groups present in Cuzco when Manco Capac arrived, then everyone but the Huallas had some kind of tie to the region from which the Incas came. Even Sarmiento tells us that the Incas, the Alcabizas, and the Culunchimas have a common origin. What we are not told, but what appears to underlie the story, is that the Ayar siblings are part of a larger group that, by circumstance or design, had encroached on the lands in the Cuzco Valley, perhaps long before. In the story it seems as if they are strangers, arriving in a new place. The Ayar siblings took the lands of the Huallas — the only group who did not claim some relationship — away by force, and the Huallas fled to an area remote from Cuzco, where they were still settled in the time of the Toledo inquiry. The Ayar siblings then took the lands of the "Sauaseras" away from them and built their own settlement there, but the "Sauaseras" remained in the area. Is the Inca version of their past a biased retelling of the expansion of a group of which they were part, recasting peoples who were related to the Incas as foreigners to foreshadow a later period when the Incas were to conquer foreign nations? If so, the story hides the gradual shift of power from some other center of power to Cuzco and suppresses any hint of the subordination of the Incas to a larger political unit. This larger group fades into the background in the Inca account.

When the story shifts in the next generations to relations with other important local lords, the rest of the political landscape begins to emerge. The Cuzco Valley is at the frontier between several groups competing at the regional level. A very tentative map can be drawn with the approximate locations of the groups mentioned in the Sarmiento narrative and from early colonial documentation (map 3). Drawing such a map is extremely problematic because it relies on images from different parts of the story which may not be contemporary with each other. Still, having some means of drawing even a hazy image of the political landscape of the Cuzco region in the period before the Inca expansion is a minor miracle.

That the Incas were part of a larger group can be argued on other grounds. In chapter 3, information was cited from the accounts of Morúa and Fernández about who was "properly" Inca. There were four groups of Incas: Hanan Cuzco, Hurin Cuzco, Tambo, and Masca.[2] This answer could only have been given after the two *sayas* of Cuzco were created. What is of interest here are

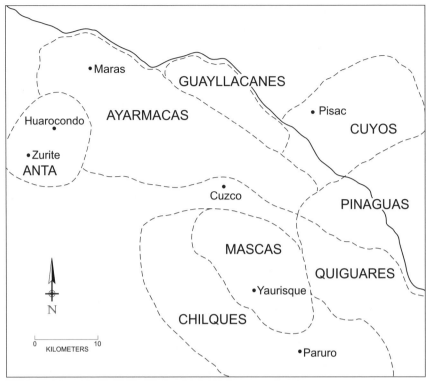

Map 3. The Cuzco region.

the last two items on the list. There were two groups of people recognized as Inca who were referred to as Tambo Inca in the account of Guaman Poma: one in the Ollantaytambo area and the other in Pacaritambo. The name Mascas appears in the name of the *corregimiento* organized in the area just south of Cuzco, called the Corregimiento of Chilques and Mascas. The Mascas were resettled in Yaurisque at the time of the Toledo resettlement program (Julien 1991:map 9, p. 79; see also p. 83). Here again is a clue that confirms an Inca tie to the Pacaritambo region.

In the Sarmiento narrative, the people who emerged from Sutic Toco were Tambos, and they settled in the area around Tambotoco. The witnesses from the Ayllo Sauasiray said they were from Sutic Toco. Are they telling us they are part of the group also identified as Tambos? What we read into the witnesses' testimony differs greatly from the interpretation of the Inca past that Toledo was trying to present. Toledo wanted to cast the Incas as violent usurpers of lands that belonged to someone else. The Inca story, with its portrayal of the Ayar siblings as powerful conquerors who arrived from outside and took over lands that did not belong to them and with its suppression of any hint that they might have been subordinate to other groups, served Toledo's purposes. He did, however, collect information, both through the interview of witnesses and through Sarmiento, that gives us a somewhat different picture of who the Incas were when they arrived in Cuzco.

Although the story of the rise to power of the Incas does not speak directly about the early subordination of the Incas to other groups, it encodes information that enables us to examine the changing position of the Incas within the Cuzco region. In chapter 2, on the transmission of *capac* status, an argument was made that the Incas were affiliated through the male line. An ideology of descent is clearly present. The dynastic line became a conduit for this status; once the dynasty recognized its importance, the status was preserved through marriage to a woman who was also descended from Manco Capac, even a sister. We have assembled the genealogical information in a body of historical narratives. Except for Guaman Poma and parts of the Murúa text that document sister-marriage from the time of Manco Capac onward, the other accounts name spouses who were not members of the dynastic descent group for the period before the time of the tenth pair (tables 3.1–3.13). Certain authors — among them Cieza, Las Casas, Cobo, Sarmiento, Cabello Valboa, and Morúa (M2) — routinely provide information about the origins of this woman. One of the possibilities inherent in the unilineal reckoning of descent — when discretely bounded groups are defined — is that patterns of marriage alliance between these groups will emerge, that is, that the women of certain groups are the preferred spouses of the men of others. Such alliance may not be symmetrical. As noted in chapter 2, there are people in the Cuzco area today who recognize a dominance hierarchy between "wife-givers" and "wife-takers," those in the former category being superior to those in the latter (Webster 1977:36–40). Sarmiento and other Spaniards who drew from dynastic sources were unaware of any status differences conferred through marriage, although there is some evidence that such differences existed (Guaman Poma de Ayala [1615], 1987:301 [303], 847 [861]–848 [862]; Arriaga [1618]; 1968:215). If we read the narratives about the period before the imperial expansion, the pattern of marriages tells us as much about alliance and subordination as the narrative itself, maybe more. The story of the rise of an important power in the Cuzco area is a story of both conquest and alliance.

Let us now examine the Sarmiento account with both the pattern of marriages and the information about conquest in mind. From this point on, we assume that Sarmiento drew from life histories and/or other materials that could be accommodated within the lifespan of a particular ruler, although these materials can have been historicized by his informants. According to the

Sarmiento narrative, the Incas established their dominance over the Cuzco Valley in the fourth generation. We will focus first on this early period.

Manco Capac marries a sister, whether she is identified as Mama Huaco or Mama Ocllo. They have a son at Tamboquiro, which Urton has identified as a site near Pallata (1990:map 2, p. 38), before arriving at the site of Cuzco (Sarmiento de Gamboa [1572], chap. 12; 1906:35). This son, Sinchi Roca, marries Mama Coca of Saño, a place in the Cuzco Valley (map 1). However, one of the groups said to have come with Manco Capac is Sañoc Ayllu. The people of Saño, then, may have ties to the Tambo region. If so, then the first spouse came from within the larger group of which the Incas form a part. Her father is Sutic Guaman. If his name is a reference to Sutic Toco, then this woman may be from the group the Incas called Tambos, since Sarmiento noted that they emerged from Sutic Toco. Various authors confirm the origins of this woman in Saño, and several name Sutic Guaman as her father (table 3.3).

If we posit a status differentiation between groups conferred through marriage, then the Incas were subordinate to the Tambos or to some group within the larger group. If this marriage reflects a preferred choice in a system of marriage alliance, then women from a Tambo group were preferred spouses for Inca men. Both interpretations are highly speculative but necessary correctives to other interpretations of marriage that do not examine the development of dynastic practice that can be read from the genealogy preserved by Inca genres or take what we know about native practice elsewhere in South America into account.

Sinchi Roca and Mama Coca produce a son, Lloque Yupanqui (table 3.3). This Inca marries Mama Caua or Mama Cagua Pata from Oma, "two leagues from Cuzco," or approximately 10 km away (table 3.4). The distance measurement is our only means of identifying this place.[3] Lloque Yupanqui and Mama Caua had Mayta Capac. Nothing much happened in this period, except that the Sun appeared to Lloque Yupanqui in human form and told him that his descendants would be great lords (Sarmiento de Gamboa [1572], chap. 16; 1906:45).

Things began to change in the next generation. Sarmiento incorporates a story about a stone object in the form of a bird that was named Inti (Indi). This object appears to have been related to Inca aggression, which began with Manco Capac and became manifest again in the time of Mayta Capac. Manco Capac brought this image with him from Tambotoco. Each Inca had some kind of sacred object called a *huaoque*, or "brother," that was handed down to his descendants. Inti was the *huaoque* of Manco Capac. Manco Capac and a number of generations that followed him resided at Inticancha. Where the term *cancha* is used, a type of architectural complex, consisting of houses arranged around a court and sometimes enclosed by an exterior wall, can be understood (Gasparini and Margolies 1980 : 181–191). Inticancha may be a reference to the place where Inti resided. The object itself was kept in a chest made of straw that was not opened until Mayta Capac, Manco Capac's descendant in the fifth generation, had the temerity to open it. Some sacred objects could speak, and this one gave advice to Mayta Capac. At this time, the Alcabizas and the Culunchimas still had some kind of autonomy; Inca domination of the Cuzco Valley was not yet complete. Mayta Capac conquered them through force of arms. The sacred object called Inti was related to warfare. Mayta Capac's descendant, Capac Yupanqui, was the first Inca to conquer outside of the immediate Cuzco area. The removal of Inti from its box, then, marks the point at which the Incas began to exhibit the aggressive behavior that resulted in the creation of an empire. Campaigns were undertaken by Capac Yupanqui and subsequent Incas against various peoples located within about 20 km of Cuzco, not yet very far away (Sarmiento de Gamboa [1575], chap. 14; 1906 : 41–42; chap. 17; 1906 : 47; chap. 18; 1906 : 48).

Mayta Capac married Mama Tacucaray, who came from a town named Tacucaray or Tancaray (table 3.5). Again, the information is problematic; not even a distance measurement is given.[4] The only author who tells who her father was is Cobo; he says her father was a Collaguas lord. The Collaguas were settled in the headwaters of the Colca River, a great distance from Cuzco. That she came from so far away seems far-fetched, particularly when subsequent generations are still marrying locally.[5]

From this period onward, the Incas begin to be actors on the regional level, although their version does not tell us if they acted independently or as subordinates of other, more dominant groups. Capac Yupanqui married Curi Hilpay, daughter of an important lord of the Ayarmacas (table 3.6). By all accounts, the Ayarmacas were the most important group in the region. The political head of the Ayarmacas was known as Tocay Capac. The term, as used here, is a title, and the name referred to other individuals who held the title at other times. From the fifth generation on, the historical account can be read for information about marriage alliance with other other local powers, chief among them, the Ayarmacas (Betanzos [1551–1557], pt. 1, chap. 27; 1987 : 131–132; Sarmiento de Gamboa [1572], chap. 11; 1987 : 33; chap. 48; 1987 : 18). If the marriage of Capac Yupanqui with an important Ayarmaca woman is interpreted in light of a status difference conferred through marriage, then the Incas were allied with the Ayarmacas but subordinate to them.

A problem began to manifest itself when Capac Yupangui's son Inca Roca married Mama Micay, a Guayllacan woman (table 3.7). Guayllacan was a regional power occupying territory on the Urubamba River near what is now Pisac (map 2). Mama Micay had been promised by the Guayllacanes to Tocay Capac. When she was given to Inca Roca in marriage, hostilities broke out between the Guayllacanes and the Ayarmacas. While they were still going on, Mama Micay bore Inca Roca a son. One of the conditions for peace was that the Guayllacanes kidnap this child and present him to Tocay Capac. Through treachery that may have been facilitated by the Ayarmaca affiliation of Curi Hilpay, the son was captured and presented to Tocay Capac. The boy, Yahuar Huacac, impressed and frightened Tocay Capac, who spared his life. With the help of another regional power, occupying the plain of Anta, northwest of Cuzco, the boy was freed. This story was told in great detail in the Sarmiento narrative but was barely mentioned in Cabello Valboa and was absent from Murúa (M2) (Cabello Valboa [1586], pt. 3, chap. 13; 1951:293–294; Morúa [1590], chap. 9; 1946:66). Later, a marriage was forged between the Incas and the Ayarmacas. A daughter of Inca Roca named Curi Ocllo was given to Tocay Capac to marry, while Yahuar Huacca married a daughter of Tocay Capac named Mama Chiquia. (table 3.8)

The marriage expresses the emergence of the Incas as a power vis-à-vis the Ayarmacas. From a subordinate position, they had acquired a position of equality or near equality. Marriage was more than an expression of relative status, however. It was the foundation of a military alliance with the Ayarmacas. In the campaigns conducted by Capac Yupanqui, the Incas appear to have been subordinate to the Ayarmacas. During the period of the next two generations, the power relation shifts, and the Incas emerge as the most powerful group in the Cuzco region. Viracocha, the son of Yahuar Huacac, goes to war against Tocay Capac and is successful. In the Sarmiento narrative, this conquest is only one among many conquests in the local area ([1572], chap. 23; 1906:54–55). Perhaps in light of later conquests, the importance of this one diminishes; however, in the context of local power relations, it marked the emergence of the Incas as the supreme power in the Cuzco region.

As noted in chapter 5, the account of the life of Viracocha was volatile, in comparison with what was preserved about other Incas. In the narrative of Cieza de León, more detail about the conquests of Viracocha is presented than in other narratives. According to Cieza, Viracocha ventured far beyond the Cuzco region, subordinating peoples up to 100 km away in the direction of Lake Titicaca. Viracocha annexed the territory of Canas and Canchis, effectively launching the Inca imperial expansion. As mentioned above, Viracocha forayed into the Lake Titicaca region ([Cieza de León 1553], chaps. 42–43;

1986:121–128). The Sarmiento story downplays Viracocha's military accomplishments. The defeat of Tocay Capac was a signal event in the history of the Inca expansion, but it, too, is not given a prominent place in Sarmiento's narrative ([1572], chaps. 24–25; 1906:56–59). What is given prominence is the attack on Cuzco by the Chancas, a political power centered near Andahuaylas, north of Cuzco, and the rise to power of Pachacuti, one of Viracocha's sons. Pachacuti is the principal actor in the version of Inca past narrated by Sarmiento and Betanzos. Sarmiento appears to have relied heavily on a life history of Pachacuti, perhaps allowing the importance given to the Chanca invasion in the life history to overshadow the events of the prior period. Cieza's account supports a view that the Inca expansion began before the Chanca attack, with campaigns in Canas and Canchis.

Viracocha married Mama Ronto Caya of Anta (table 3.9). At the time of his father's capture, there was a lord of Anta who appears to have acted independently of Tocay Capac in helping the Incas to recover the young Yahuar Huacac. Perhaps this marriage served to return this favor or to pay a debt.

An abrupt change in the pattern of Inca marriage occurs in the ninth generation. Pachacuti marries Anahuarqui, a woman from Choco (table 3.10). The marriage occurs after the Chanca invasion but before any significant military campaigns outside of Cuzco. We know no more about Anahuarqui than that she came from a place very near Cuzco. She was very likely a member of the same larger group as the descent group of Manco Capac. Why marry locally? While over the several preceding generations the Incas had used marriage to forge a role for themselves in regional politics, taking a wife from another group involved subordination on a symbolic level, if not other obligations. By marrying locally, Pachacuti did not involve the descent group in another such alliance. In fact, no more such alliances were to be made. In the next generation, Pachacuti would marry a son to the son's full sister (table 3.11).

## OTHER CAPACS

Pachacuti, during the long period of his rule, subjected many independent groups to the political authority of Cuzco through his own campaign activities or through the campaigns of his brothers and sons. Cuzco was reorganized, appropriate administrative forms were developed, and, arguably, art styles began to reflect the prestige and power of the Inca elite. A change in dynastic marriage is part of the transformation of Cuzco and will be the subject of the next chapter. Our subject here is the emergence of Cuzco and the imperial expansion. From this point on, marriage is not part of a negotiation or alliance process with other groups. What we will read in the remainder of this chapter is a story — embedded in the Sarmiento narrative — about the political organization of the peoples the Incas encountered in their campaign to extend the authority of Cuzco.

Some very important information is encoded in Sarmiento's narrative, that is, who was considered to be *capac*. In chapter 2, we explored how *capac* status was linked to a solar supernatural and was transmitted through the male line of the dynastic descent group. If other groups were identified as *capac* by the Incas, then perhaps some special status flowed through the elite of such groups. Whether or not the Incas were marking other groups who claimed a link to some supernatural, their attribution of *capac* status to other Andean lords was a tacit acknowledgment of their power. Betanzos wrote that Pachacuti planned to conquer and subject other Andean peoples to Cuzco and, particularly, "to remove the lords who were *capac*, because there was to be only one *capac* — himself" ([1551–1557], pt. 1, chap. 28; 1987:87). A claim to *capac* status — at least in Inca eyes — was exclusive. If so, claims by other lords to a similar status constituted provocation.

Because sources which drew on Inca genres in their presentation of the Inca expansion may reflect an image of Andean political organization, the focus here will be on recovering what was recorded about the peoples who resisted the Incas and, particularly, about the lords identified as *capac*. The source with the most abundant information on this topic is Sarmiento, although Cabello Valboa and Morúa (M2) refer to other Andean lords who were identified as *capac*, perhaps because they drew from a similar *quipo* source (see chapter 4). Unfortunately, these authors do not appear to have fully understood what the word *capac* meant. Sarmiento uses the term when he provides certain information at the end of a lifetime. He often gives the number of years an Inca was "capac," using the term as an equivalent for "king." Betanzos, the source of our own understanding of this concept, does not identify who had *capac* status beyond the Cuzco region. When the other authors use the term *capac*, it appears to be part of a title, constructed by the use of a name followed by the term *capac*. For example, both Chimo Capac and Colla Capac were titles that were used to refer to more than one individual. In the case of the latter, we know that one of the Colla Capacs was named Zapana.[6]

The first *capac* to be mentioned was, of course, Tocay Capac. Two others in the region near Cuzco — Chiguay Capac and Pinao Capac — were also defeated in military campaigns during the time of Viracocha but do not figure prominently in Sarmiento's account ([1572], chap. 25; 1906:58). That Viracocha began to defeat local claimants to *capac* status is another indication that the imperial expansion had already begun before Pachacuti's rise to power. Sarmiento notes that Pachacuti campaigned against Tocay Capac, resulting in his capture and lifetime imprisonment. In the Sarmiento account, Pachacuti creates Hanan Cuzco and Hurin Cuzco, and the expansion follows from this creation:

> [Pachacuti] called a gathering of his people and *ayllos* that were afterward called Hanancuzcos and Hurincuzcos, and he conformed them in a single body, so that, together, no one could or would act against them. And this done, they entered into a council over what they should do, and they agreed that they should unite and go out to conquer all of the nations of the realm, and that those people who did not submit and serve voluntarily should be destroyed totally; and above all else, they should go against Tocay Capac, the captain of the Ayarmacas who was powerful and who had not come to give recognition to Cuzco.

> [Pachacuti] hizo ayuntamiento de sus gentes y ayllos, y hizo las parciali-dades, que despues llamaron Hanancuzcos y Hurincuzcos, y conformolos en un cuerpo, para que juntos nadie pudiese ni fuese parte contra ellos. Y esto hecho, entraron en consejo sobre lo que debían hacer. Y acordaron que todos se juntasen y saliesen á conquistar á todas las naciones del reino, y que á los que de su voluntad no se les diesen y sirviesen, los destruyesen totalmente; y que ante todas cosas fuesen contra Tocay Capac, cinche de los Ayarmacas, que era poderoso y no había venido á hacer reconosci-miento al Cuzco. ([1572], chap. 25; 1906:58; chap. 34; 1906:71–72)

Perhaps Tocay Capac had reasserted his independence in the wake of the Chanca invasion.

The next lord encountered by Pachacuti with *capac* status was Cuyo Capac, the lord who had his seat near Pisac and who may have held the lands in the Urubamba Valley where Pachacuti and later Incas developed private estates. He was conquered early in the reign of Pachacuti, just after the campaign against Tocay Capac. In Cabello Valboa, the conquests of Pinao Capac and Cuyo Capac occur during the rule of Viracocha but are directed by the young Pachacuti. They occur prior to a battle with the Chancas that the Incas won and that took place prior to the Chanca invasion of Cuzco. Sarmiento is silent about Inca aggression against the Chancas prior to their attack on Cuzco and Pachacuti's usurpation of Inca rule. What the narratives record may not be successive rounds of conquest against the same groups but an overlap between the life histories of Viracocha and Pachacuti clouded by Inca bias.

Betanzos, who appears to have a version of the Pachacuti life history that followed an underlying Inca genre more closely than Sarmiento's, highlights the campaign against Soras. This campaign is either absent from Sarmiento or it is part of the campaign against the Chancas headed by Pachacuti after he took power. Betanzos describes the Soras campaign to the almost complete exclusion of information about any others ([1551–1557], pt. 1, chaps. 18–19; 1987:87–97). The disjuncture between Betanzos, on the one hand, and Sarmiento/Cabello Valboa/Morúa, on the other, is a real problem. One explanation for the difference is that Betanzos did not draw from the genealogical genre, while the other accounts are nourished by information about conquests from that source. If so, the sequencing problems mentioned above are evidence that even the genealogical genre was constructed around particular lifetimes and that the same campaigns could be claimed by two individuals: the ruling Inca and a son who carried out the campaign in his father's lifetime.[7]

Sarmiento highlights a subsequent campaign against the Colla Capac. Soras may have been significant to the Incas in ways that are not clear to us, but a very large territory fell when the Incas conquered the Colla Capac of Hatun-colla. They gained authority over the entire Lake Titicaca region and the territory southwest to the Pacific Coast (Sarmiento de Gamboa [1572], chap. 37; 1906:75–77). From this point on, their territorial reach was larger than that of any other Andean polity. What had been a competition among groups in the Cuzco area and their neighbors was now certainly an empire.

Although what Pachacuti accomplished may have been exaggerated because of his success, the intent to subject the Andean area to the authority of Cuzco was clearly manifest to other Andean peoples at this time. This conquest was also a topic in Cieza, who traveled through the region. In fact, Cieza prefaces his remarks with a digression on how he got what he wrote from native sources, "from what they think, know, and understand." He begins his story of the conquest of Colla territory immediately afterward with the words "And so, the *orejones* say . . ." (Cieza de León [1553], chap. 52; 1986:150). What follows is a story that includes elements of what Sarmiento and other writers attribute to Topa Inca, except for the destruction of Ayaviri, which is something only Cieza describes. Cieza gives due recognition to the conquest of Colla territory: at the beginning of the next chapter he notes that, because of the fame achieved by Pachacuti with this conquest, many groups came to Cuzco to recognize him and submit to Inca authority ([1553], chap. 53; 1986:153).

At the same time, both Cieza and Sarmiento give us some indication that the Incas were still bound in an alliance with the Chancas (Cieza de León [1553], chap. 46; 1986:136; chap. 47; 1986:137). Marriage may have been involved. Cieza notes that Pachacuti gave an Inca woman to Anco Ayllo, an important Chanca captain ([1553], chap. 47; 1986:137).[8] Sarmiento mentions that Capac Yupanqui, the brother of Pachacuti who led this campaign, was married to a sister of Anco Ayllo ([1572], chap. 38; 1906:78), thus providing an indirect indication of an alliance. Anco Ayllo was a captain of the Chancas, chosen by the Incas to head the Chanca troops, since the Inca "gave each nation a captain from its own people." He had been captured during the Inca wars against the Chancas and, during his captivity, had won Inca trust to the extent that they "held him as a brother" (Sarmiento de Gamboa [1572], chap. 38; 1906:77). Whatever the terms of the relationship were, the alliance with the Chancas broke down during a campaign in Parcos, near modern Ayacucho, where considerable resistance was met (Cieza de León [1550], chap. 90; 1984:254; [1553], chaps. 48–50; 1986:143–145). The Chancas outshone the Inca *orejones* in battle to such a degree that Pachacuti plotted treachery against them. Anco Ayllo got wind of it and deserted with the Chanca army into the Chachapoyas lowlands and was never heard from again (Sarmiento de Gamboa [1572], chap. 38; 1906:78–79).

Not only did Anco Ayllo desert and take his army, Capac Yupanqui then took the Inca army farther north than he had been instructed to, provoking a confrontation with Cuzmango Capac and his ally, Chimo Capac. Cuzmango Capac, who held a territory in the area of modern Cajamarca, and Chimo Capac, who had begun a program of expansion of his own in the coastal area to the west from a center at modern Trujillo, together constituted a power that might inflict a serious defeat on the Incas (Sarmiento de Gamboa [1572], chap. 38; 1906:77–79). Perhaps through a stroke of luck, Pachacuti's brother defeated these two lords in battle and captured them, ending what was a potentially disastrous conflict almost as soon as it began (Sarmiento de Gamboa [1572], chap. 38; 1906:77–80; Rowe 1946:206). Although other campaigns were fought, no political power of this magnitude remained to confront the Incas.

While the consolidation of Inca authority over such a vast territory must have required some time, the peoples who had been incorporated into the Inca empire never successfully reasserted their independence. Attempts to rebel, such as the rebellion of the Collas which broke out very soon after the conquest of Chimo Capac and Cuzmango Capac, were unsuccessful (Sarmiento de Gamboa [1572], chaps. 40–41; 1906:80–84).

In this and subsequent campaigns, Pachacuti left the leadership to others. Late in his lifetime, his son Topa Inca led the Inca armies. One important campaign against three lords identified as *capac* was carried out in the northern highlands in what is now Ecuador. The lords — Pisar Capac, Cañar Capac, and Chica Capac — offered resistance. Although these lords were said to have been taken prisoner, one of them, Pisar Capac (or another individual called by that title), subsequently offered resistance to the Incas at Tomebamba in alliance with Pillaguaso, a captain of the people from the area of Quito. Even if Topa Inca were responsible, the campaigns were sequenced in the period before Pachacuti's death (Sarmiento de Gamboa [1572], chap. 44; 1906:87; chap. 46; 1906:89).

No lords identified as *capac* figure in campaigns after the death of Pachacuti, and Inca expansion slowed considerably. The Collas again tried to assert their independence. This time, resistance was offered by the Collas of Umasuyo, a subdivision of Colla territory north of Lake Titicaca. When the Collas were first conquered, the military campaign was directed against the Collas of Urcosuyo, an adjacent subdivision of Colla territory where the Colla Capac resided (Julien 1983). At that time, the peoples of neighboring Umasuyo had submitted peacefully. Perhaps because of the resistance in Umasuyo, Topa Inca reorganized the area and created private estates there (Cieza de León [1550], chap. 4; 1984:149–150; chaps. 41–43; 1984:191–194; chaps. 52–55; 1984:201–205; Sarmiento de Gamboa [1572], chaps. 49–50; 1906:96–97). Topa Inca carried the campaign against the Collas farther south, annexing a number of peoples at this time, including the people of central Chile. The only other campaign Topa Inca led was in Andesuyo, the densely forested region east of Cuzco (Sarmiento de Gamboa [1572], chap. 49; 1906:95–96). Huayna Capac did not add substantial territory. He campaigned at the Ecuadorean frontier and annexed the province of Atacama, north of the region in Chile where his father had once been. He also organized the defense of the Inca frontier in the area east of what is now Sucre to repel incursions by independent peoples living beyond the frontiers and referred to as Chiriguanaes by the Incas (Sarmiento de Gamboa [1572], chap. 58; 1906:104; chaps. 60–62; 1906: 105–111; Rowe 1985b:215).

Although there were lords named in the narratives of Inca expansion who were not referred to as *capac*, those who were were focal points of the story. Their importance, however, was either not detected by Sarmiento or was deliberately ignored. At one point, when Sarmiento mentions Chuchi Capac or Colla Capac, he refers to him as *cinche*, that is, as a captain chosen when defense is imminently needed:

Chuchi Capac had oppressed and subjected more than 160 leagues [750 km] from north to south, because he was a *cinche*, or as he called himself, *capac* or Colla Capac, from 20 leagues [100 km] away from Cuzco to Chichas, and all of the jurisdiction of Arequipa and the coast toward Atacama [from Acarí to the Loa River in Chile] and the mountainous area above Mojos [the upper Beni River area].

Tenía Chuchi Capac opresas y subjetas más de ciento y sesenta leguas de norte sur, porque era cinche, ó como el se nombraba: capac ó Collacapac, desde veinte leguas del Cuzco hasta los Chichas y todos los términos de Arequipa y la costa de la mar hacia Atacama y las montañas sobre los Mojos. ([1572], chap. 37; 1906:76)

Sarmiento equates the status of *cinche* and *capac*! One of the points Sarmiento was out to prove in his narrative was that not only had the Incas conquered tyrannically in the recent past, but also there had been no natural lords in the Andes in the period before the Inca expansion, so his equation of *cinche* with *capac* may have been a deliberate attempt to portray earlier Andean organization as barbarous, despite the fact that elsewhere he used the term *capac* as the equivalent of "king." Sarmiento must have known that he was deliberately misrepresenting what he had been told, and we will return to his use of Inca history in the conclusions. Regardless of his project, he appears not to have understood what the term *capac* meant. His text was a conduit for messages that he did not understand.

We can read for the messages contained in a text, whether they were part of an underlying Inca genre or not. In the case of the lords who were *capac*, we may be reading a story that is implicit in the *quipo* lists of conquests by particular rulers in light of what Betanzos has told us about *capac* status. In this case, the narrative line is a product of our reading. Another narrative — the story of Inti — spans more than one lifetime and appears to override the constraints imposed by genres formatted around particular lifetimes. What we may be reading here is an Inca story that Sarmiento distributed to appropriate points in the narrative, so that the narrative sense of the Inti story comes from an underlying genre. Both interpretations of the messages contained in the Spanish historical narratives may be valid, however. These kinds of questions emerge as we read for themes and messages, keeping the various underlying genres, including the Spanish historical narrative, in mind.

# 7 Transformation

Another major theme is the transformation of Cuzco. It was an important topic in the life history of Pachacuti told by both Sarmiento and Betanzos. The Spaniards who arrived with Francisco Pizarro in December 1533 were impressed with the Inca city. What they saw reflected a deliberate effort to transform an earlier settlement into a monumental capital, like that described in the narratives of Sarmiento and Betanzos. The physical plan of Cuzco, the fine stonework, the numerous shrines in the city and in the valley beyond — all reflect an ambitious program of construction designed to reflect the power of the Inca elite. The transformation was more thoroughgoing than the eye could see, however. It involved refashioning the residents of Cuzco into an imperial elite, capable of heading military campaigns and carrying out ambitious projects in foreign areas at great distances from their homeland. It also involved educating and animating members of this elite to carry on the goals of their forebears. How this was accomplished is one of the most important themes of the life history of Pachacuti encapsulated in Sarmiento and Betanzos.

Before reading Betanzos's and Sarmiento's accounts of the transformation of Cuzco, let us look at how the topic is handled by authors who wrote "long accounts." Both Cabello Valboa and Morúa give accounts of the change effected by Pachacuti that are also substantially alike; the transformation of Cuzco was therefore a topic in Molina. It was simply not a topic in Cobo. Even though he had access to the Molina account, Cobo clearly did not incorporate material from Molina to supply what appears to have been missing in Polo. In table 7.1 the events related to the transformation of Cuzco are listed in the same shorthand used in table 4.1 (e.g., III = transformation of Cuzco; IIa–b = Pachacuti's accession/marriage; V = death of Viracocha).

What is not evident from table 7.1 but can be seen clearly in table 4.3 is that Sarmiento and Betanzos both treat the transformation of Cuzco as a single long episode. In Sarmiento the topic occupies three chapters (chaps. 30–32); Betanzos devotes seven chapters to it (chaps. 11–17). Using Pachacuti's ac-

TABLE 7.1. *Events related to the transformation of Cuzco*

| Sarmiento | Betanzos | Cabello Valboa | Morúa | Cobo |
|---|---|---|---|---|
| IIa | IIId | IIa | IIa | V |
| IIIa | IIIg | V | IIb | IIa–b |
| IIIb | IIIi | IIb | IIa | |
| IIIc | IIIf | IIId | V | |
| IIId | IIIa | IIId | IIId | |
| IIIe | IIIj | IIIg | IIId | |
| IIIf | IIa | IIIf | IIIg | |
| IIIg | IIb | IIId | IIIf | |
| IIIh | V | IIIl | IIId | |
| IIIa | IIIe | | IIIl | |
| V | IIIg | | | |
| IIb | IIIc | | | |
| IIId | | | | |

cession and the death of Viracocha — events that are tied together in all of the accounts — as a sequencing tool, both Sarmiento and Betanzos locate the transformation of Cuzco prior to the definitive accession of Pachacuti. Cabello Valboa and Morúa (M2) locate it afterward. Cabello Valboa and Morúa (M2) also intersperse the story of the transformation of Cuzco with the various military campaigns that extended Cuzco power. Logically, the transformation of Cuzco and its elite would not have occurred until the Incas had successfully launched an empire, so the version told by Cabello Valboa and Morúa is more realistic. Since this part of the Betanzos narrative is, in all likelihood, the closest approximation to a life history that we have, the foregrounding of the transformation of Cuzco is probably a feature of that life history. A single long episode may also be a feature of the underlying Inca text as well.

Although Sarmiento and Betanzos are structurally similar, as noted above, their treatments of the transformation of Cuzco read very differently. First, the Betanzos narrative follows a different sequence of events than Sarmiento's. It begins with the rebuilding of Coricancha and the making of cult images; then turns to the organization of the province of Cuzco so that the residents could be gone for long periods on campaign; then to changes in the initiation ritual and the calendar; then to the rebuilding of the city; then to Pachacuti's marriage, the definitive transfer of power, and the death of Viracocha; then to the organization of cults to earlier Incas and their endowment with lands and retainers; and finally to the organization of collective memory about the earlier Incas. Sarmiento begins with the rebuilding of Cuzco; then turns to the reform of lands in the Cuzco Valley; then to changes in the calendar; then to the organization of an Inca shrine at Pacaritambo; then to the building of Cori-cancha and the making of cult images; then to the organization of various rites in Cuzco and the surrounding area; and finally to the removal of all the people within 20 km of Cuzco and the appropriation of these lands to the city of Cuzco. Although the list of topics covered by the two authors seems similar, albeit in a different order, there is a logic to their ordering in Betanzos that is missing in Sarmiento. What Betanzos describes is both the refashioning and the consecration of Cuzco, both as a place and as a people.

Because of Betanzos's closeness to Inca dynastic sources and his compe-tence in the Inca language, his treatment of this theme may approximate its treatment in an underlying Inca genre. Here we will read Betanzos closely and try to develop an image of the transformation of Cuzco from his narrative. Other sources have been incorporated to broaden the perspective gleaned from Betanzos and to sharpen the image of those Incas who were not the fo-cus of the Betanzos narrative.

THE NEW CUZCO

Betanzos begins the story with the building of Coricancha (map 1). In the preceding chapter, the image of Cuzco that was drawn from the Sarmiento narrative is of a small agricultural community located on the site of Inticancha. A small court where Manco Capac himself was said to have founded Cuzco — named Caritambocancha — was named in the listing of Inca shrines in Cuzco (Rowe 1979 : 54). The court was located within the walls of what was later the convent of Santo Domingo. Inticancha also appears on the list, described as a small house where the sisters of the first Inca lived (Rowe 1979 : 56). In excava-tions within Santo Domingo and just to the northwest in structures on the Calle San Agustín, ceramics and architecture have been found that have stylis-tic affiliations to the period before the development of imperial styles. The ar-chaeological remains support the location of the early Inca settlement given in Sarmiento (Rowe 1979 : 54 – 57; González Corrales 1984 : 37 – 45).

Coricancha was built to house an image of the Sun. It was a new construc-tion. Four rooms of the complex were reused in the construction of the cloister of Santo Domingo, and two of them are fully exposed today (Rowe 1944 : 26 – 41, fig. 9; Gasparini and Margolies 1980 : 220 – 234). Betanzos notes that Pachacuti wanted to build a house for the Sun where an image of this supernatural would reside and be ritually fed "in place of the Sun" ([1551–1557], pt. 1, chap. 11; 1987 : 49). Sometimes Coricancha was called a "temple" in Spanish accounts, confusing the structure with a church, since this was the appropriate location for cult images. Coricancha does not figure in the listing of shrines mentioned above but does appear on another shorter list, where it is glossed as "house of gold" and described as a "house of the Sun" (Rowe 1979:72, appendix). The Sun held property and may have had wives. A residence would have been appropriate.

Principal players in the building and consecration of the house of the Sun were the neighboring peoples who had helped Pachacuti defeat the Chancas. When stones were measured in the quarry of Salu, the task of bringing the stones and constructing the house was divided among these neighbors (Betanzos [1551–1557], pt. 1, chap. 11; 1987:50). Following construction, an endowment was established to support the cult to the Sun. Pachacuti selected five hundred women to serve the cult, named a majordomo, and then endowed the cult with retainers (*yanaconas*) and lands (Betanzos [1551–1557], pt. 1, chap. 11; 1987:50).

Pachacuti then held a dedication ceremony. The Cuzco lords contributed large quantities of maize, fine clothing and camelids as well as a certain number of boys and girls for sacrifice. A large fire was lit, and the maize, fine clothing, and camelids were burned. The children, in a type of sacrifice known as *capac ucha*, were buried alive at the site. With the blood of the sacrificed animals, certain lines were drawn on the new building by Pachacuti and several of his captains. Lines were also drawn by Pachacuti and the captains on the face of the person who was to head the household of the Sun, called majordomo in the documents, and on the faces of the five hundred women who were there to serve him. Then the people of Cuzco, men and women, were to come and make burnt offerings of maize and coca. When done, they, too, received facial markings, this time from the majordomo. From that time until the image of the Sun was finished, a fast was decreed, and the sacrificial fire was kept constantly burning. When the image, the figure of a child executed in gold, was finished, it was carefully dressed by the majordomo of the Sun and given various accessories. It was fed by making offerings in a fire before it, beginning a custom that was to be carefully kept by the majordomo. From then on, only important lords were admitted into the presence of this image. A stone representation shaped like a sugar-loaf was set up in the main plaza of Cuzco. When the principal image was first finished, however, it was paraded through Cuzco. At the time of the dedication, miniature figures in gold, representing the lineages descended from Manco Capac, were buried at the foot of the stone in the main plaza. Camelids were sacrificed to the stone representation from that day forward (Betanzos [1551–1557], pt. 1, chap. 11; 1987:50–53).

Betanzos links the consecration of Cuzco to the treatment that was thereafter to be afforded to nobles in the provinces and to Cuzco. Incas from the city of Cuzco were adored as members of the Sun's descent group. Sacrifices known as *arpa* were made before them. The city itself was sacred. Travelers, no matter how important they were, had to approach the city carrying a burden (Polo de Ondegardo [1561]; 1940:146). The points along the roads where travelers first saw the city were *huacas* (Cobo [1653], bk. 13, chap. 13; 1892:20; Rowe 1967:62. n. 38; 1979:26–27, 36–37, 54–55, 56–57).

After consecrating Cuzco, Pachacuti's attention turned to the Cuzco Valley. He ordered the principal lords from the region around Cuzco who had sworn obedience to him to come to Cuzco. He had devised a system to provision the city and to permit the people of the territory around it to be gone on long campaigns without losing their means of support at home. The plan involved a redistribution of land, the marking of permanent boundaries, and the construction of storage deposits. It also involved the provisioning of foodstuffs to Cuzco. Initially these provisions were to support the people working on building projects in the valley. Soon after, Pachacuti organized the production of tribute clothing, including cloths for carrying loads of earth and stone, so that the people working on the building projects would not have to use their own (Betanzos [1551–1557], pt. 1, chap. 12; 1987:55–58; pt. 1, chap. 13; 1987: 59–63).

Part of Pachacuti's plan was to marry the lords of the Cuzco region to women of his own descent group. Their descendants, who were to inherit the lord's authority, would thus be tied by affinal bonds to the dynastic descent group (Betanzos [1551–1557], pt. 1, chap. 12; 1987:57). Another purpose may have been to subordinate these lords. As we noted in chapter 2, the relationship constructed through marriage between descent groups is not symmetrical in the Cuzco area today, and the woman's group occupies a superior prestige position relative to the group into which she marries (Webster 1977: 36–40). Pachacuti also sent his representatives to the territories of the lords and married the young men of one group to the young women of another, cementing bonds between groups. Perhaps the exchange of women between groups served to promote equality and, consequently, tended to level any hierarchical relationships that had existed. The people who were married received gifts of clothing and the household items they would need (Betanzos [1551–1557], pt. 1, chap. 13; 1987:63). The result of this social engineering project was a hinterland of discrete groups, tied to Cuzco and to each other, who would supply the basic needs of the urban population. Every four months, the people dependent on Cuzco received what they needed from the tribute that was supplied from this hinterland (Betanzos [1551–1557], pt. 1, chap. 13; 1987:63).

Betanzos then describes changes in Inca practice that reflect the new status of Cuzco itself. Pachacuti redesigned male initiation, removing it from the private realm and institutionalizing it in an elaborate round of public ritual as part of the celebration called Capac Raymi (Betanzos [1551–1557], pt. 1, chap. 14; 1987:65–70). Betanzos then describes further reform to the ritual calendar (chap. 15). A chapter on the rebuilding of the city itself follows (chap. 16). With the rebuilding of Cuzco came a new spatial representation of the concentration of *capac* status in Pachacuti's own descendants. In his final chapter on the transformation of Cuzco, Betanzos tells us about the new spatial representation, but to interpret what he says, we must first examine how the reform affected dynastic descent.

The linchpin of the reform was the redefinition of dynastic descent. We have already reviewed the reckoning of descent in a summary way in chapter 2. Here, our concern is with the institution of marriage to a woman in the dynastic descent group. The institution of sister-marriage was an abrupt departure from the past. Marriage alliance with non-Inca peoples or with related groups came to an end. What was the point? When we examine other circumstances surrounding the accession of Topa Inca, a motive becomes apparent. Topa Inca was not the brother who was first chosen to succeed. Pachacuti had initially named Amaro Topa, an older son who had already shown himself to be an effective military commander. Then he changed his mind and named Topa Inca, who had been kept hidden for fifteen or sixteen years in the house of the Sun and whom no one had seen "except as a special favor" (Sarmiento de Gamboa [1572], chap. 42; 1906:84). When it was time for Topa Inca's initiation, his father invented an entirely new rite, building another four houses for the Sun for the new ceremony. Finally, Amaro Topa was presented to his brother. When he saw the wealth and the important lords surrounding Topa Inca, he fell down in worship. Pachacuti then had Topa Inca taken to the main square with all the other sacred images in a display more magnificent than had ever been seen in Cuzco. Offerings to Topa Inca were burned in a sacrificial fire. Topa Inca's initiation followed, then marriage to his full sister Mama Ocllo (Sarmiento de Gamboa [1572], chap. 43; 1906:85–86).

Sister-marriage coincided with the recognition that the dynastic descent group was a conduit of a status that marked them as a special class of sacred beings. The Incas were descended from an important supernatural, the Sun. Sister-marriage coincided with the full recognition of the meaning of *capac* status. If the Incas chose to preserve the sacred status that passed through the dynastic line, then the most indicated marriage partner was a full sister. Since *capac* status also passed through others in the dynastic line, there were other women in whom *capac* status may have been concentrated, so we can imagine that there were other possible candidates should there not be a full sister. The author Pachacuti noted that Manco Capac could not find anyone who was the equal of his sister, and he married her to ensure that the Incas did not "lose caste" [perder la casta] (Pachacuti Yamqui Salcamaygua [early seventeenth century]; 1993:fol. 8, p. 197). The idea of "losing caste" through marrying someone of lower status is prevalent in the narrative of Guaman Poma de Ayala, who describes the ruinous state of affairs when new Spanish rules were applied in Andean communities ([1615]; 1987:454, 505, 788). Clearly, marriage within the dynastic group was a means of preserving the special status that passed through the line of Manco Capac. Also, by marrying brother to sister, in-law relationships were entirely avoided.

The avoidance of in-law relationships can also have been a strong motive for the reorientation of marriage choice. When we read the story of the emergence of the Incas (chapter 6), we noted that information about the growth of Inca power is encoded in the historical narrative. Subordinate to the Ayarmacas at first, the Incas later achieved parity, as symbolized by the reciprocal exchange of women in the generation of Yahuar Huacac. The institution of sister-marriage is coincident with the assertion of the dynastic descent group of superiority over any competing groups, another aspect of *capac* status.

Because the inequality implied by marriage alliance was not made explicit in the narrative, it must be advanced as a hypothesis only. However, on other occasions, marriage appears to have been a major means of securing a superior position over others. For example, Pachacuti's father, Viracocha, intended to defeat the principal lord of the Lake Titicaca region by allying with a local challenger to his authority. When he arrived in the Lake Titicaca area he found out that the challenger had already defeated the lord. Relations with his potential ally were friendly, but when offered a marriage with the ally's daughter while they were drinking, Viracocha quickly cried off, saying he was too old for marriage (Cieza de León [1553], chap. 43; 1986:193–194). There were other reasons not to accept this daughter by the logic of marriage alliance.

The behavior of Pachacuti in marrying women of his descent group to the political leaders of groups annexed to the empire becomes transparent if subordination is a result of such a marriage. Betanzos notes on various occasions that Pachacuti and his successors married Inca women to local lords in Cuzco and elsewhere ([1551–1557], pt. 1, chap. 16; 1987:77–78; pt. 1, chap. 34; 1987: 167; pt. 1, chap. 36; 1987:175; pt. 1, chap. 40; 1987:179). The succession was to pass through a particular brother-sister pair, but Pachacuti himself took all of his sisters as wives (Sarmiento de Gamboa [1572], chap. 47; 1906:93). Each brother-sister pair formed a new segment of the dynastic descent group. Since group affiliation was transmitted through the male line, there would have been a premium on producing as many offspring as possible. Daughters would have been particularly important: those who were descended from the line of Manco Capac on both sides because the Incas themselves did not want to "lose caste," and those descended from Manco Capac on their father's side alone because such women were politically important capital beyond Cuzco (Sarmiento de Gamboa [1572], chap. 47; 1906:93; Betanzos [1551–1557], pt. 1, chap. 16; 1987:78).

What was being husbanded was *capac* status. The transformation of Cuzco involved a recognition of this status and new rules for determining the degree of this status within the group of people identified as Inca. The recognition of *capac* status also affected the physical environment. When Pachacuti developed a new Cuzco, he divided it into two *sayas* named Hanan Cuzco and Hurin Cuzco (map 1). Betanzos relates the two *sayas* to Pachacuti's reform. After rebuilding Cuzco, Pachacuti divided residential space among the various *panacas* of the dynasty. All of the *panacas* before his own were to live in Hurin Cuzco, in the area between the two rivers, from the houses of the Sun to the rivers' confluence. This area was where the Incas had lived until the time of Inca Roca. The three captains who had helped him to defeat the Chancas and to consecrate Cuzco were to live there. The area of Hanan Cuzco, uphill from the houses of the Sun, was to be populated by his own descendants (Betanzos [1551–1557], pt. 1, chap. 16; 1987:77–78). The inhabitants were to be descendants of Manco Capac who could trace their descent backward through both male and female lines. The inhabitants of Hurin Cuzco, in contrast, were descendants of Manco Capac in the male line only.

The mothers of the three captains were not Inca. Neither were the female forebears from which the other *panacas* sprang. The division into Hanan and Hurin was more than just a division into two city districts. The city was now divided spatially and conceptually in half: the old Cuzco, occupying the same site as the early Inca settlement and peopled by the generations descended from Manco Capac who were associated with the early history of the city; and the new one, situated physically above the old Cuzco and peopled by the generations who were associated with the empire and in whom a status linked to a solar supernatural was concentrated.

What Betanzos says about the reorganization of Cuzco itself is fairly straightforward. What he says about the calendar is not particularly new, and other aspects of his description echo what is written elsewhere. What is unique in Betanzos is the insight he provides into the social engineering that accompanied the physical rebuilding of the city. Other writers — Sarmiento, Cabello Valboa, and Morúa — attribute the division of Cuzco into Hanan and Hurin to Manco Capac and/or Inca Roca. Spanish cities were divided into parishes, so the territorial division of urban space was unremarkable. Betanzos is the only author to provide us with a view of Pachacuti's representation of the increasing power of the descendants of Manco Capac in the design of urban space. Hanan and Hurin may have existed prior to the general reorganization of Cuzco, but Pachacuti took the opportunity of rebuilding the city and used it to refashion and represent the dynastic past in urban space.

## INCAS AND HUACAS

Now we know that it would be a great mistake to consider the new Cuzco to be simply a collection of monumental buildings. The monumental construction is simply an outward and visible sign of a transformation of another kind. The Incas claimed to be descendants of the Sun, an important supernatural being. Their dynastic line was a conduit of *capac* status, transmitted through the male line. Cuzco was rebuilt to reflect the sacred character of the place and the special beings who inhabited it.

The Incas were in a position to define their relationship both to the other peoples who inhabited the territory they governed and to the supernatural world. When the individuals who had been adults at the time of the Spanish arrival were interviewed or information was taken from some genre of Inca historical tradition, aspects of an Inca view of their place in the universe were encoded. Because of their loss of autonomy since the capture of Atahuallpa, their perspective on the Prehispanic past can have evolved to accommodate their subsequent history in ways that we cannot understand from the written materials we possess. Their voices have also been altered through translation into the Spanish language. However, even with these defects, when the material that speaks to this subject is assembled, some fundamental aspects of the Inca view of the universe emerge.

Cuzco itself was a sacred place, occupied by a special class of beings who carefully traced their descent from an important Andean supernatural: the Sun. The genealogical tie to this supernatural appears to have conferred a supernatural status of some kind on the Incas. "They were more than men," said one Spanish administrator (Santillán [1563]; 1879: 13, 30). The term *capac* when it followed a name meant "very much more than king" (Betanzos [1551–1557], pt. 1, chap. 27; 1987: 132; cf. Cieza de León [1553], chap. 20; 1986: 169–170).

This conclusion is abundantly supported by evidence for the parallel treatment of the Incas who were closely related to Manco Capac and other Andean supernatural beings.

Supernatural beings, as well as sacred places and objects, as a class were known as *huacas*. There were various important distinctions among them that we do not fully understand. Most were stone. Some had human form — male or female — and were children or wives of other *huacas*. Some were figures of animals. They were cared for by particular individuals who spoke with them and who were in charge of making offerings. Another class of *huacas* was the mummified remains of a group's forebears known as *malquis*. They also had individuals who cared for them and a particular ritual program. A third class of *huacas* called *konopas* was sacred to particular households. One of the children — male or female — received all of the sacred objects when they were passed on; they were not divided among the offspring (Arriaga [1621], chap. 2; 1968:202–204).

Inca rulers, from the time of Topa Inca onward, were treated in various ways as if they were like some of the more important Andean *huacas*. Their supernatural status probably derived from their relationship to the Sun and was confirmed by their defeat of any rivals. It was said to increase after the funeral rite known as *purucaya* was performed a year after the death of a reigning Inca. The rite was also performed after the death of a sister-wife, as there are specific references to the *purucaya* rite of Mama Ocllo, the daughter of Pachacuti who was the sister-wife of Topa Inca. This rite was likened to "canonization" by several authors, though the implied parallel between the mummies of the Incas and Catholic saints is specious (Betanzos [1551–1557], pt. 1, chaps. 30–32; 1987: 141–150; pt. 1, chap. 39; 1987:177; pt. 1, chap. 44; 1987:189–190; Sarmiento de Gamboa [1572], chap. 31; 1906:68; chap. 47; 1906:92–93).

In the historical narrative of Sarmiento, Topa Inca is the first Inca to be treated as a supernatural being in life. As noted in the preceding chapter, his elder brother, upon seeing Topa Inca installed in the house of the Sun, with service and treasure around him, fell to the ground and worshiped him and made sacrifices to him. Shortly after, Topa Inca was initiated. According to Sarmiento, the initiation was the most spectacular ritual event held in Cuzco up to that time; since it was subsequent to the dedication of the new Cuzco, we can assume that it surpassed the ceremony associated with that event. Topa Inca was taken out of the temple in procession, along with the image of the Sun, the mummies of his Inca forebears, and other important sacred objects (Sarmiento de Gamboa [1572], chaps. 42–43; 1906:84–86).

He was also married to his full sister, Mama Ocllo, at this time. Given its historical context, we can interpret the institution of sister-marriage both as an expression of Inca power (the Incas would no longer accept the inferior status implied by accepting women from outside the Inca patrilineage) and as an expression of the newly recognized supernatural status of the dynastic line: the way to produce offspring who conserved the supernatural status to the fullest degree was to marry full brothers and sisters or individuals descended as close to the line of succession as possible.

Oblique references to Inca supernatural status are found in various written sources. For example, Sarmiento tells us, in essence, that when Topa Inca went on campaign in the north after his coronation, the people treated him like a *huaca*. No one dared to look at his face. The people worshiped him from the crests of the hills at a distance from the road he traveled. Offerings were made as he passed. Some offered coca to him, and some pulled out their eyelashes and blew them in his direction. The latter type of offering was what even the poorest people could offer to the Sun (Sarmiento de Gamboa [1572], chap. 44; 1906:87; Cobo [1653], bk. 13, chap. 22; 1893:83–84; Arriaga [1621], chap. 2; 1968:201). In the towns he visited, burnt offerings were made in front of where he sat in the same way the Sun was "fed" (Sarmiento de Gamboa [1572], chap. 44; 1906:87; Cieza de León [1553], chap. 20; 1986:169–170). The distance kept is one indication of the sacred status of the person of the ruler. Cieza de León mentioned this treatment and noted that the rulers were greatly feared and that if a veil slipped from the litter on which the ruler was transported, a great hue and cry arose from the spectators. Elsewhere he says that what they shouted out were various honorific forms of address as a sign of adoration (Cieza de León [1553], chap. 13; 1986:160–161; chap. 20; 1986:169–170).

The term Sarmiento used when referring to the treatment accorded Topa Inca was *mochar*, a Spanish corruption of an Inca word for a particular kind of worship. *Mocha* was a kind of sacrifice offered to *huacas*, performed by their ritual specialists. It consisted of raising the left hand toward the *huaca* and opening the fingers, "as if bestowing a kiss." Only the specialists went near the *huaca* itself. The common worshipers were assembled elsewhere and participated only in a ritual invocation afterward. Supernaturals like the Sun and Thunder were worshiped in this manner, and so were the ruling Incas (Arriaga [1621], chap. 5; 1968:213–214; Santillán [1563]; 1879:35; Cieza de León [1553], chap. 10; 1986:26; chap. 14; 1986:35–36; chap. 20; 1986:58).

The Sun was ritually fed, and the ritual feeding (the making of burnt offerings) of a live being who necessarily ate food like any other live being only strengthened the parallel between the Sun and the Inca ruler. It was evident in other ways as well. The Sun had houses in the center of the new Cuzco near Inticancha, the residence of the first generations of Incas, and in many of the provinces. A great number of women were assigned to serve the Sun, as were retainers called *yanaconas*. To provide the offerings and to support the Sun's enormous household, the cult was endowed with lands and herds. Finally, the Sun possessed a large personal treasure (Cieza de León [1553], chap. 27; 1986:176–178; chap. 50; 1986:199–200; Santillán [1563]; 1879:31, 102–103; Polo de Ondegardo [1561]; 1940:183–185). Although we do not know the extent of the Sun's holdings, land in each province was worked on behalf of this supernatural, and some entire provinces were dedicated to his cult (Polo de Ondegardo 1872:19). Perhaps the holdings were directly tied to the staff and residences of the Sun in these areas. These holdings were managed by a close relative of the ruling Inca. At the time of the Spanish arrival, the Sun's major-domo was Villa Oma, a brother of Huayna Capac (Betanzos [1551–1557], pt. 2, chap. 29; 1987:291).

Each Inca had an estate that was endowed with similar resources, that is, women, retainers, lands, herds, and treasure (Betanzos [1551–1557], pt. 2, chap. 17; 1987:85–86; Santillán [1563]; 1879:102–103). Spouses may have had similar properties, either within the corporate estate of the descent group or outside it.[1] The endowment of cults to earlier rulers was instituted, or at least favored, by Pachacuti as he made gifts of property to the mummies of his forebears (Cieza de León [1553], chap. 11; 1986:157–159; Betanzos [1551–1557], pt. 1, chap. 17; 1987:85–86). The properties of the Incas involved in the expansion are most in evidence and involve some holdings located at a distance from Cuzco (Niles 1999:150–152). A description of the estate of Topa Inca provides some idea of the extent and variety of these holdings. This estate, administered by one of his great-grandsons at the time of the Spanish arrival in Cuzco, consisted of palaces on the main square at Cuzco; palaces in the country near Cuzco at Calispuquio, Chinchero, Urcos, and Huaillabamba; the province of Parinacocha on the western slopes of the cordillera to the west of Cuzco, with a subject population of 4,000 households; another province at Quipa and Azángaro in the northern Lake Titicaca basin, with 4,500 subject households as well as outlying communities located in the Carabaya area to the east of the lake, there to wash gold; and another province at Achambi on the western slopes of the Andean cordillera to the south of Cuzco, with 4,500 subject households (Rostworowski de Diez Canseco 1993:269; Anton Siguan and Anton Tito, in Levillier 1940, vol. 2:113).

Some property may have been acquired through military conquest and destruction of the resident population. For example, Pachacuti had several properties in the Urubamba Valley. This Inca, after an attempt was made on his life in the territory of the Cuyos near Pisac, destroyed the population and continued his campaign on down the Urubamba Valley. He developed several private estates in the territory he conquered at this time (Sarmiento de Gamboa [1572], chap. 34; 1906:71–72; Rowe 1990:144–145). Topa Inca, when he put down a Colla revolt at the time of his father's death, faced resistance in Asillo, the same area where he developed private holdings (Sarmiento de Gamboa [1572], chap. 50; 1906:96–97).

The corporate holdings of the Sun and particular Inca rulers were similar in nature to the holdings of other important *huacas*, although it cannot be determined whether the Incas modeled their institution on existing corporate entities or began the practice of endowing *huacas*. Clearly, Inca rulers made gifts of land, women, retainers, herds, and treasure to particular *huacas*. Important *huacas*, represented by portable images, came to Cuzco each year. They were to predict what would occur in the coming year. *Huacas* whose predictions from the preceding year had borne fruit were greatly rewarded. Presumably, *huacas* could also be punished. They could even be killed, and a *huaca* that had been destroyed was referred to as *atisca* (Cieza de León [1553], chap. 29; 1986:87–88; Santillán [1563]; 1879:34–35; Albornoz [1581–1585]; 1989:164, 196). The Incas, the Sun, and a number of regional *huacas* had dealings with each other that could include the transfer of property. For example, though the Inca could give gifts of land to the Sun's estate, it was also possible to win it back through playing a game known as *ayllusca*. The object of the game was to bring down a fabric snake that had been thrown up in the air with *ayllus*, or bolas. The game could also be played with other supernaturals (Albornoz [1581–1585]; 1989:175).

The parallels drawn between the Incas and important supernatural beings blurred the line between the natural and the supernatural world. At the same time, new lines were drawn. The descendants of Manco Capac were not the only Incas. An explanation of the unique power of one segment of the larger group served to elevate this group relative to the rest of the people who were Incas.

### THE OTHER INCAS

Within the group of people identified as Inca, very real status differences existed. When we reviewed the stories of Inca origins based on Inca sources in chapter 6, we noted that several groups were said to have resided in Cuzco at the time Manco Capac and his siblings arrived in the valley that date to the time of its "origins." Some were related to him in some way while others were not. According to the same story, Manco Capac brought ten groups of people who were not his descendants with him. That list, however, included two who were descended from his two brothers (Sarmiento de Gamboa [1572], chap. 11; 1906 : 34). The story, while it purports to be about what happened in the past, is actually an accounting of who lived in Cuzco after the reorganization and how they were related to each other. Sarmiento's account establishes that descendants of all the groups named on his list or in his narrative — except those who either left Cuzco or were exterminated when the Incas came — were present in Cuzco at the time he collected information from Inca sources.

Since the Incas of the dynastic descent group took care to preserve a genealogy and life histories of the individual Inca rulers, they are the individuals who are prominent in Spanish narratives which drew from these sources. Their lives — especially when they served as positive examples — were memorialized. Other people enter into the story, and so an Inca account of their past also contains glimpses of people and groups who made up the broader society. Since all of the residents of Cuzco were linked to its ceremonial organization, sources about rituals also name non-Inca groups as participants. Since we know that two were descended from Ayar brothers, blood ties linked at least two of these groups with the dynastic descent group. The historical narratives identify additional peoples as part of a larger Inca group. Still others were identified in the narratives as non-Incas who lived in the Cuzco Valley at the time Manco Capac and those whom he brought to Cuzco arrived. Both blood and other ties characterized the relations between the assortment of peoples who were Inca in some larger sense.

A mosaic of statuses can be glimpsed, but the kind of documentation that is needed for any nuanced treatment of these grades of difference is sadly lacking. So far, the only kind of differentiation that has been made by scholars of the Incas consists in defining a group of "Incas" presumed to have blood ties to the dynastic descent group and another group of "Incas-by-privilege" who are assumed to have been granted some kind of status like citizenship by the imperial rulers.[2] This classification is too simple.

The transformation of Cuzco, as described by Betanzos and Sarmiento, follows the revelation that the Incas were descended from a solar supernatural and that a special status passed through the dynastic line that explained their success at achieving power in the Cuzco region and beyond. Pachacuti redesigned the social and ceremonial organization of Cuzco with the same free hand he used to rebuild the city. Moreover, the physical layout of the city reflected the history and special status of the dynastic descent group. Lurking in the background are the other Incas. If one group became powerful, it could redefine its relationship to the others. One way of accomplishing this redefinition is to reconstruct the past to reflect the dominance of Manco Capac's descent group from the time of origins.

# 8 Origins

In the case of the Incas, different versions of an origin myth that accounts for the emergence of the Inca dynasty and its relation to an important supernatural have been preserved. One of them — the story about the emergence of the Ayar siblings from the cave at Pacaritambo — was seamlessly attached to an account of the past structured around a particular genealogy. Although there were other stories about dynastic origins and myths about the creation of the world that could be inserted at the beginning of a story about the dynastic line, they are not what we will analyze here. Sarmiento gives a detailed account of the Pacaritambo origin story, and our other Cuzco sources, with the exception of Betanzos, follow suit. The Pacaritambo story was collected several decades after authority over the Inca empire had been usurped by the Spaniards. It may be a reflection of the profound changes that accompanied the Inca expansion and the transformation of Cuzco. The equally profound changes that accompanied the Spanish invasion of the Andes may also have worked an effect. When we begin to look closely at the origin story, we find traces of other strata.

Gary Urton argues that the landscape described in the Pacaritambo story only became concretized to the Pacaritambo region after the Spaniards arrived, "perhaps as both a response to, and a 'maneuver' within, the increasingly historicized and concretized representations of Inka mythohistory that were being formulated during the mid– to late sixteenth century" (1990:124). He notes that Sarmiento is the first of the authors of the historical narratives to specify where Pacaritambo was: 6 leagues (30 km) to the south-southwest of Cuzco (Urton 1990:19–20). The site of Tambotoco, a hill near Pacaritambo, is about 26 km to the south of Cuzco. Sarmiento's text postdates the testimony of the Pacaritambo lord, don Rodrigo Callapiña, in 1569 which, Urton argues, literally puts Pacaritambo on the map.[1] He therefore suggests that what Sarmiento wrote is a historicized version that reflects the claims of Pacaritambo lords to noble status rather than an Inca representation of their origins.

At the same time, one point he makes — that none of the earliest versions of the Pacaritambo origin myth locates this place in precise geographical terms

(Urton 1990 : 2–3) — must be revised. The Inca story may not have included any distance measures, but the first Spaniard to precisely locate Pacaritambo was not Sarmiento, it was Betanzos, who said that Pacaritambo was 7 leagues from Cuzco ([1551–1557], pt. 1, chap. 3; 1987 : 17). He does not say in which direction, and the distance estimate is too large, but he was locating a real place. Two other early authors, Polo de Ondegardo and Hernando de Santillán, also gave distance measurements to Pacaritambo (cited in full below). Each spoke in the context of Inca origins, so we can be sure they were referring to the Pacaritambo of the origin story. Polo was actively collecting information about the Incas when he was *corregidor* of Cuzco from 1559 to 1560. Santillán wrote in 1563.

By then, Pacaritambo was a well-known place. The Spanish residents of Cuzco would all have known about it, because sacred sites near Cuzco were systematically looted in the decade after the Spanish arrival. Cieza notes that Hernando Pizarro and Diego de Almagro, son of Pizarro's partner of the same name, went on an expedition to loot Pacaritambo ([1550], chap. 94; 1984 : 262; [1553], chap. 6; 1986 : 14), an event which must have taken place in the second half of the decade of the 1530s. According to Sarmiento, Pachacuti personally went to Tambotoco or Pacaritambo, "which is the same thing," and adorned it with golden doors. From this time onward it was venerated as an important *huaca*. As such, it would have had retainers, women, *yanaconas*, land, and treasure. The presence of precious metals lured bands of Spaniards out into the countryside in the early years following the Pizarro arrival in Cuzco, and there were major looting parties to Urcos and to Aconcagua near Yauri, as well as to Pacaritambo. Pacaritambo would also have attracted Catholic evangelists, who, not long after the Spanish occupation of Cuzco, began to search out native shrines to destroy them (Sarmiento de Gamboa [1572], chap. 11; 1906 : 33; Pachacuti Yamqui Salcamaygua [early seventeenth century]; 1993:fol. 8v, p. 198; Guaman Poma de Ayala [1615]; 1987:79, 264; Bauer 1992:48–56; Urton 1990 : 32–35). Pacaritambo was "on the map" fairly early.

However, Urton is right in noting that Spanish narratives become more geographically precise only in the time of Sarmiento and Molina. Why? One reason may be that the earliest accounts simply reproduce the dynastic genealogy and include very little about the early Incas and their relations with other peoples in the Cuzco region. The *Discurso*, for example, is brief and incorporates detail only when the topic is the Inca expansion. Events in the Cuzco region prior to the expansion are not a topic at all. Cobo, if he serves as a guide to the lost work of Polo, contains more material about the dynastic past than the *Discurso* but very little on local events prior to the time of the Inca expansion.

We can generalize this problem: very little concrete information about the

Andean landscape appears in Spanish documentation until this same period. One of the difficulties with early Spanish accounts of their own activities in the Andes is that they contain almost no concrete information about location. Spanish knowledge of the Andean area grew only slowly, and the increasing use of native place-names as time passed probably reflects closer contact and more communication with native people. For example, *encomienda* awards were listed by the names of the Spaniards who held them until the 1560s. Only after the time of the *visita general* of Viceroy Toledo (1571–1575) were the grants given names that referred to the people awarded or to places. Localizing native groups is a very complex task before this period (Julien 1991:2, 124). The Spaniards who transmitted material from Inca genres may simply have recorded more information about the land as place-names came into use to refer to *encomienda* awards.

What is important to us about Urton's perspective is that it incorporates a theory of change. Not only should we be cognizant of how the origin story may have changed due to the transformation of Cuzco, we should not forget that the story may reflect the maelstrom resulting from the defeat of the Incas by an alien force with an alien supernatural. Here we will examine the Pacaritambo story using two different optics. One makes use of our analysis of the Spanish historical narratives. The other finds its evidentiary base in information collected about sacred places during the effort to evangelize native people in the late sixteenth century.

## THE ORIGIN STORY

Evidence for change in the origin story can be found in the Spanish historical narratives themselves. There are discrepancies between accounts that appear to indicate alternate versions of the story, and we can make some inferences about which version is the earliest.

Since we have examined the itinerary of the Ayar siblings embedded in the origin story along with its event structure, what remains to be examined are the characters themselves. We have already assembled genealogical information about the Ayar siblings from the Spanish historical narratives (tables 3.1–3.13). While accounts could disagree about the woman through whom descent was traced at various points in the genealogy (table 3.14), one of the most serious discrepancies involves the identification of the sister who was the spouse of Manco Capac. Most accounts name Mama Ocllo, but a number do not. Cabello Valboa and Morúa (M2a) name Mama Huaco, indicating to us that the underlying Molina account named her as well. Cobo also names Mama Huaco, indicating that Polo may have named her. Diego Fernández, the *Discurso*, Guaman Poma, and the other Morúa (M1b) name Mama Huaco. Cieza de León did not give the name of the sister who bore Sinchi Roca. The controversies over the women through whom descent passed in the case of the generations before sister-marriage was instituted are understandable, especially when these marriages symbolize a particular status relationship between the dynastic descent group and other local peoples. But why is there such difficulty in naming the woman considered to be the progenitor of everyone in the dynastic descent group?

The matter is related to how many Ayar siblings are named. Two of the authors name six and not eight Ayar siblings. Cieza names either Mama Huaco or Mama Ocllo. Las Casas names Mama Ocllo and not Mama Huaco. Of course, someone else is also missing from their list of Ayar men. Cieza names Ayar Manco and Ayar Ucho, then gives a composite name for the third brother, combining both Ayar Cache and Ayar Auca into a single person. The names Las Casas gives are harder to interpret. Ayar Manco is there. If Ayar Ucio can be equated with Ayar Ucho and Ayar Ancha with Ayar Cache, then Ayar Auca is the missing brother. Cobo gives us the names of four sisters but only three brothers. He repeats the name of Ayar Manco as Manco Capac, skipping Ayar Ucho. Cobo listed only seven Ayar siblings, reflecting his use of an underlying Polo source.

Polo wrote in 1561 that either three or four men emerged from the cave at Pacaritambo:

> I came to understand that, in the beginning when the Incas went out to conquer, the title that they had was a fable that their elders told them, that after the flood — about which I heard all over the land — three or four men from whom everyone else descended came out of a cave that they call Pacaritambo, six or seven leagues [30–35 km] from Cuzco, and, because they were the first from whom everyone else descended, overlordship of the rest would be theirs.

> Vine a entender que al prinçipio que los ingas enpeçaron a conquistar el título conque lo salieron a hazer fué una fábula que les dixeron sus viejos, que después del diluvio, del qual en toda la tierra hallo yo entera notiçia, de vna cueva que esta seis leguas del Cuzco, que ellos llamaron Pacari tanbo, salieron tres o quatro hombres de donde se torno a multiplicar el

mundo y que por aver sido ellos los primeros de donde todos avían salido les perteneçiese el señorío. ([1561]; 1940 : 152)

Polo has cast the Ayar siblings as Adam and Eve, misunderstanding the dis-avowal of a common origin of mankind that can be implied from the separate origin stories of Andean peoples collected by other Spanish authors like Sar-miento. He has also inserted a reference to the biblical flood, which may be his attempt to reconcile Inca history to his own idea of universal history. What is important to us is that he knew that there was a "short list" of Ayar men, like the one in Cieza and Las Casas.

So did Hernando de Santillán. Santillán wrote in 1563, not long after Polo was actively collecting material about the Inca past in Cuzco. Santillán notes that three Ayar brothers emerged from Pacaritambo:

> The origin of the Inca lords who ruled and conquered the provinces of Peru, leaving aside some fanciful stories that some Indians tell, is that they came from three brothers who emerged from a cave in the province of Pacaritambo and other things that, because they are not real or likely, will be left out. What seems closest to the truth and reasonable is that the first Incas came from Pacaritambo, which is 7 leagues [35 km] from Cuzco.

> El orígen de los señores ingas que señorearon y conquistaron las dichas provincias del Perú, dejadas algunas ficciones e imaginaciones que algunos indios dicen, que es haber procedido de tres hermanos que salían de una cueva que está en la provincia de Pacaritambo, y otras cosas que por no ser auténticas ni tener verisimilitud se dejan, lo que parece más verdad y lle-gado a razón es, que los primeros ingas fueron naturales de dicho Pacari-tambo, que es siete leguas del Cuzco. ([1563]; 1879 : 12)

Santillán, like Polo in his 1561 report, did not give their names.

Given the number of authors who mention an origin story with only three Ayar brothers, we can hypothesize that there was a version of the origin myth that involved three brothers and, possibly, three sisters. If the myth reflects the social organization of Cuzco at a particular time, then we should look for con-cordances between the story and the organization of Cuzco. Sarmiento is im-portant in this regard because he tells us about the origins of the groups who resided in Cuzco at the time he wrote and links three of them to the origin myth. While his narrative is structured around the descent group of Manco

Capac, Sarmiento also mentions that Ayar Cache and Ayar Uchu left descendants in Cuzco and gives the names of two or three of those alive at the time he wrote. Ayar Cache was the progenitor of Chauin Cuzco Ayllo, represented in 1572 by Martín Chucumbi and don Diego Guaman Paucar. Ayar Uchu had left a descent group called Arayraca Ayllo or Cuzco Callan; Juan Pizarro Yupanqui, don Francisco Quipi, and Alonso Tarma Yupanqui were named as living descendants. The missing brother is Ayar Auca.

In the comparison of accounts of the early Inca rulers in chapter 5, information about who among the Ayar brothers arrived in Cuzco and who became *huacas* was extracted from the narratives of Sarmiento, Cabello Valboa, and Cobo. This information, as well as parallel information from the Morúa (M2a) account that appears to draw, like Cabello Valboa, from Molina, is given in table 8.1. Cobo does not give names. Also, although he notes that one brother reentered the cave at Pacaritambo "and never emerged again" and that two brothers became *huacas*, one at Huanacauri, he is vague about where the second brother was turned to stone. He says only that the site was "not very far" from Huanacauri. An entry has been made in the table for this brother in the same column as Sarmiento, following the assumption that Cobo and Sarmiento are referring to the same narrative event.

Of course, if Ayar Auca left no descendants, then having him return to the cave at Pacaritambo, never to emerge again, may be a narrative device for explaining how it came to be that he left no descendants. It may also be an artifact of retelling a story with four brothers that had been told with three — the progenitors of three Ayar descent groups. A brother was added to the story, along with an explanation of why he left no descendants. One difficulty with this interpretation is that it is Cabello Valboa and Morúa who tell us that Ayar Auca went back to the cave; Sarmiento names Ayar Cache. Logically, Sarmiento should have named Ayar Auca, since he is the Ayar brother who left no descendants.

Which brothers reproduced and which did not is an issue that comes up elsewhere. Cabello Valboa makes a statement to the effect that neither Ayar Ucho nor Mama Rahua left descendants ([1586], pt. 3, chap. 10; 1951:268). Since Ayar Auca was walled up at Pacaritambo and Ayar Cache became a *huaca* at Huanacauri, he is telling us that only Manco Capac reproduced. Betanzos tells us that Ayar Auca died without leaving any progeny ([1551–1557], chap. 5; 1987:21). Since Ayar Cache was walled up at Pacaritambo and Ayar Uchu became a *huaca* at Huanacauri, again what is implied is that only Manco Capac left any descendants.

If the story changed at some point, we can infer that the story with three

TABLE 8.1. *Fates of the Ayar brothers*

|  | Walled up at Pacaritambo | Becomes Huanacauri | Becomes a *huaca* in or near Cuzco |
|---|---|---|---|
| Sarmiento | Ayar Cache | Ayar Uchu | Ayar Auca |
| Cabello Valboa | Ayar Auca | Ayar Cache |  |
| Morúa | Ayar Auca | Ayar Cache |  |
| Betanzos | Ayar Cache | Ayar Uchu |  |
| Cobo | a brother | a brother | a brother |

brothers is the earlier version. It explained the origins of existing social groups. The authors who tell the story with three Ayar brothers are early. That the story was captured in the years following the Spanish arrival may indicate that the story had only been retold in the recent past. However, one of the earliest accounts, the account of Betanzos, tells the story with a full complement of four Ayar brothers. Since we can tie Betanzos's material to Capac Ayllo, we can link the origin story with four brothers to that *panaca* as well. Given the importance of the transformation of Cuzco and the role cast for Capac Ayllo evident in it, we may also link the story with four brothers and sisters to the new Cuzco.

What was the point of reforming the story of origins? Here it would be helpful to know more about the social organization of Cuzco before its transformation. However, the origin story may be our only source of information on that topic. Pachacuti was said to have crafted an account of the Inca past. The story we have is a retrospective account of the steady rise to power of the descent group of Manco Capac. Given what we know about *capac* status, the full brothers and sisters of Manco Capac would have shared in it to the same degree as Manco Capac. The new story denies them that role. It overturned the implied equality between the Ayar siblings and their descendants. Manco Capac's brothers appear, but they are quickly taken off the stage. The story that unfolds is not the story of three lineages but of one. It explains why the descendants of Manco Capac were uniquely destined to rule. If genealogy was destiny, the new story denied the genealogical links of living Cuzco people with their Ayar forebear and subverted their claims — claims that could be seen to equal those of the descendants of Manco Capac.

## OTHER STRATA, OTHER STORIES

The origin story is a narrative. It can be analyzed for other strata by detecting inconsistencies in the different versions of the story and by casting it against the backdrop of what was recorded about Cuzco social organization by

Spanish authors. When we focus on the characters alone and not the story line, other sources come into play.

Two classes of sources are seldom used in explorations of the Inca origin story: the lists of *huacas* in and near Inca Cuzco and descriptions of public ritual in which these *huacas* play a role. Cobo copied a list of the *huacas* of Cuzco into his text ([1653], bk. 13, chaps. 13–16; 1893) that may have been taken from an earlier chart made by Polo de Ondegardo while he was *corregidor* of Cuzco (1559–1560). Polo said there were more than 400 shrines ([1561]; 1940:183), although Cobo included only 328. His list is therefore incomplete. Corroboration for this conclusion comes from a second and shorter list prepared by Cristóbal de Albornoz, who was active in rooting out native belief in the Cuzco region: eleven of the thirty-five *huacas* on the Albornoz list have no equivalent in Cobo (Rowe 1979:4–5). The list of *huacas*, because it is tied to a series of physical places, probably has not been distorted by the inventiveness that may characterize narratives, even though items can be forgotten or dropped from a list. Another source which sheds light on Inca origins is the description of Cuzco rituals that was made by Cristóbal de Molina ([1576] 1989). It is extremely valuable, because Molina describes something familiar to a great number of people. Inca narratives were often vehicles for the legitimation of particular claims, and the origin myth itself legitimated the dynasty's claim to descent from an important supernatural. The description of Cuzco ritual is less likely to be a vehicle for this kind of manipulation.

These sources have different capacities for conveying generic material. Narratives tell a story, while sources like the list of *huacas* may tell only about the characters. Ritual may reenact the story line of a narrative in some way, or it may relate what was once a story in a symbolic way. Our concern here is with the character Huanacauri. Huanacauri played a major role in Capac Raymi and Citua, two of the most important events of the Inca ritual calendar. He was also represented as one of the Ayar brothers in the origin story. When we examine these events and the lists of *huacas* related to this supernatural, other Huanacauris emerge.

Capac Raymi, as we have learned from the historical narratives, was when male members of the dynastic descent group were initiated. The historical narratives locate the origins of this rite in the time of Manco Capac, at the time his son Sinchi Roca was initiated. This initiation occured before the Ayar siblings reached Cuzco, while they were still living in Matagua. Matagua is at the foot of the hill Huanacauri (Rowe 1944: fig. 1 and p. 43). Before the Ayar siblings arrived at Matagua, one of the brothers had been turned to stone at the site of the *huaca* of Oma on Huanacauri. When the brother realized that he

would remain there, he told the others that he should be the first *huaca* to receive their offerings when they performed initiation.

A very elaborate initiation rite was developed, embedded in a round of ritual activities which occurred at precise intervals over a twenty-two-day period
in the month called Capac Raymi (Molina [1576]; 1989:98–110; Betanzos
[1551–1557], pt. 1, chap. 14; 1987:66–67; Cieza de León [1553], chap. 7; 1986:
17–19). The authors who describe Capac Raymi note that it was organized by
Manco Capac (Cieza de León [1553], chap. 7; 1986:17; Molina [1576]; 1989:
107, 114), with significant additions to the ritual made by Pachacuti (Betanzos
[1551–1557], pt. 1, chap. 14; 1987:63; Molina [1576]; 1989:114). Molina, in his
account of Inca ritual, describes the events of Capac Raymi in more detail than
anyone else. After noting that Manco Capac invented the ceremonies in order
to initiate his son Sinchi Roca, he explains that a dance, called *huari*, was given
to the Ayar siblings by the Creator at the time they came out of the cave at
Pacaritambo. They were instructed to dance it at this event and no other
(Molina [1576]; 1989:107).

Betanzos says that Pachacuti redesigned male initiation rites as part of his
reorganization of Cuzco:

> And another day in the morning, these lords [from around Cuzco] gath-
> ered in the house of the Inca where he communicated to them about the
> celebration that he wanted to hold, and so that there would be a perpetual
> memory he told them that it would be a good idea to incorporate certain
> ceremonies and fasts into the rite in which *orejones* were initiated, because
> something similar to that which was a sign or insignia [would be part of
> initiation] so that throughout the land they would be known from the
> youngest to the oldest resident of the city as lords and descendants of the
> Sun because it seemed to him that from that time forward the residents of
> Cuzco had to be held in esteem and respected by those of the rest of the
> land more than they had been before then and because they had to be
> called descendants of the Sun he wanted them to be made *orejones* in the
> celebration of the Sun with many ceremonies and fasts, because those
> who had been initiated before that time, they and their fathers had pierced
> their ears each one when they wanted to.

> Y otro dia de mañana se juntaron estos señores en las casas del Ynga
> donde comunico con ellos la fiesta que ansi quería hazer e para que della
> vuiese memoria para siempre dijoles Ynga Yupangue que seria bien que
> en esta fiesta se hiziesen los orejones con çiertas çerimonias y ayunos

porque *vna cosa semejante que aquello que hera señal y ynsignia para que por toda la tierra fuesen conoçidos desde el menor hasta el mayor de aquella çiudad por tales señores e hijos del sol porque* le paresçia que desde alli adelante auian de ser tenidos y rrespectados los de aquella çiudad por los de toda la tierra mas que auian sido hasta alli e que porque auian de ser llamados hijos del sol querían [*sic*: queria] que fuesen hechos y ordenados orejones en aque-lla fiesta del sol con muchas çerimonias e ayunos porque los que auian sido hechos orejones hasta alli ellos e sus padres les horadaban las orejas cada e cuando que querian. ([1551–1557], pt. 1, chap. 14; 1987:65)[2]

The public initiation of males to adult status at a particular time each year, then, was a new development related to the transformation of Cuzco.

The piercing of ears to receive golden ear spools was only part of the rite of male initiation. Initiation marked the first wearing of the breechcloth, a rite called *huarachico* in the historical narratives whose name incorporates the term for breechcloth (*huara*). Sarmiento and Cabelo Valboa both note that Manco Capac invented the rite of *huarachico*.[3] Cabello Valboa also mentions the rite of ear piercing, calling it *tocochico*, and attributes its invention to Manco Inca at the same time as *huarachico*. Whether the wearing of golden ear spools was a later addition to initiation, it is in the spirit of a rite that involves dressing the person in adult clothing for the first time and other signs of initiation to adult status. Males who were initiated received special clothing to be worn during particular phases of the rite, but there were several occasions in which the rit-ual act itself was the bestowal of gifts of clothing, ornaments, and weapons.

The rite also involved three pilgrimages by the initiates to different moun-tains around the Cuzco Valley, each followed by an assembly in the main plaza of Cuzco at which the ruling Inca, the images of the major supernaturals, the residents of the city, and the initiates were present. The mountains visited, in order, were Huanacauri, Anahuarqui, and Apo Yavira (map 1) (Molina [1576]; 1989:98–110; Betanzos [1551–1557], pt. 1, chap. 14; 1987:66–67; Cieza de León [1553], chap. 7; 1986:17–19). One of the central purposes of the visits to Hua-nacauri and Apo Yavira was to receive gifts associated with adult male status from each *huaca*. Both of these *huacas* spoke. Anahuarqui was the site of a foot race and did not have the power of speech. From Huanacauri, the initiates re-ceived their first gifts: slings and bags made in the style used by the "first" In-cas. They also got short haircuts. They received breechcloths from Apo Yavira as well as golden ear spools, feather crowns, and other ornaments. Later, in the main plaza, their relatives gave them the weapons they would use in war and substantial gifts of property. In Capac Raymi, then, Huanacauri and Apo Yavira functioned as senior members of the dynastic descent group.

Huanacauri was also cast as a principal in the rite of Citua, but this time the other members of the cast were not local mountains: they were supernaturals like the Sun and the Thunder. Citua was a ritual cleansing of Cuzco held at the beginning of the rainy season. A full complement of cult images of the most important supernatural beings, worked in precious metals, was involved: the Creator (Viracocha), the Sun (Apinpunchao) with two female companions (Ynca Ocllo and Palpa Ocllo) and the woman (known as Coya Pacssa) who was a sister of the ruling Inca taken as a wife by the Sun, and the Thunder (Chuqui Ylla). The stone cult image of Huanacauri was also brought to the plaza and played an active role. After the main cleansing rites, *sanco*, a dough of ground maize, was prepared. It was put in fountains so that they would not cause illness. The images of major supernaturals and the desiccated bodies of lineage members were "warmed" with it, apparently by placing some on the forehead:

> Those responsible for the *huaca* called Huanacauri, which is a large stone in the shape of a man, together with a ritual specialist, washed [the image] and "warmed" it with *sanco*. Then the ruling Inca, after he had finished washing, and his principal wife went to their places and put some of the *sanco* on their foreheads.

> Los que tenían a cargo la huaca llamada Huanacauri, que es una peña grande figura de hombre, los criados de la dicha huaca juntamente con el sacerdote della lavaban la dicha [?] lana y la calentavan con el çanco, y el Inca, señor principal, desde que se acava de lavar y su mujer principal, se ponían en su aposento y les ponían en las caueças, en las cauecas dellos el dicho çanco. (Molina [1576]; 1989:77)

Later, Huanacauri and the other cult images were brought to the main plaza. Huanacauri had an assigned place (Molina [1576]; 1989:78). Then the people of Cuzco arrived, organized by "ayllo and parcialidad." A celebration took place which included worship of the major supernaturals as well as eating, drinking, and dancing. At night everyone, including the images, went home (Molina [1576]; 1989:78–79).

These events involved only the people of Cuzco. The next day, another celebration was held to which people from the region of Cuzco were invited. A large number of animals were sacrificed. Four llamas — the most perfect — were chosen for sacrifice to the Creator, the Thunder, the Sun, and Huanacauri. *Yahuarsanco* (*sanco* prepared with the blood of the llamas) was set before the images in large golden dishes. So began a swearing of allegiance to the supernaturals and to the Incas by the people assembled. The oath was administered before the *yahuarsanco* was ingested. To eat *yahuarsanco*, one dipped three fingers into the dish and then placed the mixture in one's mouth. All those present partook of the mixture, including small children (Molina [1576]; 1989:79–80). Then the remaining animals were sacrificed, their lungs were examined for certain signs, and the people took the meat home, treating it as if it were something sacred. On the next day the celebration was dedicated to the Moon and the Earth. The same people participated. Then, on the fourth day, people from subject nations entered: "They came worshiping the Creator; the Sun; the Thunder; Huanacauri, the *huaca* of the Incas; and finally, the Inca, who was also in the plaza at that time" [Yban haciendo reverencia al Hacedor y Sol y Trueno y a Huanacauri, huaca de los yncas y luego al Ynca que a la saçon estuvo ya en la plaza] (Molina [1576]; 1989:94). Huanacauri is clearly a major supernatural and was presented to the peoples dominated by the Incas as such. He was fed in the same manner as the Creator, the Sun, and the Thunder: they were fed three times a day, each time by the sacrifice and burning of a camelid (Molina [1576]; 1989:98). The similar treatment is manifest in other ways. Orations were composed to Huanacauri in which his name was listed with the Creator, the Sun, the Thunder, and the Moon, and he was asked, as the others were, to preserve the population of Cuzco and to give them what they needed to assure their continued existence (Molina [1576]; 1989:101). Although Huanacauri is always subordinate to the Creator and to the Sun, he occupies a place held by no other local supernatural.

Huanacauri was also listed by Molina as a place where human sacrifices known as *capac ucha* were offered. He noted that a round of *capac ucha* sacrifices occurred at the beginning of each Inca's rule. Some of the individuals intended for sacrifice were dedicated in Cuzco and then sent to other places to be sacrificed (Molina [1576]; 1989:122; Hernández Príncipe [1621–1622] 1923). Molina first lists the major supernaturals who received this type of sacrifice, then notes that the round of sacrifice begun in this manner involved all the sacred places in the Cuzco Valley, no matter how small. His list included, in order, the Creator, the Sun, the Thunder (Chuqui Ylla), the Earth (Pachamama), and then Huanacauri (Molina [1576]; 1989:120–128).

Huanacauri, then, was represented on two levels. He was represented in Capac Raymi as one of three important local *huacas*. Like one of the others,

Apo Yavira, he gave gifts to the new initiates. The gifts they were given symbolized the past in some way — appropriate gifts from an Ayar brother who wished to be remembered at Capac Raymi. This role was played largely before the *panacas* and other residents of Cuzco. In the celebration of Citua he was grouped with the principal supernaturals recognized by the Incas. The other supernaturals were represented by cult images made of precious metals. The image of Huanacauri was a stone *huaca* brought in from a local mountain. This role was played before both the Cuzco residents and non-Inca people from outside the city. Although his link to the dynastic Inca line may have been apparent, his role as a principal supernatural — rather than a local figure — was made manifest.

Let us now look at his role as a local figure. In Capac Raymi, both Huanacauri and Apo Yavira are cast in similar roles. Apo Yavira is a character we have not heard of before. He was not mentioned in either the origin story or the historical narratives which drew from Inca sources. As a local *huaca*, he was included in the list of *huacas* incorporated in Cobo along with Huanacauri and Anahuarqui (Rowe 1979: 28, 29, 46, 52). The items on Cobo's list related to these three *huacas* are summarized in the list below. The items themselves and the numerical references to them are taken from the publication of Cobo's list by John Rowe (1979: 23, 35, 39, 41, 47, 53, 55). Additional information about the same *huacas* has been taken from Albornoz (cited in Rowe 1979: 73, 75) and Molina ([1576]; 1989: 68–69, 96, 98, 100–101, 104, 106). The names of the *suyos* are abbreviated (Chinchasuyo = Ch; Andesuyo = An; Collasuyo = Co; Condesuyo = Cu). Names and their spellings have been preserved as they appear in the sources.

Ch-4:5 Guamancancha. Near the fortress on a small hill of this name. Enclosure with two huts where fasting took place during initiation rites.
Guamancancha. A heap of stones above Carmenca.
Guamancancha. A place at the foot of Yavira where the initiates spent the night prior to their visit to Yavira.
Ch-5:7 Chaca Huanacauri. Small hill on the way to Yucay where young men preparing themselves to be *orejones* went for a certain grass which they carried on their lances.
Molina mentions obtaining grass for seating from Huanacauri itself, the month before Capac Raymi.
Chaca huanacauri. A stone over the fortress.
Ch-7:7 Churucana. Hill where sacrifices to the Creator were made.

Churucani Huanacauri. A large stone surrounded by little stones called *cachavis*.

Ch-8:2 Mancochuqui. *Chacara* of Huanacauri; proceeds sacrificed to him.

Ch-9:6 Apu Yavira. Stone on the hill of Picho [Piccho]. They believed it was one of those who emerged from the earth with Huanacauri, and that after having lived for a long time he climbed up there and turned to stone. All the *ayllos* went to worship there during the festival of Raymi. Molina notes that this *huaca* was the principal *huaca* of the people of Maras. Pachacuti was said to have incorporated Yavira into the initiation ritual as the place where those to be made *orejones* received breechcloths. Huascar was said to have given the cult image its latest form: two stones shaped like falcons placed together on an altar.
Yauirac. Many stones together.

An-4:7 Maycha Huanacauri. Stone shaped like the hill of Huanacauri, ordered to be placed in Andesuyo.

An-9:5 Ata Huanacauri. Certain stones placed next to a hill, an ancient shrine.

Co-1:6 Atpitan. Certain stones in a ravine where one loses sight of Huanacauri. These stones were men who were sons of that hill, and in a certain misfortune they turned to stone.

Co-6:7 Huanacauri. Among the most important shrines in the whole kingdom; oldest shrine after the window [cave] of Pacaritambo and where the most sacrifices were made. Hill with a stone figure said to be one of the brothers of the first Inca.

Co Queros Huanacauri, Omotu Yanacauri [Huanacauri]. Hills where they sacrificed in May, on a route to Vilcanota, via Pomacanche.

Co-7:5 Matoro. Slope near Huanacauri with ancient buildings where those who went out from Huanacauri slept.
Matagua. Place at the foot of Huanacauri where initiates slept prior to their visit to Huanacauri on the eighth day of the month.

Cu-1:7 Anahuarqui. Big hill next to Huanacauri with many idols, each of which had its origin and history. Molina notes that it was the principal *huaca* of the people of Choco and Cachona. He also notes that a race was run there at the time *orejones* were made because the *huaca* Anahuarqui was known to be so light that it ran like a bird flies.

Cu-1:8 Chatahuarqui. Small stone on a little hill next to that other one
[Anahuarqui].

Cu-1:10 Anahuarqui Huaman. Stone on a hill next to the one above
[Anahuarqui].

Cu-2:4 Rauaraya. Small hill where the Indians finished running on the
feast of Raymi. Also a place of punishment.

Rauraua. The initiates slept at a "despoblado" called Rauraua the
night of the fourteenth day and from it began the day of the races
up Anahuarqui. Rauaraua is 1 league from Cuzco, and
Anahuarqui is 2. The next day, after lunch at Quilliyacolca, they
went up to Anahuarqui and sacrificed five llamas to the Hacedor,
Sun, Thunder, Moon, and Inca. Then the girls ran back to
Rauraua and waited for the boys, calling to them. They dance
*huari*, remove the *huaracas* [slings] from the *yauris*, and whip the
arms and legs of the newly initiated. Then they return to Cuzco
behind the *raymi napa* and the *suntur paucar* instead of the royal
insignia.

Cu-5:5 Cumpu Huanacauri. Hill in line with Choco with ten stones on
top of it that were sent from Huanacauri.

Information from Albornoz about *huacas* with similar names in neighboring
valleys ([1581–1585]; 1989:179–180) is summarized in the following list.

Valley of Caquijahuana

Huanacauri, Anahuarqui, and Auiraca [Yavira]. Three stones on a hill in
memory of those of Cuzco.

Marahuasi Huanacauri. Stone where they made many sacrifices in
remembrance of Huanacauri of Cuzco.

Huaypon Huanacauri. Stone near a lake where the Cuzcos pierced their
ears.

Chinchero Huanacauri. Stone near the other one [Huaypon
Huanacauri].

Pancha Huanacauri. A stone on the hill of Pancha near the lake of
Pongo.

Racra Huanacauri. *Huaca* on a neighboring hill [to Pancha
Huanacauri].

Valley of Calca

Vitcos Huanacauri. Stone like an Indian on a hill above the town of
Amaybamba. Said to be the son of the Creator.

Though the references to Huanacauri are diverse, all of the objects identified with this *huaca* — or with Yavira and Anahuarqui — are hills or stones associated with hills. Huanacauri was represented by a single cult image. On the hill of Anahuarqui there was a collection of stone *huacas*, but there was also some kind of supernatural being named Anahuarqui who was very swift and who was fed by sacrifices. One or more of the stones may have been a physical representation of this being. A *huaca* could be represented by more than one stone, since Yavira (Ch-9:6) was apparently represented by two, carved in the shape of falcons.

We cannot assume that all the stones to which the name Huanacauri was attached were related in some way to the Huanacauri that was the principal *huaca* of Cuzco, but some certainly were. One place, Cumpu Huanacauri (Cu-5:5), was the site of multiple stones sent there by Huanacauri. Another, Maycha Huanacauri (An-4:7), was a stone shaped like the hill of Huanacauri said to have been ordered to be placed in Andesuyo. While the description does not tell us who gave the orders, elsewhere in the list of *huacas* such orders were given by particular Inca rulers. One group of ten stones at Atpitan (Co-1:6) were "sons of Huanacauri." Other stones or hills were simply called by a composite name that incorporated Huanacauri, like Chaca Huanacauri (Ch-5:7), Churucani Huanacauri (Ch-7:7), Ata Huanacauri (An-9:5), and Queros Huanacauri, as well as Omotu Huanacauri in Collasuyo. Some of these places were associated with initiation or with Capac Raymi, so if there is a common underlying relation among them, it may be that they were connected with initiation in some way.

Outside of Cuzco there were other stones named Huanacauri, particularly in Jaquijahuana, on the plain of Anta. A group of stones named after the three hills in Cuzco which were the focus of Capac Raymi were said to have been established there "in memory of" their counterparts in Cuzco. If the public celebration of Inca initiation — Capac Raymi — incorporated pilgrimages to the three Cuzco hills, and this celebration originated with the transformation of Cuzco, then the commemoration of the Cuzco hills in Jaquijaguana dates to this period or later. Ata Huanacauri in Cuzco was said to be "ancient." There may be different agents involved in the establishment of cults to the particular *huacas* known as Huanacauri, and more than one period of time may be represented.

What is interesting is that some of the information given about the mountain *huacas* reflects a particular version of Inca origins and the establishment of the Ayar siblings in Cuzco. Cobo described Huanacauri as a hill where there was a stone figure said to be one of the brothers of the first Inca who emerged from the earth with Huanacauri, and that after having lived for a long time he climbed a mountain and turned to stone (Rowe 1979:47). Cobo's historical narrative was vague about which brother became a *huaca* and where. One became a *huaca* at Huanacauri, while another became a *huaca* "not far from there," and we have assumed that he meant somewhere between Huanacauri and Cuzco since the story moves in that direction. Sarmiento mentions a brother who became a *huaca* in Cuzco. It may be that both Sarmiento and Cobo are giving us accounts of Yavira. Betanzos, Cabello Valboa, and Morúa tell a different story.

Yavira was a *huaca* that was sacred to the people of Maras, a region located between the pampa of Anta and the Urubamba Valley and the home of the Ayarmaca, whose chief lord was Tocay Capac, a major character in the Inca story of early Cuzco. Sarmiento notes that the people of Maras also emerged from one of the three "windows" at Pacaritambo, called Maras Toco ([1572], chap. 11; 1906:33). We have tried to link Yavira to the story of Inca origins, and the version told by Cobo is certainly elastic enough to include this character. However, we may have run across a character who belongs in another story as well. The stories are explanations, and we can expect that important *huacas* would be explained by different groups in different ways.

Moreover, there is another *huaca* on Cobo's list who is also connected with Inca origins named Michos Amaro (Ch-1:1) and located in Totocache (now the neighborhood of Belén). Yavira was located on the hill of Piccho, so the two are not the same. Michos Amaro was said to have emerged "with the first Inca, Manco Capac, from the cave of Pacaritambo." The sacrifices made to him "were very ancient." Further, one of the Ayar women was said to have killed "him" because of the disrespect he showed her (Rowe 1979:15). The Totocache area was where the Huallas had lived. Both Sarmiento and Cabello Valboa describe the killing of one of the Huallas by Mama Huaco. If the *huaca* of Michos Amaro commemorated this person, the Incas nonetheless made sacrifices to him. What is new in the description from Cobo's list is that this person was said to have emerged from the cave of Pacaritambo. In the Inca story, the Huallas are non-Incas.

Clearly, the landscape around Cuzco reflects other stories of social origins and other explanations of the past. The list of *huacas* contains traces of other stories or, alternatively, of other strata. Although the origin myth relates Huanacauri to the story of dynastic origins (Huanacauri is Ayar Ache turned to stone), the list of shrines and the Capac Raymi rite provide indications that the dynastic version is not the only one. Huanacauri was a complex character. From an analysis of the materials we have, it appears that he had some longevity in the Cuzco area. There are other characters on the landscape who were important to the Incas and, perhaps, to other groups. Quite naturally, the story of dynastic origins — told retrospectively by the members of the dynastic descent group about their uniquely powerful forebears — tends to obscure what can be learned about other stories.

## VIRACOCHA

The story of Inca origins changed when the Incas began their meteoric rise. Did it change again after their meteoric fall? There are two sources of change that we should not confuse. There are attempts by Spanish authors to frame the Inca past within their own conceptions of universal history. When Polo tried to describe the Pacaritambo origin story, he located it with reference to the flood and universalized the Inca origin story across the Andes. Two systems of explanation collided, and we can expect turbulence as a result. The other source of change is internal. When Sarmiento drew from Inca sources in the early 1570s, the materials he collected had been transmitted during several decades of the Spanish occupation of Cuzco. During this time, the Incas were grappling with their own defeat. The success of the Spaniards and the new corpus of belief that buttressed Spanish action may have posed new questions for explanation, prompting new responses.

So far we have assumed that the Pacaritambo origin story is the one that rightly begins the genealogical genre that was painted on wooden tablets. The Spanish historical narratives, however, incorporate other stories of origins. These stories offer explanations not just of the origins of the Inca dynastic descent group but of the origins of everything. A story that explains the creation of the world by its very nature covers the same territory as the story that launches biblical history, a story told in the book of Genesis. One of the problems we have, even if there is an Andean substratum for a creation story, is that Christian belief in the universality of biblical history would tend to rewrite any local account of creation to stress those points which confirmed or paralleled the biblical story, even if it meant adding them to bring the old story into line with what Christians knew had happened.

Let us ask a simple question here. Did the dynastic account begin with such a story, or is the creation story an example of pasticcio? Both Sarmiento and Betanzos tell an account of the creation of the sun and the moon and all of the world's peoples. Sarmiento locates the story after the universal flood. Although some people (the Cañares) told him about how their ancestors had survived the flood, the Incas said everyone perished and that Viracocha began to create the people anew. So Sarmiento tells the story under the heading "second age and creation" ([1572], chaps. 6−7; 1906 : 23−28). Betanzos tells a somewhat different story. Viracocha emerged from Lake Titicaca when it was still dark. Then Betanzos backtracked to say that this was the second time he had come and that he had created the sky and the earth the first time. He had also created people, but these people had displeased him, and he turned them to stone. The second time he created the sun and the day, as well as a new batch of people. There is no mention of a flood (Betanzos [1551−1557], pt. 1, chaps. 1−2; 1987 : 11−15).

The creator is named Ticci Viracocha in Sarmiento and Contiti Viracocha in Betanzos, but they are obviously the same personage. In both accounts, the scene moved from Lake Titicaca to Tiahuanaco, then to Cacha in Canas territory (Gasparini and Margolies 1980 : 234−254), and then to Urcos near Cuzco. After traversing the Andes, this being disappeared out to sea from the coast of Ecuador. Viracocha had helpers. In Tiahuanaco he created all of the peoples of the Andes and sent them to caves, springs, and so on, from which they emerged. Both Betanzos and Sarmiento then proceed to tell the Pacaritambo origin story. The origin story flows logically from the creation myth. Only our natural skepticism of the implied parallels between the Andean past and biblical history prevents us from concluding that the Inca genre did not begin with a story about the creation of the universe.

One account lends credence to our interpretation that the addition of the Viracocha story is an example of pasticcio. Cristóbal de Molina wrote a historical narrative of the Inca past soon after Sarmiento that we have argued was used by Cabello Valboa in his historical narrative. The parallels between Cabello Valboa and one of the Morúa texts (M2) have allowed us to reconstruct Molina's account in general outline. Molina also wrote an account of the fables and rites of the Incas for the bishop of Cuzco, Sebastián Lartaún, in 1576. This account was written *after* the historical narrative since Molina refers to the historical narrative in it ([1576]; 1989 : 49, 58, 107). The account of fables and rites contains a version of the universal creation myth that is broadly similar to the tale told in Sarmiento and Betanzos; that is, the story locates the creation at Tiahuanaco, and the various peoples of the Andes are sent from there to the places from which they would emerge and found lineages. Molina adds an episode in which the Sun reveals to Manco Capac that the Incas are his children, and the Ayar siblings emerge from Pacaritambo on the day the Sun first rises. Molina, like Sarmiento, then tells the story about Cañar origins ([1576]; 1989 : 50−56).

Since the text of Molina's historical narrative is not available, we might assume that it incorporated a version of the creation myth at its beginning. However, neither Cabello Valboa nor Morúa tell a story of the creation of mankind by Viracocha. Cabello Valboa, right after noting Molina as the source of his account, launches it with the Pacaritambo origin story. Morúa says the people tell "diverse fables" about Inca origins but then tells his fairly detailed version of the Pacaritambo story. Molina told us that the painted genre began with a story of Inca origins. His historical narrative, as transmitted by Cabello Valboa and Morúa, incorporates material from this genre. It is therefore especially significant that Molina began the story with the emergence of the Ayar siblings from Pacaritambo and not with the creation of the universe by Viracocha.

Why was there a difference between the two Molina texts? Both were relatively late, compared with authors like Betanzos or Cieza. The difference must be due to a difference in purpose on the part of the author: Molina transmitted material from Inca sources in his historical narrative; what he wrote for the bishop was an explanation of Andean belief. In the former he took what he was given. In the latter he posed a new question — how do they explain the origins of everything? — and selected material that would give an answer. Molina knew there was a supreme Creator; therefore, how had the Incas explained his creation? Molina also knew there had been a flood; ergo, how had it manifested itself in the Andes? The assumption that these questions were fundamental and could be answered in the Andes provoked new explanations based on Andean source materials.[4]

An insertion of this kind in Sarmiento is not surprising. Its insertion in the Betanzos account is much more problematic. Is Betanzos telling a new story of creation constructed of Andean materials selected and read with theories of a supreme Creator and universal history in the background, or had those who relayed source material from Inca genres done this job for him? Had the reinterpretation of origins affected the stories circulated by the *panacas*?

What Andean materials could have lent themselves to this purpose? The link with the Lake Titicaca region that is so clear in the story about universal creation is an indication that we should look beyond Cuzco for some of the materials that were incorporated in this story. Because, in a similar story that was told by Juan de Santa Cruz Pachacuti, the leading character was named Tunupa, it may be that a story with another leading character was the basis of the Viracocha creation story.[5] This question deserves much fuller consideration than can be given here. Our purpose is more limited. To understand the Inca origin story, we have examined sites on the Cuzco landscape that reveal the complexity of one of the characters — Huanacauri — and open vistas into other stories and periods. The same sources help us to recast Viracocha.

Like Huanacauri, there is more than one Viracocha on the landscape. The principal sources that contribute to this question are Albornoz and Molina. Molina gives a list of the sons and brothers of Viracocha in a very free and descriptive translation of one of the orations performed during the animal sacrifices of Citua ([1576]; 1989:83–84). The items that appear in Molina, coupled with parallel information from Albornoz ([1581–1585]; 1989:180) are given in the following list:

> Chanca Viracochan. *Huaca* in Chuquichaca where Manco Inca was.
> Atun Viracochan. The *huaca* of Urcos where there was an eagle and a
>     falcon of stone at the doorway. Inside there was a bust of a man with a
>     white shirt and hair to his waist. And the stones of the eagle and falcon
>     cried each day at midday. Their attendants said they cried because
>     Viracocha was hungry.
> This image had the following sons and brothers:
>     Corcos Viracocha.
>     Apotin Viracochan. In Amaybamba, behind [Ollantay]tambo.
>     Urusayua Vriracochan. In Tambo?
>     Chuquichanca Viracochan. In Huaypar.
> Apotinia Viracocha. A stone they say is the son of the Creator on a hill
>     above the town of Amaybamba.

Unfortunately, Albornoz does not cover the region south of Urcos, so if there was a *huaca* at Cacha, where Ticci Viracocha was said to have performed a miracle and a large Inca hall was erected (Betanzos [1551–1557], pt. 1, chap. 2; 1987:13–14; pt. 1, chap. 45; 1987:191–192; Cieza de León [1550], chap. 98; 1984:269–271; Garcilaso de la Vega [1609], bk. 5, chap. 22; 1990:203–205), it is not mentioned in his account.

Although the list is not long, there are indications that these *huacas* are similar in nature and kind to the *huacas* associated with Huanacauri. For one thing, some were stones. For another, there were a number of *huacas* which incorporated the name Viracocha as part of a longer name; as in the composite names for Huanacauri, the name Viracocha followed another name that designated which one. Also, there were multiple beings with this name, some defined as offspring of others. The *huaca* of Urcos is clearly the most important of those on the list, as indicated by its name: Atun Viracocha. This Viracocha, like the

Viracocha of the Tiahuanaco creation story, had attendants. There may have been a story associated with this *huaca* that could be retold with a Lake Titicaca basin backdrop. The obverse is also possible: aspects of a story from the Lake Titicaca region may have been superimposed on a local *huaca* associated with creation.

Once we reach this point, the complexity begins to elude our analysis. What we can detect is that the story about Viracocha as supreme Creator created turbulence in the historical narratives based on Inca sources. A clear example is the ambiguity over the nature of the supernatural most closely related to the dynastic descent group that surfaces in Betanzos. He writes:

> Although they hold that there is one who is the Creator whom they call Viracocha Pachayachachi, which means "maker of the world," and they hold that this [Creator] made the Sun and everything that is created in the sky and on the earth, as you have heard, lacking writing and being blind in understanding and knowledge, [they] may vary in this [idea] as in everything else because sometimes they hold the Sun for Creator and other times they say it is Viracocha.

> Aunque ellos tienen que ay vno que es el hazedor a quien ellos llaman Viracocha Pacha Yachachic que dize hazedor del mundo que ellos tienen que este hizo el sol y todo lo que es criado en el çielo e tierra como ya aueis oydo careçiendo de letras e siendo çiegos del entendimiento e en el sauer casi mudos varian en esto en todo y por todo porque vnas vezes tienen al sol por hazedor y otras vezes dizen que el Viracocha. (Betanzos n.d. [1551–1557], pt. 1, chap. 11; 1987:49)

The reason the confusion pops up here is that Betanzos had identified the supernatural who had appeared to Pachacuti at Susurpuquio as Viracocha, while here he is describing the construction to be dedicated to this being as a "house of the Sun" ([1551–1557], pt. 1, chap. 8; 1987:32; pt. 1, chap. 11; 1987:49–50).

Betanzos was not alone in his confusion. Sarmiento describes the figure at Susurpuquio as a person "like the Sun" ([1572], chap. 27; 1906:62). Sarmiento also notes that some of his Cuzco informants told him that the Sun and Viracocha Pachayachachic were separate beings, but others said they were one and the same (Sarmiento de Gamboa [1572], chap. 10; 1906:33). Cristóbal de Molina includes dialogue in his narrative of the apparition at Susurpuquio in which the supernatural identifies himself as the Sun ([1576]; 1989:60–61).

There are other indications of a confusion between the Sun and a supernatural thought to be the equivalent of the Christian supreme Creator. Sarmiento is positive that Viracocha is the supreme Creator. He refers to the Incas a number of times as "sons of the Sun" (his translation of *intipchurin*), but he calls them "sons of Viracocha" at one point. He identifies the Inca shrine on the island of Titicaca as a "temple of the Sun and the *huaca* of Ticci Viracocha" (Sarmiento de Gamboa [1572], chap. 59; 1906:105). The island was strongly associated with the solar cult, and Sarmiento has simply confused Ticci Viracocha with the Sun. The confusion is also evident in Polo's effort to locate the house of Viracocha. He says he searched Cuzco for the house of Viracocha without ever finding it but notes that he was told it was in the same place as the houses of the Sun (Polo de Ondegardo [1571]; 1872:58–59).

Despite the confusion over the identification of this supernatural in the historical narratives, we may be able to supply our own identification. In the Betanzos account, as noted in chapter 4, there are parallels between Viracocha's sweep through the Andes and the march of the Inca armies. These parallels are not a result of contact with a foreign system of explanation. They are an Andean motif that assimilates the Inca conquest to the actions of the supernatural most closely associated with the dynastic descent group. Let us look for a moment at how Betanzos describes the path of the Creator Viracocha. After the progenitors of all the peoples of the Andes were taken out by "viracochas" — helpers of the Creator Viracocha — to the caves, rivers, and springs from which they were to emerge, a process of calling them forth took place:

> They say he sent the two [*viracochas*] who had remained with him in the town of Tiahuanaco out to call and bring forth the people in the manner you have already heard about, dividing these two in this fashion: he sent one to the region and province of Condesuyo, which is, standing in Tiahuanaco, your back to the place where the sun rises, on the left hand, so that they, in this manner — no more, no less — would go do that to which the first [*viracochas*] had gone to do and that they would call out the Indians and natives of Condesuyo; and similarly he sent the other to the region and province of Andesuyo, which is on the right hand, standing in the manner aforesaid, back toward where the sun rises, and these two, having been sent off, they say he went straight down to Cuzco, a route between these two provinces, coming there on the royal road that passes through the highlands toward Cajamarca; along the road he, too, went calling and getting the people out in the manner you have been told.

Dizen que los dos que ansi quedaron con el alli en el pueblo de Tiaguanaco que los enbio ansimismo a que llamasen y sacasen las gentes en la
manera que ya aveis hoydo deuidiendo estos dos en esta manera que enbio
el vno por la parte y prouinçia de Condesuyo que es estando en este
Tiaguanaco las espaldas do el sol sale a la mano yzquierda para que ansi ni ni
mas ni menos fuesen a hazer lo que auían ydo los primeros y que ansimismo llamasen los indios y naturales de la prouinçia de Condesuyo y que
lo mismo enbio el otro por la parte y prouinçia de Andesuyo que es a la
otra mano derecha puesto en la manera dicha las espaldas hazia do el sol
sale y estos dos ansi despachados dizen que el ansimismo se partio por
el derecho de hazia el Cuzco que es por el medio de estas dos provincias
viniendo por el camino rreal que ba por la sierra hazia Caxamalca por el
cual camino yva el ansimismo llamando y sacando las gentes en la manera
que ya aueis hoydo. (Betanzos n.d. [1551–1557], pt. 1, chap. 2, fol. 4;
1987:13)

Although the Creator Viracocha traveled the Inca road called Collasuyo, and
it followed a northwest route from Tiahuanaco, the solar imagery is there.
When one stands with one's back to where the sun rises and keeps Condesuyo
on the left and Andesuyo on the right, one is following the course of the sun.
The Viracocha of the Betanzos "creation" story has features that suggest a solar supernatural.

There are other strata in the story of this personage/being that belong to
the period before the Spanish arrival, but they will be difficult to read because
the Spaniards and Andeans who are retelling the story have accepted Christian
explanations of creation. One question that has remained hanging throughout
our narrative is, How did the Incas construct their relationship to the Sun? By
calling themselves *intipchurin*, they were phrasing this relationship in terms of
descent. Was there a story that explained this tie? Was the story of "creation"
by a solar supernatural in the Lake Titicaca region a story of the creation of all
Andean peoples or only a story of the descent of a particular group of special
beings? We have observed that a story of the Inca past subordinated other
groups, even those who claimed descent from other Ayar brothers. An Inca
story of their relationship to this solar forebear — if we were to imagine it from
what we have learned about Inca genres — very likely put the dynastic descent
group in the foreground and forgot the rest.

# 9 Conclusions

It has been my express purpose to identify Inca sources that transmit a memory of the past. Memory is selective, and it should not be lost on the reader that a study of memory is intimately bound to a story of what was forgotten. Perhaps it is remarkable that the sources which tell us about the Inca past tell us so much about what the Inca dynastic line was trying to hide: Inca Urcon, the other Ayar brothers, even the Ayarmacas are all lurking in the background. The Inca story, if Cieza and Sarmiento were right, did not have much longevity. Just under the surface were other stories and other explanations. One of the ideas put forward in the introduction — that the story that was told about the rise to power of the descendants of Manco Capac was crafted only after an imperial expansion was launched — explains why there are fragments of other stories to be found. They were near in time to the time of the arrival of Spaniards in Cuzco.

Now that we have reread the origin myth it can be seen that the version of the origin story that found its way into Spanish historical narratives benefited a particular segment of the larger group identified as Inca. It reflects a perspective on the past that supports the claims to power of a particular group while systematically undermining others. It was part of a larger narrative, composed of a string of life histories arranged in genealogical order and painted on wooden tablets. The incorporation of some kind of story about the involvement of each Inca in contests for power provides a rough indication of how the stage on which the Incas acted changed as the political context shifted from the local, to the regional, to the pan-Andean level. The content of this narrative account provides a rough indication of when the descendants of Manco Capac emerged as more powerful than the other segments of the larger group to which they belonged: events associated with the youth of Mayta Capac mark a distinct change in the claims to power of the dynastic descent group vis-à-vis other members of the larger group to which the descendants of Manco Capac belonged and the other inhabitants of the Cuzco Valley.

If we read Inca history (this time the life history of Pachacuti), we are told that the ninth Inca, Pachacuti, constructed the painted history of his forebears to the seventh generation, as well as had a life history composed for each. To test this theory of composition we must ask if it accords with the perspective we find in the Inca genres themselves. It does, and for several reasons. Viewed as a representation of the unimpeded rise to power of one group not only within a larger group but to a much higher level, the composition had to have occurred after the dynastic group began to claim authority over a much larger Andean territory. The origin story itself, which accounts for the demise of the other Ayar siblings or their lack of descendants even though some of their descendants could still be found in Cuzco, reflects a particular perspective that would only be truly convincing after the spectacular rise to power of the dynastic descent group. The version of origins collected by Sarmiento and others reflects a perspective that postdates the establishment of Inca dominance over other Cuzco groups and that may not have been enshrined as official myth until the period of imperial expansion, when it spoke truth about the power of Manco Capac's line.

The theory of composition contained in the life history of Pachacuti accords well with the material on the earlier rulers incorporated into Spanish narratives like those of Sarmiento, Cabello Valboa, and Cobo. The life history of Pachacuti would have been composed at his death. If so, it was composed almost within the time spanned by the memories of some of the older residents of Cuzco alive during the years when material for the Spanish narratives was collected. What was told to Cieza and Sarmiento about the composition of Inca history may have been memory transmitted across only one generation. However, because Betanzos describes Pachacuti's efforts to construct a record of the Inca past, there is reason to think that the topic was part of Pachacuti's life history.

Let us accept, for the sake of argument, the theory of composition we read in the Spanish narratives. What is interesting to note is that the retelling of the origin story does not explain the tie to the solar supernatural. A new story could have linked the dynastic descent group to a solar supernatural from the outset rather than revealing this tie through a series of apparitions or dreams. The discrepancies between versions of the origin story that were incorporated in Spanish historical narratives — if they can be interpreted as evidence for successive versions of the same story — indicate to us that the retelling of the story involved only minor changes — changes, nonetheless, that upset the claims of those most closely related to the dynastic descent group. An earlier story line could have been similar in general outline to the story of the Inca emergence at Pacaritambo that was told to the Spaniards, except that it may have launched a story about three lineages and not just one.

Issues like this are important to our understanding of whether there was something we could call Inca history. What we call history works with what people know and believe about their past. Its "truth" is fundamentally a product of its ability to reflect what is known and believed. The growth of dynastic power was believable; history could be rewritten to reflect and explain it. Nonetheless, a new version would have to work with what the people of Cuzco understood of their past. It would therefore embed its messages in a corpus of material that would be recognized by its audience. We will return to these issues below.

One of the criticisms of a historicist interpretation of the Spanish historical narratives was that not enough attention was paid to the question of values (Ossio 1970). That criticism can be expanded. For us to understand what now appear to be the various forms that recorded Inca memory took, we would need to penetrate the system of values and meanings that gave these stories their reflective or explanatory power. That may or may not be possible, since the translation of the interpretation of Inca forms into Spanish may prove to be an insurmountable barrier to understanding what was meant in the original. Our efforts perforce have concentrated at a much more elementary level: that of identifying the Inca sources that underlie Spanish historical narratives. If they can be identified, we can learn something about their form and content. We can then begin to consider whose voices we hear in the Spanish narratives: the voices of the Spanish authors or the voices of their Inca sources. If we can learn something about the circumstances of composition of the narratives, we can at least construct a theory about the perspectives of those who composed them. Histories appear to be about the past, but they also reveal a great deal about the time of their composition: they encapsulate two different periods. We must take into consideration the perspective of those who composed the Inca sources.

One large assumption underlies this study, and that is that the Incas possessed some kind of historical consciousness. Of course, if they did not, then there is a *prima facie* case that Inca history is impossible. That the Incas had no historical consciousness is not something that has been explicitly argued by anyone, but underlying assumptions about this matter color the interpretations of all those who interpret the Spanish historical narratives. It is important to develop an analysis that attempts to discover the forms that Inca historical consciousness took because, through them, we may develop an understanding of its nature and purpose.

History has a purpose, even if that purpose is simple reflection. In the case of Inca history, we have kept the question of purpose very much open as we tried to identify and define particular genres. We began this study by exploring the cultural logic in which the practice of preserving a record of genealogy was embedded. Genealogy is a form of history, but it is a form which also characterizes the historical practices of the Spaniards who wrote the narratives on the Inca past, so an Inca cultural logic for this practice must be identified. The Inca account recorded who was descended from Manco Capac and his sister in the male line. A knowledge of genealogy was important to the dynasty because it was used in the calculation of a status which flowed through this patrilineage. A claim that its members were *capac* was asserted. Roughly coincident with the assertion of this claim, the genealogy of the dynastic descent group was painted on wooden tablets and housed where the rulers could control what was represented on them. It was an official history of dynastic descent.

Inca practice was intelligible to the Spaniards, but the logic guiding it escaped them. We do not fully understand the semantic domain of the term *capac*, but we do know that the Spaniards misunderstood what it meant; *capac* status was not the same as the divine status of European kings in the sixteenth century. The fact that Betanzos had to tell his audience that it did not mean what other authors thought indicates to us that we are dealing with something that was not like the divinity accorded to European kings. As Betanzos said, it meant "very much more than king." *Capac* status flowed through both males and females descended from the pair of dynastic progenitors. The strong preference for marrying the ruler to someone whose line of descent was traced to the patrilineage or even matched his own exactly was not a characteristic of European practice. Because each Inca generation defined a corporate group within the larger group identified as Inca, the matter of identifying the woman through whom descent passed was of extreme importance to the dynasty, and the genealogical account very carefully identifies who she was. Because marriage alliance was asymmetric (at least as far as we can detect from the earlier pattern of marriage in the Inca ruling line), the point came where marriage partners had to come from within the dynastic descent group and as close to the ruling line as possible so that no other group could assert claims over the Incas. Women were important in European houses and could similarly be used to construct external alliances. The new practice was less intelligible to the Spaniards than the alliance rule that appears to have characterized dynastic marriage in earlier generations.

A fundamental change occurred in dynastic practice as one group became increasingly powerful. Marriage preference changed, but with it came a new logic for reckoning status. That the descendants of Manco Capac were *capac* was not known all along to the Incas. Their special status was revealed to them.

One of the stories told by Sarmiento de Gamboa is about Inti, a stone bird that was the *huaoque* of Manco Capac. This *huaca*, perhaps like other sacred objects that passed and still pass down through the generations of particular families, appears to have been connected to Inca aggression. The story, then, tells us about when and how the aggressive behavior responsible for the imperial expansion developed. Their connection to a powerful object was there from the beginning, but the recognition of a tie to a solar supernatural had to be revealed to them. Beginning in the third generation, a supernatural appeared before an Inca and told him that, even though the Incas were not yet dominant, they would be. When the supernatural appeared again to the young Pachacuti, the ninth ruler, the revelation was fully understood. Inca power had grown because of the link to a very powerful supernatural. The relationship was framed in terms of descent, indicating that it had been there all along, that power was latent in the line that descended from Manco Capac and his sister.

If we are right about the number and nature of Inca genres, we have pieced this explanation together from three different underlying sources: the Inti story, the genealogical genre, and the life history of Pachacuti. The explanation, then, is ours. It accords with what we know of Inca meanings and values, but it is a hypothesis of our own. We are not reading the Spanish historical narratives for their resonance with European ideas about kingship and succession. Instead, we are attempting to read their underlying sources for the themes and messages they contain.

We do have to understand the Spaniards. How the Spaniards composed their narratives is of fundamental concern to us, and so is their understanding of history. Franklin Pease has assessed the latter, and his assessment provides a useful counterpoint for understanding how an Inca understanding of the past differed from that of their interpreters. Pease describes sixteenth-century Spanish historical practice. A linear concept of time was embedded in it: history began with creation and would end with the second coming of Christ. Biblical creation had given rise to a unique history consisting of singular events executed by concrete persons, whether as individuals or not. The events could be ordered and understood as a process. Over time the story came to be increasingly secular. Divinity was transferred to the persons of kings, and the story became a litany of the acts of these individuals. Royal genealogy explained the generation and maintenance of royal rights. Historical writing was also characterized by an assumption that ordered civil life derived from Greek urban organization and Roman law (Pease García Yrigoyen 1995:96).

Two aspects of Spanish belief affected the story they told about the Incas. One is the idea that mankind was created by a Creator God in a single, rela-

tively brief creation episode. A story about an Andean Creator God responsible for creating the physical world and mankind appears at the head of some
of the Spanish historical narratives, where the book of Genesis appears in the
Bible. Sarmiento had difficulty with the Inca account of creation because he
noted that their Creator had created everything anew after the destruction of
the world by the flood. In some ways, their deficient understanding of creation
is coherent with his argument that they misunderstood natural law and de-
served to be governed by Spain. Authors are also concerned with identifying
local knowledge about the biblical flood since that, too, was universal.

Other aspects of the Inca story clearly contradicted what the Spaniards
knew to be true, but the Inca story was told anyway. The Spaniards believed
that all mankind descended from Adam and Eve. Sarmiento and authors like
Joseph de Acosta had to explain how the descendants of Adam and Eve could
have arrived in the Americas; hence theories about Atlantis or a land passage
from Asia were quick to emerge. When Sarmiento explained that the Incas
crawled out of a cave only eleven generations before the Spaniards arrived, he
was not imposing his own ideas on the Inca past but telling a story that directly
contradicted them. Although eleven generations is fairly long in comparison
to the time depth of other oral accounts of the past (some groups go back to
the time of origins in as little as one generation before the present generation
of adults [Vansina 1985:24], it was extremely short by European standards.
Some later accounts of the Inca past attempt to extend the period covered by
Inca history to a span that coincides more nearly with the biblical time frame
(Guaman Poma de Ayala [1615] 1987; Montesinos [c. 1644] 1882). We can be
more certain that authors who tell the Pacaritambo story are transmitting an
Inca version of origins precisely because they knew that that story had to be
wrong.

What the Spaniards who wrote knew and believed affects their interpretation of Inca source material. Moreover, although we are familiar with biblical
creation and still accept a theory that posits the common origin of mankind,
the practice of history in the twentieth century has changed in fundamental
ways from the time when Cristóbal de Molina or Pedro Sarmiento de Gamboa wrote. For example, we have various descriptions of the being that appeared before Pachacuti at Susurpuquio. Molina describes this apparition as
being dressed like an Inca, with the headgear of an Inca, but with a puma on
its back whose arms extend over the shoulders of the being, with snakes
wrapped around the place near where its arms joined its body, and the head of
a puma extending from the region of its genitalia ([1576]; 1989:60). We can
read Molina without assuming that the being he described was the Devil —

an assumption that most sixteenth-century Spaniards would have made. Not just religious belief but what could be called science has also changed. When Sarmiento described Atlantis in the preface to his Inca history, he was speaking as Toledo's cosmographer, and he was discussing a theory that was then tenable as scientific explanation.

Reading the Spanish historical narratives is more than simply hearing whatever resonance exists between our understanding of history and the conceptual apparatus in the head of a Bartolomé de las Casas or a Pedro Sarmiento de Gamboa. It is also important to read with a knowledge of their purpose in writing and of their audience. For example, let us examine what Las Casas and Sarmiento wrote about the arrival of the Ayar siblings in Cuzco with their purposes in mind.

Las Casas and Sarmiento make a good example because their purposes are antithetical. In fact, Sarmiento wrote in part to counter the vision of the Incas constructed by Las Casas. Las Casas used sources that drew from the Inca past to argue that the Incas were the natural lords of the land. Sarmiento was out to prove that — to the contrary — they were not. Las Casas lists six Ayar siblings (table 3.1). After carefully noting that they did not have carnal relations with each other but, rather, behaved like brothers and sisters ought to, he traces their itinerary to Cuzco. His story is shorn of any details about their trip, except that at Huanacauri two of the brothers and sisters simply disappeared. He notes in passing at this point that the women may have been wives rather than sisters, perhaps because he has to explain the union of two of them to produce the next Inca generation. What is important to us is that, according to Las Casas, when Ayar Manco got to Cuzco, he was received with goodwill and given land to build houses and to cultivate. Because he seemed to be just and have a good sense of how to govern, they chose him as their king by unanimous consent ([1562–1564], chap. 250; 1967, vol. 2:573–574).

Sarmiento, on the other hand, uses nearly the same cast and virtually the same story line to construct his argument that they were tyrants. He lists eight Ayar siblings (table 3.1). Before telling the story of their emergence from the cave at Pacaritambo he describes the settlement of the Cuzco Valley at the time of their arrival, devoting a chapter to the "first inhabitants of the Valley of Cuzco." Some time before the Ayar siblings arrive, three foreign lords had arrived in the valley and were welcomed by the ancient inhabitants. Later, when the Ayar siblings arrive, Sarmiento is able to explain how the Incas gradually took the lands that belonged to these groups away from them by force ([1572], chaps. 9–14; 1906:30–43). That the Incas took possession of lands that belonged to others — and to the same others that Sarmiento identifies — is also narrated by Cabello Valboa and Morúa (M2), indicating that the same story was told in the underlying account of Cristóbal de Molina. However, Sarmiento is the only author who crafts a chapter about these people and the antiquity of their claims to the land. Sarmiento takes pains to represent the Inca advent in Cuzco as the tyrannical overthrow of groups who had stronger claims than they did to the land. Setting the stage with a chapter on who inhabited the Cuzco Valley before the Incas served Sarmiento's purpose. The Inca story — the genealogical genre painted on tablets — began in Pacaritambo.

Let us take a moment to examine Sarmiento's project in the light of what we have learned about Inca history. There is a fundamental contradiction in his project that we can detect four centuries later. Sarmiento, as noted above, had to develop a historical image of the pre-Inca occupation of the Cuzco Valley so that he could argue that the Incas had tyrannically usurped the lands of its peaceful inhabitants. In a preliminary chapter, he develops a much broader view of the pre-Inca past, encompassing the entire Andean territory. In order to argue that there were no natural lords in the Andes (in Cuzco or anywhere else), he characterizes the pre-Inca past as a time of *behetría*, a Spanish term that signifies a form of organization where no overlord is recognized. At the time Sarmiento wrote, to call something *behetría* was to acknowledge that it was an earlier and more primitive form of organization. In the Spanish past, *behetría* had coexisted with *señorío*, a form of local territorial organization headed by a noble. To further elaborate the Andean equivalent of *behetría*, he defined the *cinche* as a captain chosen when people needed a military leader. Like the preliminary account he gives of who inhabited the Cuzco Valley before the Ayar siblings came, the discussion of *behetría* and *cinches* is found nowhere else. Sarmiento certainly explained the pre-Inca past through reference to his own conceptual repertory.

What is not immediately apparent is that this vision of the pre-Inca past was a deliberate falsification. What gives the lie to Sarmiento's creation is the story of the Inca expansion contained in his own narrative. For it is in the account of Sarmiento that we find the identification of other lords in the Andes who were *capac*, that is, as we understand it, conduits for a status that made them powerful and that was transmitted through a dynastic line. Sarmiento tells us of how the Incas dealt with the Colla Capac and how a large territory fell when the Incas defeated this lord and took his sons prisoner ([1572], chap. 37; 1906:75–77). Sarmiento also tells us about the surprise military defeat of Cuzmango Capac and Chimo Capac, who together constituted a large confederation on the north coast and adjacent highlands. When Sarmiento described the defeat of the Colla Capac (also called Chuchi Capac), he equated the meaning of the terms *capac* and *cinche* (see chapter 6 for a direct citation). Supposing for a moment that Sarmiento was ignorant of what the term *capac* meant (that he had not read Betanzos), he still defined a large Andean territory, as large as some modern republics, under the authority of a single lord. Sarmiento the cosmographer was not ignorant of the physical expanse of this territory. He casts the Colla Capac as a *cinche*, even when his narrative suggests to us that this is absurd.

Sarmiento's contradiction opens a space through which we can see the Andes from an Inca perspective. There were other lords who were *capac* who were obstacles to the expansion of Inca power. The world of *cinches* and *behetrías* vanishes, and another political landscape emerges. How the Spaniards misunderstood and misrepresented the Inca past is there for us to find, but it is something that has to be studied, not assumed. Nor should we assume a priori that the Spaniards had a higher standard of truth than the Incas.

Some scholars who are interested in the Spanish historical narratives accuse their authors of misunderstanding what they heard and recasting it in conformance with their own understandings of the past. There is more at work in the rewriting of the Inca past than simple misunderstanding, however. The structure of an Inca story can be used to launch antithetical arguments about what happened. We should read past these manipulations, however, and try to recover the structure of an Inca story.

One question that has been raised here but that has not been given the attention it deserves is whether or not Inca genres served to explain the past. The version of the origin myth and the stories about earlier rulers preserved in the narrative of Sarmiento can be read as an explanation of the clear superiority of the descendants of one pair of Ayar siblings over any others and over everyone else they encountered. It suppresses other claims and conceals the subordination of Manco and other early Incas to other local groups. If we accept that stories about Inca origins or about the past deeds of important rulers constitute explanations of how things came to be or why some are powerful and others are not, then it is a short step to accepting that Inca genres reflect what the Incas thought actually happened, at least as a backdrop to the messages that were also incorporated. Ideas about the supernatural that reflect belief rather than explanation were also present.

The incorporation of belief into explanation and the relation between both and a relative standard of truth is no less a concern of Spanish or colonial Inca accounts of the Inca past. If you believe in the creation of the world by a universal Creator God and that that God laid the framework in the minds of all mankind to understand Christian truth and observe natural law, then local practice everywhere should reflect the existence of such a framework. Since mankind was only created once, and since it was destroyed once by a universal flood, then support for these historical facts should be encountered locally. When Las Casas and Sarmiento tell us about an Andean Creator God who made everything and about a universal flood, they agreed with each other; they agreed because they shared a common understanding of how things had "happened." How we interpret what was written about the Incas is not simply a matter of assessing whether a particular version of the past actually happened or not. That the eating of an apple caused the downfall of mankind is not inherently more true than the story about the Ayar siblings crawling out of a cave in Pacaritambo. It was and is enough for a story to represent what people can accept as true, whether its truth derives from belief or knowledge.

Finally, memory alone is not history. At its most basic, history is the creation of a formal process of recording and transmitting a story that reflects the past in a believable way. We need to identify a format for representing the past or preserving historical knowledge before we can talk of history. The Incas had developed their own forms of recording and transmitting representations of their past, forms that responded to a native historical consciousness. There is an Inca history.

# Notes

## 2. CAPAC

1. Anthropologists have used a great deal of ink to describe affiliation practice in light of general models. Recent criticism of the theoretical construct of "primitive society" (Kuper 1988) causes one to enter this field with some trepidation. One of the most serious criticisms is that the models are essentially static. Where temporality is incorporated, it is the conjectural history of evolution (Thomas 1989). I am using the analysis of a specific status over time to shed light on the logic of Inca practice. This analysis may be relevant to other groups, especially since the Incas recognize other peoples as claiming *capac* status, but, in accordance with recent critiques of classical anthropological studies of social organization (Schneider 1984 : 97–112; Trautmann 1987), I do not wish to create a generalizable model from Inca practices.

2. Rowe concluded in 1946 that "evidence for descent in the male line is overwhelming" (254), although in recent years parallel descent (reckoning through both the male and female lines) has gained acceptance (Zuidema 1967 : 240–255; Lounsbury 1986 : 131; Silverblatt 1987 : 4–5). Here my concern is with dynastic practice. That the Incas reckoned descent from apical ancestors through the male line is abundantly evident.

   The issue of whether patrilineal reckoning has survived is not a topic in this book, but it is one that comes readily to mind when Inca practice is examined. It should be addressed by those who work with the lapse of time between the sixteenth century and the present. The reckoning of some statuses through the father's line has been noted by ethnographers who work in the upper Amazon. For example, patrilineal reckoning is common in the Vaupés region of lowland Ecuador and Colombia (Arnhem 1981; Hornborg 1988).

   In Pacaritambo, in the highland Andes, a continuity in *ayllo* structure can be traced from the sixteenth to the twentieth century (Urton 1990 : 72, 76–77). The *ayllos* are "reproduced primarily in patrilineal fashion," children being considered members of the *ayllo* of their father (Urton 1990 : 76). The *ayllo* functions principally as a corporate landholding institution. Certain parcels of land are jointly owned by members, and though the property resembles private property in terms of transmission from one generation to the next, the land may not be sold or alienated. These same corporate groups redistribute high-altitude potato lands (Urton 1990 : 78). In Kaata, in the highland region on the border between Peru and Bolivia east of Lake Titicaca, claims to land are also reckoned through the patrilineage (Bastien 1978 : 159). On the island of Taquile in Lake Titicaca, descent is reckoned in the male line (Matos Mar 1956 : 215).

   In Q'ero, a highland community on the eastern flanks of the Andes near Cuzco, the term *ayllo* refers to the whole community. Within the larger community are groups that persist over several generations whose members trace descent in the male line from a sibling group, a seeming parallel to Inca practice. The definition of affines — *cacay* — is also similar to Inca practice. *Cacay* are both mother's brothers and wife's fathers, a situation common when women marry into one group from another. Webster notes the classification of people into groups of "wife-givers" and "wife-takers" (1977 : 33, 36–42). He does not clarify whether the definition of these groups reflects the perspective of the individual, in which case a kindred is what is reckoned, or whether there is a system of marriage alliances among discrete kin groups (but see p. 41). Several Spanish terms, including *yerno*, are used in Q'ero as substitutes for Quechua equivalents while preserving their

Quechua meanings. Webster also notes the widespread definition of affinal groups in the Andean highlands (1977:39). In Tangor kin is reckoned bilaterally, but there is a strong tendency toward patrilocality. People with the same last name concentrate in particular neighborhoods. Tangorinos associate certain qualities of character with these residential groups and say they are "family" as opposed to other such groups whom they term *hapa*, or "not family" (Mayer 1974:304–305).

3. The work of Gary Urton in Pacaritambo, the place associated with the emergence of Manco Capac and his siblings in the historical narratives, is a noteworthy exception. Urton appends a document to his study that makes an argument from genealogy, but it does not lead to an understanding of the contribution of women to the status defined by descent. There is a serious problem with the claims made in the document as well as with its date. It is a copy of an original purportedly composed in 1569, copied first in 1692 and again in 1718 (Urton 1990:129–140). The original, however, must postdate 1572 since it refers more than once to the "eight parishes of Cuzco," a fact which only became true in that year. The parish of San Jerónimo is specifically mentioned; that parish did not exist until 1572 (Urton 1990:133). Perhaps 1569 was a mistranscription of 1579, since "sesenta" was often mistaken for "setenta" when a document was copied. However, the 1569 date is mentioned five times in the document, so the error would have had to have been repeated each time the date was transcribed. The other problem is that the petitioner, Rodrigo Sutec Callapiña, argues only that he is descended from don Fernando Chuqui Sutic of the *ayllo* Anchacari of Pacaritambo, his paternal grandfather, and don Martín Yupanqui of the *ayllo* Carhuacalla of Pacaritambo, his maternal grandfather. His claim that he is "directly descended" from Manco Capac through the male line requires him to name a *panaca*, but his naming of the *ayllo* of Anchacari precludes that possibility.

Sutec Callapiña's argument is vague at best, but the document may still be a copy of an original — even if it has been doctored — made sometime after 1576, when Gabriel Paniagua de Loaysa was appointed *corregidor*. He began to exact *tambo* and other services from Inca nobles who had been previously exempt, stimulating a series of complaints from those who claimed descent from Manco Capac (Archivo General de Indias, Lima 472). Pacaritambo or groups within it may well have been accorded a special status by the Incas that had continued during the early colonial period. If so, it was granted on some other basis than that the claimants were descendants of Manco Capac, if we are right in our assessment of Callapiña's claims.

What is intriguing about the document is the information provided about Sutec Callapiña's maternal line. He traces the descent of his mother through her father to her grandfather Quilaco Yupanqui of the *ayllo* Carhuacalla. The name of Quilaco Yupanqui's spouse, Callapiña's great-grandmother, is Coya Cori Coca. If the word *coya* is a title, this woman may have been someone who traced her descent from Manco Capac on both father's and mother's side (see the section on Inca women, this chapter). In the Betanzos narrative, Pachacuti is said to have given his daughters to the lords of the Cuzco region for wives ([1551–1557], pt. 1, chap. 12; 1987:57). Cori Coca died during the rule of Huayna Capac, so it is possible that she was one of these daughters. Guaman Poma was very aware of the importance of his own paternal grandmother, Juana Curi Ocllo *coya*, a daughter of Topa Inca ([1615; 1987:[832–833]), so the lack of any argument about the status of Cori Coca is noteworthy.

4. Sarmiento de Gamboa ([1572], chap. 37; 1906:75–76; chap. 38; 1906:79; chap. 40; 1906:82; chap. 44; 1906:87; chap. 46; 1906:91 and Julien (1998a:26–33). Pachacuti Yamqui Salcamaygua also uses the term principally as a title. In his story about the Inca

foundation of Cuzco on its present site, he notes that the place came to be called "Cuzco pampa and Cuzco llacta, and the Incas afterward titled themselves Cuzco capac or Cuzco ynca" (1993: fol. 8). The term is also used repeatedly in connection with Inca insignia. Like Sarmiento, Pachacuti Yamqui Salcamaygua also names Andean lords by their titles, such as Tocay Capac, Chuchi Capac, and so on.

5. Here and elsewhere I am referring to the progenitors of the dynastic line as "Manco Capac and his sister-wife." She is named as Mama Ocllo in some accounts (Sarmiento) and as Mama Huaco in others (see chapter 3). The discrepancies suggest not a disagreement over who she "was" but change in the origin story (see chapter 8).

6. What Betanzos wrote cannot be reconciled with what we know about Vica Quirao, whose name was used to refer to the *panaca* of Inca Roca, the sixth Inca. Inca Roca was the first Inca to build his own houses; they were in Hanan Cuzco. In the context of this statement, we can understand Betanzos to mean that purity became a concern and, in effect, that those born before this time were Hurin in the sense of tracing their ancestry back to an Inca pair where only the man was a descendant of Manco Capac.

7. Again, Betanzos is using a term counter to its meaning in other sources. Capac Ayllo was the *panaca* of Topa Inca, not Pachacuti. However, in that Topa Inca and Mama Ocllo were Pachacuti's children and the concentration of *capac* status began with them, all of the descendants of this pair were descended in a direct line from Pachacuti. In a very real way the members of Capac Ayllo were his descendants, too.

8. The underlined portion was not transcribed in the 1987 edition of Betanzos but is present in the original manuscript.

9. Another term supplied by Betanzos that begs for attention is *pacsa*. *Coya pacsa* was glossed by Cristobal de Molina as the woman of the Sun, and she was the sister or daughter of the ruler ([1576]; 1989: 77). Could this person also be the principal wife of the ruler at the same time? A *memorial* dated to 1551 describes the "principal woman" as *paxia*, perhaps the same term (Rowe 1966: 38). Betanzos translated the word *pacsa* as "moon." Cristóbal de Molina also mentioned a statue of the moon called Pacsa Mama ([1576]; 1989: 100), so that the name referred to more than one personage, in any event. The word for moon in Aymara is *pacsi* (*Doctrina christiana* 1585: chap. 7, fol. 9v).

10. Rostworowski de Diez Canseco (1993: 135): "muger legitima en su ley que fue de Ynga Yupangui señor que fue deste reyno."

11. The three brothers are Amaro Topa, Topa Yupanqui, and Topa Inca Yupanqui (Rowe 1985b: 223). Two authors mention specifically that they are the sons of both Pachacuti and Anahuarqui (Murúa [1611–1615], bk. 1, chap. 21; 1987: 80; Sarmiento de Gamboa [1572], chap. 37; 1906: 77; chap. 40; 1906: 83; chap. 42; 1906: 84; chap. 47; 1906: 93).

12. Susan Niles argues convincingly that Betanzos (or Angelina) slips Yamqui Yupanqui into the place occupied by Amaro Topa Inca. Retelling the story was possible in part because Capac Ayllo had been decimated by Atahuallpa's generals and was easy prey; not only its land but its history could be stolen (Niles 1999: 19).

13. Tito Cusi, in his narration of events that took place during the life of his father, relates an incident in which Gonzalo Pizarro demanded that Manco give him the *coya*. Manco substituted a very principal woman, named Ynguill, the companion of "his sister, the *coya*, who resembled her in almost every way" and whom he dressed like the *coya* (Tito Cussi Yupanqui 1988: 179–184). This may have been Francisca Ynguill, who became the wife of Juan Pizarro, or another woman. In any event, the story illustrates the importance of these women to the Incas and the knowledge on the part of the Pizarros of what it meant to espouse a woman with this status.

14. Equeco, a town near Anta, was divided into Hanan and Hurin Cuzco, so it is not inconceivable that Anta also had these divisions (Rowe 1995:124).
15. Cf. Temple (1948a:117–118, 123) for other references to this event. She follows Ocampo on the date of the baptism and is mistaken.

## 3. GENEALOGY

1. Gasca mentions a Cayo Topa who was a grandson of Huayna Capac in a letter (27 June 1547; CDIHE 1842–1895, vol. 49: 309). A Cayo Topa described himself as a "son of Tupa Inca Yupanqui and a nephew of Huayna Capac" in a donation of land to the Mercedarian order (8 October 1549; Barriga 1938–1954, vol. 2: 161–166). He may have been the son of Auqui Topa Inca, a brother of Huayna Capac (Rowe 1993–1994:103).
2. Cobo also dealt with Inca religion (book 13), incorporating material similar to what Acosta included in his publication of Polo (1585). Perhaps this was what he got from Polo and not the Inca history. However, what he says in his introductory chapter seems to indicate otherwise. He frames the presentation of Polo's work in a discussion of Inca history. First he notes that the common people knew very little about the past:

> They do not know how to answer or even if there had been Inca kings in this land, and asking the same [questions] to any of those who, of the lineage of the Incas, live in Cuzco, they immediately give a very punctual account of everything, of the number of kings there were, of their descendants and conquests, and of the families and lineages who remain. So it is that only the accounts on this subject that have been gathered in the city of Cuzco should be heeded, from which I will not depart in all of this writing, and especially from the account that, ordered by the viceroy don Andrés Hurtado de Mendoza, the marquis of Cañete, and by the first archbishop of Lima, don Jerónimo de Loaysa, was done by the *licenciado* Polo Ondegardo in 1559 when he was *corregidor* of that city, gathering together for the purpose [of writing it] all of the old Indians who had been alive at the time of their gentility, including principal Incas and their priests and *quipocamayos* or historians of the Incas. They could not have been ignorant of Inca government, rites, and customs, since they were alive during the time of the Inca kings and were actively involved in all the things they were examined about, and because [they had] the testimony of their *quipos* and paintings which were still in existence [then].

> No saben responder ni aun si hubo reyes Incas en esta tierra; y preguntando lo mismo a cualquiera de los que del linaje de los Incas moran en el Cuzco, al punto da muy cumplida razón de todo, del número de reyes que hubo, de su descendencia y conquistas, y de las familias y linajes que déllos han quedado; y así no hay que hacer caso más que de las informaciones que desta materia se han hecho en la dicha ciudad del Cuzco; de las cuales no me apartaré yo en toda esta escritura, en especial de la que por mandado del virrey don Andrés Hurtado de Mendoza, marqués de Cañete, y del primer arzobispo de Lima, don fray Jerónimo de Loaysa, hizo el licenciado Polo Ondegardo el año de 1559, siendo corregidor de aquella ciudad, haciendo junta para ella de todos los indios viejos que habían quedado del tiempo de su gentilidad, así de los Incas principales como de los sacerdotes y quipocamayos o historiadores de los Incas. Los cuales no podían ignorar lo tocante al gobierno,

ritos y costumbres de los suyos, por haber alcanzado el tiempo de los reyes Incas y ejercitado en él todo aquello sobre que fueron examinados, y por los memoriales de sus quipos y pinturas que aún estaban en pie. (Cobo [1653], bk. 12, chap. 2; 1956, vol. 2:59)

The question of whether Polo incorporated a genealogical account of the dynastic line similar to what is found in other Spanish historical accounts should be posed here. After Cobo mentions the Polo manuscript, he mentions two others, one by Sarmiento (though he does not mention Sarmiento by name) and the other by Molina. In chapter 4 we compare the event structures of Sarmiento, Cobo, Cabello Valboa, and one of the Murúa manuscripts (see table 4.3). The latter two are structurally very similar and appear to have followed the event structure of the lost Molina manuscript (see chapter 5). Cobo's narrative does not reflect the structure of any of the other narratives of Inca history he mentions. He could have begun anew, as he notes that the Incas of Cuzco still gave an account of their dynastic line similar to what his authors had recorded:

> It would be very simple for me to follow in the footsteps of serious authors, worthy of our faith, without trying to conduct a new investigation into this subject; however, on account of having resided some time in the city of Cuzco, and at a time so close to the time of the Inca kings that I met more than a few Indians who had been alive during the time of their government, and many of them descendants [of these kings] in whom I found a fresh memory of those times. Taking advantage of the opportunity, I informed myself from these sources as much as I wanted to know about this particular, and I found nothing that contradicted what Polo had found out. I principally knew and communicated with an important Indian of Inca blood who, because of a certain matter he had with the viceroy, had made a report of his descent which I read; and I found the same line and number of Inca kings that the *licenciado* Polo had put in his report.

> Bien pudiera irme yo por los pasos de autores tan graves y dignos de toda fe, sin tratar de hacer nueva pesquisa sobre esta materia; mas, por haber residido en la ciudad del Cuzco algún tiempo, y éste tan cercano a el de los reyes Incas, que alcancé no pocos indios que gozaron de su gobierno, y muchos déllos descendientes suyos, en quienes hallé muy fresca la memoria de sus cosas; aprovechándome de la ocasión, me informé déllos cuanto deseé saber en este particular, y no hallé cosa en contra de lo averiguado por el licenciado Polo. Porque, primeramente, conocí y comuniqué mucho a un indio principal de la sangre real de los Incas, que para cierta pretensión que con el virrey tenía, hizo información de su asendencia, la cual me leyó él mismo y hallé la misma linea y número de Incas reyes que pone en su relación el licenciado Polo. (Cobo [1653], bk. 12, chap. 2; 1956, vol. 2:60–61)

Cobo confirmed the details of a dynastic genealogy incorporated in the Polo manuscript, a genealogy which Cobo has already noted was similar to what could be found in Sarmiento and Molina. Cobo said he could collect a genealogical account from living Incas. Did he collect the structure of his Inca history, a narrative account of the Inca past that includes quite a bit more than just the dynastic genealogy? Or did Polo supply the story line? Even if he used Polo for the story line, he appears to have taken some material from other authors, for example, the information about Mayta Capac's wife which is also found in Oré, a source Cobo had. Cobo's dependence on various manuscripts inhibits our reading of his Inca history as a direct transmission from a lost manuscript of Polo, but because of what we know about his dependence on manuscript sources, the likelihood that he used one of his manuscripts to structure his account of the Inca past is correspondingly greater.

3. Sarmiento had been commissioned to collect information for a geographical description of the Andean region. The manuscript was in preparation (Sarmiento de Gamboa [1572]; 1906:xxxiii) and may have been completed. Its whereabouts are unknown.

4. Toledo mentioned that the cloths were painted by "Indian painters" in a letter to the king in June 1572. He noted as well that they "did not have the curiosity" of those in Spain and also that, to hire them, it was only necessary to provide them with food and a mantle (Iwasaki Cauti 1986:67).

5. There were two Molina manuscripts, one, as Cobo says, done soon after Sarmiento collected his Inca history and the other a manuscript on the "fables and rites" of the Incas. Cobo does not distinguish between them, but Molina does. He notes in the first paragraph of his work on "fables and rites" that he had already given a manuscript to Lartaún:

> Because the account that I gave to your Illustrious Lordship of the dealings, the origin, life, and customs of the Incas, former lords of this land, and how many there were and who were their women and of the laws they gave and the wars they had and of the peoples and nations they conquered, and in some parts of the account I deal with the ceremonies and cults they invented, although not in any detail, it seemed appropriate to me now, especially since your Reverend Lordship has ordered me to do it, to take on a bit more work so that your Reverend Lordship could have some idea of the ceremonies, cults, and idolatries that these Indians had. For that purpose I gathered together a number of the ancient people who saw and carried out the said ceremonies and cults in the time of Huayna Capac, and of Huascar Inca and Manco Inca, and some of those who had been teachers and religious practitioners in those times.

> Porque la relación que a vuestra Señoría Ilustríssima di de el trato, del origen, vida y costumbres de los Ingas, señores que fueron de esta tierra y quántos fueron y quién fueron sus mugeres y las leyes que dieron y guerras que tuvieron y gentes y naciones que conquistaron y en algunos lugares de la relación trato de las ceremonias y cultos que ynventaron aunque no muy especificadamente, parecióme ahora principalmente, por mandármelo vuestra Señoría Reverendísima, tomar algún tanto de travajo para que vuestra Señoría Reverendísima vea las ceremonias cultos y ydolatrías que estos yndios tuvieron. Para lo qual, hize juntar cantidad de algunos viejos antiguos que vieron y hizieron en tiempo de Huaynacapac y de Huascarynca y Mancoynca hazer las dichas ceremonias y cultos, y algunos maestros y sacerdotes de los que en aquel tiempo eran. (Molina [1576]; 1989:49)

The other manuscript already existed; if we can at least trust the sequencing in Cobo's chapter on sources, Molina's other account was written sometime between 1572 and 1576.

6. One of the Morúa texts has been published under the name Murúa ([1611–1615] 1987). I have kept that spelling in the bibliographic entry but have consistently used Morúa to refer to this author in my text.

7. Las Casas used Bartolomé de Segovia, whom he called "el buen seglar," a work by Cristóbal de Castro, published works by Xérez and Cieza de León, and other sources written by Dominicans, whom he refers to as "nuestros religiosos" (John Rowe, personal communication).

8. The account of Montesinos, with its long king list, has not been included. It obviously cannot be reconciled with the list of twelve generations that was so frequently collected in the early decades of the Spanish occupation of Cuzco, and it is much later. Because an Inca version of their own past was so short, some authors tried to extend it. Montesinos tried to extend it through multiplying the Inca dynastic list (Pease García Yrigoyen 1995:48). Guaman Poma stretched the dynastic list to span the entire Christian era: Sinchi Roca, the second Inca, ruled at the time of the birth of Christ (Guaman Poma [1615]; 1987:91).

9. Philip Ainsworth Means was the first to call attention to the story about how the Ayar siblings tricked the people into accepting them as "sons of the Sun" by wearing garments that reflected the sun's rays (1928). The story appears in Cabello Valboa ([1586] 1951), Oré ([1598] 1992), the *Discurso* ([1602–1608] 1920), Ramos Gavilán ([1621] 1988), Anello Oliva ([c. 1630] 1895), and Montesinos ([1642] 1906). The idea that the Incas tricked people into accepting them was probably not part of an Inca account; it appears only in late-sixteenth-century/early-seventeenth-century accounts.

10. Román y Zamora follows Las Casas in his presentation of the *panacas* ([1575], chap. 11; 1897:25–26), as we would expect (Pease García Yrigoyen 1995:312).

11. Right before Fernández presents his *panaca* list in a summary treatment of Capac Raymi, when male initiation rites were held, he notes that "only the Incas" were involved and describes them as belonging to four groups: "Anan Cuzco, Hullin Cuzco, Tambo, and Maxca" ([1571], vol. 165, bk. 3, chap. 6; 1963:84). Despite the spellings, he is naming Hanan Cuzco and Hurin Cuzco along with two groups from the region south of Cuzco. Morúa includes this material right after his *panaca* list; he gives the names of four groups of people who were the "true" Incas: "Hanan Cuzco, Urin Cuzco, Tambo, and Marca [Masca]" ([1605], bk. 1, chap. 15; 1946:80). Morúa's spellings of certain names on the *panaca* list ("Piauragua," "Vaca Capac," "Aoca," and "Hatren") also indicate a textual dependency.

12. Neither Las Casas nor Gutiérrez were ever in Peru. A written text probably underlies both accounts, one that they consulted outside of the Andes.

13. Rowe has an explanation for the incorporation of the name don Juan Tambo Mayta Panaca in a Polo account: while Polo was *corregidor* of Cuzco, he heard a lawsuit to which this person was a party (1993–1994:104). This person, then, was alive at the time Polo was collecting historical material about the Incas. He was also mentioned by Sarmiento as a living member of the descent group of Mayta Capac. Sarmiento also notes that Tarco Huaman was a son of Mayta Capac ([1572], chap. 17; 1906:47–48). Is it possible that Acosta used a Polo source or sources that included a *panaca* list and/or an account of the genealogy of don Juan Tambo Maytapanaca? Rather than arguing that Polo got it wrong, it seems more likely that Acosta misunderstood Polo.

What Acosta and Cobo wrote was different enough to support a conclusion that the two used different Polo texts. Acosta met Polo in 1575, the year of Polo's death, and may have gotten several manuscripts from him at this time. According to Cobo, Polo had sent his Inca history to Archbishop Loaysa in 1559. When Acosta returned to Lima after meeting Polo, Loaysa was dead. Perhaps Acosta did not have access to the manuscript Loaysa had, a manuscript that Cobo later used.

## 4. LIFE HISTORY

1. The remains of the Inca rulers were in Lima when Toledo arrived (Hampe Martínez 1982), so if there was still a connection between *quipos* and the Inca mummies, this material was examined in Lima. Sarmiento does not explicitly note where he conducted his interviews, although it seems most likely that he worked on his history in Cuzco in 1571 ([1572], chap. 9; 1906: 31–32).

2. He is less clear about the division of the *suyos* within the Hanan/Hurin division, since his interpretation is given in terms of the "North Sea" and "South Sea" — the Atlantic and the Pacific. One clue is that he describes Andesuyo as "above, toward the mountains." Perhaps Condesuyo was "below, toward the ocean."

3. False Estete (1924: 55). This account has been attributed to Miguel de Estete (Pease García Yrigoyen 1995: 18–20). The attribution has caused confusion because there was more than one Miguel de Estete.

4. Susan Niles has described some of these performances in more detail than is offered here (1999: 9–11, 28–51). Our concern is with how Inca history was imprisoned in the book. Niles looks much more broadly at the reenactment of the Inca past and its physical memorialization; she does so as a backdrop to her study of Huayna Capac's building program in the Cuzco region.

## 5. COMPOSITION

1. Remains of the arch were located by John Rowe on the street that leads from Limacpampa to the Avenida de la Cultura (personal communication).

2. Cabello Valboa's numbers were used by John Rowe in 1945 to suggest a plausible chronology for the length of rule of the last three Incas and hence the duration of the period of empire. Many students of the Incas have used those dates uncritically. The dates themselves are not important. What is important is whether or not the Spanish historical narratives record a series of actual rulers or not. If the rulers ruled and succeeded each other in the order given, then any dates that reflect a time span that is not out of line for real people who lived for some period of time after they reached adulthood would be plausible. This matter is one of the more difficult issues among specialists of the Incas, some of whom want to overturn the historical sequence implicit in the Spanish historical narratives without adequately testing it against the material record.

## 6. EMERGENCE

1. Sarmiento wrote various relations, memorials, and letters. His own style is full of references to other scholarly works, particularly those of classical writers (Sarmiento de Gamboa 1988: 23–26).

2. Morúa has Tambo and Marca ([1605], bk. 1, chap. 15; 1946: 79–80; cf. Fernández [1571], vol. 166, bk. 3, chap. 7; 1963: 84).

3. Pietschmann cites Paz Soldán (1877: 960). Bauer (1999: 55) refers to an Omaspampa, citing Cornejo Bouroncle (1957). Niles also finds the identification of Oma with Omaspampa to be reasonable (personal communication).

4. Tancaray may be the Tawqaray above the modern Cuzco airport (Susan Niles, personal communication).

5. The name of the spouse of Mayta Capac and her Collaguas origin may have been taken from Luis Jerónimo de Oré (Rowe in Hamilton 1979:ix–xi; [1598], chap. 9; 1992: fol. 41).

6. Sarmiento refers to him most frequently as Chuchi Capac ([1572], chap. 37; 1906:75–77). In Cieza he is called Zapana ([1553], chap. 37, p. 110; chap. 41; 1986:121).

7. Where another source of information about campaigns was available, for example, the *quipo* recording the conquests of Topa Inca, perhaps the sequencing problems could be remedied.

8. Cieza says he gave her "una palla del Cuzco" ([1553], chap. 47; 1986:137). Garcilaso provides a context for the term *palla*. The *coyas* were daughters of the ruler "por participación de la madre," that is, they were descended from the ruler and a woman of his bloodline. He then describes *pallas* as the "concubines of the ruler who were of his descent group [*parentela*]" or "women of royal blood" ([1609], bk. 1, chap. 26; 1990:45). The definition fits women who are descended from the line of Manco Capac on the father's side alone or women who were Inca on both sides but not first-generation descendants of a ruling pair.

## 7. TRANSFORMATION

1. The spouse of Pachacuti was given two small towns near Cuzco, women, and *yanaconas* (Betanzos [1551–1557], pt. 1, chap. 17; 1987:85). Pachacuti's *huaoque* also had houses, land, women, and *yanaconas* (Sarmiento de Gamboa [1572], chap. 47; 1906:94). On holdings of particular Inca women, see Niles (1999:150–152).

2. Garcilaso called them "estos incas, hechos por privelegio" [1609], bk. 1, chap. 23; 1990:41), and others have adopted this designation, calling this group "Incas by privilege" (Rowe 1946:189, 261; Zuidema 1995:222, 252–253; Urton 1990:28; Pease García Yrigoyen 1992:72).

## 8. ORIGINS

1. There is a problem with the 1569 date of the document (see note 3, chapter 2).

2. The transcription has been made from the original manuscript. In addition to other small changes, a fairly lengthy passage was left out of the 1987 edition of Betanzos. The italics indicate the skipped passage.

3. The accounts we have say very little about female initiation, although both Sarmiento and Cabello Valboa mention that it was invented by Manco Capac. If it coincided with the first menstruation, as others note, it may have been impossible to coordinate it with the ritual calendar. At Capac Raymi, women of the same age as the male initiates were involved in the events, particularly in a pilgrimage to the mountain of Anahuarqui. They were given clothing similar in patterning and origin to the clothing provided to the male initiates. The clothing worn by the girls was appropriate to adult women. These girls could have been newly initiated. In the description of Capac Raymi Molina says nothing about female initiation, though the manner in which young women were incorporated into the event suggests a connection.

4. Elsewhere the reference to Viracocha Pachayachachic as a supreme Creator deity has been credited (Rowe 1960; Pease 1973). The question will be difficult to resolve, and the exploration of the issues involved in this matter here does not pretend to address the matter fully.

5. Aspects of the story told about Viracocha are similar to stories told about Tunupa and may have been the basis for the Viracocha creation story (Gisbert 1994 : 35–39; Pachacuti Yamqui Salcamaygua [early seventeenth century]; 1993: fols. 3v– 6v, 9v, 15r–16r).

# Bibliography

## UNPUBLISHED DOCUMENTARY SOURCES

Archivo General de Indias, Seville, Spain
Lima 29, No. 6.
   Testimonio en lo de don Carlos, don Felipe y demas yngas del Cuzco. Cuzco, 1573.
Lima 110
   Carta del doctor Loarte, el lic. Polo y el cabildo del Cuzco al virrey Toledo. Cuzco,
   [1572].
Lima 270
   Carta de Juan de Vera al Consejo de Indias. Cuzco, 9 abril 1572. Fols. 532–533.
Lima 472
   Prouision de los yngas de la çibdad del Cuzco. Cuzco, 7 noviembre 1579. 16 fols.
Patronato 90B, no. 1, ramo 11
   Probanzas hechas por don Diego de Almagro contra Hernando Pizarro. 1541.
Patronato 90B, no. 1, ramo 55
   Probanza de doña Françisca Pizarro y filiaçion de ser hija del cappitan Joan Piçarro
   hermano de el marques don Francisco Piçarro. 1596.


## WORKS CITED

Abercrombie, Thomas A.
1998   *Pathways of memory and power: Ethnography and history among an Andean people*.
     Madison: University of Wisconsin Press.
Acosta, Joseph de
1940   *Historia natural y moral de las Indias* [1590]. Ed. Edmundo O'Gorman. Mexico
     City: Fondo de Cultura Económica.
Albornoz, Cristóbal de
1989   Instrucción para descubrir todas las guacas del Piru y sus camayos y haziendas
     [1581–1585]. C. de Molina, C. de Albornoz; *Fábulas y mitos de los incas*, Ed.
     Henrique Urbano and Pierre Duviols, pp. 163–198. Madrid: Historia 16.
Allen, Catherine J.
1988   *The hold life has: Coca and cultural identity in an Andean community*. Washington,
     D.C.: Smithsonian Institution Press.
Anello Oliva, Giovanni
1895   *Historia del reino y provincias del Perú, de sus Incas reyes, descubrimiento y conquista por
     los Españoles de la corona de Castilla* [1630]. Ed. Juan Pazos Varela and Luis Varela y
     Orbegoso. Lima: Imprenta y Librería de San Pablo.
Aranibar Zerpa, Carlos
1963   Algunos problemas heurísticos en las crónicas de los siglos XVI–XVII. *Nueva
     Corónica*, vol. 1:102–135. Lima.
Arnhem, Kaj
1981   *Makuna social organization: A study in descent, alliance and the formation of corporate
     groups in the north-western Amazon*. Uppsala Studies in Cultural Anthropology 4.
     Stockholm: Almqvist & Wiksell.

Arriaga, Pablo José de
1968    Extirpación de la idolatría del Perú [1621]. *Crónicas Peruanas de Interés Indígena*,
        Ed. Francisco Esteve Barba. Biblioteca de Autores Españoles (continuación),
        209:193–277. Madrid: Ediciones Atlas.

Ascher, Marcia, and Robert Ascher
1981    *The code of the quipo: A study in media, mathematics, and culture.* Ann Arbor:
        University of Michigan Press.

Barriga, Victor M.
1938–1954   *Los mercedarios en el Perú en el siglo XVI.* Arequipa: Editorial La Colmena. 5 vols.

Bastien, Joseph
1978    Marriage and exchange in the Bolivian Andes. *Actes du XLIIe Congrés International
        des Américanistes* 4:149–164. Paris.

Bauer, Brian S.
1999    *The sacred landscape of the Inca: The Cusco ceque system.* Austin: University of Texas
        Press.
1992    *The development of the Inca state.* Austin: University of Texas Press.

Betanzos, Juan de
1996    *Narrative of the Incas* [1551–1557]. Trans. Roland Hamilton and Dana Buchanan.
        Austin: University of Texas Press.
1987    *Suma y narración de los Incas* [1551–1557]. Ed. María del Carmen Martín Rubio.
        Madrid: Ediciones Atlas.
1880    *Suma y narración de los Incas* [1551–1557]. Ed. Marcos Jiménez de la Espada.
        Biblioteca Hispano-Ultramarina 5. Madrid: Imprenta de Manuel Ginés
        Hernández.
n.d.    Suma y narracion de los yngas que los yndios nombraron capac cuna que fueron
        señores en la çiudad del Cuzco y de todo lo a ella subjeta . . . [1551–1557].
        Fundación Bartolomé March, Palma de Mallorca.

Boone, Elizabeth Hill, and Walter Mignolo
1994    *Writing without words: Alternative literacies in Mesoamerica and the Andes.* Durham:
        Duke University Press.

Brading, David A.
1991    *The first America. The Spanish monarchy, Creole patriots and the liberal state,
        1492–1867.* Cambridge: Cambridge University Press.

Cabello Valboa, Miguel
1951    *Miscelánea antártica: una historia del Perú antiguo* [1586]. Lima: Universidad
        Nacional Mayor de San Marcos, Facultad de Letras, Instituto de Etnología.

Calancha, Antonio de la
1974–1982   *Corónica moralizada del Orden de Nuestro Padre Sant Augustín.* Ed. Ignacio
        Prado Pastor. Lima: Ignacio Prado Pastor. 6 vols.

Caso, Alfonso
1949    El mapa de Teozacoalco. *Cuadernos Americanos*, year 8, no. 5. Mexico City.

Cieza de León, Pedro de
1994    *Crónica del Perú. Cuarta parte* [before 1554]. Ed. Pedro Guibovich Pérez, Gabriela
        Benavides de Rivero, and Laura Gutiérrez Arbulú. Lima: Academia Nacional de la
        Historia, Pontificia Universidad Católica, Fondo Editorial. 4 vols.
1987    *Crónica del Perú. Tercera parte* [before 1554]. Ed. Francesca Cantù. Lima: Academia
        Nacional de la Historia, Pontificia Universidad Católica, Fondo Editorial.
1986    *Crónica del Perú. Segunda parte.* [1553]. Ed. Francesca Cantù. Lima: Academia
        Nacional de la Historia, Pontificia Universidad Católica, Fondo Editorial.

1984    *Crónica del Perú. Primera parte.* [1551]. Ed. Franklin Pease García Yrigoyen. Lima: Academia Nacional de la Historia, Pontificia Universidad Católica, Fondo Editorial.

Cobo, Bernabé

1983    *History of the Inca empire.* Trans. and ed. Roland Hamilton. Austin: University of Texas Press.

1890–1895    *Historia del nuevo mundo* [1653]. Ed. Marcos Jiménez de la Espada. Seville: Sociedad de Bibliófilos Andaluces. 4 vols.

CDIHE

1842–1895    *Colección de documentos inéditos para la historia de España.* Madrid: Imprenta de la Viuda de Calero. 112 vols.

Cornejo Bouroncle, Jorge

1957    Tierras de la fortaleza. *Revista del Archivo Histórico del Cuzco* 8:199–202. Cuzco.

*Discurso*

1920    *Discurso sobre la descendencia y gobierno de los Incas; informaciones sobre el antiguo Perú* [1602–1608]. Ed. Horacio H. Urteaga. *Colección de Libros y Documentos referentes a la Historia del Perú* 3 (series 2):3–53. Lima: Imprenta y Librería Sanmartí y Cía.

*Doctrina christiana*

1585    *Tercero catecismo y exposición de la doctrina christiana, por sermones.* Lima: Antonio Ricardo.

Domínguez Faura, Nicanor

1994    Juan de Betanzos y las primeras cartillas de evangelización en la Lengua General del Inga [1536–1542]. *La venida del reino: religión evangelización y cultura en América, siglos XVI–XX.* Ed. Gabriela Ramos, pp. 65–74. *Cuadernos para la Historia de la Evangelización en América Latina* 12. Cuzco: Centro de Estudios Regionales Andinos "Bartolomé de Las Casas."

Duviols, Pierre

1997    Respuesta de Pierre Duviols a Tom Zuidema. *Saberes y memorias en los Andes: In memoriam Thierry Saignes.* Ed. Thérèse Bouysse-Cassagne, pp. 125–148. Institut des Hautes Etudes de l'Amérique Latine, Paris. Lima: Institut Françaies d'Etudes Andines.

1980    Algunas reflexiones acerca de las tesis de la extructura dual del poder Incaico. *Histórica* 4, no. 2, December:183–196. Lima: Pontificia Universidad Católica, Fondo Editorial.

1979    La dinastía de los Incas: ¿Monarquía o diarquía? Argumentos heurísticos a favor de una tesis estructuralista. *Journal de la Société des Américanistes* 66:67–83. Paris.

False Estete

1924    *Noticia del Perú. Colección de libros y documentos referentes a la historia del Perú,* vol. 8 (series 2). Ed. Horacio H. Urteaga. Lima: Imprenta y Librería Sanmartí y Cía.

Fane, Diana

1996    *Converging cultures: Art and identity in Spanish America.* New York: The Brooklyn Museum, Harry N. Abrams.

Fernández, Diego

1963    Historia del Perú [1571]. *Crónicas del Perú,* vols. 1–2. Ed. Juan Pérez de Tudela Bueso. Biblioteca de Autores Españoles (continuación), vols. 165–166. Madrid: Ediciones Atlas.

Garcilaso de la Vega, el Inca

1990    *Comentarios reales* [1609]. Mexico: Editorial Porrúa, S.A.

Gasparini, Graziano, and Luise Margolies

1980    *Inca Architecture*. Trans. Patricia J. Lyon. Bloomington: Indiana University Press.

Gillespie, Susan D.

1986    *The Aztec kings: The construction of rulership in Mexican history*. Tucson: University of Arizona Press.

Gisbert, Teresa

1994    *Iconografía y mitos indígenas en el arte*. La Paz: Editorial Gisbert y Cía.

González Corrales, José

1984    Arquitectura y cerámica Killke del Cusco. *Revista del Museo e Instituto de Arqueología*, no. 23:37–45. Cuzco: Universidad Nacional de San Antonio Abad.

González Holguín, Diego

1952    *Vocabulario de la lengua general de todo el Peru llamada lengua qquichua o del inca* [1608]. Ed. Raúl Porras Barrenechea. Lima: Universidad Nacional Mayor de San Marcos, Imprenta Santa María.

1842    *Gramática y arte nueva de la lengua general de todo el Perú llamada lengua Qquichua o lengua del Inca* [1608]. [Genoa: Pagano.]

Guaman Poma de Ayala, Felipe

1987    *Nueva crónica y buen gobierno* [1615]. Ed. John V. Murra, Rolena Adorno, and Jorge L. Urioste. Crónicas de América 29. Madrid: Historia 16. 3 vols.

Guillén Guillén, Edmundo

1994    *La guerra de reconquista inka. Historia épica de como los incas lucharon en defensa de la soberanía del Perú o Tawantinsuyo entre 1536 y 1572*. Lima: R. A. Ediciones.

1976–1977    Documentos inéditos para la historia de los Incas de Vilcabamba: la capitulación del gobierno español con Titu Cusi Yupangui. *Historia y Cultura* 10:47–93. Lima: Museo Nacional de Historia.

Gutiérrez de Santa Clara, Pedro

1963    Quinquenarios o historia de la guerras civiles del Perú [after 1575]. *Crónicas del Perú*, vols. 2–4. Ed. Juan Pérez de Tudela Bueso. Biblioteca de Autores Españoles (continuación), vols. 166–168. Madrid: Ediciones Atlas.

Hamilton, Roland

1979    *History of the Inca empire: An account of the Indians' customs and their origin, together with a treatise on Inca legends, history, and social institutions by Father Bernabé Cobo*. Austin: University of Texas Press.

Hampe Martínez, Teodoro

1982    Las momias de los Incas en Lima. *Revista del Museo Nacional* 46:405–418. Lima: Museo Peruana de la Cultura.

Harrison, Regina

1989    *Signs, songs and memory in the Andes: Translating Quechua language and culture*. Austin: University of Texas Press.

Hernández Príncipe, Rodrigo

1923    Mitología andina [1621–1622]. Ed. Carlos A. Romero. *Inca* 1:25–78. Lima.

Hornborg, Alf

1988    *Dualism and hierarchy in lowland South America: Trajectories of indigenous social organization*. Uppsala: Uppsala University.

Iwasaki Cauti, Fernando

1986    Las *panacas* del Cuzco y la pintura incaica. *Revista de Indias* 46, no. 177:59–176. Madrid.

Julien, Catherine J.

1999    History and art in translation: The *paños* and other objects collected by Francisco de Toledo. *Colonial Latin American Review* 8, no.1 : 61–89. Oxfordshire: Carfax.

1998a   *Die Inka. Geschichte, Kultur, Religion*. Munich: C. H. Beck.

1998b   La organización parroquial del Cuzco y la ciudad incaica. *Tawantinsuyu* 5 : 82–96. Canberra.

1993    Finding a fit: Archaeology and ethnohistory of the Incas. *Provincial Inca: Archaeological and ethnohistorical assessment of the impact of the Inca state*. Ed. Michael A. Malpass, pp. 177–233. Iowa City: University of Iowa Press.

1991    *Condesuyo: The political division of territory under Inca and Spanish rule*. Bonner Amerikanistische Studien 19. Bonn.

1985    Guano and resource control in sixteenth-century Arequipa. *Andean ecology and civilization: An interdisciplinary perspective on Andean ecological complementarity*. Ed. Shozo Masuda, Izumi Shimada, and Craig Morris, pp. 185–231. Tokyo: University of Tokyo Press.

1983    *Hatunqolla: A view of Inca rule from the Lake Titicaca region*. Series Publications in Anthropology 15. Berkeley: University of California Press.

Kuper, Adam

1988    *The invention of primitive society: Transformations of an illusion*. New York: Routledge.

Lamana, Gonzalo

1997    Estructura y acontecimiento, identidad y dominación, los Incas en el Cuzco del siglo XVI. *Histórica* 21, no. 2 (December) : 235–260. Lima.

Las Casas, Bartolomé de

1967    *Apologética historia sumaria* [1562–1564]. Ed. Edmundo O'Gorman. Mexico City: Universidad Nacional Autónoma de México, Instituto de Investigaciones Históricas. 2 vols.

Levillier, Roberto

1940    *Don Francisco de Toledo, supremo organizador del Perú: su vida, su obra (1512–1582)*. Buenos Aires: Espasa-Calpe, S.A. 3 vols.

1924    *Gobernantes del Perú. Cartas y Papeles. Siglo XVI*. Buenos Aires: Biblioteca del Congreso de Argentina. 11 vols.

Lisi, Francesco Leonardo

1990    *El Tercer concilio limense y la aculturación de los indígenas sudamericanos*. Acta Salamanticensia, Estudios Filológicos 233. Salamanca: Ediciones Universidad de Salamanca.

Lohmann Villena, Guillermo

1997    Unas notas documentales sobre Juan Diez de Betanzos. *Arqueología, antropología e historia en los Andes. Homenaje a María Rostworowski*. Ed. Rafael Varón Gabai and Javier Flores Espinoza, pp. 127–131. Lima: Instituto de Estudios Peruanos, Banco Central de la Reserva del Perú.

Lounsbury, Floyd

1986    Some aspects of the Inca kinship system. *Anthropological history of Andean polities*. Ed. John V. Murra, Nathan Wachtel, and Jacques Revel, pp. 121–136. Cambridge: Cambridge University Press.

MacCormack, Sabine

1998    The Incas and Rome. *Garcilaso Inca de la Vega, an American humanist: A tribute to José Durand*. Ed. José Anadón, pp. 8–31. Notre Dame: University of Notre Dame.

1997    History and law in sixteenth-century Peru: The impact of European scholarly traditions. *Cultures of scholarship*. Ed. S. C. Humphreys, pp. 277–310. Ann Arbor: University of Michigan Press.

Matos Mar, José

1956    La propiedad en la isla de Taquile. *Revista del Museo Nacional* 26:211–271. Lima: Museo de la Cultura Peruana.

Mayer, Enrique

1974    Más allá de la familia nuclear. *Revista del Museo Nacional* 40:301–330. Lima: Museo de la Cultura Peruana.

Maúrtua, Victor M.

1906    *Juicio de límites entre el Perú y Bolivia. Prueba Peruana presentada al gobierno de la república de Argentina*. Barcelona: Imprenta de Henrich y Comp. 15 vols.

Means, Philip Ainsworth

1928    *Biblioteca andina*. Transactions of the Connecticut Academy of Arts and Sciences, 29:271–525. New Haven.

Molina, Cristóbal de

1989    Relación de las fábulas y ritos de los Incas [1576]. C. de Molina and C. de Albornoz, *Fábulas y mitos de los incas*. Ed. Henrique Urbano and Pierre Duviols, pp. 5–134. Madrid: Historia 16.

1943    *Fábulas y ritos de los Incas: las crónicas de los Molinas*. Los pequeños grandes libros de historia americana. Ed. Francisco de Loayza. Lima: Librería e Imprenta D. Miranda.

n.d.    Relación de las fabvlas i ritos de los ingas [1576]. Biblioteca Nacional, Madrid. Ms. 3169, fols. 2–36.

Montesinos, Fernando

1882    *Memorias antiguas historiales y políticas del Perú* [1642]. Madrid: Imprenta de Miguel Ginesta.

Morley, Sylvanus G.

1983    *The ancient Maya*. 4th ed., rev. Robert J. Sharer. Stanford: Stanford University Press.

Morúa, Martín de

1946    *Historia del origen y genealogía real de los Reyes Inças del Perú* [1605]. Ed. Constantino Bayle. Madrid: Consejo Superior de Investigaciones Científicas, Instituto Santo Toribio de Mogrovejo.

Murúa, Martín de

1987    *Historia general del Perú* [1611–1616]. Ed. Manuel Ballesteros. Crónicas de América 35. Madrid: Historia 16.

Niles, Susan Allee

1999    *The shape of Inca history: Narrative and architecture in an Andean Empire*. Iowa City: University of Iowa Press.

1993    The provinces in the heartland: Stylistic variation and architectural innovation near Inca Cuzco. *Provincial Inca: Archaeological and ethnohistorical assessment of the impact of the Inca state*. Ed. Michael A. Malpass, pp. 145–176. Iowa City: University of Iowa Press.

Nowack, Kerstin

1998a   *Ceque and more*. Bonner Amerikanistische Studien 31. Markt Schwaben: Verlag Anton Sauerwein.

1998b   The intentions of the author: Juan de Betanzos and the "Suma y narración de los

Incas." *50 años de estudios americanistas en la Universidad de Bonn. 50 years of Americanist studies at the University of Bonn.* Bonner Amerikanistische Studien 30:513–526. Bonn: Seminar für Völkerkunde, Universität Bonn.

Nowack, Kerstin, and Catherine Julien

1999    La campaña de Toledo contra los señores naturales andinos: el destierro de los Incas de Vilcabamba y Cuzco. *Historia y Cultura* 23:15–81. Lima: Museo Nacional de Historia.

Oré, Luis Jerónimo de

1992    *Symbolo catholico indiano* [1598]. Ed. Antonine Tibesar. Lima: Australis.

Ossio, Juan M.

1973    *Ideología mesiánica del mundo andino*. Lima: Ignacio Prado Pastor.

1970    The idea of history in Felipe Guaman Poma de Ayala. Bachelor's thesis, Linacre College, Oxford University.

Pachacuti Yamqui Salcamaygua, Joan de Santa Cruz

1993    *Relación de antigüedades deste reyno del Pirú* [early seventeenth century]. Ed. Pierre Duviols. Cuzco: Centro de Estudios Regionales Andinos "Bartolomé de las Casas," Institut Français d'Etudes Andines.

1879    Relación de antigüedades deste reyno del Pirú [early seventeenth century]. *Tres relaciones de antigüedades peruanas*, pp. 229–328. Madrid: Ministerio de Fomento, Imprenta y Fundación de M. Tello.

n.d.    Relación de antigüedades deste reyno del Pirú [early seventeenth century]. Biblioteca Nacional, Madrid. Ms. 3169, fols. 131–174.

Pärssinen, Marti

1992    *Tawantinsuyu: The Inca state and its political organization*. Societas Historica Finlandiae, Studia Historica 43. Helsinki.

Paz Soldán, Mariano Felipe

1877    *Diccionario geográfico estadístico del Perú*. Lima: Imprenta del Estado.

Pease García Yrigoyen, Franklin

1995    *Las crónicas y los Andes*. Pontificia Universidad Católica del Perú, Instituto Riva Agüero, Lima. México City: Fondo de Cultura Económica.

1992    *Perú. Hombre e historia*. Lima: Fundación del Banco Continental para el Fomento de la Educación y la Cultura, Ediciones Edubanco. 3 vols.

1973    *El dios creador andino*. Lima: Mosca Azul Editores.

Pérez Bocanegra, Juan

1631    *Ritvual formvlario e institvcion de cvras*. Lima: Geronymo de Contreras.

Polo de Ondegardo

1940    Informe del licenciado Polo de Ondegardo al licenciado Briviesca de Muñatones sobre la perpetuidad de las encomiendas en el Perú [1561]. *Revista Histórica* 13:125–196. Lima.

1872    Relación de los fundamentos acerca del notable daño que resulta de no guardar a los indios sus fueros [1571]. *Colección de Documentos Inéditos . . . de Indias*. 17:5–177. Madrid: Imprenta del Hospicio.

1585    Los errores y supersticiones de los indios sacados del tratado y averiguación que hizo el licenciado Polo. Appendix to *Confesionario para los curas de indios*. Lima: Antonio Ricardo.

Porras Barrenechea, Raúl

1986    *Los cronistas del Perú (1528–1650) y otros ensayos*. Biblioteca Clásicos del Perú 2. Lima: Banco de Crédito.

Protzen, Jean-Pierre
1993    *Inca architecture and construction at Ollantaytambo.* New York: Oxford University
        Press.
Ramos Gavilán, Alonso
1988    *Historia del santuario de Nuestra Señora de Copacabana* [1621]. Lima: Ignacio Prado
        Pastor.
Rappaport, Joanne
1990    *The politics of memory: Native historical interpretation in the Columbian Andes.*
        Cambridge: Cambridge University Press.
Román y Zamora, Jerónimo
1897    *Repúblicas de Indias: idolatrías y gobierno en México y Perú antes de la conquista* [1575].
        Ed. D. L. d'Orvenipe. Colección de libros españoles raros o curiosos que tratan de
        América, vols. 14–15. Madrid: V. Suárez.
Rostworowski de Diez Canseco, María
1999    *History of the Inca realm.* Trans. Harry B. Iceland. Cambridge: Cambridge
        University Press.
1993    *Ensayos de historia andina: élites, etnías, recursos.* Lima: Instituto de Estudios
        Peruanos.
1988    *Historia del Tahuantinsuyu.* Instituto de Estudios Peruanos, Historia Andina 13.
        Lima: Ministerio de la Presidencia, Consejo Nacional de Ciencia y Tecnología
        (CONCYTEC).
1953    *Pachacutec Inca Yupanqui.* Lima: Editorial Torres Aguirre.
Rowe, John Howland
1995    Los incas no reales. *Revista del Museo e Instituto de Arqueología — Museo Inka,*
        no. 25 : 121–126. Cuzco: Universidad Nacional de San Antonio Abad.
1994    El barrio de Cayau Cachi y la parroquia de Belén. Horacio H. Villanueva Urteaga,
        *La casa de la moneda del Cuzco, homenaje de la facultad de ciencias sociales y los amigos
        del autor,* pp. 173–187. Cuzco: Universidad Nacional de San Antonio Abad.
1993–1994  La supuesta "diarquía" de los Incas. *Revista del Instituto Americano de Arte,*
        no. 14 : 99–107. Cuzco.
1990    Machu Picchu a la luz de documentos del siglo XVI. *Histórica* 14, no. 1 : 139–145.
        Lima: Universidad Católica del Perú.
1987    La mentira literaria en la obra de Martín de Murúa. *Libro homenaje a Aurelio Miró
        Quesada Sosa* 2 : 753–761. Lima.
1985a   La constitución Inca del Cuzco. *Histórica* 9, no. 1 : 35–73. Lima.
1985b   Probanza de los Incas nietos de conquistadores. *Histórica* 9, no. 2 : 193–245.
        Lima.
1979    An account of the shrines of ancient Cuzco. *Ñawpa Pacha* 17 : 1–80. Berkeley:
        Institute of Andean Studies, University of California.
1967    What kind of a city was Inca Cuzco? *Ñawpa Pacha* 5 : 59–76. Berkeley: Institute of
        Andean Studies, University of California.
1966    Un memorial del gobierno de los Incas del año 1551. *Revista Peruana de Cultura*
        9–10 : 27–39. Lima.
1960    The origins of Creator worship among the Incas. *Culture in history: Essays in honor
        of Paul Radin.* Ed. Stanley Diamond, pp. 408–429. New York: Columbia
        University Press.
1955    Movimiento nacional Inca del siglo XVIII. *Revista Universitaria del Cuzco,* no. 107
        (second semester) : 3–33. Cuzco: Imprenta "Garcilaso."

1946    Inca culture at the time of the Spanish conquest. *Handbook of South American Indians*. Ed. Julian Steward. 2:183–330. Washington, D.C.: Smithsonian Institution, Bureau of American Ethnology, Bulletin 143.

1945    Absolute chronology in the Andean Area. *American Antiquity* 10, no. 3 (January):265–284. Menasha.

1944    *An introduction to the archaeology of Cuzco*. Papers of the Peabody Museum, vol. 27, no. 2. Cambridge.

Salomon, Frank

1997    Los *quipus* y libros de la Tupicocha de hoy: un informe preliminar. *Arqueología, antropología e historia en los Andes: homenaje a María Rostworowski*. Ed. Rafael Varón Gabai and Javier Flores Espinoza, pp. 241–258. Lima: Instituto de Estudios Peruanos, Banco Central de Reserva del Perú.

Salomon, Frank, and George L. Urioste

1991    *The Huarochirí manuscript: A testament of ancient and colonial Andean religion*. Austin: University of Texas Press.

Sánchez Cantón, F. J.

1956–1959    *Inventarios reales: bienes muebles que pertenecieron a Felipe II*. Archivo Documental Español, vols. 10–11. Madrid: Real Academia de la Historia.

Santillán, Hernando de

1879    Relación del origen, descendencia, política y gobierno de los Incas [1563]. *Tres relaciones de antigüedades peruanas*. Ed. Marcos Jiménez de la Espada, pp. 1–133. Madrid: Ministerio de Fomento.

Sarmiento de Gamboa, Pedro de

1988    *Los viajes al estrecho de Magallanes*. Ed. María Justina Bravo Sarabia. Madrid: Alianza Editorial.

1906    *Geschichte des Inkareiches von Pedro Sarmiento de Gamboa* [1572]. Ed. Richard Pietschmann. Abhandlungen der königlichen Gesellschaft der Wissenschaften zu Göttingen, philologisch-historische Klasse, n.s. 6, no. 4. Berlin: Weidmannsche Buchhandlung.

n.d.    Segunda parte de la hisstoria general llamada yndica la qual por mandado del excelentisimo señor don Francisco de Toledo virrey gobernador y capitan general de los rreynos del Piru y mayordomo de la casa rreal de Castilla conpuso el capitan Pedro Sarmiento de Gamboa [1572]. Universität Göttingen.

Schele, Linda, and David Freidel

1990    *A forest of kings: The untold story of the ancient Maya*. New York: William Morrow and Co.

Schele, Linda, and Mary Ellen Miller

1986    *The blood of kings: Dynasty and ritual in Maya art*. Fort Worth: Kimbell Art Museum.

Schneider, David

1984    *A critique of the study of kinship*. Ann Arbor: University of Michigan Press.

Sherbondy, Jeanette E.

1992    Water ideology in Inca ethnogenesis. *Andean cosmologies through time*. Ed. Robert V. H. Dover, Katharine E. Seibold, and John H. McDowell, pp. 46–66. Bloomington: Indiana University Press.

Silverblatt, Irene

1987    *Moon, sun, and witches. Gender ideologies and class in Inca and colonial Peru*. Princeton: Princeton University Press.

Temple, Ella Dunbar

1949–1950  Los testamentos inéditos de Paullu Inca, don Carlos y don Melchor Carlos Inca. *Documenta*, year 2, no. 1:630–651. Lima: Sociedad Peruana de la Historia

1948a  Azarosa existencia de un mestizo de sangre imperial incaica. *Documenta*, year 1, no. 1:112–156. Lima: Sociedad Peruana de la Historia.

1948b  Don Carlos Inca. *Revista Histórica* 17:134–179. Lima.

1940  La descendencia de Huayna Cápac. Conclusión del capítulo "Paullu Inca." *Revista Histórica* 13:31–77. Lima: Instituto Histórico del Perú.

1937a  La descendencia de Huayna Cápac (continuación). Paullu Inca. *Revista Histórica* 11 nos. 1–2:204–245. Lima.

1937b  La descendencia de Huayna Cápac (continuación). Paullu Inca. *Revista Histórica* 11, no. 3:284–323. Lima.

Thomas, Nicholas

1989  *Out of time: History and evolution in anthropological discourse*. 2nd ed. Ann Arbor: University of Michigan Press.

Tito Cussi Yupangui, Diego de Castro

1988  Instrucción del Inga don Diego de Castro Tito Cussi Yupangui (1570). *En el encuentro de dos mundos: los Incas de Vilcabamba*. Ed. María del Carmen Martín Rubio. Madrid: Ediciones Atlas.

Trautmann, Thomas R.

1987  *Lewis Henry Morgan and the invention of kinship*. Berkeley: University of California Press.

Urbano, Henrique

1997  Sexo, pintura de los Incas y *taqui onqoy*. *Revista Andina*, year 15, no. 1:207–246. Cuzco: Centro de Estudios Regionales Andinos "Bartolomé de las Casas."

1981  *Wiracocha y Ayar, héroes y funciones en las sociedades andinas*. Biblioteca de la Tradición Oral Andina, no. 3. Cuzco: Centro de Estudios Regionales Andinos "Bartolomé de las Casas."

Urton, Gary

1998  From knots to narratives: Reconstructing the art of historical record keeping in the Andes. *Ethnohistory* 45, no. 3 (summer):409–438.

1997  *The social life of numbers: A Quechua ontology of numbers and philosophy of arithmetic*. Austin: University of Texas Press.

1991  The Stranger in Andean communities. *Cultures et sociétés Andes et Méso-Amérique: mélanges en ommage a Pierre Duvioles*. Ed. Raquel Thiercelin, 2:791–810. Aix-en-Provence: Publications de l'Université de Provence.

1990  *The history of a myth: Pacariqtambo and the origin of the Incas*. Austin: University of Texas.

1981  *At the crossroads of the earth and sky*. Austin: University of Texas Press.

Valcárcel, Carlos Daniel

1983  *Tupac Amaru y la iglesia. Antología*. Lima: Comité Arquidiocesano del Bicentenario Tupac Amaru, Banco de los Andes, Edubanco.

Vansina, Jan

1985  *Oral tradition as history*. Madison: University of Wisconsin Press.

Varón Gabai, Rafael

1997  *Francisco Pizarro and his brothers: The illusion of power in sixteenth-century Peru*. Norman: University of Oklahoma Press.

Villanueva Urteaga, Horacio

1970    Información ad perpetuam dada en 13 de enero de 1567 ante la Real Justicia de la
        Ciudad del Cuzco, Reino del Perú a pedimento de la Muy Ilustre Señora Doña
        María Manrique Coya. *Revista del Archivo Histórico del Cuzco*, no. 13:149–184.
        Cuzco: Universidad Nacional de San Antonio Abad del Cuzco.

Webster, Stephen S.

1977    Kinship and affinity in a native Quechua community. *Andean kinship and marriage*.
        Ed. Ralph Bolton and Enrique Mayer, pp. 28–42. Special Publication of the
        American Anthropological Association, no. 7. Washington, D.C..

Wedin, Ake

1966    *El concepto de lo incaico y las fuentes*. Studia Historica Gothoburgensia 7. Uppsala.

Zuidema, Reiner Tom

1995    *El sistema de los ceques*. Lima: Pontificia Universidad Católica del Perú, Fondo
        Editorial.

1967    "Descendencia paralela" en una familia indígena noble del Cuzco (Documentos del
        siglo XVI hasta el siglo XVIII). *Fenix* 17:39–62. Lima.

1964    *The ceque system of Cuzco: The social organization of the capital of the Inca*.
        International Archives of Ethnography, supplement to vol. 50. Leiden: E. J. Brill.

# Index